Meditations of a Modern Mystic

by

Maurine Doerken

Breathe through the heats of our desire thy coolness and thy balm; let sense be dumb, let flesh retire; speak through the earthquake, wind, and fire, O still, small voice of calm, O still, small voice of calm.

Hymn 653, The Hymnal 1982
Words: John Greenleaf Whittier
Music: Repton, Charles Herbert Hastings Parry

TABLE OF CONTENTS

INTRODUCTION:
WHEN THE UNIVERSE ASKS YOU TO CHANGE, IT MAY TAKE LONGER THAN YOU THINK

In the truest sense of the word, I am a journalist: I keep a journal and I write about the events of my time. When I was in my mid-twenties, a family friend suggested I commence a written record of what I experienced because I was in "the most interesting years" of life. Now that I have reached what indigenous traditions call elderhood, I believe that all the years are interesting, not just or only those of youth. However, I took my family friend's suggestion and started keeping a journal at the age of twenty-five. I now have well over one hundred hand-written volumes occupying substantial space on a library shelf.

The peculiarity about keeping a journal is that you quite literally record a journey through time. You get to witness yourself – and your unconscious – through time's changing lens. For me journal keeping has also been a pilgrimage toward listening to my heart and has evolved into a kind of education in growing my heart's intelligence. I never suspected this would happen when I first took pen in hand.

That we think with our hearts is no longer idle speculation. Neuro-cardiologists have discovered that between 60% to 65% of the cells in that organ are neural cells, not muscle cells as once thought. These neural heart cells are identical to those in our brain and operate through the same connecting mechanisms. So there is, quite literally, a "brain" in our hearts, and I believe it is important that we learn more about its language, how it speaks, and how we listen to that "still small voice within."

What follows is a journey through time about my own dance between the darkness and light and how I am

1

learning to allow the brain in my heart to conduct the score. I chose to start with the journals from my middle years because I believe they hold a unique perspective. In youth, one looks forward with questions and wonder. In old age, one looks back and reminisces. But at the mid-point in life, one can look at what has happened and still look forward to what may yet come.

My personal thanks to Father Lawrence Shelton of St. Anselm's Parish in Los Angeles with whom I studied Ignatian Spirituality and who has been my Spiritual Director for over a decade. My thanks also to Dr. Jack Zimmerman for his rigorous, intelligent, and no-nonsense psycho-spiritual care. Both individuals have provided patient and compassionate guidance that I appreciate more than they will ever know.

Aside from the many writers and artists whose works I have quoted in the following pages, I want to acknowledge in particular the following authors and their works:

The Book of Runes by Ralph Blum and *The Healing Runes* by Ralph Blum and Susan Loughan.

Animal Medicine Cards: The Discovery of Power Through the Ways of Animals by Jamie Sams and David Carson.

Goddess Guidance Oracle Cards by Doreen Virtue, Ph.D.

Sacred Geometry Oracle Deck by Francene Hart.

It is my hope that those who read these journals will take heart.

Maurine Doerken
Sebastopol, California
2013

PART I:
THE MIDDLE AGES, Vol. 3
(Excerpts from Journals 78-89)

To write is to love: it is to inquire and to praise or to confess or to appeal. This testimony of love remains necessary. Not to reassure myself that I am...but simply to pay my debt to life, to the world, to other men...to speak out with an open heart and say what seems to me to have meaning.

Thomas Merton

July 7, 2002

There's always something.

Tomorrow I am scheduled to have surgery on my right carotid artery. The whooshing and thumping I have been experiencing in my head over the past nine months turn out to be a very serious condition. My artery is over 90% blocked, and the doctors believe it is a result of all the radiation I had fifteen years ago when I had cancer. The suddenness of this hasn't allowed me time to get upset, yet I am vastly relieved this condition has been diagnosed before rather than after a major stroke.

Somebody up there, or several, must really be watching over me because it's not as if I haven't been trying to get to the root of this problem for some time now. Last December I went to a cardiologist who wondered why I was in his office. Then I checked with my gynecologist thinking it was raging middle-age hormones. Last March I went to the emergency hospital one night because the sound in my head was so loud I thought I was going to have a stroke (!). The doctor on call listened to the artery in my neck then ordered a CAT scan of my head which, of course, didn't reveal anything because the problem wasn't in my head. Then two weeks ago I went for my annual cancer check up and mentioned this "annoying sound" to my oncologist. Dr. T. listened and suggested I go to an ear nose and throat specialist to check things out. But I could tell from his manner that something was up. You get to know these things after spending so much time with doctors and in hospitals. A special sonogram was ordered, and as the technician scanned both sides of my neck, even I could hear the difference. All the whooshing and thumping and pulsing and pumping I have been listening to and that have been keeping me awake nights is my blood being squeezed through such a narrow opening.

The test was on a Thursday afternoon and when I got a message on my pager at noon the following Monday, that sinking, sickening feeling came over me again. Bad news. Doctors don't call you at noon on Mondays with good news. Good news they leave to the evening or next appointment or for their nursing staff to make the follow up call. Bad news doctors tell you themselves. I was transported back fifteen years to the call I got from my doctor that a routine chest x-ray had picked up a large shadow requiring more tests. Bad news and Mondays go hand-in-hand.

As I was listening to my internist, I took notes because I don't trust myself in situations like this. Over ninety percent narrowing. Vascular surgeon. Three recommendations whom to call. I got off the telephone, turned off my computer – suddenly email jokes didn't seem so very urgent – went into the family room, and broke down in tears.

There's always something.

Dr. S. arranged for me to see a surgeon immediately rather than having to wait the usual three to four weeks for an appointment. When I saw the surgeon, he corroborated that he had seen this same problem in other people who have been exposed to radiation. The Fourth of July BBQ with my aging, tottering parents was cancelled. Back at Dr. S.'s again for my pre-operation workup, his comment, "This is a big wake-up call for you; we're going to have to do some more tests." Tests to see if I've sprung any more leaks or blockages from those cancer treatments long ago. And it isn't as if they didn't tell me back then that fifteen to twenty years down the road I might experience complications. (Dr. S. was also very impressed with my kundalini serpent tattoo. "Your kids must think you're a cool mom.")

Let's hope!

I think, too, with a ghoulish kind of foreshadowing: three parents of students at the school where I work have had strokes this past year. One died, another was severely debilitated, the third came out relatively unscathed. But I remember thinking as I was counseling the young people about their own fear and grief: a cautionary tale, don't let this happen to me. Stress, not just radiation, can be a killer, too.

P. and I had another fight the night before last about the same old, same old stuff. If I am as unnurturing and unfeeling as he claims, why do the kids seem so okay with me and never complain the way he does? And I know that a part of this is his fear talking about the up-coming surgery. But I also realized during one particular phone conversation where he was putting down me and my work, that I had had it. I hung up the phone, too angry to talk, thinking: he has no right to say what he did in that condescending tone of his. Correction: he has the right, but it is not the truth; it is only his *belief*. Is he hoping that I'll somehow "snap out of it?" That I'll "come to my senses" and "behave?" Be different? Be what he wants me to be?

It also occurred to me when Dr. S. said what he did about this being a wake-up call that I may not be blessed with the longevity my parents have had. It is quite possible that what was done to extend my life in my thirties, paradoxically, may have a shortening effect at the other end of the journey. While I feel confident all will go well tomorrow, there are going to be some changes made.

July 13, 2002
I made it through the operation and picked up another four-inch scar. The body count now is nearly four feet in all. On the way home from the hospital, I actually started chuckling to myself. I turned to P. and said, "I have a neck

scar and a tattoo. Now all I need is an eye patch and a parrot and I'll officially be a pirate!"

Shiver me timbers. Har har!

While the surgery went as expected and there were no complications – the main concern being having a stroke while on the operating table – I got violently ill as a result of the anesthesia and pain medication. At one point in the early evening, some ten hours after the operation, I bolted awake from sleep, only to projectile vomit all over myself, the bed, and hospital table in front of me, accompanied by similar loss of control of my bladder, both ends of the alimentary canal in revolt. All I could think of was how I looked like Linda Blaire in *The Exorcist*. How I found that thought funny is beyond me, but I was laughing as two nurses tried to clean me up, along with the bed and nightstand. Four hours later as I was still retching, wave upon wave of hacking, dry-heaving nausea, I could barely keep my head up. At this point all vestiges of humor had utterly vanished. By the next morning, thanks to some intravenous anti-nausea medication, I began to return to the land of the living, and by noon I was discharged from the hospital.

It strikes me as very odd how this event has impacted me, so different from what I went through fifteen years ago. When I was diagnosed with cancer, I had three surgeries with general anesthetic, two of which were extremely invasive and painful. I was in the hospital nearly two weeks for those two operations alone, followed by nine weeks, five days a week of intense radiation therapy; the vomiting, the hair loss, the nasty case of hives, not to mention still having four children ages seven and younger and a busy businessman husband to care for. From the discovery of the tumor to completion of treatment was nine months, a new birth of sorts, followed by depression and psychotherapy afterwards.

While having cancer at thirty-six was objectively far more serious in many ways – not that having a major stroke isn't – this event feels more compelling because I appreciate much more now the finiteness of time and the reality of the diminishment of the body. It feels more mortal and real now, intimate and quietly truthful in a way. While having cancer in my thirties was without doubt a major emotional, psychological, and spiritual watershed, it was also a conversion experience that didn't really convert me. Well, it did and it didn't. It's hard to explain.

I think it is because in our thirties our egos feel so much in control, so determined to see things through, and so confident in our sense of being able to make things happen. At mid-life I have come to realize, and I continue to be taught with great humility, how my ego most definitely is not running the show. It is not the ultimate arbiter of events, never has been, and never will be.

I was resting in bed the other day, reading a book about women and madness (*Out of Her Mind: Women Writing on Madness*), and I came across this:

> Mrs. Cheneworth hung herself in her own room after retiring from the dancing party last night. Her measure of grace was not sufficient to enable her to bear the accumulated burdens of her hard fate any longer. (From chapter "Modern Persecution or Insane Asylums Unveiled")

I got to thinking: What is anyone's measure of grace? Can grace run out or be used up? And this has absolutely nothing to do with an arbitrary or capricious deity but the idea that while God's grace may be sufficient, is it necessarily endless? How can I feel into whether or not my measure of grace is enough to do what I need to do, to accomplish what I was sent here to accomplish? Something I'm still trying to figure out. And this has nothing to do with me per se, other than being an instrument to be played upon, and everything to do with God. Will my particular measure of grace be sufficient for what God wants to accomplish through me?

In between all this mental preoccupation are a husband and four rapidly growing children ready to take flight, the last soon heading to college. This will finally leave P. and me alone to figure ourselves out as a couple. I do not understand, and I am weary of trying, how we can feel as close as two human beings can feel one moment and then seconds later as alien and foreign to one another as galaxies flying apart.

And it is not as if I don't want to be in a relationship. I just don't know what to do about the part of me that wants to be in relationship with me, to have more ownership over my own body and being – as much as we humans can claim ownership over anything in light of divine ownership of all.

But I think for women this is a particularly and peculiarly relevant point:

We are looked upon, in ways both subtle and blatant, as property/chattel by our family members and men; daughters and sisters and wives to do the care work, the cleaning up, and servicing of others.

Biology looks upon us and requires that we be the vessels of life and therefore we ultimately are at life's demand, not our own; women who manipulate this often pay the price of loneliness, ostracism, and/or regret, myself included.

Our bodies keep betraying us, or if not betraying us, at least keep morphing beyond our control. We don't menstruate, then we do; we get pregnant and stop menstruating; we have babies and start menstruating again; then we stop having babies and periods altogether.

Hormones up, hormones down, hormones gone crazy, hormones gone period. Men, by contrast, undergo far fewer physical changes and their sense of entitlement and ownership of their bodies, their maleness and its primacy I think are archetypally entrenched.

So breaking free of family expectations and needs; partner expectations and needs; tribal expectations and needs; off-springs' expectations and needs; biology's expectations and needs to get to the point of being in ownership of me: at once both selfish in an understandable way and paradoxically self-indulgent. I do believe the planet requires as much collaborative energy as it can muster right now as opposed to the solitary way. Nevertheless, this whole feeling of "me" ownership is there.

****

While at the post office today, a disturbing event occurred. A young man (white) in his early thirties started hurling all kinds of racial and ethnic slurs at some of the people who where there. He thought an older man (Asian) had cut in front of him in line when the postal worker had, in fact, asked the man to not wait in the queue again but return to her for help.

This information, however, did absolutely nothing to stop the young man's abusive invective. He simply upped the volume and vociferousness of his attack. "Fucking third world people! I'm sick and tired of them coming in and taking over *my* country! They've got no fucking respect. Go home to where you belong, you fucking assholes!" Blacks, Jews, Hispanics, Asians, you name it: he hit them all. When a woman next to him suggested that such comments were not helpful, the young man turned on her and said, "Don't you fucking get started on all that liberal bullshit. Fucking go home. All of you!"

He was from New York, hated LA, hated all the "chinks" and "Latino assholes" and especially the asshole in the parking lot who had dinged his expensive car. I found myself getting angrier and angrier as I listened but recognized that I, too, was intimidated by this guy: 225 pounds of hostile male muscle, way too much testosterone cruising through his veins. What's a woman to do? After about five minutes, some of the people waiting for service actually started laughing and snickering at the guy, especially after his comment about other people having no respect. He stormed out in a loud stream of fucking this and fucking that.

I returned to my car, drove to my next destination, and started to cry. It was so upsetting witnessing that blast of unbridled fury and hate. And this was just a post office; imagine all that goes on around the world on a daily basis!

All the way down 14th Street I kept repeating to myself:

Love always conquers hate.

Love always conquers hate.

Love always conquers hate.

And I remembered something a friend of mine sent me after 9/11:

> The ultimate weakness of violence is that it is a descending spiral, begetting the very thing it seeks to destroy. Instead of diminishing evil, it multiplies it. Through violence you may murder the liar, but you cannot murder the lie, nor establish truth. Through violence you murder the hater, but you do not murder hate. In fact, violence merely increases hate. Returning violence for violence multiplies

violence, adding deeper darkness to a night already devoid of stars. Darkness cannot drive out darkness; only light can do that. Hate cannot drive out hate; only love can do that. (Dr. Martin Luther King)

As I got out of my car, I thought my dark glasses would hide the fact I had been crying, but apparently not. An elderly woman approached me and asked, "Are you all right, dear?" And I blurted out, "No!" and proceeded to tell Faye, age 72, what had happened.

Faye could not have been more dear. She listened and told me how much my story touched her. We talked about cancer, both having had the disease. She even showed me her scar. Mine was too big. I would have had to undress. We hugged, and Faye left me teary-eyed at Santa Monica Seafood.

I need some tools, a protective spiritual shield to help get through experiences such as these. That and the realization how quickly we – how quickly I – polarize around that kind of negative energy. I was pissed and angry at that man in the post office, ready to call him a fucking asshole, too. And then I would be doing precisely and exactly what he was doing: making individuals and groups of individuals into objects of scorn and derision.

What bothered me the most was my own anger and fear, especially fear of what this person might do. Certainly not an unreasonable concern for a petite middle-aged woman around a hot-tempered young man. But it does go to the heart of how one behaves and responds from a spiritual core. Who needs the unflappable, rock-solid response of love more: the old man who was being verbally abused or the young man hurling all the hate?

I need to learn how to go deeper with this. Our human emotional responses are so hair-trigger at times, and we assume they are right simply because we have them. Witness all the brutality that is taking place daily in the Middle East. After the smoke of suicide bombings settles, the body parts collected, and victims and martyrs honored – all that is left on a human level is grief. Grief and a profound sense of waste and loss.

Silence may be the appropriate response at times; at others absolutely not. One must step up to the plate of life and say, "This is not the way." But that needs to be said with love, and I wasn't feeling love in my heart in that moment at the post office. I was oscillating between anger and fear, not centered.

What I am left with is this:

- How does one respond in a spiritually congruent matter to events such as these?
- How does one avoid doing exactly what one condemns in others?
- When is it appropriate to remain silent?
- When must one speak out with love and passionate conviction?
- What are the nuts and bolts of how each and every one of us can participate in this required shift in consciousness?

I remind myself: love always conquers hate. My prayer for that young man. And for me.

August 2, 2002

I went to see my spiritual director, FS, and spent most of the time talking about writing rather than my spiritual life, or writing as my spiritual life. At this point, I am trying to become rule-less. I find it challenging enough being loving; that's rule enough for me. The ego is a large and mighty beast indeed.

I told FS I have been having real discernment issues regarding this whole pen and paper business. I think of the money I have spent on all the scribbling that could go to helping others, and it bothers me. It was then that FS asked me if I had ever heard the story of St. Francis and his conversation with Jesus.

No, I answered. I'm spiritually illiterate.

Well, said FS, legend has it that Christ appeared before St. Francis and asked him to build a church. There was a dilapidated, ramshackle building in a nearby field which St. Francis spent a year refurbishing, stone by stone, with great effort, care, and devotion. When Jesus appeared before Francis a year later, he told the monk, "That's not what I meant. People! Build my church with people!"

Moral of the story:

All the time you think you are doing the right thing, or God's will, only to discover that that wasn't what was being called for at all. Not at all.

I got the point of the lesson, of course, though I can't say I was particularly happy about it. And I also can't afford to be reckless, or feckless, with my time. Realizing, too, that constant, ever-present shadowboxing against the nemesis of self-abnegation and self-denigration. It seems we women – or at least this one – often serve life-long apprenticeships in our own tentativeness and marginalization. The constant, ever-present struggle to speak out, to be heard rather than giving in to the hissing deflation of "why bother?" and remain silent. It is the silence that is soul-killing.

Something from a compilation of Merton's diaries (*The Intimate Merton*) that I liked:

> Whatever this vocation is, it involves a whole different attitude to the future. A sense of calm. A sense that I am going to do something hard, murderous to my pride and my senses. That it doesn't make sense to fear it or

love it: *I must refer everything to God.* (italics mine, from entry dated 11/1/41, All Saints' Day)

Murderous to my pride, indeed; my desire for success, or even recognition. All that must go and the roots of these weeds, and wounds, run deep. Like the story of St. Francis: how we can misinterpret the cues and signs, quite innocently. So we do what we think we are supposed to be doing only to discover that that wasn't what was called for at all, and yet even in that error something nevertheless is accomplished, though we may not know what it is or how. This is the mysterious economy of God.

What I was trying to tell FS, and he me, is this: It's not what I thought, not how I imagined it would be and paradoxically it is precisely and exquisitely what I need, this wandering internally; a kind of perplexity, which in turn becomes a spiritual petri dish for transformation and change.

I was also thinking about something else Merton wrote: something to the effect that you have to be grateful for goodness before you can know or appreciate goodness. I want the goodness but have forgotten, or at least neglected, to concentrate on the gratitude. First, last, and always gratitude. Gratitude for being that has absolutely nothing whatsoever to do with doing or accomplishing. So, of course, that's exactly the lesson that keeps coming my way. Ah, humility, humility…Which comes first: humility or gratitude? Both. Neither. All of the above.

So I keep trying to meditate in the morning, to get quiet and calm, but the internal chatter is relentless!
R-E-L-E-N-T-L-E-S-S.
Today this is what happened instead:
"My life as a pirate began
When the gypsies pitched camp in my yard,

With the smell of garlic and onions wafting my way.
I could hear the snake-like rattling of their tambourines,
But it was their laughter that shanghaied my soul.
Captive then, out the door walked I
And never, ever looked back."

Trying to be "spiritual" and all I meet with is the irrepressible! As Merton says: I must refer everything to God – chatter, silliness, broodiness, all: the ongoing babble in my head. And as FS said, we too often forget God's divine comedy in this. We so like to focus on the struggle, and our own self-importance, that we overlook our own utter and precious foolishness. It's all about love laughing at the end of the world, being shanghaied by the gypsies of soul, and never looking back.

August 12, 2002
Yesterday I went to a meeting at the Quaker House on Harvard Street in Santa Monica – a memorial service in remembrance of those who died at Hiroshima and Nagasaki and what those two bombs, Little Boy and Fat Man, meant to the world. It was a warm Sunday afternoon, at any other time what would have been an invitation to mid-summer laziness.

There were about fifty people gathered: young and old, men, women, and children, Quakers, Christians, Jews, Buddhists, and Muslims. My friend JP spoke, giving a brief history of the bombs dropped on August 6th and 9th, 1945 and working his way up to the present. For him, nuclear weapons are a denial of God; they reflect how we humans have taken on the role of omnipotence in defiance of anything greater than ourselves, lacking any sort of humility by our wanting and expecting to be in ultimate control.

I sat in the chair in silence, as is the Quaker custom, looking out at the green leaves on the trees in the patio surrounding the retreat house. There was a tactile sense of air and space and light, thick almost, and alive. I sat looking at the other people in the room, some with heads bowed, others looking out with meditative gaze, and I thought: "We are the immune system of the human family gathering to counter the disease of terrorism, hate, and fear. We are the goodness cells, and we are more powerful than anything that partakes of the darkness so prevalent today." There has been a surfeit of violence over the last one hundred years; we have glutted ourselves on it. Now the goodness cells are gathering to harness and protect the light, the light of love and the light of spirit. *Because this is what Spirit both requires and demands!*

And this Spirit, in whatever form, in whatever faith, in whatever belief system, contemplative practice or path – Hindu, Muslin, Christian, Jew, Sikh, Buddhist, humanist – the name or label doesn't matter; it is heart music willing itself to be heard. And there will be nothing that can stop this heart music because it is more powerful than anything else. Think of the few thousand people on this planet who comprise the cells of terror and hate. Then compare that number with the millions, the billions who do not harbor such malice and enmity or ill will. Like the prelude to *Das Rheingold*, this heart music is building slowly and steadily, cell by cell, person by person, drop by drop, wave by wave, building the immune system of the human family so that heart music and love can be made.

August 18, 2002

Bora Bora, the Society Islands. A universe away from LA and the last few days of our family vacation before everyone goes his or her separate way. Being in a place like this for even a short while changes one's being and psyche profoundly. Away from phones, cars, highways, TVs and noise – indeed, they have only one road here and one generator to power the entire island – the only sound that of the gentle, diminutive waves lap, lap, lapping at the shore; the occasional suck and pop of tropical fish as they rise to the surface to catch bugs and food. And the trade winds moving, at once soft and fierce.

Against all precaution, considering my sensitive skin, I have been lying out in the sun, even went snorkeling for three hours the other day but forgot to put sunscreen on my legs. This has presented quite a problem in the sitting down department, yet the brown skin and color looking back at me in the mirror appear healthy and fit, not the pasty white I came here with. Too much time inside my study and, of course, recovering from the surgery and not being well.

The sheer physical beauty of this place is unparalleled: a volcanic island, surrounded by a reef and lagoon; water so many different shades of blue I can hardly count them: light blue, turquoise, aquamarine, sapphire, royal blue, and more. And coral structures underneath the water that run the gamut of color as well: pink, yellow, brown, grey, mustard, light green, lime, off-white, and black. The tropical fish are even more varied in size, shape, and fin ornamentation. I have seen sting rays, star rays, several moray eels, one quite large and menacing in appearance, and an octopus, not to mention scores of fish.

Other than a few excursions, I have managed to be a complete beach slug, immobile. I have read only two books, not even; rather finished two I started in LA, one on terrorism and some journals by Merton. I was struck by the latter's meditation on death and aging: how facing death, truly facing our ending is necessary for us to embrace our lives, and particularly the gift of freedom, to their fullest. Only by knowing, by absorbing the finality of ending and our not-beinghood can we begin to live in vertical, God time. Merton refers to this embracing of death as a quality "of faith and uprightness of heart."

Yes, faith and uprightness of heart.

I jotted down the following:

A pure heart.

Empty.

Patient.

Obedient.

Without intent other than the above.

To be open to God's will.

And love.

Truly, those twenty words represent the work of a lifetime. Or several.

The children – not children, I keep reminding myself, young adults – have just come to inform me of flooding in Europe and of a Nigerian woman who has been sentenced to death by stoning for having a child out of wedlock. My youngest daughter's rage in particular. Mel. is becoming a woman; she is beginning to understand all the barriers, small and large, blatant and subtle, around what it means to be a woman, to be female, even in American culture, let alone in Africa, still by and large patriarchal and tribal, as is much of the world.

Her angry question: "I wonder what they are going to do to the man?"

What indeed.

August 20, 2002

One bus ride, a boat ride, an eight and a half hour jet ride, and an airport shuttle later, back in LA. I feel as if I have returned to Bedlam. Which, in many respects, I have. I am beginning to think and feel that the only thing that matters anymore is kindness and being present. And music with humanity as "the musical instrument of God." How will this God music be played through me? I'm afraid I'm not a very cooperative instrument at times.

Since returning home:

More conversations with Mel. She is beginning to open up to me about her life, her hopes, anger, and fears. Anger, yes, because she already intuits that who she is, the life she has, or will have over the next decade or so, will abruptly come to an end when she marries and has children. Mel. also sees quite clearly that this does not, by and large, happen to men; their work and careers, not to mention their physical bodies, remain more intact. She sees the inequity of this, and it makes her mad.

As it should.

As it must.

P., being male, cannot understand what Mel. is going through "when she has absolutely everything!" Yes, this is true but it does nothing to address the reality, the experience of *being female,* that there are women in Africa and elsewhere who still get stoned.

I have also been thinking about Merton's concept of a *point vierge,* the virgin point at the center of each of our being:

> ...a point untouched by illusion, a point of pure truth...which belongs entirely to God, which is inaccessible to the fantasies of our own mind or the brutalities of our own will. This little point...of absolute poverty is the pure glory of God in us.

The pure glory of God within us. When we reach the still point, which is God and which belongs to God, we also embrace more fully what is precious and valuable within ourselves, undiminished and unique at our core.

Thinking, too, more and more about my sense of vocation because the childrearing phase of my life is over. This sense of vocation – voce, voice. If not still struggling, I am at least wondering about my particular vocation, what it is meant to be now. How will it be made manifest, this God music moving through me? If I am patient and open and quiet enough to listen, spirit will become concentrated in my heart.

August 24, 2002

Yesterday I went to Cedars for some more tests, a special CAT scan to see about my heart. The results were not good. There are several noticeable calcium deposits on both my coronary arteries, plus smaller deposits elsewhere. I am in the 98th percentile for women my age, which means that only 2% are worse off. I had expected some scarring and tissue damage from all the radiation but not this. Heart trouble. I guess you might say that is true in more ways than one: turmoil of the heart.

I now have to go in for a thallium treadmill test to see what the next step is.

My internist called me immediately with the results. Sadly, I'm growing accustomed to the Monday noon calls. Even before he had a chance to speak, I said, "More bad news?" I am grateful I took his advice and did not have the scan done before our vacation. I wonder if he expected such dismal results?

The first words out of his mouth: "I don't want you to think open heart surgery. I want you to really hear me on this one."

Well, *that's* comforting. If this much damage has occurred in only fifteen years, how much longer do I have?

I think the family is more stunned than I. The children, especially, I can tell are scared. But ultimately I suppose, and hope, even if it takes more hacking and slashing, the problem is correctable. I have, however, been musing about the folly of human endeavor. In my study there is a pile of papers about nuclear items and political action alerts, a pile of contacts for "remaindering" my step-parenting book, another pile for the nuclear book momentarily ready to go to press, and another of unopened mail, mostly bills. And here I sit in my early fifties with a heart in serious trouble.

Like I said: ruminating on the folly of human endeavor.

What's a life for anyway?

Certainly not self, I am learning more and more, but to love God and be loved and share that love with others. As I wrote in my last entry: kindness and being present, gratitude and music, to relish the heart music we leave behind.

August 28, 2002

Went to take the treadmill test. After arriving, the technician injected my veins with liquid thallium – just what I need, more radioactivity – and for the next two and a half hours they took pictures of my heart.

It turns out I have coronary heart disease, but it is an anomaly, brought on by none of the usual causes (heredity, dissolute lifestyle, etc.). Even the technicians and nurses looked at me quizzically, asking "What are you doing here? You're way too young for this sort of thing."

Apparently not.

And yet…

I feel centered, calm, peaceful, and light – as if I have discovered a secret key to the universe. How can so many contingencies and variables and coincidences conspire to preserve just one life? I was thinking, too, how in many ways I brought this state of affairs upon myself, all the negativity I held pent up inside from the past, not being able to say no – or yes – at the necessary moments, the blockage of darkness building within, then the radiation required to intervene on that process. And now, fifteen years later, the consequences of that previous intervention coming to light. It is all connected, all of a piece. This assessment is not about self-blame or self-pity. Far from it. Rather just looking at a sequence of events from their inception to their logical, perhaps even foregone, conclusion.

September 4, 2002

St. Andrew's Abbey in Valyermo, the high desert. My birthday. I decided to escape from the routine of family for a couple of days to meditate and pray.

My first impressions:

Voluminous clouds in the sky, breezes building through the poplars and oaks that surround the monastery, that very special kind of wind-song: more and more it speaks to me now, draws me toward it. I cannot think of a more fitting way to spend this particular birthday, especially after the good news of last week's test results. While there has been extensive scarring and inflammation due to the radiation, there are no significant blockages at this time. I passed! I feel a readiness that goes deep, open to God in a way I never have been before, and I want to be present to this.

As I was wandering around, I came across a statue of the Madonna and Child in the monastery garden and an upwelling of gratitude for my mother moved me, a relationship that has been so problematic over the years. But today, my birthday, I felt profound gratitude that she had given birth to me, that she had given me the gift of life. I honestly do not believe I have ever felt quite that way about my mother before: the fact that I came through her into all this beauty, this garden, the trees, plants, water, wind, sound, birds, people, the big, fat, obviously well-fed white duck loafing around the small pond looking for easy handouts; my life, my family, my children who came through me, just everything. Grateful for this day, this hour, this moment in the softness of the late afternoon sun, sitting on a blanket on the grass with bugs whirring around my ears, the monastery bell chiming for vespers.

It is all such a miracle.

And such a mystery.

After dinner I decided to go on a walk that extended into the last vestiges of light. When I started out, sunset was in full bloom, a panoply of pink and blue clouds across the western sky. As I was taking this in and the fresh air of twilight, scented with desert pines, I became enamored with the various sounds coming off the trees and landscape and started to wander down a dirt road.

I came across a side path with a sign marked "Cemetery" and an arrow pointing "this way." I debated for a moment about following the small road because of the coming darkness but decided to take a chance. So I started down, or rather up, the road. I walked for a number of minutes as the terrain steepened, requiring that I pick up my pace. I could see in the distance an archway of stone, which I assumed was the entrance to the burial grounds. It was farther than I anticipated, and while I might have had just enough twilight to reach it, I knew I would not have enough to return to the Abbey, let alone any time to sit and mediate on the mortality of life. So I turned around and headed back toward St. Andrew's thinking, "tomorrow."

When I finally returned, it was completely dark except for a few nightlights on in some of the buildings. I decided to see if the chapel was unlocked, which it was, dark except for a tiny flame lit in a single wall mounted candle. I tiptoed inside, despite the fact that I was alone, and knelt in one of the pews to pray. Kneeling in the darkness, whispering words of gratitude, the desire to be of service. Kneeling in the darkness with a sense of peace, the feeling of coming home. When I returned to my room, I read for quite a while from *The Cloud of Unknowing*. I can only hope the following is true:

> For God will never disappoint those who truly abandon worldly concerns to dedicate themselves to him. You can be certain of this: he will provide one of two things for his friends: Either they will receive an abundance of all they need or he will give them the physical stamina and a patient heart to endure want.

The next day I managed to hike back to the graveyard. The cemetery itself was divided in two sections: one for the monks and one for the oblates, with a plain, stark stone altar in between the two. One never knows the day or the hour, but there is a finite signature of time to this arena of consciousness. How precious then each day and each hour, though so few of us, myself included, keep this meditation long in our hearts.

September 9, 2002

I came to work early this morning thinking I had a 7:30am meeting with a parent, only to discover that it is scheduled for next week. (Memo to myself: When in doubt, check your calendar.)

On the freeway, buzzing from coffee on my way to school, a Pete Townsend song came on, "Let my love open the door to your heart..." I cranked up the sound and started singing, not only because I like the song, but because that is what it feels like is happening to me: love opening the door to my heart. And I wish I could say it has been P. or the children, though they certainly are a part of it, but I also know they are not the only reason. How steadfastly I have resisted their love in certain ways, thinking I had to prove myself, to be the mistress of my own destiny and fate – all that me/me/me ego – and a life-threatening disease have contributed to this opening, no doubt.

But I know, too, that the real opening has been effected by something beyond P. and the children and historicity and cancer and that is Love, the Prime Mover. And while it is true that it has been up to me to accept the invitation, I have been guilty of a lot of kicking and screaming and petulant thumb-sucking along the way. Then there are moments, such as cruising down the freeway at 7:15am in the morning on the way to work, listening to rock and roll that it hits you, knocks your socks off and takes your breath way, and you get a glimmer, the slightest sense of connection with the power of this force that is love and the deep, deep humility and beyond that the endless gratitude for the grace of it and the blessing.

I am beginning to feel a profound difference internally. And, of course, I also haven't had all that much to do with it other than show up and be present. No, on second thought, that is not precisely accurate either. I have wanted to experience this shift toward greater congruence and internal peace very much and have spent a lot of time devoted to spiritual "weight training" as it were. FS has seen to that.

Transitioning.

Slowing down.

Letting go.

Wondering what my next "job" will be.

Getting quiet and still.

The goal: to get soundless and deep, to experience what wants to be set free, what word-notes and sounds want to come forth. And as if on cue this, in my mailbox at school, "Doing Nothing" by Thomas Merton:

> Some of us need to discover that we will not begin to live more fully until we have the courage to do and see and taste and experience much less than usual...There are times, then, when in order to keep ourselves in existence at all we simply have to sit back for a while and do nothing...The very act of resting is the hardest and most courageous act [a man] can perform.

Or a woman.
Blessing.
To embrace all as blessing.

October 17, 2002

Since my last entry and the delivery of my nuclear book, our government, my government seems hell-bent on going to war with Iraq. Congress appears, with few exceptions, to have rolled over and capitulated to Bush's bellicose demands. All this talk about terrorists (others) and weapons of mass destruction (others) when a very good argument could be made that we, the United States, Land of the Free (only we don't think freely) and home of the brave (though we function, by and large, on fear and anxiety) is the world's preeminent terrorist: the most weapons, the most guns, the most bombs, the most munitions, the deadliest nukes, the largest, most well-appointed military machine in the history of humankind, the largest purveyor of weapons around the globe

We citizens have more guns than any other country in the world; we kill one another with greater alacrity and regularity than any other people in the world. Our airwaves and movies are obsessed with law, order, and violence. We use the vast majority of the world's resources and seemingly do not care as long as "the American way of life is preserved." And we have the nerve, or rather the unconsciousness, to call others terrorists. I think the thing that disturbs me the most, even more than our lack of self-reflective analysis, is our hypocrisy as a people. Or our government that speaks and acts in our name.

Well, not in my name.

I can hardly watch the news anymore. We are so distracted and kept in the dark about the things that really matter. Why don't we see coverage of the protests in Europe against what America is planning? What about the millions marching in our own streets not being reported? I sometimes wonder why we humans seem so hell-bent on hastening our own end. Do we not know that death comes all too quickly without any help from us? Do we not have some sense of the gift it is to be alive? Is self-destruction *that* attractive? And I understand the "yes" part of that on a personal level. There may very well be some ideas, perhaps many, worth dying for, but it is hard to accept that greed, arrogance, moral self-righteousness, and fear are among them.

I think the challenge facing us all is to get to the space within of compassion even for the persecutors, the rigid, authoritarian structures that inevitably must – and will – fall, just as the Berlin Wall fell, in order for the new life, a different way of being to emerge. In many ways, this is happening already, beneath the surface, under the radar screen of media detection, but happening nevertheless, those goodness cells I spoke about gathering and coalescing. To learn how to embrace all the badness as a necessary component of this emotional, psychological, spiritual evolution. How, out of all this darkness, comes an opportunity to shift, to focus on wonder and blessing, calling for us to act, to participate in a spirit alive to humanity and the life force that flows through us all. To get to the point of coming alive to spirit and the animation of the universe in God.

I am so not there yet and it most certainly is a mental discipline being able to go around blessing the suffering and stupidity of others. But I get the *idea* of this, how it absolutely does require and more importantly engenders a shift within that generates power and energy rather than the contraction and absorption that occurs when focusing on "the problem." Out of this comes the opportunity for right action in the world.

This is a year of transition for me, physically certainly since the operation, simply not willing to force myself as much, refraining from turning on the after-burners, like a clock once wound spring-tight, slowing down, the hands-on job of parenting almost over. I think of a friend who cried when her children left, not because she missed them but because she was so relieved to see them go that she felt guilty! After 21 years, the anticipation of getting my life back, the poignancy of letting go of the job description of the past two decades, but also a certain quiet eagerness growing as well. And, of course, parenting is never over; it just becomes different.

November 7, 2002

How does one go about getting back to what one once was? After a detour of such length and duration – twenty plus years of child rearing and parenting – is it even possible? And if possible, is it desirable? How the idea of what our life will be like vs. the reality of the life we live is quite often not only completely different from what we dreamed but perhaps even diametrically opposed to it. The dream I once had for myself: writer/novelist/artist dedicated to being outside the ordinary and expected – and in my youthful judgment, of course, the pedestrian and mundane. And what is the life I have actually lived? Very conventional and traditional in many ways, three books about rather – or very – school-marmish subjects; a wife of nearly twenty-one years and mother of four. Cooking, schlepping, decorating the house for the holidays, birthdays, events, responding to "Mom/Honey, could you please (fill in the blank)?"

It simply is not what I expected to do or to be. Yet here I am. And in that lack of expectation is a profound lack of self-understanding, at least at the stage of life entitled youth. My dreams of what I wanted to be and thought of being were a defense against what was: in the end my own restraint and fear, however subtle, were more debilitating than the power of any dream to embolden me or make me more daring.

And perhaps, too, more laziness than I was once willing to admit; the personal sacrifices that have to be made for that kind of success are not something I have been willing to do. It isn't even laziness. More that I like to daydream too much. I don't possess the requisite ego selfishness, not in a bad sense, that keeps its eye on the goal rather than the process along the way. I simply do not have that kind of relentlessness in me. Unlike Balzac, I do not write sixteen, eighteen, twenty hours at a clip, though I do spend a fair amount of time "ruminating, broodulating, eatulating, and strollulating" without doing much of anything useful, at least in the writing department. While the latter may or may not qualify as the writer's temperament, the former most certainly does and one which I have yet to activate; and if not yet, it does feel unlikely to let myself loose in now.

But you never know.

God has a way with impossibilities and long-shots if it is in His/Her plan. I guess the moral of that existential dilemma is this: never bet against miraculous intervention but don't count on it either. What I am waffling on about here is accepting that I gave up the trajectory I once was on, or thought I was on, or thought I wanted to be on many years ago and this says more about me, my character deficits and strengths, too, than the trajectory itself. I honestly do not know if it is possible, or desirable, to will something into being if it is not Will's intent for whatever it is to come into being. There is a razor thin line between perseverance, willfulness, and stubbornness in both the good and bad sense; between rightful devotion vs. wanting things to go your way.

A line from Freida Kahlo I like: "sharpened to the point of infinity."

Yes, my soul as a divine pencil, being sharpened to the end.

November 15, 2002
A vivid dream last night:

I meet G. who represents being alive and creative to me. We are in a palatial estate like P.'s and my former home in Carmel Valley. At first it feels as if this place belongs to G. but my study is there, filled with books and light, so the space must be mine as well. We meet in a large room where G. wants to make love but I tell him I am pregnant with my 5th child which will be difficult to bear because of all the surgery I have had. We embrace lying on the floor with such feeling that I have an orgasm. It is long, deep, and intense. As we kiss, there is a kind of instantaneous click, like the sound of tumblers fitting into place and coming together. Afterwards, G. says it was great sex, even though there was no physical penetration. I say no, it wasn't sex but great love making.

G. tells me that his personal assistant will be looking for him to keep an appointment, so we haven't much time. I want to show him my study, so I take G. by the hand and lead him to it. It is like a secret garden behind closed doors. He is impressed by all the books and totems, the artwork on the walls.

I then see a huge buttercup yellow butterfly outside one of the windows and say, "Wait!" I rush to the window and open it. G. cautions me to be careful as the butterfly flutters in and lands on my arm. It is gigantic, enormous, the size of a hawk or eagle. The color is a stunning, brilliant yellow; rich yet delicate, ephemeral yet vibrant and pulsating. It rests on my arm for a number of moments before taking flight. I gaze upon it with delight and wonder, as if it is talking to me, then watch it fly away.

I am both pleased and comforted to know that when a dream really needs to get through, it will. The image of this butterfly was so potent, so powerful and beautiful that it does feel that a large transformation is in store. Do I stay in the comfort and familiarity of old patterns or do I break free? Every new world we are "born" into requires that we spread our wings, however tentatively, and fly.

December 3, 2002
Personal velocity: how this concept captivates me! How each of us has a specific pace and speed at which we move, unique to us alone, and also perhaps a personal vector that we are traversing, traveling on through time at our unique personal velocity. Personal velocity and personal vector: how much or how little of these two attributes do any of us share?

Things have not been good of late. No, that isn't accurate. Being alive is good. I still cringe when I see people in the market or on the street who have had strokes. P. and I continue to struggle with one another, aspects of each other's characters that are unfathomable, sometimes to the point of war, and hypocrite me writing about peace. No doubt some of the complaints P. has about me are true and at times some of the things he says are downright condescending, abusive even. That to him I so lack the testing of character, that my belief system and philosophy "have no basis in the real world, all theory and no practice." How he does underestimate me in this regard! And even worse, the scornful, simmering lack of respect. In his eyes I come across as a disputatious, contentious bitch, which I no doubt can be. But unless these perspectives are informed by "the realities of the business world" (the only real world in P.'s view), he dismisses mine as untutored. We simply do not appear capable of breaking this destructive dynamic.

I was telling him the other day:

If there is a flaw in a diamond, no matter how many times you cut and polish it, you can never get rid of the original flaw. It will always be there. One either learns to love the flaw just as it is or get another diamond. And there has been a basic flaw in our relationship since the beginning, the "deal" we made. Now that the children are grown, more and more of the fissures are showing. But there is something about me P. experiences as so threatening. My worldview? My stubbornness? My what?

What I notice now is that I no longer react to these episodes – so like the pattern of domestic violence but without the physical component – with anger, fear, or internal collapsing. I feel centered, though these episodes remain deeply disturbing, destabilizing, and sad. How is it that two people can so lose sight of the goodness in one another?

I was walking around the neighborhood the other night, thinking I cannot continue to live with a man who feels this way about me, who feels I am so naïve, so unsuccessful, so unproven, so underachieving. It is a fundamental issue of self-respect and remaining congruent with my character. I need to start over. Or start, period. This is where the spiritual discipline comes in because it is of the heart, not the head, and it is the heart that must speak. Staying the course but also knowing when things have run their course, when and where the course is at its end.

All this private turmoil amidst aging parents who are failing rapidly and petrified of what comes next, a brother who is far away, and off-spring and houseguests who are home for the holidays amidst turkey, stuffing, and mashed potatoes. Twenty-one years of living with someone not a lie exactly but based on a false premise, a flawed foundation – more a business relationship than a deep abiding soul-love.

Maybe it's not about personal velocity at all. In the physical realm, yes; but in the sacred realm perhaps not because the light of the heart travels in a different dimension. How I need this heart light now! How the world needs it too, light vectors and goodness cells connecting.

December 10, 2002

I had planned on spending last Saturday locked in my study working, but instead P. and I had a three-hour talk. I had been giving serious thought to our marriage contract and what the next step would be. Would I just revert to living in a room the way I did some twenty plus years ago in London when we first met? But, of course, it is not twenty years ago; it is now. And in spite of all my confusion, I have to confess to a certain eagerness about the possibility of a newly emergent self.

But I recognize, too, that this is a cop-out in a way – the idea that you need to be physically alone to become "you." It is more the reverse of that: once you truly make the commitment to be your true self, you will be alone anyway, whether or not you are in solitude or with multitudes of people. In many ways, it is infinitely more challenging to become oneself in the context of a relationship. Sometimes I think staying is much harder than going. Going is primarily complicated at the material level. Staying requires an emotional grittiness and toughness that can feel fathomless at times. And yet I know, too, that leaving can be the one act, the one gesture that absolutely is required because I did that in my first marriage and I was right, however painful and difficult it was at the time.

But, but, but...I am trying to feel my way into this process and something remains incomplete. I can tell that much, though I cannot pinpoint what that something is. Dependency? Dominance? Authority? Submission? And because the world (and P.) are so dominated by money and the marketplace level of existence, it is easy to assume that he is the dominant one and I the submissive; that he is in charge and I am dependent. While there is no doubt that I would miss many of the material comforts, I won't be held hostage. The journey of self and soul is larger than that.

If I cannot or do not become the person I am meant to be within the context of this relationship, what makes me think that I will somehow miraculously become that person outside it? The same issues will be there; the same work will be required. I guess it all boils down to this: be who you are, where you are, now. But it is also true you sometimes have to lose sight of land before getting to the shore of a new life. The butterfly must leave the cocoon in order to fly.

****

I was reading the other day how the words "worth" and "worship" share the same root; that worship is an expression of worth-ship, of worthiness. This is the fundamental level I am grappling with: learning how to pay attention, to make the conscious decision each day to create small pockets and places of time to recognize and remember my worth-ship and to worship that worthiness. Not in a narcissistic sense, but learning how to keep myself in the equation, to not flee mentally or lose myself by deferring to others or thinking I somehow do not matter or that what I say – or do or write – will not be taken seriously or will be criticized and ignored.

I also know how indifferent the world can be. And though that may be true, it is also true that one does not have to capitulate to that smaller truth when there is a larger truth calling. I think this is what keeps me in this relationship: it is the testing ground of worth-ship precisely because it is so foreign feeling to me at times. And this has nothing to do with feminism or women's and people's liberation or politics. Well, maybe it does, but that is not the point. It has to do with a spiritual unfolding, a spiritual uncovering and liberation that resides within the heart. Because it is only from the heart level that any of this makes sense to me, that this feels complete and holistic to me. Otherwise, it all just disintegrates into he said/she said; we think/they think polemics and duality, the battle of being right vs. the commitment to being loving and kind. The whole world is embroiled in this particular struggle, right now in Afghanistan and Iraq especially, but elsewhere, too.

Some guiding principles for my immediate future:

Accuracy with regard to my family; for me, a fierce tirelessness. There is never any end, any goal other than processes evolving, velocities and vectors deepening. I think this is why the word "perseverance" appears so many times in the New Testament; a devoted tirelessness to the task of self-restructuring with God, of self-restructuring into the image of God.

For my foundation: compassion, the only virtue, and not even virtue really, though it may be one, but rather compassion as an activity of love. It is the only thing, value, concept, act, endeavor, idea, and organizing principle that will keep me honest, humble, and sane. And to remember to apply it to myself as much as I do to others.

Music: "the electrical soil in which the spirit lives, thinks, and invents." There is no other art form like it. I think this is so because we humans are meant to be musical, to sing, to resonate and vibrate at a core level with divinity, or with the small, infinitesimal ray of divinity that is given to each of us, however hidden in darkness it may be. There needs to be more time for music, more music period; music alone is one of the best reasons I can think of to want to be here, moving with rhythm and notes and sound, playing Bach and Clementi in the late afternoon. That is what a life is for: to rejoice and vibrate and sing!

Even the notes of the scale have a spiritual connotation:

Dominus (Do) – God in humanity.

Regina Caeli (Re) – Queen of Heaven (the moon).

Microcosmos (Mi) – Earth.

Fatus (Fa) – Destiny (the planets).

Sol (So) – the Sun.

Voie Lacte (La) – the Milky Way.

Siderial (Ti) – the stars, galaxies, and cosmos.

Domiuns (Do) – God the Creator.

The sounds of celestial music indeed!

So as this year closes with wars and rumors of wars; with power bases shifting and shuffling; with talk, talk, talk; nuclear this, problem that: we as a species are reaching critical mass. And if we do end up blowing ourselves and the world apart, as Henry Adams feared, will we do so without learning the lessons we need to learn? That we are here to live in reverence and respect and love for one another with the nanosecond of time we are gifted with.

January 9, 2003

While on our family ski vacation, P. dropped the bombshell that he wants to terminate our marriage by revoking the pre- and post-nuptial agreements we signed over twenty years ago. In other words, he wants a divorce. But here's the kicker: he still wants us to live together as if nothing has changed. But this will change *everything*! Like Pandora's box, it will set in motion a series of events over which neither one of us has any control. It is quite possible we will not survive this "experiment" of his. And P. has built a multi-million dollar empire doing just that: predicting and controlling outcomes.

You can nullify a contract.

But how do you nullify a vow?

I am positively reeling, stunned and simultaneously not surprised at all, but still very sorrowful and sad. I am profoundly sad for all the things I have said and done that I shouldn't have and equally sorry for all the things I should have said and done but did not. I love P. but I haven't been very loving at times. So much defensiveness and disputatiousness on my part. I must own this, and I do feel contrition for it.

Talk about being on a shake down cruise: the best and the worst of times! Health issues, marriage collapsing, children leaving, parents imploding; there are moments when all this has felt positively Jobian to me. I am almost afraid to ask "what next?" for fear that I will be hit with another thunderbolt. How do I learn the discipline of being surrendered while everything around me is so out-of-control? How do I remain calm in the midst of chaos and change? And there is much grief in letting go even if you know it is right and required. It is like launching oneself into a river with a rudderless boat and trusting in the Providential nature of God to get you where you need to be.

January 18, 2003

I don't really know what to think anymore. Organizing the dissolution of our marriage – in legalese the "memorialization of the contract" – has brought up so much shit for me, and while shit may be a natural process, it still stinks. For several mornings in a row I have awakened in tears. Tears of sadness? Tears of confusion? Tears of injustice? Tears of anger and rage? Does it matter?

P. believes settling our marriage contract, a.k.a. paying me what I'm due, will allow us to destroy the false premise upon which our marriage was originally based – that fractured diamond – by razing it to the ground, in order to build an entirely new relationship, not as husband and wife in the legal sense, and therefore somehow "forced" to be together, but rather as partners on a soul journey. At least, that is what he says.

But it is hard, hard, hard for me not to feel now that the parenting/maternal job is over that I'm being "fired." P. may feel this way on some level too, though he has been the one to set the rules of the game, so he's calling the shots and having it his way. You're worth this, I'll pay you that; you get this, I keep everything else. It is a mental/emotional/spiritual discipline not to fall into a War of the Roses mentality.

Because ultimately this is not about money, even though every divorce is about money and who gets the kids. No: *it is about freedom!* I refuse to play the victim here. The real issue is how I did and did not take care of myself in this relationship. It all points back to me and my own self-responsibility, or lack thereof. Nobody put a gun to my head to sign all those documents so many years ago.

I do think P. is being naïve or unconscious or both to believe that we can terminate this marriage legally, go on living together as if nothing has changed, and as he puts it "explore what we both need." These are all euphemisms for the fact that he wants an open relationship. He wants to be with me while seeing others. But what do I want? My head is reeling and whirring so much I can't even think what the answer to that might be.

In the meantime, my parents' declining health and inability to function require my immediate attention and my off-spring are all eager to get on with their lives, which is as it should be. When you're young, you simply cannot relate to getting older and being old, almost as if it is a foreign country you will never visit, let alone inhabit. Then you wake up one morning, and you're middle-aged, and your face is a passport stamped with wrinkles, ready for entry. And you wonder what your life has been about. In the meantime, P. is in Hawaii at a conference, wheeling and dealing with the movers and shakers of wealth. He says he loves me but his work is his one true mistress, his constant passion and companion.

I have been aware of a number of reactions, some blatant, others subtle, that I have experienced since this process was set in motion:

A vast sense of relief that I do not have to care for and oversee the house if I don't want to, like a faithful steward arranging for all the details of living and maintenance: food, supplies, cooking, preparations, workmen, repairs, events, entertaining, cleaning. I can walk away from it all.

I do not have to listen to P.'s constant complaints about food in restaurants or travel accommodations or about other people unless I want to, unless I experience this as endearing, which I do not.

That my mental faculties have become so disjointed and distracted, not to mention natural deterioration due to age, because of the constant interruption of family and communal life, that I will need a lengthy retreat, perhaps even a silent hermitage to get quiet again in order to actually hear myself THINK, to hear what my soul needs, what my soul has to say.

A growing neutrality. There is no real disappointment or elation anymore, just feedback from the universe. And trusting God.

And then, of course, within moments of that last thought, real and true as it is, I can feel as if I am going to scream, pace the floor like a tiger (tigress), and/or be in tears.

February 2, 2003
The winds are howling outside, inside the winds of change.

P. and I signed the divorce papers in a small West LA mediation office, a Jiffy Lube for divorce, after twenty-one years and one month of marriage; irreconcilable differences cited as the cause. It does indeed feel as if the world, and mine especially, is disintegrating because we simply aren't patient enough to learn how to get along. I remind myself of the Gayatri Prayer:

> You who are the source of all power/Whose rays illuminate this whole world/Illuminate also my heart/So that it can do Your work.

Remember, Maurine, you do nothing by your own power; it is Love that works through you, that loves through you. This is the ultimate goal of the spiritual warrior, the disciple of spirit.

Yes, and having felt the absolute rightness and clarity of this counsel, it was still bloody hard going into that low cost, no frills divorce clinic, signing those papers, and seeing it all in black and white, neat and stark on the forms. P. as "petitioner" and M. as "respondent," the only other legal basis for divorce in California being incurable insanity, which is hard to prove in court, and P. of course wanted to avoid court and lawyers at all costs because of his money. I wonder: Is marriage a form of incurable insanity? Fighting the battle over who's going to be right? Who's going to win the argument or the divorce or the war? How much violence is perpetrated in the world today over who's going to be right!

On one level, however necessary this may be, on another level it feels infinitely sad and tacky and confusing to me. We didn't even talk about what this would mean, what the possible ramifications and outcomes might be. P. just steam-rolled everything through because it is what he wanted and "couldn't go on unless this was done." From first mention of his "out-of-the-box" idea to signing papers only four short weeks, my head still spinning. But how *do* we go on?

A hot day, too, the hottest on record, the middle of winter with heat blasting. Even the weather wouldn't cooperate with just a little gloom. Going into a small, nondescript two-story office building, Room 210, Divorce Resource, Inc. "affordable family divorce." P. knew I wouldn't contest this, though I knew I could with his millions. It's a joke. As JF said when he saw the final accounting of my life on paper: x amount for so many years, x + x for so many others, he actually used the word "punitive" to describe what I ended up with. A business deal that didn't pan out as P. expected? And the irony, too, that what has driven P. wild about me at times – my passivity, my not taking risks or fighting back – is also the very character aspect, flaw, weakness, deficit, and/or trait he needed to count on for me to *not* make waves, for me *not* to hire somebody like Gloria Allrad to defend my rights. Not to mention losing three to five years or more battling in court, not to mention we would probably never be able to look each other in the eye again, let alone speak to one another, not to mention what such a battle would do to our children, not to mention the fact that I honestly do not think my body could tolerate the stress of engaging in World War III.

I have to confess, though, that there was something so seedy and sneaky about it, like trying to hide or cover something up while no one else was looking, like a back-street abortion, get it over quickly, don't tell anybody, shhh. A small waiting room, fifteen by ten, with a receptionist from Blackpool, England, a small beige embroidered pillow hanging on the door with the message: Eat, Drink, and Remarry.

I doubt it.

The woman who was helping us saw how my hands were shaking and offered me a diet coke and box of tissue. A part of me was surprised how upset I was but then again, why wouldn't I be? I was being legally and emotionally clobbered. As P. sat there calmly explaining his view, his agenda, the woman had the experience, and kindness, to say: "Well, that's how you see things. It's usually harder for the person on the receiving end."

No kidding.

At one point as she was recording the list of P.'s property and holdings, the mediator looked at me, her eyes communicating, "What's going on here? You're getting what?!" I just looked back without uttering a single word, only a slight nod of my head, and she got it. I'm not sure exactly what we two women managed to communicate in that non-verbal exchange but she "got" it and I got that she "got" it.

Middle-age meltdown?

The man moving on?

The man wanting it his way?

The man wanting to protect his financial empire?

The man wanting to see who else is out there?
Why even bother arguing?
Just give me the fucking papers to sign.

February 5, 2003

Starbucks, Malibu, early morning. I have been awake
since 4:00am. Not able to sleep or stop the endless internal
chatter about this and that, along with great sadness over
things breaking up and falling apart. Birth, in whatever
form it takes, is painful. Painful!

When we left the mediator's office, I didn't want to
talk to or even look at P. I was hoping to get away in my
car before he spotted me, but I didn't quite make it. He was
concerned and surprised at how upset I was, though I could
tell he, too, found the whole experience unnerving, not
what he expected. For him, it was like "performing
surgery" and "cutting away the diseased parts." But
sometimes surgery metastasizes the disease and the patient
dies.

Shaking I said, among other things, "What exactly
have we been to each other? Just a womb and a sperm
donor? If that's so, shame on us both!" He wanted to go out
for lunch. Who could eat after that? Thanks but no thanks.
I left P. standing in the parking lot. I told him I wouldn't be
home that night; it's what I needed to do to take care of me.

After I squealed out of the parking lot in front of
Trader Joe's, I went to the market and cleaners. Of course,
what else is new? Even when the chess game ends, there
are more errands to run. When I got home I listened to
Jonathan Franzen on NPR. I thought earlier that as the first
act of my newly divorced life I would show up at the radio
station to reconnect with the writer part of me and get an
autograph on *How to Be Alone,* his latest book. But I ended
up being much too upset and the paper work at the
mediator's took longer than expected. So I went home

45

instead, except it wasn't my home anymore, and listened to Franzen on the radio.

"It's ok to be a writer."

"People who read are the only people I feel passionately about. They are my family."

"It's ok to be a misfit."

Amen.

Then off to do more errands: picking up a small amp and head mike for an upcoming speaking engagement. Standing in West LA Music thinking: "This is the closest I'll ever get to being a rock star." Then off to Kinko's to pick up more copies of my writing partner's and my script.

When I got home I hurriedly threw a T–shirt, my toothbrush, and a pair of clean underwear into a bag, along with a candle of a couple intertwined, which was given to me years ago by a friend. I knew I had to do some sort of ritual later that night, and then headed north on PCH just as the sun was setting, so tired, such a draining day. I hadn't eaten since breakfast and was hungry and emotionally spent. But rather than rushing to yet another destination to do yet another errand – retrieving my reading glasses, which I had left at my parents a few days prior when I was helping them sign documents to sell their house. And how poignant too that scene was! Having to guide their hands where to sign because they are becoming so feeble and blind that they could not do it themselves. Thinking to myself: everyone signing papers now, for one reason or another.

I finally had to stop. I simply could not rush anymore. So I pulled into the shopping area at Cross Creek in Malibu, just as the last rays of the sun were dying and took myself out to dinner, luxuriating in a well-deserved and much needed Cosmopolitan and Italian food while leisurely reading an article from *The New York Times Magazine* about American hegemony.

After eating, I went to a movie and upon exiting the theater around 9:00pm, I stood for a moment debating whether or not I wanted to go to Taverna Tony's, one of the local hang-outs. The Santa Ana winds were stirring, and I couldn't see myself being convivial with people around a bar. So I drove to Michael Landon Park, locked the car, and walked across the soccer field and past the baseball diamond where my kids had played so many games, kicked and hit so many balls, and felt the warm breezes kiss my face as I watched the stars. Looking up at Orion's Belt I thought: it really is such a gift to be here. A peacefulness came over me and suddenly I felt quite tired. I drove through Malibu Canyon and checked into the Day's Nite Inn, a motel just off the 101 Freeway. After changing and putting on my T-shirt, I lit the candle of the couple intertwined and said a prayer for P. and me, a prayer asking for forgiveness for all the things I/we have done wrong in this relationship. At 1:30am I blew out what remained of the half-spent candle and went to bed.

The next morning after a restless night I checked out the yellow pages for the closest Starbucks, where this entry started – remind me to buy stock – and sat with a cup of coffee and a zucchini walnut muffin reading some scriptural passages that bring me comfort. Driving out to my parents to pick up my glasses, I once again was reminded, "Look up!" The hills off the freeway were so green, like spring, though the dead of winter everywhere else. "Look up," the injunction to look up, like the stars the previous night. No matter how bad things get, we must all keep looking up. And to be honest, as hard as signing those papers was, there also was a part of me that felt unburdened and relieved.

Nothing is ever simple and straightforward. The nuances and complexities of things can be infinitely subtle and subtly intricate, all those vectors and velocities colliding. I have been on a veritable rollercoaster of emotion for weeks now: deep, deep sadness, a grief and anguish that physically hurt, to feeling buoyant and anticipatory, at times even excited, to feeling remorseful and righteously humble over all the things I have done wrong or neglected to do or have been at fault for and sincerely culpable about in this relationship, to crying – no sobbing – until my head hurt, to being okay and praying for internal peace and surrender.

Talk about a triple E ticket ride!

Yesterday was particularly hard. I forced myself to go to yoga and broke down in class. Afterwards, I called FS, weeping over the phone, sharing the part of me that is so hurt, so devastated by this and also wondering what that part is about, the part that is not afraid to say I don't want to lose P., that I love him, not to mention what to tell the kids. We cannot pretend this doesn't change things and while the marriage may be P.'s and my business, the family and how it will be affected is theirs. FS and I spoke for nearly an hour. Correction: I burbled and sputtered between blowing my nose dozens of times with his patient, kind, concerned listening. How I needed that! FS's counsel to just sit with the rubble and devastation of this, along with the absolute craziness of the idea: dissolve the marriage in the hope of salvaging the relationship? Burn the village to save it?

After I got off the phone, my head ached from all the tears, so I took some aspirin and a very hot shower, then I took myself out and I did not rush home to fix dinner.

****

An afterthought:

While skim reading sections of the *Illuminated Kama Sutra,* the last in the book devoted to Courtesans, I was taken aback by how much it applied to my relationship with P., how I had "sold myself out" for security and he had "bought" me to have children and create a family. This brought up so much about the idea that marriage traditionally has been seen as a "deal," an exchange of sex and procreation for goods, dowry, and money. But in any exchange where money and goods take place, a pattern of hostility, guilt, and resentment can be set in motion between the debtor and provider, between the one doing the "hiring" and the one who allows him or herself to be "hired."

Based upon the past two decades and the core truth of our marriage: that P. wanted a wife, drew up a list of must-have attributes, went out "shopping" and found me and that I allowed myself to buy into his plan, consciously or unconsciously doesn't matter. I take that back. It does matter; at least if it is conscious you are not that surprised when the shit hits the fan. If unconscious, then there truly is hell to pay.

I have to admit there were times when I felt like a worker on a plantation where the rich, powerful "massah" came out and pointed "I'll take that one" – meaning me – or the fertile peasant maid the king wanted for his bed. That is how completely bereft of personal volition I was in my life when P. and I met after the end of my first marriage.

What really struck me was the list of 32 ways to get rid of an unwanted lover: how many have I been guilty of over the years? And P. too: never being around, always working, getting angry and upset over trivial things, his volatile temper. Just a few from the list we both are guilty of committing:

- sexual spurning
- being indifferent toward subjects he/she knows about or is interested in
- staying separate

- sleeping alone
- always taking everything he/she says the wrong way
- repudiating the things he/she says with contradictory comments
- focusing on inherent short-comings that he/she can do nothing about
- persecuting him/her for flaws that are common to most men and women

I stopped there. The burgeoning catalogue of faults, both his and mine, was too depressing to confront.

February 8, 2003
Another restless night.

My conversation this past week with JZ once again brought my placating pattern right smack-dab before my eyes: my defending P.'s position and rationalizing his actions, not focusing on my own; the split in our personalities, both P.'s and mine, and, of course, his sadness, too, over hearing the news. His acknowledgment that he is probably the only person I could be having this conversation with because of the history he, P., and I share. I do need some wise elder counsel at this time. JZ believes P. hasn't surrendered fully to the feminine and without this there can be no true healing. And that I, for whatever reason – fearing my own power or avoiding it – haven't demanded or required this of him. My sharing with JZ the feeling that P. has thrown down the gauntlet, and I must now pick it up and do what I must do.

Which means moving out when the dust of my parents' relocation and Mel.'s flying off to greet the arms of her new life at collage are accomplished. JZ said several things that struck a chord, especially that I need to resume my life as a woman of letters. The woman of letters I am. It touched me that he said that, that he sees and acknowledges this about me, something P. never did or if he did, only begrudgingly as my "expensive hobby." When I told JZ some of the chronology of the past six months – my surgery, etc. – he commented that P. may be scared of my physical weakness and that he is "cutting his losses," so to speak, or to use P.'s words "doing surgery to cut out the diseased part."

Can this possibly be so? Is there that much unconsciousness at play here? On one level I understand exactly what JZ means. I have had the same feeling myself, not so much that P. is "getting rid" of me because of my recent health problems but because he feels it is time to move on and get on with his life, the clock ticking, and he doesn't want any legal connection to inhibit his freedom. Now that my "services" are not longer needed as the mother, breeder, housekeeper, caretaker, well here's the check and golden handshake, oh faithful and trusty servant.

In a perverse sort of way, I honestly do believe a part of P. is sincere about this "stepping outside the box" in a last ditch effort to see if his crazy idea just might work. But, of course, that is what he *must* believe in order to protect himself from his own unconscious, darker truths. And it is what I must accept to alleviate the shock and hurt that he could actually do what he has done, just cut me off, snap, like that.

I must move out in order to answer the question: Is it P. I truly want or the lifestyle? Because if I miss the lifestyle more than the relationship, with or without the legal papers, it's all over anyway. I told him I think spring break would be the best time to tell the children. They will have some time off from the pressures of school to digest the news – if, in fact, it is news to them. In a moment of comic hilarity, I can actually see one or several of them saying, "What took you so long?" But that is probably being overly optimistic. Though they may understand and not be that surprised, they still will be sad. It is sad when a family breaks apart.

Maybe all this is just an elaborate excuse to protect ourselves from the truth that everything is over by holding on to the idea or hope or fantasy that this will allow us to come together again in a different way. One never, ever knows. I am embarking on a journey whose destination I do not know.

February 15, 2003

Not much of a Valentine's Day, and I am trying not to be sentimental or maudlin about it. The only requirement now is trust. I am beginning to calm down a bit, though waves of sadness and grief still arise. The internal judge/defense attorney arguing my side of the case is taking a recess for now.

It has been a busy week, starting with a seriously depressed suicidal teenager at school, followed by a workshop on step-parenting. And, of course, it was pouring rain the day the workshop was scheduled. The heavens opened and the El Nino forecasters have been predicting finally arrived. I left the house shortly after 8:00am thinking that would be ample time to reach my destination, set things up, and collect myself. But at 9:45am I found myself standing in a deluge of water without an umbrella at a phone booth, asking for directions, my cell phone having decided at that precise moment to go dead. The mental health facility where I was to speak had failed to mention that their building was set back from the street, behind a Jack in the Box of all places, and therefore could not be seen from the highway. Oops!

I entered the room only minutes before "going on," carrying a podium, portable chalkboard, and bag filled with handouts and books, looking like something the cat dragged in. I am glad I have a sense of humor. There is nothing so tempting in life to set oneself up for a fall than taking oneself too seriously. However, I am pleased to report that the presentation went swimmingly – no pun intended – and I actually sold six books.

O ye of little faith!

What else?

Still dealing with the paper work of divorce. In the final analysis it all boils down to signing on the dotted line. I am working to maintain a public persona of calmness and to get on with my life. In private, behind closed doors there are poignant moments of profound grief for what is dying. The few of my friends whom I have told are sad about what has happened. But none is surprised.

I am learning more what it means to not just make peace but *be* peace, be *at* peace. It is a different level of presence within. I think peace is what is achieved or rather peace is what flowers when one can remain in a state of compassion. Compassion is a love that goes so deep that you would do anything to shed light into places of darkness.

A love that goes so deep.

A love that goes so deep you are willing to be present to what is.

March 1, 2003

A sleepless night due to an adverse reaction to some medicine, along with my weakened condition from being sick with the flu. I found myself sobbing, gut-wrenching sobs on the floor of my shower in a fetal position, bereft at the thought of losing P., of not being with him, playing out in my mind's eye getting a place, being alone, going back to work – it's not as if I don't work now but it would be different – not having to report to anyone or deal with the many intricacies of relationship, and so on. And I found myself wailing like a hurt, wounded animal, not so much about what I would lose in terms of lifestyle or comfort, which probably would not be all that different because I, myself, live quite simply.

No, it wasn't that but getting to the point of recognizing the absolute and sovereign importance of love in one's life: not just being in love, at this point too romantic and immature a notion, but the honoring of love, the gift of love, of being a loving person, of sharing that; I have been guilty of dishonoring that. Nothing, absolutely nothing – no success, however one defines that; not proving one's point or being right or being able to do whatever one pleases – none of that is worth sacrificing love. And I don't mean clinging to a love that is not right or from a position of neediness and fear because that would not be love anyway but something unhealthy based upon manipulation and coercion rather than generosity and freedom of spirit.

I honestly felt as if I experienced a complete nervous breakdown in the course of only a few hours. I felt as if I had been sent into exile, that my soul, by leaving P. or thinking about leaving him, had been separated from God, and that is positively the worst thing that can happen to anyone in the spiritual realm. Not that P. is God or that I am. But rather the separation from Love and the gift of love is such a separation, such a profound rift that the soul quite literally can die without it. So I lay on the tiles of the shower floor with hot water streaming over me and sobbed and sobbed, inconsolable, a visceral, physical hurt, a rent in the fabric of my being.

Coming to the reality that we are unceasing beings existing in the eternal unfolding of God's universe and that relationship and family are among the primary vehicles of redemption in that universe; this is what we are called to bear witness to: how to exist in Love. Nothing else matters or is of true worth or worthiness or worth-ship.

****

P. and I met again in the divorce mediator's office and signed the final papers severing our legal relationship. P. handed me my check, my "severance" pay. By this act we have set the time clock on our relationship back to zero. Have you ever heard of anything so bizarre or strange or crazy in your life? We have "killed" our marriage in order to see if we have a relationship; no marriage contracts or prenuptial and postnuptial agreements or duties or responsibilities to children as the reason for being together. Just P. and me and God.

I do know this: Whatever the outcome, it will be because of love and in the service of love and therefore for the good of us both, together or apart. I have to confess that I have had to undergo a most piercing and brutal moral inventory of all the areas where I have truly and honestly fallen short. And this process has been painful in some very real and distinct ways: my argumentativeness, my overactive judge, my ironic commentary, which P. never got anyway; at times my inappropriate deference, passivity, and accommodation; my inability to see myself as fundamentally good and therefore capable rather than fundamentally flawed and not worthy of love. It makes me think of what FS said: how separated I am from my own goodness. If I had a stronger sense of it, I would no doubt have better self-preservation skills.

Ultimately it boils down to this: Can you love me just for me? An imperfect, fallible creature with strengths and weaknesses. Can I forgive myself for my past errors and faults? Can I forgive P. for his? Can we forgive each other and start anew? Can we choose that, be *that* strong? For the weak can never forgive; forgiveness is an attribute of the strong.

If I have learned anything from the extreme oscillation of emotional events over the last few months it is this:

I must trust Spirit and the fundamental goodness, beneficence of things.

I must allow myself to come from a position of joy and abundance in spite of immediate contextual events, however painful on a human level they may be.

What I first experienced with such hurt and feelings of rejection, understandable and valid to be sure, I am now beginning to see that it comes down to love freely chosen, love freely given. That's it.

March 8, 2003

Spent the day at a Reiki workshop because it is time to gather in more healing tools. It is becoming more apparent to me that a chain of events has been set in motion over which I have little control and all my fussing and whining won't make one jot of difference. The journey is far from over, but old patterns die hard, entropy being what it is, and setting the appropriate intention is critical. It is time. Now. For me.

What has had to die within? The needy child? The hesitant, reluctant being? All this no longer acceptable to the demands of Spirit. A new energy is required and a new energy shall enter, of this I am sure. I just don't know, nor can I predict, how long this process will take. Truth is inherently confrontational, and even in someone such as myself who prides herself on seeking the truth, falsehood can have a fast and vast hold.

Energy follows thought toward truth or falsehood, depending what we focus on, what we hold in our intention. Which channel do you want to align yourself with? This is at once a nerve-wracking process and an exciting one. What is required is not a new me but a new power within me. I have never before felt so completely at the mercy of total trust. I don't even want to talk about work anymore – a book here, a book there; a contact here, a contact there – though I did say a prayer of gratitude for an order of twelve books. What I have come to is this: the work is the healing, and the healing is the work. Full stop. The healing of self, the healing of other, person by person, place by place. The planet positively groans right now for this kind of healing, this requisite coming to a different level of interaction. Or maybe it is about getting back to where we all started from in the first place: whole, complete, loving, and at peace.

Energy follows thought. What are the thoughts we wish to think as individuals, a country, or a species? Thinking about the war and how war bruises the psyche more than we can possibly imagine, to say nothing of lives lost. No one wants to confront the psychologically wounded when a war is started: a single life, a single death, and all of us die a little more somewhere in our being. Maybe we humans are coming to the point where we simply will not be able to afford war anymore. All of our resources will need to be garnered to safeguard and protect one another, especially those in greater need, and the planet itself.

Yet I fear with our short attention spans and our move on to the next disaster mentality we will get easily bored and not pay attention. How very swift are the forces of destruction! And how slow those of creation. Time favors each in its own way but from utterly opposite ends of the continuum. This, too, is a deep meditation.

And this is not to disparage those in the armed forces who put themselves in harm's way. I do not want them to have to do that for me, to make that sacrifice for me or for anyone. I feel for the makers of war as well as those who suffer at the hands of those makers. Force and military might may buttress the physical weakness of the individual and state but it diminishes personal power and spiritual authority. Non-violence renounces physical power but gains proportionally in the spiritual realm. It is this we must focus on. We are moving from a paradigm of external force to one of internal power.

I have a sense that no matter what happens either to me or the world there will be goodness behind it because ultimately love conquers hate and wrong thinking. There is no power more powerful than that, despite what one is exposed to in the world, especially on the news, the Merchants of Anxiety and Dread, or Inanity and Frivolity. What is required now is being more compassionately attentive. It seems to me that non-violence and healing can only spring from non-agenda because of the "sheer morality of its claim" as Martin Luther King said. It is what is required at an objective level without politics or ego-driven schemes.

Love always conquers hate and energy follows thought. We must be very mindful of our thoughts. They carry far more power than we realize. That is the reason why prayer and meditation hold such promise – and power – because they focus positive thought and help diffuse negative thought. Einstein's E=mc2 is the most salient mathematical equation of our time, not because it gave insight into the nature of matter and how we could manipulate it, but because it gives us a clue as to the potent nature of thought, of consciousness and light, not as physical principles but as *spiritual realities*. This is what we need to wrap our minds and hearts around now. And to know that the speed of this love-light traveling is the fastest phenomenon of all.

March 22, 2003

The first official day of spring: the equinox and our planet poised evenly between light and dark. Let us hope that as our sweet earth moves toward greater light, we humans will, too. It is at times so difficult holding together all the disparity and contradiction presented in the world of duality, and yet somehow hold them we must, all those different personal velocities and vectors. The disparity of bombs dropping and killing people, mostly innocent who don't want to die, soldiers included. This darkness and death followed by the joyfulness of spring – all the growth and green and flowers budding forth – allowing oneself to feel and appreciate it and experience gratitude for it while yet knowing that war is going on half-way around the globe. How does one bear witness to all these co-existing levels of reality?

Praying for guidance about what my mission in the world is. The mission of spirit has become far more important to me than any other, though devotion to writing may be a part of that mission. The only way to meet and accept spirit's invitation is to rest in a state of being undefended. And whatever answers come from this undefended place will come from the heart, not the head. *Anahata*: heart, "the unstruck drum." What strikes the unstruck drum? What causes this vibration of life to rise and fall? The primordial prayer: God.

April 26, 2003

What does it mean to rediscover passion within oneself? All those nooks and crannies where passion has been buried and stored? All the places where it has been hidden and locked up? That is what this journey is about: the recovery and rediscovery of passion, long dormant and long silenced. A time now for new beginnings and rekindled song. Over a month since my last entry, a month of individual trial, to say nothing of the world's. It feels almost impossible to fight the river of global events we are being swept up in. How to resist this current? For it is all about resistance, not fighting. Resistance must never cease.

I feel as if I am in transit from one plateau of being to another. Wherever I land I can rest assured of one thing: it will be very different from the place I am now. I can no longer operate, nor choose to operate, from a position of anxiety, worry, what if or fear, though there remains a profound and sober concern for what is happening in the world. I pray for the state of the world's collective heart and the psychic, spiritual challenge of bearing witness to so much waste, mindlessness, and greed yet still hold on to the belief, dare I use the word knowledge, that somehow, someway all this is bringing us to the point of transformation ultimately for the good.

This, of course, has a most immediate and powerful application to the relational odyssey I am on. I received the official petition from the court yesterday. A slight clinch in my gut but not too much. There is no looking back now, only moving forward. My days have been absorbed in helping my parents' transit to their new life: the last stop before the final exit. Dealing with my parents has far overtaken whatever journey P. and I are on, closer now in many ways. What was it about signing those papers and seeing the words "irreconcilable differences" that gave us both such a kick in the butt? Hard to fathom.

And me – what of my deepest needs? I certainly am not sitting home alone pining away or feeling needy or hurt or jealous. At least not now. Thanks to twenty-one years of wifely "pay" for the first time in my life I can honestly ask: What is it I want? What is it I need? What will make my heart sing? I saw a bumper sticker the other day that has become a mantra for me. It read: "Remember Who You Wanted to Be."

REMEMBER WHO YOU WANTED TO BE!!!

Remembering who you wanted to be means remembering who you were and even more importantly who you are. I have stuck that mantra on post-its everywhere to help me be in transit back to myself, to remembering – literally putting back the member parts – of who I was, am, and still want to be: my personal velocity restored.

May 11, 2003

Mother's Day.

When I opened my bedroom door this morning, the first thing my gaze fell upon was a beautiful 18" by 24" oil pastel drawing of a glass vase filled with roses. Beside it was a small bud vase with a Double Delight rose and a note from Mel. "I love you." Yesterday I received a card from my second son W. saying he would "take a sniper's bullet" for me. I have to confess, this brought tears to my eyes. All that hard work and effort and time and devotion and struggle and joy and ambivalence over mothering: after twenty-one years bearing such sweet fruit.

In the meantime, P. is off to Florida with a female associate, his "business wife" as I have dubbed her. Just because someone isn't having sex with another person, doesn't mean the relationship isn't intimate. Get real, Maurine, they're probably having sex. Who are you kidding? But then again, P. and I are not legally married anymore, so how to respond? I don't know how to do this new relationship. I don't know what the ground rules are or what I want/need them to be. P. says I am the angel who has his heart, and I am glad to hear him say that. But sometimes I feel as if he is some sort of Chinese emperor with me as #1 Wife, and therefore a place of great honor, but that he is also collecting concubines who serve other needs for him.

I cannot say that I am angry about this, more jealous and perturbed, but mostly vulnerable and confused. If two people aren't together at least 51% of the time, is it still a relationship, married or no? I don't have any hooks or structures to build from. Is the role of spiritual guide and occasional lover enough?

After prayers this morning, I wrote this:
"I hear my heart beating,
Without haste, with rhythm and cadence precise.
Perhaps it knows already, like predestination,
Its final contraction and breath,
The last tha-thump pump.
I wonder:
How many beats are left in this unstruck drum?
Would knowing make me act differently,
When it is precisely *not* knowing that should?"

May 26, 2003

I have slammed into the wall of accumulated stress, and I mean slammed into that wall hard. I am writing down appointments incorrectly in my client book, forgetting things, losing my train of thought, dealing with panicky and forgetful parents – it must be rubbing off – an absent husband who is no longer a husband, I'm not sure what either of us is at this point, and a child who wants to get the hell out of Parental Dodge. Tomorrow when I see my internist Dr. S. I am going to ask for medication. I am hoping for Thorazine. I already feel as if I am mumbling stupidly and drooling. Might as well have the drugs to finish me off.

I spoke again with JZ. He told me I am being naïve; that all bets are off. P. has declared his intentions to have an open marriage, only it's not a marriage anymore. I think his exact words were, "Wake up and smell the coffee, honey, you've been laid off!"

Sitting in my car parked on a street in our neighborhood where my cell phone actually works, knowing that what JZ said is true and I have been a willing, albeit naïve, accomplice in P.'s agenda. Yes. And my sweet angel self not having the fire of Kali to smack him into shape, or even understand what's truly going on.

I saw FS too and he said something that has resonated so completely with me, along with some of the things Rabbi S. said about Kabbalah. It is the true Truth despite the truth of the chaos of my temporal reality. And that is the eternal reality of God; the eternal reality of the Erotic Principle making love with Love. Suffering and hurt, however real they are, do not supersede this transcendent, eternal reality. It is all God. Everything, everywhere is God. There is nothing but God. Full stop.

So when I am tossing and turning at night and cannot sleep or my parents are calling me for help or P. is gone and I wonder what the hell is happening I repeat to myself: the eternal reality of God. There is no other thing but that. There will never be anything but that. This has helped me tremendously over the past few days, a source of comfort at a time in my life that is off the Richter scale in terms of stress and earthquake-like discombobulation.

June 7, 2003

As summer approaches, I am aware that I have approximately three months to figure out where I am going to move. The reality of the divorce is sinking in.

In the meantime, my father calls me daily, several times a day, with detailed reports of his appetite or lack thereof and bowel activity as he rides the rollercoaster of age and approaching death. I asked Mother if Dad understands that he is dying – at last someone in the family finally used the "D" word. And Mother, being my mother, couldn't bring herself to say "yes," that would be far too direct. But at least she intimated that he "had been thinking about" his older brother and what happened to him before he passed away, i.e. sleeping a lot, not wanting to eat. In the meantime, Mel. graduated from high school with a stunning valedictory speech. That's my girl!

Later Mel. commented that her grandma is so old she looks "creepy." Mel. didn't even want to hug or kiss her or her granddad who is even worse. I told her I understand. I don't like touching my parents either. And now they are afraid. It is a sad, sad thing to reach this point in life, to see one's parents failing and moving toward the end, and to have so few feelings of deep-seated tenderness for them, rather only a sense of duty. I feel a poignancy for the reality of their human condition, that we all must die and that journey evokes compassion and empathy within me, but not much more. While my parents provided me with food and shelter, they did not give me any real nourishment. I am actually rather surprised by my detachment, precisely because they have always been so enmeshed and needy of me. And while those destructive patterns have been somewhat at bay over the middle years of my life, they have returned with a vengeance as their death approaches. I sometimes think people can live too long.

In the meantime, despite all this personal upheaval and turmoil, I managed to attend the LA Book Expo America. Still holding on to the idea that I am a writer, either a sign of great moral fortitude or an act akin to Nero fiddling while Rome burned. I attended some marketing seminars and cruised the booths and displays, picking up cards and information. At one point I met Michael Moore and gave him a copy of *One Bomb Away*. He seemed genuinely pleased and surprised, "Did you do this?!" Maybe he will look at it. I am working to put my faith in the universe and God to get me where I need to be with the requisite tools I need to have when I get there.

July 10, 2003

I can't believe it has been a month since I put pen to paper. It feels like only a few days. I remember sitting down one morning to work, to sort out some of the many notes I have pegged to storyboards that have been staring at me for months. And the next thing I knew three hours had gone by – not with writing or pondering what comes next in structure or character development – but on the phone with my brother and cousin making arrangements to move my parents into the retirement community they should have moved into years ago. Dad had a serious fall the day of their 60th wedding anniversary that clearly shook him up. And it occurs to me I haven't even recorded that painful, bittersweet event!

Walking into their room at the club to see Father's face bunged up, wearing diapers and leaning on a cane. It took all the strength of will I could muster to act as hostess for the 35 guests who arrived to celebrate, in between ducking around the corner where no one could see me to weep. Later that night when I finally got to bed I cried for all that has never been, all that never will be, and all that has been lost in my relationship with them. Crying also with compassion for the degradation of the body, what this poor body goes through in the end. It is not pretty. Watching what will come next for me, like through a peephole, a window into the future.

Anniversary over, then on to the move. Zip, zip, zip. Doors opening and closing, mostly closing now. So after the party, the next two weeks of my life got chewed up helping Mom and Dad pack and move; glad and relieved that at last they will be in a safe environment, and yet angry too at the Technicolor, panoramic highlighting of my family's crippling pathological dynamics.

Maurine to the rescue!

The day of the actual move Mother and I got into what? I can't call it a fight, but I came absolutely unhinged by a hurtful remark she made – and this after moving and carrying boxes and furniture and stuff for three days in 95 degree heat, working as hard as any day laborer in any field to help them.

We were talking about their estate sale and when to have it and I suggested the sooner the better, so they could get it over, relax, and enjoy their new home. And my mother, being my mother, in all her unconscious, poisonous darkness, said snidely, "Oh, so it can be convenient for you to go on your vacation."

I dropped what I was carrying and started to shake with shock, in complete and utter disbelief. I simply could not fathom it, where she was coming from. Screeching:

"Mother! How can you say that to me after all I have done for you and Dad! How dare you say that to me, how dare you!"

There my mother stood in the kitchen, stooped, virtually blind, tired, and frail, blinking as if she had been slapped. She started to sob, even more bent over, holding her hands over her face, saying how sorry she was, she hadn't meant to hurt me, how could she do that, please forgive her.

I went over to her and put my arms around her, trying to comfort her, and said that we both were tired and that everyone had been under a lot of stress. Feeling, too, for her plight as she continued crying in my arms:

Leaving her home of nearly thirty years.

Watching her husband of sixty years fall apart before her eyes.

Not being able to see well and having to rely on others.

Afraid of what comes next.

I told Mom to stop working and go upstairs to take a shower, that I would handle things. She hobbled up the stairs still crying.

Then on the home front, the offspring called for a family council wanting to know what is going on between P. and me. We talked about having to find a new way of being together – if we can – and about my getting an apartment and moving out, which they all thought would be a good idea. They weren't at all surprised. Kids never are. They have instinctual radar for this sort of thing. But P. and I still didn't tell them we are legally divorced. Neither one of us can face that truth on some level.

And, as if this weren't enough, my having to grapple with all sorts of insecurities and fears reminiscent of my break up with my first husband years ago. Not to mention how utterly human it is to feel hurt, vulnerable, and tired, no doubt not functioning with a complete mental deck at this point, and as the children so kindly, yet bluntly pointed out at our family council "overreacting to little things."

No fucking shit!

I remind myself as I ride this rollercoaster that all the splits in our personal psyches parallel the splits in the global consciousness as well. I cannot begin to imagine where I will be when this ride is over. All I can say is: when the Universe wants you to change, there is no arguing about it, there is only surrender. One can go willingly or kicking and screaming, but if change is needed, change is what will occur – no ifs, ands, or buts. And I know change can take a long time, longer than we think in this land of I-want-it-yesterday instant gratification.

****

I went to see FS again and shared with him how difficult it has been to reconnect with what we talked about the last time we were together: the eternal reality of God.

Part of that is I haven't, on a practical level, set aside time to do so, which says a lot about me and my priorities. But even more than that, how devious and relentless this mind is at pulling things apart, all that what iffing, stewing over intangible crap. FS suggested using the process of Ignatian Examen we worked on several years ago when I did the 19th Annotation with him, just to lay all the muck and mire down before God.

So I did, asking for guidance and direction. I started by praying about how upset I've been. Feelings of anger and hurt, feelings of being left behind and edged out, of others being more valued and desirable than I.

And before I knew it, I was scribbling down the following, like dictation:

What nonsense! Quite literally: it makes no sense. This sort of mental unrest is the work of evil. Evil in the truest sense of the word: of being antithetical to life. You are none of those things. You just let yourself think you are. The mind is a crafty thing, ever-ready to move you away from God. You put yourself in a state of dis-ease, of being ill-at-ease. You do it to yourself! Nothing external is doing this to you. I repeat: you are doing this to yourself!

You are equal, powerful, loved, every bit as good as; you need to relinquish all thoughts that contradict this truth, any thoughts that separate you from God and the love of God, any thoughts that make you feel lost, abandoned, or left behind. And to be most attentive and vigilant how subtle these messages can be. You are equally valued, uniquely treasured. Nothing can prevent that truth, nothing can interrupt that reality except you!

You need to see how and when you have not lived up to the potential of strength, love, and soundness of mind that are within you and are your birthright. How and when you have denied or not fully accepted the power of God's love ever-working, unceasingly working for your good –

even in spite of you! – and the good of others. There is no enemy except the ones you create within your own mind and heart.

Be attentive to how and when you give your ego and the emotions it generates more power than you give God; how you make your reactions into gods rather than let God be God. This is not to deny your feelings, for you are human and feelings are feelings. You need to recognize them but not give them so much power and authority that they overwhelm your connection to Spirit. Rather than being angry, hurt, or harboring feelings of lack, you need to be gentle and loving with yourself the way God is with you. This is what God wants you to learn from these experiences and reactions. Pay close attention!

Later I called FS and told him what happened.

August 1, 2003

I have moved out. Sort of. There is still a lot to do before I can make the move complete – painting, installing blinds, etc. But at present I am sitting on a small aluminum beach chair in my newly rented apartment – all 600 square feet of it. It reminds me of the home I was born in, circa the 1950s: wood floors, large metal furnace grates for heat; you have to turn a key, no thermostat. I remember as a child lying on top of the grates when I was cold in order to get warm and watching the flame dance below me. Even the closet in the bedroom is like the one I had as a child: sliding wood doors with cupboards above and drawers below.

As I handed over the check for the first and last month rent, plus security deposit, a part of me inside screamed: "What the hell are you doing??!!" I was so scared my hand was shaking. But I handed the money over anyway. And irony of ironies: I signed the lease on July

31st, the Feast of St. Ignatius. FS would appreciate that, no doubt.

So here I sit in my new space, a small sanctuary of quiet. No phones. No TV. Only minimal garbage supervision and household upkeep, back to a low maintenance life. A friend of mine asked what I plan on doing after all the dust of moving settles. I replied: reread my three books, two screenplays, and 80+ journals and remember who I wanted to be.

Remember the woman of letters I am!

September 28, 2003

I have had to pinch myself several times and say out loud, "You actually did it!" I do feel at home in my new place. And a most telltale sign: when I go back to P.'s, I have found myself trying to use my apartment key to unlock the front door. And yet, of course, very odd being here too, alone after twenty-two years of domestic hubbub and frenetic busyness, not to mention holding someone close at night. Just coming down from all that momentum and speed will take time and not a little conscious presence on my part to derail the habitual patterns of the past.

Which makes me think of something I read the other day about intention:

> Concerning all acts of initiative and creation, there is one elementary truth, the ignorance of which kills countless ideals and splendid plans: *that the moment one definitely commits oneself, then Providence moves in too.* All sorts of things occur to help one that would never otherwise have occurred. A whole stream of events issue from the decision, raising in one's favor all manner of unforeseen incidents and meetings and material assistance, which no

man [or woman] could have dreamed would come his way. (italics mine; W. H. Murray, *The Scottish Himalayan Expedition*)

We do not need to know, and cannot, what particular piece of knowledge or what particular action will present itself to help us and our intention along. But one thing is sure: committed, focused intention is an act of creative consciousness.

October 2, 2003

Sitting in my tiny living room, looking out my front window at the green shrubbery and grass, a small brown squirrel investigating the ground for food. The past few days have been lovely in a way that only October can be. How I am relishing my moments here! Dreams about birthing babies, fire, and wet cunts.

I am beginning to settle into a kind of routine, one that is slower and more quietly melodic, yet at the same time realizing that it is going to take quite a while to deprogram myself from the past. I am beginning to meet some of the other tenants. I understand I am referred to as "the new girl." How I laughed! Using the word "girl" to describe me is no doubt a form of endearment, certainly not one of truth. And yet in many ways, I do feel like a new girl again. I just don't look the part. My upstairs neighbor, Arlo, used to play the bass guitar and sing. Now she is a massage therapist. I feel right at home.

And the joy of living in a world without TVs and telephones! I turn off my cell phone by 8:00pm. It recharges while I recharge to reading and listening to music. My home entertainment center consists of a boom box for tapes and CDs and four shelves of books. After such a long detour, I'm finally back on track, giving my attention to what I love. For attention is a form of love. Where your treasure is, there indeed lies your heart.

More important that any of this, however, is the state of peacefulness I am growing into. The only thing that can disturb this is my mind. I am learning how to lasso it when it starts to run wild. I am learning how to become both amused by and compassionate toward my self-defeating, self-abnegating behavior. "Oh, there goes that 'you're so stupid, what's gonna happen now, everybody else has what it takes but me' dithering, blathering voice again. Well, I'm not going to listen to you now. Or ever." Like learning how to ride a bicycle or having your first orgasm, until you experience it, it is only an idea. But once you have, you never forget how it feels. Maybe it just comes with age. Who knows? But the new girl on the block is feeling pretty damned good.

P. and I have had several intense conversations since I moved out, not intense in the sense of hostile or angry, but getting to the juice of things. If truth be told, a part of me likes being single again, likes being in charge of myself again – as much as anyone can ever be in charge of his or her life. Last night I went to yoga at dinnertime, not having to think about fixing anyone's food, came home sopping wet, filled the bathtub with hot water and lavender oil, and then ordered take-away from a Thai restaurant around the corner. (They have a killer green curry with tofu, eggplant, and basil.)

I like this! This is cool, having my life back.

October 28, 2003
I actually spent last night with P. after we went to a Kabbalah class. It was comforting and familiar, even though we did not make love, and yet it felt odd, too. I told him I am trying to think/feel with my heart and body rather than with my head. While up in Northern California

visiting my artist friend DC, I ran across an advertisement in a coffee shop for a Zen retreat that talked about *sesshin*, a Japanese word which means "to touch the heart-mind" or "gathering together the heart-mind." That is what this process feels like. I need to learn how to be different with myself. Again, how we all need to learn how to gather in this heart-mind with each other. Otherwise, I do believe we and this planet are doomed.

How do we bring this consciousness, non-violent and patient, into the world? Not just igniting matter so it becomes bombs to destroy but more importantly igniting the spirit energy *within* matter? If we can blow this spiritual part up, make it bigger, like an enlargement in photography, perhaps we can avoid blowing up everyone and everything else. How much of this gathering of the heart-mind do we need on the planet before a transcendent rather than destructive critical mass is reached? A few hundred thousand? Several million among the over six billion beings on this earth? I only know that I need to become very slow and very quiet at some very deep part of me, now.

November 17, 2003

During prayers yesterday morning, I remembered a dream about sitting in my beach chair, writing, then looking heavenward with the feeling of coming home.

Coming home.

We are all on our way home.

P. and I are still talking. He wants to have a spiritual/soul connection and indeed, what other journey is there to take? But as I told him yesterday: there is a lot of darkness and pain from the past that simply cannot be swept away by signing a few documents with the stroke of a pen. In many ways we hurt one another deeply, our relationship so clearly off the mark, emotionally abusive in a number of ways. How does one get over that? How does one go about healing and forgiving that? By looking right at the pain and dysfunction themselves. And it can take time for the layers to arise.

After rereading my journals it is apparent to me that I was, and probably still am, hopeless when it comes to men; that my malleability and acquiescence in and around the male of the species are large to say the least. Like Ah-do Annie in the musical *Oklahoma*, I'm the girl who can't say no. Meeting P. was like being hit by a tsunami. I held on for dear life; there was no way of fighting it or him. It felt like life and going with possibility after the end of my first marriage.

P. says all he wants at this point is my honesty, which he is getting in spades. I cannot live in the world he lives in. I cannot move at the speed he moves. I like being alone too much. I like being with me too much. I like my own pace and rhythm. This applies to multiple levels of reality, not simply the realm of physical accommodation. Contemplative loner that I am, I want to rest in the moment, this moment, this day, every action to be engaged in simply a moment of the NOW.

And yet, if what the rabbi says is true – that wherever we are or have been we somehow, in some way were keeping a divine appointment – then I guess I needed P. in my life. Four kids, seven homes – eight if I count this apartment – cancer, two fires, various dogs, cats, snakes, birds, turtles, and God only knows what else have toughened me up just a bit. A friend of mine said I should change my name to "Done-It-All." But it is much more about reconnecting to my story, reacquainting myself with the plot line of my life. I suppose the difference is that before I felt so tentative and timid about it. Now it feels it is my spiritual duty to rediscover this personal vector and song.

****

Went to hear a talk about some of the deeper meaning in the Torah (a dose of "wisdotainment" as the speaker jokingly called it).

He started with a Sufi story about a young man searching a cobbled street with lights. A master approached him and asked the young man what he was looking for and the young man replied, "A key."

The Sufi master asked, "And where did you lose it?"

To which the young man answered, "Over there in the dark."

This, of course, amused the Sufi so he asked, "But why then are you looking for the key over here under the street lamps if you lost it over there?"

And the young man replied, "Because over there it is dark and I cannot see."

The moral of the story: the keys to the kingdom can only be found by looking deeply into the darkness; learning how to embrace the spirituality of the dark side; the shadow, the thief, our trickster energy; what the rabbi called our *ra* force, in order to get to the wisdom within.

That is why so many stories and fairy tales, in one form or another, are about this light/dark/more light paradigm. Peter Pan has his shadow; Wendy sews it back on. Eve engages Adam's shadow and both become more real. If you can love the stranger within yourself, then you are better able to love your friend and neighbor. The stranger is not something external; it is an internal phenomenon. How many times do I have to be reminded of this? The problem with most of us is that we project this internal stranger, this *ra* energy onto others and call it "bad." But if you can integrate it, then you will be able to see more clearly; there will be more light. We need to learn how to identify and relate to the "other" rather than relating only to what we see on the surface.

So:

Love your *ra*.

Love the stranger within yourself.

This is how you love God.

This is how God loves through you.

The rabbi also talked about a tradition of the Temple where the ceremony of the incense is one of the most important. In many ways, this ceremony is symbolic of the process of embracing the darkness within and making it more fragrant because one of the ingredients in the incense is quite awful. When burned, however, this foul smelling substance turns sweet. The moral here is about bringing our unconsciousness to the light of fragrant love and burning through it to gain greater understanding.

In the Bible it talks about how the light is greater than the darkness but a closer translation of the Hebrew is not that the light is greater than the darkness but greater is the light that comes *from* the darkness, that comes after a false and untutored innocence. How we must all learn to descend into our darkness and interior black holes – do they ever end? – to bring all that sludge back into the light of consciousness and day.

December 14, 2003

In my little apartment after church, rain falling outside. In the kitchen making Christmas candy, that special holiday smell, almond brittle simmering on the stove. Standing by the window listening to the soft music of the rain and looking at the tree outside, laden with pendulant raindrops, just aching to fall and plop to the ground. As I examined the moist tree branch, not one, or two, but three hummingbirds braved the wet and cold to visit the small feeder filled with bright red fluid I have outside. I stood very still, not wanting to scare them away. How fragile and tiny they are, almost surreal in a way, little wings fluttering in a frenzy that allows them to hover, move forwards and backwards, up and down in space, unlike any other creature.

My animal totem book tells me:

If you have hummingbird in your life (I have three!), get ready to laugh and be musical and enjoy abundant gifts. The hummingbird dances to celestial music and is in harmony with it. Though small, the hummingbird embraces the highest aesthetic: small creature, large heart. Drop any attitude of judgment and relax. And paradoxically as you do this, you prepare yourself for a burst of energy, the energy and vibrancy that are released from letting go.

Letting go.

How much have I been letting go!

And still need to let go, no doubt.

****

Days later. Thinking about how much I have struggled with the emotion of envy in my life, particularly around the success of writer friends. My own personal battle with this particular demon: all the internal bitching, moaning, complaining, agonizing, and/or worrying. I am responsible for this; no one else. More fickle than any man or woman is this mind, like an errant, spoiled child throwing tempter tantrums, from small, petulant thumb-sucking pouts to full-blown, floor-kicking, fist pounding rants. My southern grandmother called them hissy fits.

Here is the progression:

- Envious thoughts lead to an envious me.
- Petty, conniving thoughts lead to a petty, conniving me.
- Sad thoughts to a sad, mournful me.

- Grateful thoughts to a me of blessing and delight.
- Caring thoughts to a more caring me.

I do believe it is as simple – and hard – as that.

But how the mind wrangles about, dances, sidesteps, twists, and turns away from its own particular death throes. For free will is nothing more, or less, than the step by step, moment by moment, day by day power to choose what to think, even more so than to choose what to do. Freedom of thought is far more compelling and ultimately more important than freedom of action. And harder to achieve.

So:

We experience what we think, so think peaceful thoughts, kind thoughts, loving thoughts – and if you don't think that is hard to do on a daily basis, just give it a shot.

Do not blame others; accept existential self-responsibility and become absolutely psychologically fluent in the language of your shadow; for disowned internal energetic patterns are among the real trouble makers of this and other times.

Learn to love yourself. It is positively frightening the paucity of appropriate self-esteem and self-acceptance there is in the world today, especially in the so-called advanced cultures, and lack of self-love is a breeding ground for the seeds of envy to sprout.

From self-love stems the ability to love others, or at least to respect and honor others as legitimate, precious, and necessary expressions of life.

Be as joyful and joy-filled as possible while you engage in the above.

January 19, 2004

My mother, Sara Margaret Freeman Bollinger, died on Sunday, January 4th of a sudden massive and unexpected heart attack. I have avoided these pages like the plague, not because of the frenzy of activity and plans and phone calls and preparations and listening to condolences that such an event entails, but because I have wanted to avoid the finality of putting into language: my mother is dead, the being who brought me into this world and carried me for so many years, in one form or another, is now gone.

My mother is dead.

The loss of a parent, and I think especially one's mother, is perhaps one of the most complicated, intricate, illusive, and compelling experiences in life. Since we received the shocking phone call from my bewildered father – his mate of sixty years lying dead on the den floor – a complex and sometimes baffling wave of emotions has run through me. At first, nothing, then tears, then resolve, then remorse – why hadn't I talked with her earlier that day on the phone? – to gut-wrenching grief, to a winsome sadness for all that never was between us and now all that never can be, to calm, to disbelief, and finally to silence. And I know, too, that I haven't even begun to tap into the oceans of feeling that lie within connected to that word: Mother. And even more so, those associated with "Mommy." Not only is my mother dead, but my mommy is, too. And those two words can be worlds apart.

When the call came through, Mel., her oldest brother D., and I were sitting at the kitchen table, chatting over a leisurely meal. P. was gone again on business. When D. picked up the receiver and said, "It's Granddad," the three of us smiled and started to half-laugh. Of course, Dad always calls right when we sit down to eat, whether at 6:00pm or 8:00pm. I took the phone and Dad said, "You need to come. It looks like your Mother is dead." And then the paramedic came on the line, "She was already gone when we got here. No breath, no pulse, and with a do not resuscitate on file, we didn't even try to bring her back." Dead six months to the day after helping Mom and Dad move into their lovely new apartment and retirement community.

After calling my brother in Salt Lake City to let him know, I got into the car with D. Mel. stayed home; she said she couldn't face seeing Mom's dead body. An hour later I walked into the scene: my father weeping uncontrollably on the sofa, the police and a security guard on hand. Mother's body lay covered on the den floor, and with a detail I know would have mortified her southern-belle soul: one bedroom slipper was on and the other off, askew to the side of her body. One shoe off, one shoe on. I replaced the remaining slipper, but no longer any Cinderella there. At least when the morticians carried her away, it would be with that one, last small dignity. Then began the bureaucracy of death: paperwork with the policeman, calling the mortuary to come collect the body, consoling Dad.

After the policeman and security guard left, I went over to Mom's body and uncovered it to say good-bye. I can't really say that her face looked calm and peaceful nor did it appear to be in any pain or shock or anger or fear. It was more an expression of surprised unexpectedness: eyes and mouth slightly open, Mom's poor almost blind left eye squinting. What did she see at the very end?

I touched and caressed her; she was still warm. I told her I loved her. "I love you, Mommy. I love you." I kissed her forehead and blessed her, telling her it was okay to go, that I knew where she was going is a wonderful place, truly wonder-filled, calm, peaceful, serene, loving, and kind. I read a few verses from Romans 8, which Mom had been reading that very morning in her large-print *Silent Unity*:

> Thus, condemnation will never come to those who are in Christ Jesus, because the law of the Spirit which gives life has left you free from the law of sin and death.

The Spirit has set you free, Mommy; your soul has been set free.

I whispered some prayers over her; D. held her hand. I wish I had thought to close her mouth and eyes. I wish I had spoken with her one last time on the phone when Dad called earlier that day. Why didn't I say my usual, "Heh, Dad, let me say 'hi' to Mom" because he has a terrible habit of just hanging up on me without letting Mom talk.

I wish I could have hugged her one more time.

I wish we could have been closer, she and I.

I wish.

I wish.

I cannot say I have regrets about my mother. She may have understood things about me I never will and I about her. At this point in my journey I do not think it is possible for one human being to ever truly understand another, at least at the level of thought. We are all so unique and idiosyncratically quirky.

But I do harbor many wishes about and for my mother. I wish her father hadn't died when she was two and a half years old, scaring her for life. I wish her mother, my grandmother, had not abandoned my mother emotionally and turned my mother into her companion, using Mom to fill the void left by my grandfather's death. I wish Mom's sister hadn't brutalized her and tyrannized over her as a child and adolescent. I wish my grandmother had let Mom play with her beautiful porcelain "dollie" rather than forcing Mom to keep it in a box "so it wouldn't get dirty." I wish my mother had been allowed to be noisy instead of always being told to sit in the corner and be quiet. I wish my mother had accepted the offer of going to graduate school at the University of Chicago instead of feeling she had to stay in Oklahoma to take care of her mother. I wish my grandmother had encouraged Mom to go. I wish my mother hadn't suffered from glaucoma and had such trouble with her eyes. I wish my mother had liked my dad after spending sixty years with him.

I wish.

I wish.

I wish I weren't writing this damned entry. Everyone, simply everyone thought Dad would go first. At 93 he is the one who has had quadruple bypass surgery; he's the one who haunts doctors' offices; he's the one with a cardiologist. All the attention that has been focused on him and his needs while Mother sat quietly – and at times, I must admit, not so quietly – in the background. At nearly eighty-nine, with the exception of failing sight, Mom was still as sharp as a tack and interested in things, worried about the state of the world her grandchildren are growing up in. I always assumed there would be more time with her, at least to talk, if not to do things. We had even toyed with the idea of taking a road trip together this spring to visit a dear friend. Mom's mother, my Nana, lived to be nearly one hundred. I just always assumed there would be more time.

More time.

But you never know when the last moment, the last breath, the last ray of sunlight or moonlight will be glimpsed. One can make no assumptions about time and the immutability of death. I know Mother dreaded being alone. Indeed, she had never lived alone in her entire life, and especially with her diminishing sight, she was so reliant on Dad. It would have been very difficult for her, despite the caring, communal living facility into which they had moved, to be by herself. In certain respects, I believe Mother felt it beneath her southern dignity and pride to live in a place with "so many old people." The irony, of course, is that Mom and Dad were among the oldest ones there. But to the very end I think Mother did not consider herself old and finally decided "I've just had enough" and checked herself out of this earthly hotel.

According to Dad, Mom and he had decided not to attend dinner that evening because they wanted to watch their beloved OU football team play. They had spent the day reminiscing about all the wonderful travels they had made around the world. They were having a cocktail, Dad with his head in Mom's lap as he often did, when Mom said she needed to get up. Apparently she struggled quite a bit trying to get off the sofa, took a few wobbly steps, then collapsed at Dad's feet. She was still conscious when Dad tried to help her. He asked Mom if he should call security, but Mom told him, "Don't bother." Dad waited a few more minutes, expecting Mom to get up, but when she didn't, he then called. Security arrived within minutes, said that Mom was going and called the paramedics, but she was already gone when they arrived.

Like I said, it was as if she had just had enough. Mom stood up to leave and left, neither with a bang nor a whimper. She simply departed for good. Not one to take chances, I do believe in that moment Mom risked all. I don't know why I think this, but I believe for just a moment Mom was wavering after she fell to stay or go, to return to her body or leave and in that one moment she made the decision "don't bother" and left. For someone who did not like surprises, how Mom surprised us all! Maybe she even surprised herself with what courage and strength she had inside. From Mom's *Memoirs*, I understand her mother left in pretty much the same way: lucid to the end and then gone. I just thought like her mother, that my mother would be around for some years to come. But it was not to be.

Dad, D., and I had to wait for over an hour before the morticians came. During this time, Dad was crying, no not crying, keening with grief. I tried to console him while D. made phone calls on his cell phone, and I on mine. When the gentlemen in black arrived from Pierce Brothers, I couldn't help but think, "Right out of *Six Feet Under*."

God forgive me!

More paper work, making sure to remove Mom's jewelry, loading her body onto the gurney, and wheeling her out for the last time. Then collecting a few items for Dad and driving him back to our house in Santa Monica to be with us. After I got Dad safely in bed, I came downstairs and sat in front of the TV, channel surfing, numb.

The next three days were a flurry and blur of activity: meeting with the mortuary people to make arrangements for Mom's memorial service and cremation; calls, calls, and more calls; arranging for a minister to speak; making preparations for the reception after Mom's service, food, drink, renting chairs, etc.

The day after Mom's death but before the memorial service, Dad and I returned to their apartment to pick up a few things he needed. How many times had he and I been out running errands to return back to Mom, whom Dad referred to as "Mother," and now there was no Mom or Mother or Sara Margaret or Mommy there. Walking Dad through the dining hall back to their special corner table was painful to watch. All the eyes turned toward us in sadness and commiseration and an unnamed, or perhaps not so unnamed, fear "Will I be next?" "When will it be my turn?" How hard it was keeping myself together! And realizing, too, that for once in my life Dad had completely and utterly relinquished control into my hands to be in charge.

The morning of Mom's memorial I laid out a tribute to her on our dining room table: pictures from her childhood, young adulthood, marriage, motherhood, being a grandparent. I actually had the strength to say a few words at her service about one of our last conversations together. We talked, among other things, about how she realized that we are all part of the whole and how she wished she had known this sooner: that we are one. And I insisted that the preacher read the following from Mother's *Memoirs* as part of the traditional Anglican homily; it was from the last two pages of her handwritten book, what Mom called her family history.

> Our personal winters – our dark nights of the soul, are like the earth's winters: times when everything appears dark and dead...In fact, those times have offered an opportunity for rest and renewal before the period of greater growth and expanded lightness of being...Spirit is just as present in experiences that arrive looking stark as in those that appear lovely to us at first. We can learn to see beauty more clearly everywhere...Like winter into spring experience is a powerful opportunity for new growth, more love and more joy...(anonymous quote)

The last lines of Mom's 20th century memoir read:

> Many exciting things have happened during my lifetime. I've always felt that I have been greatly blessed – very proud of my background and of being an American. If I have any advice to offer: Follow your dreams; respect yourself; have respect for others and like the person you see in the mirror. The only regrets I have are from what I haven't done. Time is precious. May God bless.

The day after Mom's service I was positively exhausted. My brother returned with Dad to his retirement community and spent the next three days with him. I honestly do not remember what I did. I know I must have done something. Renewed a screenplay registration? I know I probably wrote a few thank you notes to people who sent flowers, made more phone calls, put Mom's memorial pictures away, and saw my youngest daughter back to college.

Mom's cremation was scheduled for Tuesday, January 13, ironically the date of her older sister's birthday, the sister who had been so mean to her, so many times. I was the only one in attendance, the only person who had permission to witness the scene. So off I went at 9:30am in the morning, heading east on the 10 Freeway, with Mom's *Memoirs* in tow toward Vermont and Venice Blvd. in downtown LA. I had yet to read them in their entirety, something I am quite sorry about. I had time to read another friend's book manuscript and a cousin's screenplay but did not take the time to read about Mom's life and talk to her about it while she was alive. How we all just smugly or stupidly expect that there will be more time.

More time.

I entered the Chapel of the Pines, a large dome-like mausoleum, at 10:00am sharp and rang the service bell. While I waited for someone to come, I entered the sanctuary and around the circular frieze was the carved inscription: "Beyond this fleeting day/Behold a dawn more fair/For there is a splendor/Like as of the sun and the moon."

I thought: a splendor like unto the stars.

A young woman named Kimberly arrived with more paperwork and a special numerical tag to identify Mom's remains, one in a sealed envelope for me and its mate to be burned with her body for later verification of the ashes. I asked to see Mom's body again, to pay my final respects. Then I hesitated, wondering if the body had decomposed or was much altered. I most certainly did not want that to be my last visual memory of my mother. But Kimberly checked and assured me "your Mother looks fine." Thankfully, the morticians had closed her eyes and mouth. I touched Mom's marble-cool forehead and kissed her gently. I held my hand over her heart, "Bless your sweet heart, Mommy. Bless your heart. Good-bye." I started to cry and Kimberly put her arm around my shoulder. She and the attendant put the lid back on Mom's cardboard coffin, like a gigantic shoebox, and put her into the crematorium. They told me it would take up to four hours. For such a tiny body! All four feet, eight inches of her? How could that be? And I shuddered too, wondering, bewildered, a ghoulish thought: however did the Nazis manage it? One tiny body vs. six and a half million!

After the man closed the door on the furnace, I went back upstairs and read Mom's *Memoirs.* At one point I got so cold I had to move outside onto the cement steps to absorb some sunlight and warmth. I spent not even two hours reading Mother's 128 hand-written pages: some background genealogy, some childhood events, moving from Tennessee to Oklahoma, adolescence, college, marriage, the war years, having children, about her friendships, home, moving, travel, and, of course, golf. Rarely did anything go deeper than a most superficial level. I think that's one of the reasons I had put off reading them. Mom attacked her world with the linear events of chronology and time. Only a sentence here or there spoke to any depth of feeling but I did laugh several times. Mom was capable of a good sense of humor. The last two pages were the most Mom revealed. The rest was pretty much a Joe Friday "just the facts, ma'am" approach.

And I know Mother was capable of depth. Wherever did it go? Wherever did it run to and hide? But I know it is one of the things she somehow passed on to me. Whatever depth I may possess, I know the seed of that germinated through my matrilineal line. My sweet mother had depth and for whatever reason chose not to cultivate it. My father's people were plain mid-western shop-keeping folk: good and decent and kind but shallow. Which is the sadder come from?

Then back on the freeway to drive nearly sixty miles out to Dad to check on him, to see how he was doing. And I spent the next seven hours seeing to his needs, emptying soiled diapers and trash, running errands with him: doctors appointments, banking, stopping to talk to whomever would listen to the story of his loss, how he and Mom met, how he proposed, and so on. Not once during that seven hours did my father turn to me and ask, "How are you doing, Maurine? I'm sure it must have been difficult for you this morning." Not a word. Just a few tears when I mentioned the word "cremation." By the end of seven hours of listening to Dad talk non-stop, I thought: "This is why Mom checked out. She was exhausted from listening to him."

God forgive me, again!

After a rough first week, Dad bounced back quickly and has been doing remarkably well. Even as I write this he is on an outing with other individuals from his retirement community to visit the new Frank Gehry Walt Disney Concert Hall, followed by dinner downtown. I think a part of my father, unconscious no doubt, is actually relieved Mom is gone. He does not appear sad and certainly not depressed or morose. He even talks about how hard it would have been on Mom if he had gone first because of her poor eyesight, which is true. It would have been very hard for her. But I also think there is a secret, hidden part of him that is, as I said, relieved that at long last the silent – and not so silent – war between the two of them is over.

Am I being harsh? Cruel? Judgmental? Objectively accurate? Or am I simply being honest, brutally honest about what was between them? One of the several positive out-comes of the termination of my marriage has been the absolute death knell of even the faintest whisperings of such soul-killing interactions. If you are going to spend sixty or twenty or forty years with another human being, you had damned well better like that person, not just love him or her. I have no doubt that my parents in their own way loved one another. They just couldn't stand each other's personalities unless they were traveling or playing golf. Toward the end my father actually started calling my mother "The Prophet of Doom" and would poke me in the arm every time he said it to make sure I got the point. And yes, my mother, without doubt, could be one of the most negative of human creatures at times. But I don't think my dad ever once asked my mom why she was so sad. He just always blamed her eyes.

But then again, if my father had asked, would Mom have been able to articulate all the stored hurt? And at such a late stage in the game, would it ultimately have mattered or made any difference? And yet how we all long to be known in that deep way; what it means to have an *anamcara*, a soul friend, a person to be trusted over a whole lifetime with one's innermost self. The Druids were the first soul friends and had a saying, Irish no doubt: "Anyone without a soul friend is like a body without a head." Or a head without a heart.

That's rather the way my parents were: like a body without a head. Possibly they could have been more, but it feels as if the Depression and World War II and the fact that they both lost a parent in childhood were the grand themes of their lives, their soul cohort imprint. It didn't leave room for much else.

****

89

Last Thursday I collected Mom's ashes from the mortuary. Since it is right around the corner from my little apartment, I walked to pick them up. More signatures and paperwork, like identifying and collecting lost or misplaced luggage. The receptionist handed me a tiny wrapped case, smaller than a shoebox, discreetly covered with a faux green velvet cloth with a drawstring. There I was at 5:00pm in the afternoon walking down Arizona Ave. in Santa Monica carrying the last physical remains of the being who labored to bring me into the world. I brought Mom back to my tiny hermitage and put her on the top shelf in one of my kitchen cupboards – a kitchen so reminiscent of the home where I was born. I poured myself a glass of wine and drank a toast, "Here's to you, Mom."

I then took one of the pictures the morticians used to identify Mom's body and framed it. It was taken on her last Mother's Day, standing next to a vase of flowers I had given her. Next to the picture are the last vestiges of a beautiful flower arrangement sent by P.'s company in Mom's honor. It's as if I am trying to hold on to the last remnants of her: her warmth, her flowers, her smell. On a chair in the corner of my bedroom is her porcelain doll, the one my grandmother never let Mom play with. When I asked Mom if her doll had a name, she said no, so I have named her Isabelle. I say good morning to Isabelle when I wake up, along with saying hello to the pictures of my children.

And the words from the last page of Mom's journey do haunt me:
Follow your dreams.
Respect yourself.
Have respect for others.
Like the person you see in the mirror.
The only regrets are from what I haven't done.
Time is precious.

May God bless.

My mother said she always dreamed of being a wife and mother. She knew that was what she wanted. And that she did achieve. But over the last few months, in what was her growing despondency, Mom had mentioned to me on several occasions: "What do you suppose my life has been good for? What have I accomplished? What have I done, really?" And I would suggest for her to go into her heart and ask God that question. The only answer Mom said she could come up with was having my brother and me and by way of extension her grandchildren.

Our individual lives feel so very small in the end, even inconsequential. Less than fifty people attended Mother's memorial service. What a tiny, infinitesimal drop in the ocean of time! But while our individual lives may feel so very small, the love we experience does not. Life is grand beyond measure and time. To live forever means to have lived just once. That's all it takes. *Ewig sein ist gewesen sein.* I cannot comprehend that she is gone.

February 8, 2004

Since the holidays, the last weeks have been a blur to me, January entirely lost. Like a groundhog, I only now feel as if I am poking my head above earth again – and a week late at that. The reality of Mother's death is beginning to sink in. One moment in particular I remember: smelling her powder and perfume that I saved after her death. The scent dropped me to my knees: the "Mommy" smell.

Not to mention all the details of dealing with death: changing bank accounts, removing Mom's name from the daily things of life, transferring title over to Dad, helping him cope, going through Mom's things for him, reading condolences and sympathy mail, writing notes. The moment of death may be fleeting but the truth of what death means for those left behind takes time. In many ways,

I think it changes us who remain much more than the loved one who departs.

It makes me think, too, of a moment I shared with Mel. and D. the night following Mom's memorial service and reception. I went to them and asked flat out, "Do you have any pot?" knowing full well they did, and the three of us crawled out onto Mel.'s balcony, sat on the window ledge, and shared a ritual toke, roles for once dropped. After half a baby puff I'd had enough and was wondering out loud what the next door neighbors would think if they saw us. What kind of parental role model am I? Aiding and abetting? At least the children are all adults now, no longer minors. And in truth, it was more like their aiding and abetting their emotionally unplugged mother.

Afterwards I crawled back into the house, leaving D. and Mel. outside, went into the bedroom, and started to pace back and forth, up and down, back and forth. What a sorry mess! Mom just dead, here I was back in the house I'd left just a few months ago, sleeping with P. again, and smoking pot with my children. Did I say something about confronting your shadow?

D. and Mel. came looking for me to see if I was okay. There the three of us were standing in the small foyer to my bedroom and I pulled both of them close to me, one child in each arm, and their looking down at all 5 feet 3 inches of me. I hugged them close, so close and told them how proud I am of them – as if I, of all people, could come down on their heads for anything after all I've done; how proud their grandmother was of them – she definitely would have come down on their heads – and how much I wanted them to live their lives as they see fit, how life is so very short and you really have to grab hold of it while you can. It is over in a nanosecond, an *Augenblick*, the blink of an eye, at least this physical booster rocket stage. My own experience with cancer and my mother's passing have taught me that there is no death really, just the transformation of form and energy. But you are required to let go and catch that last breath wave good-bye.

It has been said that to be Irish is to know that in the end the world will break your heart. It has also been said of the Irish that they are the only people who could not be helped by psychoanalysis. Bless them and my Flanary blood! I don't know whether it is my southern Irish roots that are welling up inside me since Mother's death, like some west coast Katie Scarlett O'Hara, but in the end I think *to be human* is to know that the world – life – will break your heart no matter what. And this is not necessarily a bad thing. My mother's heart simply broke. She died in less than a minute. She and her heart simply gave up the ghost, the Holy Spirit that animated her left.

In the end, having our hearts broken is what the job description of being human, whether Irish, Hindu, or Swahili, is about: that cracking open of the interior fortress surrendering to pain, to loss, to vulnerability, to life, to death, to joy, to God, to the Infinite Whatever-Is-Beyond.

I was thinking, too, of Mom's *Memoirs* and the jottings of another long ago Irish scribe:

> Sad it is, little black book, for a day will
> surely come when someone will say over your
> page: 'The hand that wrote this is no more.'

How I thought of Mom. So while I may not be a particularly evolved or conscientious parental role model in the marijuana-smoking department, I hope for my off-spring and their off-spring and their off-springs' off-spring that these little black books of mine, like my mother's and like Terence, will speak: "I am a human being, so nothing human is strange to me."

All the falling off and apart that is required!

February 20, 2004

Lots of random dreams last night. Images of Mel. as a precious three year old, dressed in her pink and blue princess costume, laden with jewelry, waiting by the side of the road, playing; images of my dead mother in younger, happier times; images of my rapidly failing father, frail and struggling; images of me in deep, tempestuous waters, river rapids and torrential rain trying to navigate to safe harbor, trying to get home. So many images of loss, of what is no more, of what, by necessity, must be relinquished and let go of; my being buffeted by the storms and uncertainties of life – loss of youth, loss of innocence, the loss of children, marriage, and family – and yet somehow, too, being able to navigate to safety.

At one point my boat was drenched by the river rapids, taking on too much water, and a voice from the shore shouted: "Keep the bow up, point it up!" I did and was okay. I suppose in the end and all the way through this journey called life we must keep our heads up, keep our eyes and ears and hearts focused on looking up, the Greek *anothen* – to be renewed from above, again and again and again.

Back once again on a more regular basis in my little apartment, rekindling a sense of my own rhythm after all the chaos and disruption of the holiday season, kids home from college, and of course, Mother's death, not to mention tending to and caring for Dad. I cannot say that I have learned to like what I have been through with my parents over the past few years especially. But I do feel I have learned how to be more at peace with what I have had to do.

In the meantime, I have been working to redesign my website to make it more marketing friendly. Bit by bit I am trying to follow through with some of the ideas culled over the past year from seminars, reading, and the LA Book

Expo. A part of me cringes as I plunk down more money. I am working to still the ever-present negative voice of "what folly!" – my mother's "why bother?" – inculcated so thoroughly in me at such a young age. I am slowly weaning myself from that mindset of lack and discouragement and learning to entertain, if not yet fully accept, that this is something I have to do to learn whatever it is I need to learn.

So one of my more immediate personal spiritual practices is blessing each check I write vis-à-vis my fledgling publishing business rather than cringing. I remind myself over and over about the power of words and intention; of being focused with greater presence how I go about attending to this intention. And how subtle it is how we humans, at least this one, will go to far greater lengths to avoid what we fear than grab after the brass ring of what we most truly cherish and desire, *that* treasure. Or to put it another way: how we paradoxically fear what we most desire. And I am not talking about desire on a superficial level, but a deeper longing, the kind of desire that makes our hearts sing; the kind of desire that comes from why each of us is put here in the first place: to bring forth that desire is the most real and honest and true thing about ourselves.

There is a Jewish teaching that says in time we humans will have to account for all the good things that God has created for us that we refused to acknowledge and even more importantly that we refused to enjoy. Nowhere is this saying more applicable than how we fail to enjoy that which is most ourselves, to embrace that which is most unique within us, and "return" to that still point. It is all about learning how to dismantle the fear of being who we are, who we are meant to be, and rekindle our soul's story, our sacred autobiography. Andre Malraux said that the 21st century will either be spiritual or it won't, the implication being that this quality of spirituality will be an essential component during this time.

If this is so, then why are we all shooting and killing one another, gods killing God, whether in our own homes or half-way around the world? People are not enemies or objects or ideologies; *they are spirit!* Granted there are some, perhaps many, who are far removed from their light and very frightened. I am not at all convinced, however, that shooting them, or they us, is the most efficacious way of dealing with this particular problem. Not to mention the fact that killing and destruction are just so expensive, on all levels – human, economic, moral, psychological. We simply haven't learned yet how to combine all the disparate stories and lyrics, vectors and velocities into a more harmonious song.

It seems to me that in order for this spirituality to evolve we must learn how to face our fears of being and doing the good we were sent here to do, however large or small, however personal or global, to be the goodness cells we are meant to be. The 21st century will require that we learn how to release fear in massive, non-violent, non-destructive ways, otherwise it and all the systems we have orchestrated and created to defend against this fear will consume and destroy us in the end.

I can see how taking this little apartment has been about just that: facing fear, however nebulous and intangible, or perhaps more accurately, a willingness to face the unknown, a willingness to risk hazard and uncertainty. And the peacefulness that somehow paradoxically grows when one does this! I suppose that is one of the reasons why Jesus so loved the sinners and tax collectors and prostitutes: they weren't hypocritical about their darkness and because of this, more real. It's all about how to get more real.

February 22, 2004

I ended the last entry rather abruptly because I had to go collect food from a local restaurant and take it to my church for our homeless meal program. In certain ways, I am homeless now, too. Or at least a wandering pirate-pilgrim. I haven't done this tithing of my time since Mom's death, and I realized as I gathered the food, drove it to church, unloaded it, and wrapped all the pies, desserts, meat and chicken into plastic freezer bags what a meditation this is for me: my quiet Friday morning ritual resurrected from the chaos of change. Alone in the kitchen, the church meeting hall quiet, wrapping food that otherwise would have been thrown away; collecting and gathering food for people who have little to nothing, most of whom I will never even see. One tiny little link in a chain of people that somehow manages to provide 150 individuals each week with hot meals.

I got to thinking about the whole concept of hospitality: treating others, both friends and strangers alike, with warmth and generosity. How this world could use a little, or a lot, more hospitality. I realized how much I had missed doing this small service and how much this gathering and storing of food fed me. It made me reflect on something I wrote down the other day, Princess Marya speaking from *War and Peace*: "One must put oneself in everyone's position. To understand everything is to forgive everything!"

I don't know if it is possible to understand everything. To try to understand everything with the mind is not possible, certainly. Only with the heart is this particular kind of understanding available, I do believe. It is the understanding that arises out of compassion and being without judgment – a quality I am still working on and probably will work on for the rest of my days.

I have been taking another course at the University of Judaism about the possibility of converting. For me, it is the logical extension of the other work I have been doing and my belief that in order to understand Christianity, you have to go to its Jewish roots. While there is a great deal about the dogma and theology of Christianity I do not accept – can I even call myself Christian when I don't accept some of its major tenets, the Nicene Creed, and a Father God. Why not a Mother God? Or for that matter a Father/Mother God? Or Chairperson of the Board God? – nevertheless it is my culture and as much as anything else, the art and music with which I am familiar. I cannot imagine giving up my culture in order to embrace another religion whose culture feels so foreign to me. Not to mention that I can neither read nor speak Hebrew. Not to mention that I love Jesus, whether or not he literally is the son of God. Who he was as a man means infinitely more to me than what he might be as a god. In this sense I agree with the Jews: God is God; man is man. And while God may invest each particle of creation with a portion of divinity, it is not necessarily a reciprocal process.

The only reasons I have stayed within the walls of so-called organized religion are:

It is a discipline to attend on a regular basis and discipline is something I need whether I like it or not.

It keeps me at least marginally humble, looking out at the congregation, just like everyone else, putting one foot in front of the other, trying to figure things out.

It is the only place where I get a chance to sing, even if badly.

I seriously appreciate Jesus' invitation to walk with and learn from Him.

It's all a work in progress, no doubt. And with Lent coming up what wonderful, holy thoughts and desires. Yes, desire. What is my heart's desire, that one true longing that resides beyond the neediness of ego-based envy and fear? Where one's true treasure is: how Spirit communicates from this sincere point of longing, a longing that is humble in tone, not arrogant or vain. Articulating this becomes one's goal. To become fully what we are is to fulfill creation's desire to incarnate uniquely in each and every one of us. And how that thirst, that longing become the focal point of communication, communion, and prayer because God not only wants to greet us in the Tent of Meeting but also in the Place of Blessing.

It is all blessing, whatever form it takes. God as the Paraclete calling us forward; God as both the Comforter and Uncomforter; the One who loves us enough to bail us out of our messes and misguided choices; the One who loves us enough to not bail us out of our messes and misguided choices; God as the Vulnerable One weeping over our messes and misguided choices; God as the Supreme Agitator and Discomforter, calling us to redirect our messes and misguided choices; to turn blessing and grace into social justice; the One who niggles at us and pokes and prods us to take action in the world. Only we can do it.

So here I am right in the middle of mid-life and the challenges are these:

The purifying of expectation, what I thought I wanted and what I actually have achieved.

The letting go of dreams, especially the tyrannical ones: I will be a famous writer.

The embracing of dreams that have been deferred: I will be a famous writer.

The embarking on utterly new and unexpected dreams: I just want to sell the books in my garage, or give them away.

Learning how to make friends with my self, to make peace with being good enough. I am not a famous writer but I am a writer nevertheless.

And how envy diminishes as good enough is embraced! Indeed, gratitude for good enough is a remarkably potent antidote to the disease of envy. Besides, if God wants to bless me, shower me with blessings, to quench the thirst of what I truly desire – not what I think I want or need but what will truly bring peace to my spirit – how can I possibly lose? The truly deep desires and longings, those implanted in our souls, not those fabricated with our minds: these are what fuel the journey. For "the glory of God is the human person fully alive." (St. Irenaeus, 2nd century)

And what are the attributes of being fully alive?

Vibrancy

Centeredness

Rootedness in one's own life

Vitality

Radiating a quiet – or loud – joy

Humor

Hospitality

Flexibility

Presence

A peacefulness and acceptance of things as they are, though still committed to working toward the betterment of creation.

Loving without judgment, though not without discernment.

Internally focused rather than externally driven.

What it means to be spiritually vital: to weather the painful disorientations of life, which will come and which are many, whether in youth, mid-life, or old age, and have the willingness and bravery and gratitude to be reoriented to the Above again and again. How the Exodus story applies to us all: to be released from whatever is holding us in bondage – a bad relationship, compulsive thoughts, addictive habits; letting go of the old and secure, though possibly the infantilizing and unhealthy, in order to wander unknowingly through the wilderness of ourselves until we enter the Promised Land, whatever that might look like for each of us. In many ways, bondage is really nothing more, or less, than freedom misused. And to know that Spirit is present in all places; wherever Spirit is *is* Holy Ground, the idea that ultimately all reality is gracious; God is present even in the darkness, the badness and rough times.

Is there any other way to survive? And yet how we struggle against this beneficent principle so much of the time! At least I do. Or worse, we forget that this beneficent principle is there to sustain us when we have lost our familiar footing and are required to cross unknown seas, life's unchartered waters.

As in my dream: look up!

February 24, 2004

Last night as I was lying on the rug in my small living room, listening to the Anglican evening prayer service and doing some meditative breathing, a feeling of such what – I don't even know what to call it – came over me. I burst into tears, saying, "I'm sorry, I'm sorry," as if I were apologizing to God because I feel as if I have not yet fulfilled the commission or reason for my being here, being saved from disease and being sent back into this world to do the work God has given me to do.

It was the oddest sensation of experiencing simultaneously blessing and gratitude AND the feeling that I have also somehow let God down; that I have not yet reached full throttle or full personal velocity; and if not perfect pitch at least my right vibrational speed, somehow still off the mark, the true meaning of the Hebrew word for "sin." So I lay on the rug weeping, "I get it, I get it, thank you, I get it," feeling good and yet humbled at the same time in the sense of being kindly chastened.

I think about something I heard the other day about the Chinese character for patience: it is a combination of the word symbols for both heart and knife. That is what it felt like, as if my heart were being cut with a knife, not in an extraordinarily gross or painful way, but delicately by the hands of a Master Surgeon guided by vast experience and knowledge.

And that was part of the feeling lying on the rug. So much! So much! *And still not there!* The last stages of my heart being carved by the knife of patience, and literally, too, how my body has been so carved up, surgical knives and scalpels literally cutting around my heart. My tearful reaction was so spontaneous and so unexpected, this feeling that I have somehow let God down and yet, too, His/Her patience with me still even though I have not done or accomplished what I am meant to.

Surrender is endless.

Patience is endless.

And gratitude at present is not endless, but it should be.

Over and over and over again being brought back down. The last vestiges of laziness and bad habits, maybe not even as harsh as that, more a lack of moment-to-moment mindfulness and presence. Yes, that feels like it, being called to an even deeper presence within my life and my time here. This sense of time with my life more than half over and yet also, too, the feeling that I haven't even begun to tackle my *tikkun,* my own particular gift that will help repair the world.

And it is not about my not wanting or not being willing to be a faithful and devoted servant. It is about getting even more grounded and embedded into the moments of each day, harnessing *that* treasure, and making manifest what is not yet realized externally through that moment of time. It is as if the Divine needs the keyhole of each moment to be opened through the individual in order for the Unmanifest to be made manifest. I like that image: each of us a divine keyhole through which Creation enters as a key of light, unlocking our own individual light within time.

February 27, 2004

Up early, a bright clear morning after all the recent rain. Went outside to get my cell phone that I left in the car last night to phone a repairman, my refrigerator having decided to "un-fridge" everything. As I was unlocking the car, a large and very vocal black crow was perched in the tree overarching the curb and sidewalk. He (or she) kept cawing and cawing at me. I gathered up my phone and some other items and proceeded back to my apartment, not really paying much attention, only registering how loud the bird was.

But the crow followed me to the tree just outside my living room window, cawing even more loudly and persistently: CAW! CAW! CAW! It really did feel as if the bird were trying to tell me something. It was so intent upon this, in fact, that I stopped, turned, and answered laughingly, "Well, good morning to you, too!" at which point the bird flew away.

I came back inside, ground some coffee beans and put on the kettle to heat water, called the appliance repair service to set up an appointment for the fridge, and then decided to look up crow medicine, thinking: hummingbirds out the kitchen window, crows out the front.

I had to laugh:

Crow, an omen of change, living in the void with no sense of time, the merging of inner and outer reality, lightness and dark. Crow medicine signifies knowledge of a higher order of right and wrong than human laws and reality.

Oh, God! How much does it take to clobber me to attention?

As I allow my personal integrity to be my guide, my sense of feeling alone will diminish. My personal will can then emerge so I can stand in my own truth, being willing to walk my talk, and know my life's mission.

I sat on the small Victorian sofa in my tiny living room, shaking my head, and peering heavenward. Don't tell me that God doesn't have a sense of humor! So a crow comes along and caws at me to shape shift reality, telling me to learn how to be comfortable with discomfort and paradox. And how true, too, that quality of outlaw energy that crow carries; better not yak too much unless you have a good back up plan. I guess that's where God and the Divine part come in: too much the outlaw and you end up going to jail or eating crow. (This may be where the expression "eating humble pie" comes from.)

I found myself wanting to qualify the mainstream part. Can't I be a little more marginal than that? Just a little more on the fringe, please? How's about this for a tagline:
Marginal
Mystic
Middle-aged
Mother goes
Manic:
Beware of possible Maternal Mayhem.

****

A friend of mine remarked to me the other day, "Oh, so you're going through a conscious divorce."

To that I say: rubbish! There isn't anything conscious about divorce. People get divorced because of all the unconsciousness they brought with them into their relationship in the first place. Divorce is not about consciousness; well, maybe it is after the fact. Divorce is about undoing all the unconsciousness – the drives, motivations, needs, and fears – that lurked in the darkness that propelled us to say "I do." Until we say "I don't."

Divorce is also about money and property. Since P. and I had that arranged on paper beforehand, there wasn't much to talk about except sign on the dotted line, marriage over, deal done. I have a lot of female friends who still are angry with me for not fighting more and taking P. to court. But if you don't marry for wealth and money, how then do you divorce for them? I'm still trying to figure that out.

But the universality of my friends' angry responses has intrigued me: the ego wanting justice when freedom may be more important than cash? Could such a document, all those pre- and post-nuptials and quit-claim deeds, be rendered nugatory? That's a good word, meaning worthless, of no force, inoperative. Any agreement may be rendered nugatory by something that contravenes its execution. But I didn't fight for nugatory, even though I could have.

What's a life worth? The cliché of the middle aged female being turned loose after the breeding and child rearing years are over. Since I was living on about $100 a week and teaching in 1980s London, I was hardly what you might call "on the make." People do not become teachers or go into the profession of education to get rich. Far from it. They probably are more interested in having time than money.

But people who have a lot of money generally want to protect what they have. Since I did not at the time, that is a moot point. But it does bring me back to my original question: What's a life worth? How do you affix a value to who you are and what you do? Actuaries and insurance companies figure it out based upon what a person produces, but that has nothing whatsoever to do with any intrinsic worth as a human being, which is priceless, beyond measure.

Since what I did was teach, P. decided that the best way to determine my "worth" was to base it upon what I did as a profession. As his CPA put it "a non-taxable lump sum buy-out," my marriage pay. I didn't think much about it or question his logic at the time. I do remember feeling uncomfortable with the idea but signed all the documents anyway to show my good faith, along with all the training in passivity I had as a women, overtly and covertly, and doing what others, especially men, wanted.

Why didn't I fight more? Well, a deal's a deal, you give your word, you sign a document, you commit to something with good faith and integrity, you don't go changing the rules in the middle of the game, all that fair play stuff. Right? There is some honor in that, isn't there? Or is it just another variation on the theme of submission and submissiveness, of not wanting to rock the boat or argue or fight?

But I also learned that it's not what you deserve; it's how well you negotiate. Clearly I got an "F" minus in that category. Was it cowardice on my part because I was afraid of going against what the man wanted? What the man thought was fair? Was it inexperience with this level of the business world? Yes, no, maybe. The only person who understood why I didn't fight the marriage documents is a friend who also is a cancer survivor. You just look at things differently after going through that. You learn that time is more valuable, infinitely so, than money. All the time that would have been eaten up by depositions, legal letters back and forth, court appearances, continuances, vs. vs. vs. vs.; they would have been a form of cancer themselves.

Besides, why spend years in court battling only to have the lawyers get most of your share? More to the point, would a legal battle rectify the unconsciousness that allowed me to sign all those documents in the first place? The moral level, the ethical level, the legal level, the heart level: each has its own demands and rewards; each its own standards and requirements. I chose the heart level. That probably makes me a legal level loser.

Does that make me a coward?

Or brave?

The point is: I signed the papers when a part of me somewhere deep inside knew I shouldn't but I did anyway. Just the way I said "yes" without really thinking about what I was committing to. What are the psychological dynamics of one who wishes to follow a policy of dominance? Is the answer to that one who has been, or at least feels he/she has been dominated? What are the psychological dynamics of one who feels powerless and submissive? One who feels he/she must cover these up with an appearance of control? I also learned the hard way that just because you have insight into these things doesn't mean you necessarily act upon them. Change can take a long time.

I've always liked the sound and cadence of the traditional marriage vows. For better, for worse; for richer and poorer; in sickness and in health: now that's a commitment. Call it the raisin test: Will you be there to help feed me and change my diapers when I am all shriveled up? To hold my hand at the last breath and journey's end with love in your eyes and heart? That takes a lot of courage. And compassion and perseverance and patience – commodities our culture does not encourage or seemingly even value much anymore. But life values them even if we don't. What challenges intimacy faces in a society that moves with such haste and pace, like a relentless juggernaut, an unending flood of images and sales pitches and technology! The coin of love in this country is not time but speed. And greed. And celebrity.

'Til death do us part...' But the death of what exactly? There are many different kinds of death besides the physical one. What does the death of love feel like? Different for everyone, no doubt. Which death do you think will come first: the psychological or the emotional or the physical? The idea is to be liberated *before* our bodies die, and that also means being liberated from a love that no longer works, one that is no longer loving. How much personal choice is involved in this? Sometimes psychic death, the death of who you thought you were can feel just as terrifying as the physical one.

In hindsight I can see all the bad habits P. and I got into to solidify the loneliness of our being together. What about the "business" of love? Or the joy of it? What is the meaning of this in my life now as I look at the etiology of this break-up and my own reorganization? And, of course, like the road to hell, I had a lot of good intentions. And no doubt P. did, too.

So much for good intentions as I sit here alone and he's off with someone.

Walking on thorns, a marriage bed of thorns. Yes, it has felt like that at times over the last few years and before. I am now beginning to sense – and what is deeply disturbing about this discovery, not in a negative way, but a discovery more of wonderment – is a developmental stage I should have gone through years, if not decades, ago after the end of my first marriage. I have an easier time forgiving

AD and me. We were so young and hormonal and it was all so Romeo and Juliette like. Life feels more forgivable and forgiving when you are young simply because you are young and think there is an endless amount of time spreading out before you. At mid-life you look at the clock ticking in a completely different way.

I did not learn how to think about my own wants and needs, something I should have done after my first husband and I parted. And not only to think about what I wanted and needed but to be okay with thinking about it. Is this propensity to be acquiescent a female trait or rather a peculiarity of my own dysfunctional upbringing? Probably a combination of both. I learned early on how to manage other peoples' psychological and emotional needs but not my own. I simply learned to assume that mine did not count; indeed, whenever I expressed any they somehow went unheard, unrecognized, or simply did not matter. I did not have much, or any, practice learning how to pay attention to my own heart, though I became quite adept at picking up on the emotional cues of others.

Is this something so deeply embedded in the world psyche in its collective attitude toward the female of the species, that we are here to serve and be of service to others? There is incredible spiritual power behind the act of devotion and service. But this power must be an act of choice and volition rather than one of mindless expectation or smug assumption that this is the way we women are or what we must do.

If I had had any practice in pausing and listening to those internal murmurings when P. and I first met at least I could have said, "Let's take some time to get to know one another better before taking the plunge." I had no business getting involved again so soon, let alone married. Let alone married to someone who already had a child, and an obstreperous one at that.

But here's the rub – and there usually is one. Or several. Even though I knew I wasn't ready to get married again and it wasn't the right time do say "I do," I did anyway because I couldn't say "I don't" or "I won't" or "not now." I absolutely was incapable of saying "no." It may be a reasonable, even compassionate, thought to reflect upon how our actions and choices affect others. It's called soul searching. But only worrying about the impact of one's actions on another's soul without looking at one's own best interests is hardly compassionate toward oneself now, is it?

What is so telling about that thought, what is so obviously lacking is that I never paused to consider, nor did it even occur to me to consider, what my feelings were, what would or would not be right or good or healthy or loving *for me*. After a whirlwind romance of only two weeks, I went back to England where I was living and still not legally divorced from my first husband. At the time I had a vague feeling of unease, as if propelled by some unconscious compulsion, an inexorable sense of being driven by something beyond my control, something beyond my conscious understanding. It felt as if I simply did not have any voice in the matter; it was already a *fait accompli*.

And while I know objectively in my mind that there is always a choice, I was unable to access that truth on a feeling level. It felt that once a certain combination of actions was set in motion there was an inexorable categorical imperative that took over, leading to the foregone conclusion of marriage. I wonder how many women have harbored similar feelings, inarticulate and below the surface? And men, too. When talking with female friends and colleagues about this "I-couldn't-say-no-to-him" mantra the poignant reality is that many know exactly what I mean. They have experienced variations on the same inability to articulate "no." It isn't even about not having the courage – well, maybe a little – but much more about feeling we don't have the right or permission to go against what others, especially men, want.

****

I met with FS again yesterday. He talked about a seed, long dormant, now just beginning to germinate and grow. And I am most grateful that this seed has at least started to sprout. Who am I to question Divine economy or timing? But the all-too-human me cannot help but wonder why now? Why didn't I learn this in childhood as a part of my birthright into freedom of choice as a spiritual being, forget about being female or American?

The Grand Inquisitor may be accurate in his observation that humankind wishes nothing more than to have the burden of personal responsibility lifted from its shoulders. I don't know whether this is more true for women than it is for men. I have heard women talk about wanting a man to take care of them. But I have also experienced how much men want women to take care of them and their needs, too. So I'd say it is equal but coming for different directions.

I recently read Erica Jong's *Fear of Fifty* (maybe I should write a sequel entitled *Fear of Sixty*?) and related to a number of things she wrote vis-à-vis men and women: how this "please disease" and training in niceness kills the heart of so many of us females. All that ancient, primordial imprinting about the male being more valued. As Jong says, it is as if somehow our very womanhood, the fact that we are female is a fault or flaw.

Jong talks about all the different "phallacies" we women engage in with men. A few of my favorites:

Phallacy No. 1: "If he loves me, he'll be faithful forever."

Yeah, right.

Jong's response to Phallacy No. 1: "His loving you has nothing to do with his being faithful."

Yeah, right again.

Phallacy No. 2: "A woman needs a man to feel whole."

When the truth of the matter, according to Jong and most women I know, is that women are by far the more self-reliant sex. Men are the dependent ones. But by and large they are in denial of their dependency, and we women actually enable and encourage this denial.

Phallacy No. 3 "If you use your power to support a man, he'll always support you."

Don't get me started on that one.

Phallacy No. 4 "Men love it when you tell the truth about your relationship." But when you tell them the truth, they often go "Huh?" or "Wow! I didn't know that!" But whose truth is it anyway?

Phallacy No. 5 "Men love women who never oppose them and cater to their every whim."

Well, I say some do; some don't. But the idea that men don't like women who "humor them constantly, succumb to all their whims, and never tell them what to do," I need to think about that, for sure.

Phallacy No. 10 "Men are rational, women irrational."

Enough said on that one. Man's "rationality" is what is killing this planet; woman's "irrationality" is the only thing that will save it.

Jong says we women can no longer afford what she calls "spiritual laziness." Spiritual laziness, indeed. That's what this journey of self-exploration is about.

March 11, 2004

Sitting in the Literati Café on Wilshire Blvd., listening to big band music, followed by John Lee Hooker, those Mississippi Delta Blues. Have just come from my office after seeing a client. Feeling what? Somewhat despondent but trying not to be. So much the feeling of being in unchartered territory, untethered from all I have known before. Mel. home for spring vacation and surprised that I expressed sadness over my mother's death, her experience being that I wasn't that close to my mother and then, of course, my irrational fear that she will feel the same way about me.

I tried to explain to her how human interactions are so much more complex and complicated than that; diametrically opposed feelings and emotions can exist simultaneously and both be true. My mother may not have been the mother I either wanted or needed but she *was* my mother. She carried me and bore me and there is something so primal and fundamental about that bond and fact.

I remember receiving a condolence letter from a friend after Mom's death in which she talked about how close she was to her mother, how she dreaded her mother's passing, and how she couldn't imagine what I must be going through. Her letter saddened me; not everyone has her experience. I certainly didn't. My mother did not know how to feed me, which though that still would have felt bad, would have been more tolerable if she had simply acknowledged the fact of her own limitations and been more loving and accepting. But her emotional and psychological needs were paramount, not to mention the conscious and unconscious demands created by the unhappiness of her own childhood and marriage.

I tried to share with Mel. that part of my sadness stems from the fact that with the death of my mother is the death, however unlikely or unrealistic, of the possibility of our relationship ever being any different. I always assumed I would have more time to do healing work with Mom once Dad was gone. How wrong, how wrong I was! I felt a tremendous compassion for my mother toward the end, her frailty and fears. But our roles were still the same: my care-taking her neediness and negative, pessimistic worldview; my trying to cheer her up. How I wished I could have been privy to the sense of humor Mother's friends so praised her for!

That is why I can return to my apartment at night both crying and blessing God. I can cry for the lack of closeness with my mother and still express gratitude for experiencing the relationship itself. Nothing exists in a vacuum. Human relationships are always in process. And like I said: complicated.

March 22, 2004

Just returned from a three-day conference entitled Call to Action, a progressive coalition of Catholic activists. For all the dogma of traditional Catholicism, I was impressed with the forward-thinking and openness of the people I met, in many ways more open than the so-called liberal Anglican church. I attended the conference not only because I am interested in social justice but also because I wanted to connect with others, show up and be present, and hopefully sell a few books.

I had a small exhibit entitled "Spiritual Activism" and after the second day of not selling anything, I walked out of the conference hall into the parking lot with a smile on my face, thanking God for *yet another* opportunity to learn humility. The goal is not to sell books; the goal is to be of loving service. Period. And, of course, the next day I sold three, not breaking even with expenses, but still experiencing a feeling of gratitude, not because I sold anything but because I got the lesson. The message is simple and clear: we are all in this together. Our tribe is the entire family of humankind, 6.2 billion people, 6.2 billion souls, 6.2 billion divine sparks.

Why are we here at all? Because some Force outside us willed us, willed everything into being. We didn't get here on our own. And what is that Willing-into-Being about? How are we to respond to It? So we can choose, of our own volition and free will, goodness, kindness, and loving compassion rather than fear, contraction, anger, and hate. And this will-to-goodness, this choosing to rise above instinct only we humans can do.

We fail to appreciate the divine significance and sanctification of choice and the moral/philosophical challenge it both implies and demands. We possess the power to think about goodness and what is not goodness, and at times there is a whisper thin line between the two where one's individual conception of goodness becomes another's idea of evil. In essence, that is what the world is arguing about today.

In order for non-violence to succeed one has to be a non-violent person. It is not just an idea, a conceptual framework from which to see the world; that kind of non-violence, that kind of love, that kind of mercy in action *is* the Kingdom of God, *is* the Empire of Good. And the splits in the collective psyche are huge! I think about the application of this conception of non-violence in my own life and it starts first, of course, with me. I am learning how to be non-violent with myself for the first time in my life. What a concept! And what a pity so many of us learn this self-battering, self-punitive, self-loathing, peace-destroying voice, all the menacing dos and don'ts of achievement, avarice and/or envy, wanting or coveting something to fill the hole of self-disavowal.

I am learning how to become more attuned and obedient to another call. Like the old saying that charity begins at home: so, too, does peace. And I have come to realize that this is the only place peace can start and the only place peace can be truly powerful. It is where the singular note of energetic vibration gets struck and sounds within. There cannot be a peaceful world without peaceful people. The buck truly does stop/rest with me. I only have to focus on me. How liberating this truth is! I can leave others' peacefulness – or lack thereof – to them. And God.

Yesterday after the conference and after only four hours' sleep Saturday night, I decided to go to a movie, and as I was leaving the parking lot I realized something about healing the wound that has been at the core of my relationship with P. and that in some ways, or many, is still there despite the fact that my moving out has helped. I realized that the healing of this wound is the primary responsibility, *my* responsibility whether or not P. and I continue together, and of course we cannot continue in any meaningful way unless this archaic wound is healed.

Tears came into my eyes because I realized how I have been battling the wound of my past, making war with it, and reacting against it rather than simply embracing it and loving it. This is very different, quantitatively and qualitatively different, than denying it, ignoring it, or accepting it in a defeatist way.

The only way to love is to be loving.

The only way for peace to enter the world is to be peace-giving and peace-filled.

Like I said: a lot of psychic splits requiring a lot of healing. Some of the tools requisite for this healing, both personal and collective, first and foremost, for me at least:

1) Patience: patience as a reflection on a daily basis of a deep interior quiet and tranquility.
2) Personal power, especially over my own thoughts; being mindful of peace-disturbing, anxiety-generating thoughts, bringing them into awareness

and then letting them go, the idea of breathing in the negative and breathing out the positive. #1 and #2 really work in tandem, back and forth, like a spiritual dance.

3) Persistence: keeping at it with love, over and over again. This is what discipline, true discipleship means.

4) Perspective: to trust that God will get me where I need to be, where He/She wants me if I keep engaging in the first three.

And when I fall off the wagon or out of the spiritual saddle, to get right back on. This, too, is a discipline because discouragement and despondency are antithetical to being peaceful and yet they also provide more opportunities to exercise patience and perspective.

Much to ponder.

March 28, 2004

A glorious spring morning. Through the open windows of my apartment float the sounds of birds and the rhythmic whirring and clicking of the automatic dryer across the walkway in the laundry room. And from across the alley and the little Lighthouse Church come voices singing: "Holy, Holy, Holy!" Yes, all of this, so holy.

A difficult, tumultuous week. After living apart for the past six months I realized P. and I could easily drift our separate ways and that it is time to make a conscious effort toward building something new after letting the dust and debris settle on the razing of the past. What do we choose to do? Sitting at opposite ends of the spectrum on just about everything, do we want to have a food fight or a banquet? For the two of us combined bring a lot to the table of life. I honestly felt that we were beginning to round the corner, to take some baby steps toward healing, and then only a few days later an eruption like the ones we used to have. It feels so insidiously sick: six months of such committed hard work and soul-searching, only to be dashed in a matter of minutes and going on an emotional/psychological binge after all that hard-earned sobriety.

After the rubble settled, I got into a hot shower and felt ill, utterly defeated, thinking, "Another nail in the coffin. I simply cannot do this anymore." Of course, I said that last August, thinking my moving out would make a difference – which it did, sort of – and then last Friday night there we were back again to square one. Or so it felt to me. I honestly do not know what I do or say to set P. off so and, of course, his excuse of being tired and stressed from work is no excuse at all, only symptoms of a deeper problem.

So what happens when you vow to yourself that you will never let something happen again, and then it happens? You get *very* quiet. One minute P. is sitting across the dinner table from me, telling me I look like an angel, then thirty minutes later he is furious and smashing things all because I said, "Honey, take a deep breath and count to 10."

I simply cannot fathom it, nor do I wish to spend more of my time trying to. One does begin to comprehend the great challenge of becoming a truly non-violent organism internally. As bad and disturbing as all our death oriented structural system is, it is only a reflection of this deeper internal fear, hostility, and warring. How to calm and still *that*?! The emotional violence must stop.

We need to ask ourselves how to move beyond the wound. Not denying it, not repressing it, not acting out of it but embracing it, healing it, and letting it go. How to make the unconscious, both small and large, conscious? How to heal the wars that rage within our hearts? How many variations are there on this theme being played out across our planet today: husband to wife, wife to husband, lover to lover, parent to child, child to parent, country to country, religion to religion?

The violence must stop!

March 30, 2004

Awake at 2:00am in the morning wondering about so many things: the seemingly bottomless pit of money and energy this book marketing enterprise is consuming, as if I am caught in a monumental process over which I have no control. Thinking, too, how I let these concerns, legitimate as they may be on one level, disturb my slumber, followed by my attempts to self-sooth and calm down. Tossing and turning in the middle of the night; hot, restless, and sweaty, my mind not to be stilled. At a total loss what to think about, what to do or say. I waver between "This is so over, why bother with any more effort, the writing is on the wall, no more talk, this is it" to the voice that says "stay present without judgment, let your heart do the listening, be patient."

So I toss and turn in the middle of the night, not knowing which way to go. And the curious thing about all this is that as this being who can't sleep and bounces around the mattress agitated beyond measure about contingencies, finances, relationships, and what to do next is met by another part that feels all right, anchored, just breathe in and out, in and out, put one foot in front of the other, day by day. What, finally, is liberation? From the past, from parents, from children, from spouse, from false ideologies, from self?

Breathe and trust.

Breathe and trust.

And then, of course, there is that part of me, like Scrooge, who dismisses all the tossing and turning to digestive disruption brought on by "a bad spot of cheddar"

– in my case, not eating dinner until 9:00pm after seeing clients.

And so I turn on the light in the far reaches of the night and instead of tossing and turning, I breathe and read: Pierre from *War and Peace* having a dream, and a voice talking:

> The most difficult thing is the subjection of man's will to the law of God...No one can be the master of anything while he fears death [or fears anything at all]...And all things belong to him who fears it not.

Yes. She who fears not.

April 3, 2004

At a Reiki retreat in Arrowhead, a small group of only twelve people, and we are a motley crew indeed: incest and abuse survivors, cancer survivors, relationship survivors. But survivors nevertheless. It feels good to be out of LA if only for a short while. There is something so comforting about the cloud and fog shrouded pines. Nature is more than we humans deserve considering how we abuse and neglect it so. I have felt remarkably peaceful since being here, more and more a pilgrim: putting one foot in front of the other and seeing what happens. Sounds simple, doesn't it? And yet I am finding it precisely not simple, exquisitely not so. Though simple in theory, it is perhaps one of the most difficult and demanding of spiritual disciplines to accomplish as a process, not a goal.

And, of course, the opportunities for humility in all this are endless, endless, endless. I keep having to bring myself back down to one foot in front of the other, don't think, don't anticipate, don't second guess, don't judge, be present, walk, carry peace within yourself, breathe. This, I believe, is perhaps the most necessary part of living honestly. I only hope that I can carry this energy back to LA as I attend a business marketing meeting and then another with P. The curious paradox for me in this most baffling of relationships is that I do not see P. and my being together, at least not in the same way as we have been, nor do I see us being apart – in the way one traditionally imagines divorced people to be. It is a puzzlement. No concrete answers, no insightful "Ah has!" Sometimes floundering in the dark is precisely what we need. We may not want it, but it is what we need.

So it's back to one foot in front of the other, trusting that Spirit will get me where It needs me to be; that Spirit has me where I need to be at this exact moment and each moment if I can just remain an open channel.

Open!

The following from an article I read recently that broke my heart:

The story of a 32 year old man, a Hamas member for fifteen years, who claims that his activities making rockets "are what give me satisfaction and peace in my heart." The idea that knowing what he does – killing others, innocent or guilty, culpable or not – brings him peace: how do we embrace and heal *that*? This man, a fugitive living on the run, has five children whom he rarely sees. Will these young people think their father a hero, or will they regret his not kissing them at night before going to bed?

How does my trying so very hard to hold the peace here, half way around the world, affect that 32-year old Hamas militant? Or to the many others who are willing to dedicate themselves and their lives to killing? And yet somehow it feels as if my holding the peace does matter very much, like praying for that angry young man in the post office; that it acts as a counter-balance to all the negativity, a form of covert "counter-terrorism," peace cells building.

April 18, 2004

As I sat down in my arm chair to read my little *Runner's Bible*, it fell apart in my hands: the binding gone, the cloth cover worn threadbare like a frayed rug or the cuff of a favorite shirt; water stains from when W. as a toddler threw it in the toilet and tried to flush it down the john; all the smoke marks and smudges after rescuing it from the Malibu fire: my beloved little pocket Bible that has literally saved me in so many ways, over so many days in pieces in my hands. And I started to weep, thinking about Mom, how much time do I have left? All that has happened in the last year and a half, all the chaos and change.

For the last few days I have been feeling very fragile, tearing easily, trying hard to draw upon my inner resources, but I haven't been as successful as I usually am at pulling myself up by my spiritual bootstraps. And when my Bible fell apart in my hands, it was the proverbial last straw.

One of the several notes I had stuck in my journal: the fact that truth never adapts or accommodates itself to our feelings or beliefs about what is. Truth never serves our individual wills, though we usually expect, and certainly want it to. As a teacher of philosophy once put it, "Reality is the brick wall you smack into when you're wrong." The only reality that can said to be truly real is spiritual reality, not human reality, though the latter certainly exists. I *am* tired today and my feet *do* hurt. Spiritual reality is not human; we humans are only the vessels for this other transcendent reality. We become the personal embodiment of spiritual power. But once we start to think we know best how to use this power, in that very notion we lose it. Time for Humility 101. Again.

An odd thought just occurred to me; it's like spiritual chiropractic. Crack, crack, crack, putting that spiritual spine back into alignment. How we all need to incorporate – literally put within our bodies – the notion of *kokua*, a Hawaiian word a friend told me about. It means thoughtfulness, grace, respect, dignity, being centered. These are qualities that take place by and large outside the mind; they spring from a different vibrational field within. It occurs to me that I need to foster more of *kokua* toward myself in my own life.

How does one accept all this "as is?" Not to condone what is going on but somehow to accept it in order to transmute tribal mentalities and worldviews, whether east or west, different perspectives clashing, a battle of contesting egos and wills taking place upon the world stage. To write that most, if not all, of this mess is the result of men wanting to force their own parochial ideologies on one another is ultimately non-productive. One might as well ask: How did we women become so disempowered that we allowed our men to get this out-of-whack and berserk? We are all responsible; maybe in some ways we women even more so because we know better, we are more aligned with life.

I cannot help but reflect upon some of the things Tolstoy wrote about war and conflict toward the end of *War and Peace*: that it is those who possess the illusive and hard to describe "X" factor of will who will ultimately win, regardless of the numbers involved. I suppose the salient question is how much of this "X" factor of will does each of us possess? There is a process afoot. I hesitate the use the word "battle" because that word reinforces polarity and dualism, but there is a process afoot whereby this "X" factor in the hearts and minds of the world's people will come to bear as we watch psychological conflicts being played out on the world stage and within our own lives.

And it may not be sheer numbers that are required, though as MLK said, the sheer morality of the claim of non-violence will persuade many. No, the number of this critical "X" factor of will may be far smaller than many of us realize or appreciate.

Imagine: a single prayer could save the world!

Will it be you who says it?

April 27, 2004

Another restless night. I sleep for three to four hours, then like clockwork I awaken somewhere between 2 and 3 o'clock in the morning, not able to sleep, eyes open, thoughts churning. After listening to my thoughts rattle around inside my head for half an hour, I finally got up. I *am* jealous of P. seeing other women. I *do* love him and would like for us to be able to forge something vital and robust after all the hurt and misunderstanding of the past. But I also know I am not in control of this process. I can only show up and be present, speak my truth lovingly, and trust that God will get us where we need to be. In the meantime, this whole experiment in relationship is an opportunity to dance with my shadow, which I have been doing a lot lately in the wee hours of the night.

I remind myself of this as my mind is racing and I feel primal territorial reactions stirring while P. incorporates other women into his life. Me, I feel like a hermit. A friend even remarked that my apartment has a monastic quality to it. I'm trying to repair myself while P. is out partying and "getting his needs met." I guess I'm getting my needs met too, only in a different way. It is not about denying the thoughts and reactions I am experiencing about his socializing and womanizing; they do provide important feedback. It is rather about not letting them dominate my mental dance floor.

A part of me misses being P.'s wife, a part of me misses calling him "husband." There is such a special sense of intimacy and belonging associated with those two words. And the fact that the other women P. is seeing know we are separated and perhaps know we are legally divorced is the breeding ground for hope springing eternal for other plans. Nature abhors a vacuum and there are those ready, willing, and able to swoop in to soothe the deserted and/or lonely and/or abandoned mate, something P. capitalizes on, too. Me, I've actually gone back to wearing my wedding ring just to put men off.

I am such a one man woman.

I just don't know if P. is a one woman man.

What I'm talking about here are primal connections of intimacy and territoriality and soul. I'll be damned if I don't fight for what I believe in, not out of neediness or feelings of disempowerment but because it is my primal foundational connection to Spirit.

Talk about war and peace!

Talk about that red raw beast, the green-eyed god-damned straight from the heart!

It is time to shape shift reality like crow.

I have noticed in this process how quick I am to judge. Thoughts simply cannot afford to be squandered on *any* form of negativity. That old familiar sense of self-deflation and hurt? Of lack? Of not being good enough, not worthy? And isn't that what my voice told me? To not pay attention to those feelings of deflation. My shadow dance more like a ballet; for every thought that has a dampening impact, trying to counterbalance it with a spiritual thought salve, soothing the part that has difficulty with trust. Our minds truly are the most powerful tools on earth. Or weapons, depending on their focus.

I can see how long it takes to become grounded in God, embedded in that reality, a constant process of bringing oneself back over and over again. Talk about discipline! I step on my own toes a lot, one move forward, two moves back. The ouches are not as clumsy and oafish as in the past, but for that very reason they are harder to execute gracefully. Over and over, beginning again and again with a one-two-three. Shifting from a horizontal human perspective to a vertical, spiritual one.

Only God knows what will happen, and I must trust, whatever the outcome – painful or joyous or somewhere in between – that it will be right. What I want may not be what I need and what I need may not be what I want. I can only remain surrendered to what is.

Slogging through *War and Peace* (only 50 pages left), this struck home:

> Life is everything. Life is God. All is changing and moving, and that motion *is* God. And while there is life, there is the joy of the consciousness of the Godhead. To love life is to love God. The hardest and most blessed thing is to love this life in one's suffering, in underserved suffering.

Yes.

May 19, 2004

P. spent nearly a week at my little apartment after some surgery while painters ransacked the other house. I slept in a sleeping bag on the floor in the living room while he was in my tiny bed recuperating in a trance-like state as he absorbed the energy of this place. "It's like a sacred temple." He didn't know how to respond.

Mother's Day. Far more painful than I anticipated; all the children gone and the first without my mom; hard, hard. Son D. graduating from Berkeley: how can this be? He was just a boy or at least an obstreperous adolescent three seconds ago.

And for me personally deep grief as more archaic patterns emerge and my not being able to do much – or anything – about them except let them be, let the grief and the darkness and the muck of the past and its purging keep rising to the surface, surrendering and letting go. That, coupled with the usual frustrations of the day-to-day world (painters, cleaning, sorting out on a grand spring house-cleaning scale), plodding, if not retrograde movement, on the book and professional front. My father failing more and more. No longer legally married but still in a relationship.

Is it any wonder I feel numb most of the time?

It feels like this is the final battle over my middle earth, the terra firma of my soul and psyche. As melodramatic as it sounds, this does feel like a crucifixion of sorts, and I must simply hang on, hang on, hang on until all the old everything dies. It has been a painful time, and I know it is not over yet. How I long for the morning when I will awaken with peace and a sense of quiet joy in my heart rather than the nothingness I now feel – not dread or anxiety or panic or anything – just this sense of "Oh, another day, what to do?" And I know, too, that this descent into the darkest parts, like Inanna and Ereshkigal, is required, something I must surrender to, like when I was a child body surfing along the coast and would get slapped by a wave that I couldn't handle. No use fighting it, you just had to go limp and let its energy dissipate and subside, and hope you came up on the other side without drowning.

Yes, that is what this process feels like, and I know that when I get through this last monstrous shaking of the dark dragon's tail I will come into my power. The old stuff, the old system simply must go – whether in me personally or how it is being reflected around the entire planet: *it must go!* If I can get through this Gordian knot of self and soul perhaps it will aid the collective energetic shift that is being called for, that is yearning to groan its way into being. Again, liking or not liking this process, embracing it willingly or unwillingly is not the point because what is required is what is required. But I must say from this tiny little perspective of mine, it is one fucking hell of a bitch of a ride!

So I keep going through my days with tears of grief and sadness welling up and saying to myself, "Okay, more house cleaning to do." For in the final analysis, identity and empowerment are *the* core spiritual issues: "Who am I?" "How am I to be effective in the world?" "What is my mission, my own particular charism?" These are questions that must be answered. So this crazy, mind-warping time is about being stripped of all external identity and becoming totally disempowered and out-of-control as a paradoxical way of leading to a deeper level of identity and empowerment about which I have very little understanding at present.

Like Alice in the rabbit hole, I just keep falling. And amidst all this internal chaos people tell me I have such wonderful energy! This, too, baffles me because I have been feeling so sad at times, so lost and blue and disjointed. How little I must recognize or appreciate my own goodness in all this and this, too, is part of the wrenching process, for me to come to this embracing of self apart from parents, children, and ex-husbands. The *only* thing life or God gets out of you is you, the person you become, not what you accomplish in the world, though certainly what one accomplishes is a reflection of the individual at his or her core. This plane of existence is all about personal transformation. Will I become a blessing or a curse? Will I be able to bless the curse and darkness as they lead hopefully to the light and blessing of day?

May 23, 2004

Yesterday I spent a grueling 12-hour day finishing my training and initiation into the final level of Reiki. I am now officially a Reiki Master Teacher, and though exhausted I want to record a meditation about soul work I did before it completely evaporates from my mind.

I am walking down my life's path, noticing how it has been, where I have been in nature or by the sea, where my path has been narrow or wide, crooked or straight when I come to a bridge. As I cross the bridge, I look below into the clear waters of a stream and see an image of myself from the past, a previous life. I immediately envision a Druidic priestess, clothed in a white mantel and robe cascading to the ground. I connect to the electric blue of her (my) eyes which radiate energy and the kind, loving smile she gives me, heart-to-heart.

As I continue over the bridge, I meet another guide. I see myself at an even younger age, four or five, a radiant child, laughing and gay, with the white platinum blond hair I had at that time. This little Maurine takes me by the hand and gives me a parchment scroll in which there is information that is important for me to know. At first the name on the scroll reads "Maurine" but then it changes to my first name "Sara," which means princess, and I think about the true significance of that: being regal, my own royalty and sovereignty, that authority within.

As I unroll the scroll, a multitude of tiny multi-colored butterflies, like a rainbow, emerges, along with rays of light. Little Sara continues to laugh, that giggling, tinkling chime kind of laughter that only children possess. I realize my soul's journey, my soul's work is to be light. To be light in the sense of bringing light into the world but also in the sense of walking lightly and gently upon the earth. The little butterflies, symbols of beauty and transformation and fragility, continue to flutter out.

I ask Sara if there is anything else I need to know and a strange thing happens:

A large, softly glowing white luminescent, slightly pulsing circular portal opens up before me and I am transfixed. I am not frightened or surprised by this but quietly attracted, curious. Did I somehow expect this? The image is so vivid and enticing; it beckons me. I walk over to the portal/vortex and put my right hand on its circular doorway rim. The sense of infused, soft white light is palpable, loving and kind. I have the feeling that at some point in order to evolve closer to the light this corporeal casing will have to be left behind to enter the portal of transformation; that the body, in effect, will have used up its usefulness, like a butterfly's cocoon, and will have to be shed, and that this sloughing off and away of the body will be a good, no joyous, wondrous event.

The journey back to love.

The journey back to light.

And so I stand on the threshold, watching myself as I look into the void which isn't a void at all but an entirely different reality. Or rather the next stage on a continuum of reality about which we humans have only the tiniest blip of understanding.

My soul meditation ends with my standing before this circular portal, this round vortex of light. When is each of us asked to transform our bodies and step into that portal? Until then, I must be light, both noun and adjective, where I am. And laugh a lot while I am doing whatever I am doing. Indeed, laughter itself creates, generates light, lightness of being. Doesn't a good laugh make you feel lighter? Doesn't a good laugh take your burdens away? What is it that Pablo Neruda said? That laughter is the language of the soul. And the irony, or paradox, of how often we must wade through the tears in order to get to the laughter.

Letting go. Letting go. Letting go. The battle for the Middle Earth of Maurine: where my mother was, where she left off, where I begin and continue, where I leave off and where my daughters continue; all that female lineage, how we learn to make it into a blessing rather than the curse of self-denial or worse, killer restraint. Asking Mom to be an ally in my soul's journey now from wherever she is in a way that she wasn't able to do in this life.

As I write this with tears in my eyes, sitting in the chair in my small bedroom, Mom's ashes are in an urn in the corner underneath a woven shawl of chakra colors. I like to think that Mom is at the end of the rainbow, all the energy of those vibrant colors flowing into her soul and that she is giving to me now in a way that is open-hearted, not driven by need. I need her blessing now more in death than I ever did in life. I don't know how to explain this any other way. I do believe there is a grief that goes too deep for tears.

June 10, 2004
More sparks flying off as the dross is released. I don't even know what to say anymore: I'm lovers with my ex-husband? A part of me is still angry about a number of things, especially what feels to me like P.'s lying to himself and his motives about initiating this process; i.e. getting legally disentangled so he feels less guilty about seeing other women and also wanting to protect his money. I am on the verge of tears most of the time, frequently not even aware how close they are to the surface; how raw and tender I am in some places, tough as a railroad tie in others.

My memory has become an absolute sieve: forgetting thoughts mid-sentence; forgetting phone calls and conversations I just had. I even forgot a friend visited me for an entire week in January right after my mother died. Like being in labor, this process of transformation is excruciatingly painful and there is nothing I can do except get through it, just keep pushing and grunting until the new birth pops out. And then what a sense of relief and release! How I am looking forward to that last push and grunt where the new me will open her eyes and blink. I don't believe I have ever prayed so fervently over such an extended period of time in my entire life. And the thing that is so hard, so very challenging about the spiritual life is needing/wanting some sort of feedback or encouragement from the universe, God, Spirit, whatever you want to call this Other Entity with whom prayerful conversation takes place.

Some sort of feedback that you are on the right track or at least some indication, however slight or small, positive or negative, that one is, in fact, on the path that spirit intends rather than coming from a place of ego gratification or willful stubbornness or petulant child-like whining and thinking it is spirit because that is what you want. The only other time in my life when I have been in a comparable place of such nakedness, of being so stripped of everything, when I truly felt the immediate and intimate movement of spirit was when I had cancer. And while I know that one cannot demand anything of God other than to be surrendered to His/Her will, one does need to have some sense from the Above what His/Her particular will is for the particular individual sending forth that heartfelt supplication.

I just reread Thomas Merton's prayer:

My Lord, I have no idea where I am going. I do not see the road ahead of me. I cannot know for certain where it will end. Nor do I really know myself, and the fact that I think I am following your will does not mean that I am actually doing so. But I believe that the desire to please you does in fact please you. And I hope that I have that desire in all that I am doing. I hope that I will never do anything apart from that desire. And I know that as I do this you will lead me by the right road, though I may know nothing about it. Therefore I will trust you always though I may seem to be lost and in the shadow of death. I will not fear, for you are ever with me, and you will never leave me to face my perils alone.

I wish I could write that I am at a commensurate level of faith and trust. I am afraid I waver a lot of the time. What are the signs, internal and external, that we are leading a God-directed life? Joy, patience, loving-kindness, all those attributes that are called fruit of the spirit. But what about the periods and oh-so-humanly real, decidedly real times when one finds oneself in intense desolation, living, walking, moving, and breathing in a spiritual desert where those fruit are precisely *not* to be found? The only thing I can come up with, the only answer I can ground myself in is how to be loving in the moment.

How to be loving with myself? How to bring more Venus, Love, Eros energy into my own life and being? A part of me wants to flee all this. Another part of me says, "Tough it out." Another part of me feels drugged, buzzing inside; another part feels as if I am actually growing more stupid, especially having difficulty listening because of an internal sensation of being perpetually distracted. Not good, not good. The more confusing and disrupted the surface, horizontal level of my life becomes, the more I am losing a sense of my own depth. If Spirit finds its way into the world through passion and joy, what makes me passionate and joyful? How do I start, or restart, cultivating *those* fruit?

June 17, 2004

The following is the only writing I have done in weeks. From Isaiah 61: 1-5:

> ...the Lord has appointed me to preach good tidings unto the meek; he has sent me to bind up the broken hearted, to proclaim liberty to the captives, and the opening of the eyes of them that are bound...to comfort all who mourn.

All who mourn and are broken hearted. Asking in supplication: Dear God,

I have been thinking so much about P.; feeling separated, something lost; deep mourning, lots of crying, talking in my head trying to explain things, rationalizing to control my hurt and anger. Where is Your hand working in all these feelings, reactions, and emotions?

To show on some deep level how connected you still feel to P. That you feel violated and betrayed and need to learn from this how to respond. That you are a tender-hearted person, too trusting perhaps. You are doing all this to yourself. How can you learn to be loving and gentle with yourself? How many women could do what you are doing? How many would have the courage to go through what you are going through? You are in a large process guided by me, always remember that, to enter deeper and deeper into your heart. How can you become more loving with yourself as you walk through this valley of pain? How do you learn to turn the other cheek while fully embracing the tears on your own?

Every time you have a thought that hurts, witness it and immediately let it go, cut the thinking off and turn toward yourself and your needs in that moment. Say a kind word to yourself or recite a passage of scripture. Pray for

your own healing every time you split away from yourself toward others, come back to yourself and me and follow what makes you feel more peaceful and centered internally. Expectation of any kind implies, however small, lack of faith and trust in me. Put your absolute faith and trust in me! Your flowering is in my hands, you are being held through all this tenderly and lovingly. This is what you have a tendency to forget. All the hurt and pain: they are asking you to turn to me and know that you are loved.

Can you forgive yourself for being the human that you are, the human who is subject to all the emotions that humans have? Can you learn at a core level that you are not these emotions and responses? It just feels that way in the moment because of their intensity. When these reactions come up they are a signal for you to:

Witness and observe them.

Realize they are not you, that nothing can threaten you.

Do not get caught up in mental rationalizing because that is what upsets you.

Calm yourself.

Take a deep breath.

You are being held through this.

Do all actions with and in the name of Love.

June 22, 2004

Yesterday P. wanted to make sure I was out of the house before one of his female friends arrived. How it feels to me he wants to keep his worlds separate. How my gut churns and broils, like he's playing with both them and me. Why not introduce me? We're supposed to be working on our relationship, right? Now P. gets not only friendship but ego strokes and gratification from other women, being looked up to and admired, and he clearly does not want me in on that.

How I awakened at 2:30am in the morning to find him on my computer going over emails from eHarmony. How guilty and sneaky he appeared – as if he had been caught out. It makes me furious he doesn't tell these other women that he's still trying to rebuild a relationship with me. It makes me feel as if he's playing both sides of the game, dangling "I just want to be your friend" (no serious relationship) while these other women are more than willing to be nurturing, loving, supportive, hoping perhaps he'll change his mind until he does want one. Maybe.

My feelings of being the fool, the chump, his wanting the best of both worlds while I'm on fire inside. I may be the most important woman in P.'s life (so he says) but it also feels as if I'm in a pack jockeying for position. P. is not being honest with himself or me.

How is God's hand working through this state of absolute shock I feel myself experiencing, like I've been duped and that I've willingly allowed myself to be duped. How is this working for my good?

I have given you the gifts of a trusting nature, kindness and generosity of spirit. Now is the time to concentrate on these unique gifts. All the anguish you are experiencing is calling you, urging you to rise above the human drama that is transpiring. Though not intended to hurt or make you enraged, these human feelings and emotions are the trial by fire, the purgatory process.

You must purge and release all self-doubt. You are being called to become grounded in a higher order of reality. You must do whatever you can to get calm. It is doubly hard when friends counsel otherwise – anger, retaliation, confrontation – that may not be either required or productive because they lack your generosity of spirit. Your compassionate heart will always feel for others. It is time now for you to turn that compassionate heart toward yourself.

Remain steadfast with me. Peace will come. Peace is ever-present. You know that when you awakened in the hospital after cancer surgery. Whenever you start to go off, insert that moment into your consciousness because you understood that Love is the Transcendent Power, the essence of all creation. Concentrate on how you can love yourself; the essential work is self-love.

Some ways to achieve this:

Snap off any sense of guilt or that you are unworthy.

Cut off any sense of "There's something wrong, I need to be doing something else."

Be humble and grateful that you are blessed to be in the position you are in. Your work in the world will come when you are ready because to do my work you must love yourself.

Learn to move with more grace and graciousness.

Take care of your body; it is your temple and already has been through a lot.

Love and embrace the world as part of who you are, gift it with your loving presence.

Continue to open your heart.

The most important action for you to take is rooting out any weed of doubt, self-doubt about the rightness of your being and where you are. Embrace each moment for the gift that it is and give thanks. Cut off any feeling of lack in whatever form it presents itself but especially any sense of lacking anything within yourself. Stilling this thought process is the most important and necessary act of love you can do right now.

September 12, 2004

Back from a trip to Eastern Europe to celebrate D.'s graduation from college and his official send off into the "suit and tie" crowd. While away, I had the sad realization that a profound tie has been broken. I guess it has taken me this long to feel divorced, that and finding out about P.'s affair with E.

I thought after a year in my little apartment I would be more than ready to move back in with P. But I have decided that hope can be a form of denial because we generally hope for something to transpire, and therefore it can be a subtle, or not so subtle, form of control; i.e. wanting a specific outcome. The only valid hope is hoping to follow the will of God. And how much of the unknown can be involved in that and how much we humans tend to resist the unknown because of our habitual need to feel safe and in charge. I am packing the rest of my personal belongings to put into storage until I can decide – or am guided to – the next step.

I also returned to my father being hospitalized for the second time in less than a week for two falls and have to face the task – again! – of packing his belongings and moving him into another area of the assisted living facility. While I was away I actually prayed, "Bill, it's time to let go." No anger or resentment just the truthful acknowledgement that there is a rhythm to things. After experiencing Mom's sudden death and now witnessing Dad's decline, I do believe Mother was the lucky one. And I am grateful for God's infinite mercy in taking her first because she could never have handled watching her husband weaken and diminish the way he has, especially since he was the commander of their marital ship.

This is the first time in weeks I have set pen to paper, and I wonder if words will even come out the end. Are there any words left? And if there are, will the cranial retrieval connections work well enough to bring them forth? Why write anyway? Joseph Heller's *Portrait of the Artist as an Old Man* is right on the money – minus the hormones and hot flashes and sleepless nights.

And yet it is true in spite of all this, in spite of everything that has happened on this mid-life shake down cruise I am experiencing for perhaps the first time how to bring joy into my life. And while all these multiple losses are sad and they do bring tears, there is also a sense of deep, profound liberation from all the roles, demands, expectations, and shoulds. The real job now is to listen to and train this spiritual core. Trust about the wisdom and ultimate beneficence of the universe is growing. It is awakening to and entering into a world much deeper and richer and kinder than the world of ego and mind. And yes, I still experience all the reactions and emotions this flesh is heir to, but I am learning to watch the human comedy in a different way. At least for now.

And how very blessed I am that I can do this! Appropriate self-valuing is the key.

This was brought home to me like a 2 x 4 to the head last week as I was helping my father reorganize his life. Months ago we made an agreement that I would act as power of attorney and executrix for Mom and Dad and that Dad would pay me several hundred dollars a month for this work. He hasn't paid me anything for quite a while, yet I noticed several checks written to my brother for thousands of dollars to help him with his business. When I mentioned this to Dad, he said, "Oh, yes, let me give you some money." He handed me a check for $100.00. Is it any wonder that when P. handed me a marriage contract assigning me a certain value that I signed it? Or that some twenty-plus years later for all practical purposes he handed me a pink slip, marriage and mothering job over, I signed that, too?

I was very carefully taught. I can only pray that my own daughters have been very differently taught.

October 1, 2004

P. broke down weeping on Rosh Hashanah, wondering if he even deserved to get me back after all the pain he has caused me, especially his relationship with E. – all the "confused projection" on his part as he called it. It is indeed a poignant time: so many leave-takings. It feels less and less likely that we will come together again, though we will always be partners of sorts because of the children. But who knows? It ain't over 'til it's over and there is always the interface between personal choice, individual surrender, and the divine "X" factor of will Tolstoy wrote about. Not much to worry or fret about in light of that. You learn the lessons you need to learn, you fulfill the contracts – energetic, spiritual, legal, and temporal – that you came in to fulfill. And then you move on.

This past weekend was the first time in months that I could actually feel myself slowing down. Saturday I spent a quiet afternoon sorting through a closet full of papers, my one tiny little closet in my tiny little apartment, and still it was bursting to the seams. The sense of spaciousness around me while I was doing this was visceral, followed that evening by the first rainstorm of the season.

Last Monday after a lovely dinner with P. and some honest, open-hearted communication, I returned to my place, put on some Gregorian chants, and started getting ready for bed, when unexpectedly there was knocking at my door. It was P. and when I let him in, we fell into each other's arms, kissing as we haven't kissed in a long, long time. The next thing I knew P. said, "That's it. You're coming home with me." And I looked heavenward, saying: "I hope this isn't a mistake."

And we made love that night like never before. My pelvic region felt on fire, as if it had been ignited, and this sensation lasted throughout the next day. I asked myself when alone again, "What happened last night?!" After all my resolve to stay away from P., I did not feel bad or weak-willed or remorseful or self-chastising. On the contrary. Because what happened was so spontaneous, so unplanned, and so devoid of neediness and game-playing, it felt right. I could really love the man I was with that night. Yet I know too that neither one of us is ready to enter this deeper level of intimacy. Still half-baked. For now.

And I know also that I like my low maintenance life. I like becoming reacquainted with my own rhythm. I like not having to deal with the demands of the material world P. deals with – all its noise and stress and phone calls and drama. I like the lightness and simplicity of my life.

October 20, 2004

Thinking about how to most wisely use the time I have left and yet knowing, too, I have no real control over that. All that I can do, all that I am required to do is to bring to my life three "willingnesses":
   1) the willingness to be who I am;
   2) the willingness to let her out;
   3) the willingness to be proud of who emerges.
      All else will unfold from these.

It does feel as if a new plant is sprouting, like FS said, poking its head above the surface for its first encounter with light and water and air. Does love at the level of personality have to die in order for love at the transpersonal level to be born?

Spiritual flashcards for today:

I have been given a unique mission to accomplish, even if I don't know what it is.

Doubt of any kind must be abolished.

I must not judge others or myself.

I must not hold grudges or irritation of any kind.

I must focus on abundance and goodness.

All my relationships and interactions are a reflection of the Divine. (Especially those who piss me off!)

I must train the tuning fork of my mind to resonate at higher frequencies.

In order to accomplish this, I need to concentrate on the attributes of God, of Good.

In an intelligent, creative universe there are no accidents, including me.

To be of service whenever and wherever I can and take every opportunity to concentrate on planting seeds.

I must listen to my heart; my heart speaks the truth, not my head.

I must live with gratitude.

All the power and love of the universe are working on my behalf.

Because of this I need to:

Be generous.

Be passionate.

Practice forgiveness.

Practice surrender.

Practice silence.

Remove resistance.

Concentrate on being kind rather than right.

November 9, 2004

This feels like the only thing of value that comes through me these days:

Gracious Heavenly Spirit Father/Mother Whoever You Are: Help me understand more clearly what my work is, what You want of me.

Peace, quiet, presence. You must not have an agenda of any kind. You must trust that all is unfolding according to my plan. It is not what you do, it is how you go about loving what you do. All action must be filled with my grace. This, and this alone, is what makes life sacred and worthwhile. It is so hard for you simply to be, to do nothing if necessary, other than stay focused on me. You need to become more alert to the subtle ways in which I work. Most miracles go unnoticed because people (you) expect something large and grand to occur. You need to become more attuned to that which is around you – not by giving up your power but as a way of grounding yourself completely in the power of life itself. You still expect too much, for things to happen your way.

Your prayer must always be "Thy Will Be Done." The books in your garage that so concern you will enter the world at the appropriate time in ways you may not imagine. In your prayer the sincerity of your longing is what communicates, not any sense of neediness or lack. How can you pray for anything without absolute trust? You pray daily giving thanks, and this is as it should be. But a part of you does not pray for what you long for because a part of you still doubts that you deserve and are entitled to all the gifts of birthright as one of my beloved children.

Pray as if you deserve all! Pray as if all is already accomplished, exactly as is right for you. You must believe whole-heartedly the truth of this. It is right for you to want things deeply. Your desire is part of the special gift that you are, the unique message you carry. Pay attention to this desire and what inspires you. Too often this desire gets confused or mistaken for neediness or ego-gratification, but true desire, desire devoid of neediness and ego, is of God. Pray from the point of passion and your true heart's desire. This type of prayer is always heard.

Most people pray for what they want and do not give thanks or prayers of gratitude. You give thanks and prayers of gratitude but you do not ask your Heavenly Father/Mother God enough for what you want. It is right that you ask. It is not all up to you to achieve what you want. You must learn how to receive my blessings and right action for you and in order to do this you first must ask. You are worthy of asking. You are worthy of receiving. You have no idea the riches and blessings I can shower down upon you if you but fervently ask and believe that all is already accomplished according to my plan. Open yourself to receive. Concentrate on being open to the power of the entire universe. It is yours for the asking. Believe and receive!

November 16, 2004

Gracious Heavenly Father/Mother:

What is it I need to learn about desire that I do not understand?

Desire is why you were built, why you came into the world. The desire that is in you I planted. It is my yearning to express through you. This desire is what gives you purpose and meaning. It is through the desire I planted that this gift comes into the world. That is why you are precious because only you have this specific desire gift

Your true desire nature is one of joy, enthusiasm, bubbling excitement, light. It is never heavy or ego-driven, though in your case you may need to call upon your mind to implement the birthing of this spirit planted desire into the world. You will know you are following your true heart's desire by the lightness and buoyancy you feel. You will feel better and better as you seek and follow this desire.

All God-Directed, Spirit-Directed desire is good. You tune into this type of desire by paying close attention to your body and how it feels: light, purposeful, not rushed, rhythmic, paced, peaceful, yet imbued with excitement at the same time, a tingling sensation, energetic. You have begun to sense this. Your prayers of thanksgiving indicate as much. Now it is important that you continue to do what you have been doing. You are on the right path. Your willingness to serve and be present, to give of yourself unbegrudgingly and with genuine sincerity will reap rewards you cannot at this time imagine.

Pay closer attention to the small things that happen in your life. These small seeds will grow into larger ones with time. Know that your desire is like a seed. You must nourish it and water it for it to come to fruition. Your desire must reflect everything, all that you are, all that you have been gifted with. This is so that others will see me through you, the totality of you and not just what you label "work." Who you are becomes a reflection of me, the Divine Spark within you. Desire is not about work. Desire is always about love in its deepest, purest, and broadest sense. Focus on what you love and hold firm to that.

Become a more astute listener. Continue at your quiet pace. You will know that you are sufficiently prepared because there will be no fear. Love and your desire will fuse. Your specific work in the world will flow from that.

December 3, 2004

I have been thinking about the spirituality of matter and matter being transformed by mind: it is all of a single piece – the erotic quality of matter and mind, of all life; this is the new direction, the emergent consciousness we and the planet now need. The word "Eros" literally means "to be on the inside" or "being on the inside." I think one of the greatest challenges for humanity, and me, is learning how to be on the inside because once we get that straight, once we are able to bring our internal being into erotic, loving harmony, the exterior world cannot help but reflect this shift. As within, so without. As above, so below. The purpose of our being here is to participate in bringing this consciousness into the world. The reason for our being here is an invitation, a call to be protectors and guarantors of humanity.

145

And it takes only one small spark, a single flame to ignite many. This is the ultimate power of one, the singular God-force within. "The one who dwells within you" as poetry and passion; the sustaining force that runs through and permeates all, that provides a womb for the world; that which knows all names, nurtures all being, and from whom nothing is hidden. The cauldron fire of all desire and all imagination. This is the act of nourishing, sustaining, and "growing" God.

Imagination, image, imago, likeness: God created man/woman in His/Her image and how we humans imagine God will either save and restore us or destroy His/Her creation. First we must choose life and its sacredness. From that primal moving point, Merton's *point vierge*, all else will flow.

"Remember the words I have placed deep within your hearts, before you were even born."

Yes! The Erotics of Giving.

February 23, 2005

Random stuff, quotes and thoughts from reading and elsewhere:

Something about the notion that at critical moments in one's life it is always possible to differentiate what belongs to oneself and what does not. I disagree. It has been my experience that there is no "always" in life, except death. I have found moments of absolute clarity are so rare, and even when they do arise we have a tendency to backslide and second-guess ourselves. I think T.S. Eliot describes the process of life and decision-making far more accurately: hints and guesses and hints after guesses. Plus endless humility. And then, of course, there's prayer.

Speaking of prayer:

The prayer that does not succeed in modulating our wishes; in changing the passionate desire into still submission; the anxious tumultuous expectation into quiet surrender, is not true prayer. The life is most holy in which there is least petition and desire and most of waiting upon God, but in which petition often passes into thanksgiving. Pray till prayer makes you forget your own wishes and leaves or merges it into God's will. The Divine wisdom has given us prayer, not as means to obtain the good things of earth, but as a means whereby we learn to do without them, not as a means to escape evil, but as means whereby we become strong to meet it. (Mrs. E.G. White)

I am not sure how the above fits in with my inner voice's injunction to pray for my heart's desire. The spiritual journey is so paradoxical at times: desire, then let go; seek and then surrender; relinquish in order to receive. God does expect a lot from us discombobulated humans!

Then something about true happiness coming from one of three things: an excess of energy, the cessation of pain, and the absolute certainty that one is doing the will of God. A big "if" that. How much evil has been perpetrated in the world by those of us who are certain of our own self-righteousness. The only time I feel I am doing the will of God is when I am loving toward others. And most of the time I am not truly loving in the sense of being completely focused and present. Quite frequently my acts may be loving but my head and thoughts are elsewhere. To my mind, as long as we are human, that rebellious, willful human part will make itself known. It feels blasphemous to me to declare that we are able to act with absolute certainty when it comes to the will of God. Absolute certainty does not equate with the ineffable and mysterious of all that we cannot know or understand. Which is a lot.

An interesting thought regarding Jung and the numbers 3 and 4:

Jung believed humankind is just beginning an evolutionary process from the stage of consciousness represented by 3 to that represented by 4. He based this theory on the Catholic Church's decision in the late 1940s to include Mary with the all-masculine Trinity, thereby creating a Quaternity. He postulated that the work of the truly "modern" individual is to make the transition or expansion of consciousness from 3 to 4; from a consciousness that is devoted to doing, working, and accomplishing to one that is characterized by being, peacefulness, and tranquility. Jung believed that 4 can contain 3 but not vice versa; therefore, one who is at level 4 consciousness is capable of handling all the practical aspects of life but is not bound by them, whereas the individual at level 3 cannot understand the qualities and attributes of 4.

Are we moving collectively from a Trinitarian to a Quaternarian view? From an orderly, masculine perception of reality based upon the ideal of perfection, seeking, restlessness, and searching to one that includes the feminine as well, one of wholeness and completion?

Hmm....

Finally, something I read the other day that fits well with what I have been going through:

> The early part of adulthood is devoted almost entirely to discipline. One prepares for profession, learns the social graces, cultivates a marriage, and improves one's earning capacity – and all of these activities invariably create a large shadow. There are elements we had to

leave behind, elements that had to be 'unchosen' in order to produce a cultured life. By middle age, the cultural process is mostly complete – and very dry. It is as if we have wrung all the energy out of our character and at this point, the energy of the shadow is very great. We are suddenly subject to explosions that have the power to overturn the product we have worked so hard to create. We may fall in love, break up a marriage [!], storm out of a job in desperation as we try to relieve ourselves of this monotony. These are extremely dangerous moments, but they can set the stage for a whole new phase of life, if we learn how to take the energy of the shadow and use it correctly. (From *Owning Your Own Shadow* by Robert A. Johnson)

That's it in a nutshell.

PART II:
NEXT STEPS
(Excerpts from Journals 90 – 99)

Men are not free when they are doing just what they like. Men are only free when they are doing what the deepest self likes. And there is getting down to the deepest self! It takes some diving.

D.H. Lawrence

March 2, 2005

Back from a brief trip to New Orleans for Mardi Gras, daughter A.'s choice of belated college graduation trip. And what fun we had! Watching A. strut down the street, all 4ft. 10 in. of her, making pronouncements about life, her courage to keep on keeping on, how much she is like her dad. I made a list of some of the things she said.

HOW TO BE A DIVA:

Rule #1

You can never have too much glitter.

Rule #2

I may not always be right but I'm NEVER wrong.

Rule #3

When in doubt, use more make-up.

Rule #4

You must say 'FABULOUS' a lot.

Rule #5

FABULOUS! FABULOUS! Simply FA-BU-LOUS!

Rule #6

Walk into a room as if you own it.

Rule #7

Don't ever drink anything that looks like a rainbow.

(She got quite inebriated one night after consuming such a multi-colored concoction at Pat O'Brien's.)

Rule #8

I repeat: NEVER! (see Rule #7)

Rule #9

Shoes are God's gift to divas – the higher, the better.

A.: the kid who's not my kid who really is my kid. And me: the mom who isn't the mom who really is the mom.

March 23, 2005

"The Lord will perfect that which concerns me." (Ps. 138:8)

Gracious Heavenly Being,

Yesterday with some colleagues it became even more apparent how I hold myself back. There is some barrier still there, not taking myself seriously enough to believe I matter or deserve all. How or why is it that I still...that I am what?

There are certain bad habits, old patterns of being and doing that are filtering out of your being. It is time for you to become more focused on wanting. You have learned to remove the ego part. You have learned that your self-worth is not dependent on anything you do or achieve in the world. This is the first essential step. Now it is time for you to become more consciously focused on cultivating the inner God-given, God-driven desire. Just as you have been diligent in embracing your life, bringing more peace into it and eschewing fear and worry, now is the time to apply that same energy and discipline to this next phase. Remember what I told you about asking and receiving. In order to receive, it is important to ask with sincerity what it is you truly want.

Take the time to take yourself seriously. You must prepare yourself to embrace what I have planned for you and to do this you must become very concrete. Pay close attention to how you look at things. Stop yourself before you automatically respond. Ask your desire what it needs and wants to accomplish. Do not worry about the "how" yet. That will unfold. You are just beginning to articulate the future direction. Do not be discouraged if you do not achieve it immediately or in just the way you imagined. That is not as important as your taking the step to set the goal. Every goal you set is a statement of your belief in your worthiness and your trust. Do not let the past infiltrate this present. Stay awake. All is ready now!

April 15, 2005

After a brief trip to the East Coast to catch up on family, P. and I returned to LA and the whirlwind of what I call "P.'s World." P.'s world is always busy and driven by business problems, personal issues, meetings, and putting out "bond fires." There is always something. "Maurine's World," on the other hand, is minimalist. It does not require much attention. It is much slower and more quietly paced. There is less hustle, bustle, noise, and rushing about. And I realized:

I much prefer Maurine's World.

I have not been spending enough time there (here?).

There also occurred an incident while on the East Coast, one of P.'s blustering complaints in a restaurant about food, wine, service. I got up, excused myself from the table, and went into the restroom. Once inside I looked into the mirror and declared, "I'm so not into this!" As I come to know and enjoy Maurine's World more, I don't know how to fit into P.'s world and go back to the default button of old patterns emerging.

The other day I was having lunch with a friend and confessed thoughts of having sex with someone else just to see what it would be like after all these years. A friend said, "Why not? P. has." Yet even though P. and I are not legally married, it still would feel like a betrayal to me. I may have to get over that thought. When A. and I were in New Orleans, one of the first things out of her mouth after checking into our hotel room was wanting to know if I'd had sex with anyone else. I nearly dropped my teeth. Another friend said recently, "Maybe P. isn't able to honor your womanhood in the way that you need."

Hmm…

Question: Is a woman who is legally divorced from her husband but who still sleeps with him and takes a lover guilty of infidelity? Moral infidelity? Emotional infidelity?

Spiritual infidelity? Is he? At this point, what is infidelity? Lying to oneself.

Maurine's World...to be continued.

June 9, 2005

Gracious Spirit:

I come before you today asking for continued guidance. I still feel so adrift.

You must learn to enjoy yourself and your life. Look upon every single moment as a gift of grace. The energy of this kind of focus, this kind of love is electric. It will communicate wherever you go even if you do not utter a single word. You still have a tendency to withhold yourself and your sensitivity. Remember that while you are no better than others, you have a gift to share. Your loving heart speaks more than you know. Love is the true language of the universe, love and love alone.

This is why your joy and your exuberance are such precious gifts that you need to cultivate. The serious side of you has been in the forefront for a long time. Now it is time for the joyous, loving, laughing part of you to shine. The light spirit in you will spark this in others and the world so needs this light connection now because of all the darkness that appears to be pervading the planet. Do not let this appearance of the way things are daunt you. Hold on to the peace you feel.

You have proved a sense of devotion and perseverance through time. This will open doors that may feel uncomfortable to you in your human form. That is why it is especially important for you to have fun and enjoy yourself in whatever way you can. Awaken each day and ask yourself: "What do I want to do today to have fun?" And ask this without any sense of guilt. Love your life just as it is right now.

This is a time of tremendous transition. You must not be afraid of coming into your power, because you understand that it is really my power opening up inside you. You have worked hard to quell the destructive call of arrogance and ego. The space that has been opened is now available for me to enter and use as a vessel of spirit. It is not you but I who am in control. You have learned this, perhaps the hard way, but learned it you have. This is the mystery of Incarnation. Your body truly is the temple of my spirit. Let it be joyous as a child is joyous.

Follow this instruction without hesitation. Have faith and confidence that as this new power enters and begins to surge through you that there is no fear or worry because I am in control. I will be with you when you hit the spots where your shyness makes you want to contract. As you learn to turn this quiet shyness into spoken vulnerability, your work as a teacher will expand. There are times when you may be at a loss for answers but you know that even in that mystery of unknowingness love still permeates all.

July 13, 2005

More grief is slowly arising about Mom. Over the past few weeks, thoughts and memories of her have been filtering through. I was looking at a tapestry I made and it popped into my head a comment she made about her paintings when we were preparing their home for the estate sale prior to their move. "Oh, nobody's going to want those old things." Or "Do you suppose anyone will want these?" In the moment, I said, "Of course, I do!" and gathered them all up. But reflecting back, my heart broke inside me, the sense of futility in her voice, and the desperate yearning: "Won't anybody please notice these, notice me!" The sad sense of "what has it all been for anyway?" The look of her when she said that: tired, tiny, frail, the defeat of it all, life.

Then there's Dad:

More and more forgetful and deaf, weaker by the day; all he wants to do is stay in his little room and sleep, the outside world unnavigable for him. There is a part of me that wonders what meaning he can find in life anymore. There is another part of me that feels both compassion and a certain distant foreboding. What will I be like when I get there? And then there is another part of me waiting for the phone call telling me it's over. In some sense the relief there will be when that happens and the knowledge, too, of ending. Losing one's parents is a large event.

I am glad to be by myself today, the first time back in my little apartment in a long time. I am looking forward to being alone for the next few nights, appreciating more and more the internal process I am engaged in. I am leaving the world of being lost in the mind behind.

The mind is such a small part of the totality of things, and such a shit-stirring part at that. As I grow older, I have fewer questions and more humor about things despite my ongoing concern for the state of the world in general, the planet and its people. This also makes me boring, no doubt. I suppose the challenge is being able to surrender to that something without knowing what that something is. Faith is not a noun but a verb.

Read a book by Rabbi Harold Kushner, *How to Live a Life that Matters*. He quotes something from the Book of Jeremiah that struck a chord:

> Lord, you seduced me and I was seduced.
> You overpowered me and I was overcome…If I
> say 'I will not speak anymore His name,' there
> is a fire burning in my heart, within my bones. I
> exhaust myself trying to hold it in but I cannot.
> (Jr. 20:7-9)

July 15, 2005

A busy day yesterday. I spent the entire morning catching up on things – sorting through emails, working to get through piles of paper on my desk, phone calls, a little writing. Finally got my business taxes done and was pleased to see that I made almost twice as much money as last year, but still not much. I am so far in the red at this point it's not even funny. I know how to read books, how to write books, how to critique and edit books, how to get books published, and how to give them away. But what I don't know how to do – at least not yet – is make money from them. A minor detail, no doubt, but one that does feel rather important since this is supposed to be a business.

By 7:30pm my day was officially over, so I went out to get some dinner. Afterwards, on my way home, I was stopped by a young man, obviously nervous, saying "Excuse me…" I thought when he said he was new in town that he was going to ask for directions. But out poured a breathless, faster-than-fast litany about how he'd finally managed to make it to LA, find a place to live, get a little work, all the while twisting his baseball cap, which he had taken off to talk to me, nervously in his hand, sotto voce "God, how I suck at this!" i.e. asking for money.

I cut him off before he could finish, reached into my pocket, and gave him a $5 bill, all that I had left from dinner. The young man was both surprised at how easy his pitch worked and vastly relieved he could stop talking. I smiled and walked on, thinking "What is it about me?!" Like fleas, if there is one in the room, it will find me. Kids, puppies, babies, old people, poor people, sick people, needy people: they do seem to find their way to my door. Do I look kind, non-threatening, innocent, a pushover, an easy mark? Probably all of the above.

As I turned the corner, I checked to make sure the young man wasn't following me. He wasn't. Yet for some reason tears came to my eyes. Not over the fact that he wasn't following me, but why? A tad of frustration, perhaps, that somehow I expect my goodness to be rewarded? On some deep, wispy residual level that I still am not completely congruent and in alignment, the idea that I still want something to happen that hasn't happened. That I am still not fully present to the sacred gift of each moment? Or the gift of myself? Somehow another expectation that does not even have a name rose up in that moment that I still do not trust enough to trust completely.

August 2, 2005
For the first time in years I gained weight at my annual physical. Middle age spread is upon me! Vanity, vanity, all is vanity. Funny, I never thought much about my looks when I was young and actually rather good-looking. It has taken middle age for the vanity bug to bite. What we humans can and cannot escape: there's always something.

It has been two years now that I have had this little apartment. I am beginning to feel a little more settled in this new world of mine. It is so very odd how P. and I seem to be much better at being friends and lovers than we did being husband and wife. I don't know why but I acknowledge this as true. I wonder if despair is the only thing that truly allows us to say good-bye? One could say that surrender, love, and death achieve the same results, and while they may have elements of despair in all of them, love, surrender, and death also have something more, an inexplicable "X" factor of otherness.

Some bumper stickers observed while stuck in traffic:
"KEEP YOUR DISSIDENCE"
"WHEN THE POWER OF LOVE OVERCOMES THE LOVE OF POWER, THE WORLD WILL KNOW PEACE"

Yes, the politics of love over and above the politics of power.

One thing is clear:

The only reality of significance is love, how we participate in being a circle of lovers – man, woman, parent, child, friend, and stranger. The only thing that can save us and this poor, disintegrating planet is love, *not* politics. Or better said: the only thing that will work is politics grounded in love, not greed or arrogance or fear. More and more I am letting go of external achievement in the world, and instead using the bellows of my heart to fan the fire of light and love, of loving light within.

Another check in with my Guide. If only I were better at listening to His/ Her/Their advice!

Gracious Spirit:

I know my only work is to do Your will, yet I have such difficulty discerning what that is. The last time I approached You, I felt elated that my novel was finished. Yet the feedback I have received from others tells me it is not. My suggestions for redoing the TV book were rejected by an agent in New York. Last night at the play I attended for Physicians for Social Responsibility, not a single nuclear book sold. You spoke of doors opening, but it does not feel that way. What is Your truth for me now?

You must approach each day individually, using it as you can without thought of any goal. You will find as you do this, you will accomplish more than you know. Yours is a long journey, and while I know this tests your capacity as a human being because humans want outcomes, goals, and finish lines, this is not the journey I have in mind for you. You need to use the moments of each day without thought of outcome.

You live in a world that demands and praises results. The world I need for you to inhabit does not. Your frustration is understandable from a human plane but from

161

a divine perspective it is not. You must act with the assurance that your goal has already been achieved. You are simply putting the finishing touches on what is already accomplished. That is why you must live daily, take small actions each day. You forget the parable of the mustard seed: something so tiny growing through time into something so large. You are at the beginning stages of learning how to embrace the dailyness of things: small rituals, little meditations; these are very important. Because you live in a world that overvalues the large, it is challenging to inhabit the world of small things. But it is precisely through these small things that I do much of my work.

Engage in small, consistent actions, and let me orchestrate the rest. Perseverance and patience with a deep-seated smile in your heart, knowing all will be well is what you need to concentrate on. You are learning things that you may not even be aware of but your training continues. It is important that you do not judge or evaluate yourself and your work by worldly criteria.

Keep taking small actions. You are doing this more but because you do not fully believe in the power and efficacy of small things, you trip yourself up by wanting large things to happen. Just keep doing the small things and the large ones will take care of themselves. As a human I know it is difficult but it is essential that you continue to do what you are doing and be joyful while you are doing it. I am here watching more than you know.

August 17, 2005
It has been a busy few weeks since my last entry, about which I remember absolutely nothing. The fundraiser I spearheaded for the commemoration of Hiroshima and Nagasaki went well. Sold some thirty books, all profits going to Palisadians for Peace.

In retrospect, it is absolutely ridiculous how nervous I get in front of people, especially ones who are rooting for me. But I also learned a valuable lesson. After the event, I realized one of the gifts my mother bequeathed me was how to be a gracious hostess, welcoming others and making them feel appreciated and at ease – even if I don't feel that way myself! I don't think I have ever acknowledged this special quality of southern hospitality. It is a legacy my mother imparted to me that I kicked and screamed about in the past but that I understand and honor more now and want to apply.

Another valuable lesson: anxious about no one showing up, I told myself at one point to shut up! I had done everything I could: sent out bulletins to the local newspapers and emails to progressive groups to inform their members, plus distributing flyers to friends. Okay, God, I've done as much as I can, now it's up to You. And surprise, surprise: everything flowed. You *do* need to do your homework in order to pass the test, but the rest truly is in God's hands. Life is a co-creation of this divine spirit and human interaction. It is all about generosity and giving away what you've been blessed with. If I cannot sell books for me, then I will sell them to make money for others. If I cannot sell them to make money for others, I will give them away. My prayer has been to get books out of storage in my garage and into the world, and that prayer *is* being answered – just not in the manner I imagined.

But a prayer answered is a prayer answered, and the only appropriate response is gratitude. I am learning to release expectations, trust that Spirit does indeed know better than I, and open myself up to the mysterious flow of things. Miracles and divine activity *are* constant. Constant! We humans simply need more tutelage in picking up on the grace and wonder of small things, just as my Guide said. We may need to think and act large, but we need to learn how to see the fruit of this large thinking in small, everyday ways. We miss so much grace otherwise.

This is the unpredictability and unknowingness of surrender. When you truly release all – I mean ALL; there can be no fudging or almost with surrender; it must be a complete, total, sincere, heartfelt letting go – then paradoxically a space is created where the seeds of truth can grow. It is all about freedom and the most important freedom of all is that which one experiences internally; this particular kind of freedom brings with it a peacefulness and centeredness that are without price. These energetic vibrations simply do not, cannot lie. And they cannot be stolen or taken away.

I find myself wanting to become clear and clean, taking on my body in a way that is new to me. In certain respects, it feels as if I am just getting started with my life. It feels, strange as it may sound, as if I have finally incarnated into my body, as if my soul and body are finally getting into sync. I am beginning to appreciate the mystery of spirit being incarnated in flesh. It is as if the soul of me, which has been so out there, way ahead of itself, has finally found a home in this physical, corporeal form. It is an ODD feeling! What I thought was "being here" before wasn't really "being here" at all. Congruence, that's what it feels like, as if everything is finally coming into congruence.

September 20, 2005

Another birthday come and gone and still alive along life's way.

Not so for those who died from Hurricane Katrina and those who continue to die around the world from war. Where's the real homeland security when you need it? Off chasing terrorist ghosts. Or oil. My solution, of course, is simple: change the Department of Defense to the Department of Peace and Reconstruction. Pay everyone to build things up rather than raze them to the ground, to help people renew themselves rather than figuring out ways to harm them. Sustain and support the majority and it will aid threshing out the few who are a threat. Like the Bible says: everybody just wants his/her own fig tree and a bit of land. Enough for everyone's need, but not everyone's greed. What could possibly be worse than the way we are handling things now? It might even work.

Came across this the other day from the Interfaith Community for Justice and Peace about the word *jihad*, from the Arabic word meaning effort; a fight for the sake of God. But it doesn't stop there; there are multiple layers of meaning:

The first is to put God at the center of one's life, every hour of every day.

The second is to resist peer pressure, especially negative peer pressure, from those who say you cannot make a difference.

The third meaning is to stay on a straight path, remaining steadfast; patience is a form of *jihad*.

The fourth has to do with striving after righteous deeds and taking positive action. In this sense, taking care of one's aging parents is a higher form of jihad than joining a mobilization effort or fighting.

The fifth meaning is living as a Muslim, conveying the message of Islam but not proselytizing or trying to convert others.

The sixth type is defending one's community. Islam is not pacifist; it does permit violence to defend oneself or one's country. It resists oppression but not aggression. The first step in this process is to hate injustice and act to change it.

The seventh meaning is considered the most important but is also the least understood. It is to free another from the injustice of tyranny. When a community faces injustice but cannot defend itself, those nearby who have the means to help have an obligation to do so. But the Koran is clear that the defense of some cannot be used to justify the harming of others.

Sounds reasonable enough to me, the only stumbling block being the definition of non-aggressive violence and injustice. We attack Iraq saying we are defending ourselves; they say we are being preemptively aggressive. We look upon women being stoned or ritually castrated as injustices, while others see these actions as acceptable custom. And round and round it goes.

I was thinking about something from the end of the movie, *The Shawshank Redemption,* about the principles of geology, the character Red talking about it being the study of pressure and time as it acts upon the earth's surface. And I thought: pressure and time, the keys to both revolution and non-violence. It's a foregone conclusion: we shall overcome because of pressure and time. Resistance but not violence.

- Applying kindness in the midst of passion.
- Not knowing all, or even some, of the answers yet being able to maintain a spirit of goodwill and spontaneity in spite of this.
- Being fiercely self-reflective, shadow hunting.
- Being engaged in Eros in the deepest sense of the word: the art of loving and being compassionate toward all creation.
- Engaging in non-dual reality. There is no enemy, no other; we are all part of one body, one universal field of dancing energy.
- Being able to see far, to be a prophet or a visionary, without getting caught up in what Lennon called "all the plastic reaction."

All this takes pressure and time. Consistent pressure and time and more and more people waking up to walk the walk: the long walk to justice; enough people, applying enough pressure, and committing themselves to this non-violent project through time.

Which brings me to a last thought: how to be more joyful in the process, literally: how to bring more joy into the planet as we engage in this, how to do the work of pressure and resistance with joy and delight.

Which brings me to another last thought about the Garden of Eden:

In Hebrew "Eden" means delight. So to witness life from God's point of view means to see things from a perspective of delight as part of the fabric of all creation. The story of Adam and Eve is not so much a story about good and evil but rather a story about disappointment and lost delight.

So, how to bring forth more delight?

September 21, 2005
Gracious Spirit:
Yesterday I felt so odd, as if the personal vector I am on is still off, that I need to reassess my plans. My plans must coincide with Your plans if they are to bear fruit. How to proceed?

You must train yourself to listen to your heart, train yourself as a warrior or athlete would. How do you know that you are listening to your heart? You must pause and go deeper; await the feelings that come through your body, not just your mind. A warmth, a peacefulness, a sense of lightness will be signals for you. Your body knows answers in ways your head never can. Take time to check in: how do you feel, not what do you think.

Your fears about self-betrayal must be checked. Anything that is fear-based does not come from me. However, your concern about not drifting back into old patterns is legitimate. Concern and fear are not the same;

the former requires discernment, the latter rejection. There are no timetables here. You must live vertically, not horizontally. The umbilical chord must rise to heaven, not stretch through linear time. You must continue to learn how to enjoy the spaciousness of each day.

Your sincere caring for the world and all that is transpiring is a good thing, but you still need to refine the fusion of passion with trust. You will feel rather than know when the time is right. The feeling will become a kind of knowing that is not subject to rational analysis, though it will be mindful. You must trust Spirit's unfolding. The fact that you are beginning to question certain positions you have taken with a kind of forcefulness or adamancy is an indication that you are becoming more aware. Watch out for taking positions that masquerade for wanting things to go your way without first becoming quiet within and able to ask: What is truly called for?

Your relationship with P. is still in a process of unfolding. Your biggest challenge will be how to honor the past and not let it hound you as you move forward toward the future. It is important for you to continue to protect your solitude, but not to be defensive or greedy about it. Defensiveness and greediness of any sort, no matter how subtle, are warning signs that you lack trust. At this stage you must be alert and concentrate with greater subtlety.

You are being instructed about the ways of fulfillment that are mine and mine alone. You are learning how to think differently. Get quieter, go deeper, listen in a different way. Do what you can, but don't do something just because you think you need to. Take action because you feel it is the right thing to do. You are not required to do anything other than to be with and in your heart, listen to it, for its beat belongs to me. If you are centered in that, guidance will flow with an ease that will surprise you. Listen to your heart and its still small voice. It is ever-present, ever-there, and will speak if you but take the time to listen.

September 29, 2005

Awakened at 4:00am this morning after an amazing dream:

I am traveling in the Andes. The terrain and countryside are absolutely magnificent; the grandeur and beauty of the snow-topped mountains, stars so bright and close I feel as if I could touch them. There is a calmness and beauty to it all, and yet a quality of danger and treacherousness as well. At one point, I see a cart carrying people topple and the passengers fall head-over-heels down the snow-covered slopes. I know that some of them are going to die.

I am surprised how cold it is – cold, cold, cold – even though it is summer. I ask someone what it is like during the winter if it is this cold now. I am traveling with another woman, a guide of sorts, and she takes me up to a small village high at the top of a mountain. It is so steep that even the houses are on a slant. We stop finally at the hut of the local librarian. He is busy scurrying around operating an elaborate set of bellows that he explains are to keep him warm. Large, round hollow tubes go deep down into the crevasses and fissures in the mountain to capture and circulate the heat from the earth's core. I notice I am having trouble breathing because we are so high up and the air is thin. The man's hut and library area are combined. I notice he has an elaborate Xerox machine and am amused by this oddity. I wonder how the natives managed to cart this large piece of equipment up the mountain!

We go outside and I meet some of the other villagers. I notice that the women's breasts look funny: one breast floats up, while the other is pressed down. The phenomenon is happening to my breasts, too. I ask what this is about, and one of the natives explains that this is due to what they call the vortex – that we are at a site of great magnetic forces and this peculiar effect on women's breasts is one of the results. He goes on to tell me that the vortex also causes the people who live there to age more rapidly, and he proceeds to go into intricate calculations using ancient Indian methods in order to explain this to me. I notice his wife is pregnant and yet she looks old. The man has strange teeth; they have been sharpened to a point with some sort of file. Others in the village have teeth like this, too.

My guide and I then leave and wander through magnificent country. At one point, we come upon a large mountain lake, the water a dark, dark blue, and my guide almost falls in. She is nearly bitten by a huge fish, but I grab her just in time, only for the both of us to get deluged with water from a mountain stream. The two of us laugh; the water and the experience of the large fish trying to bite us are exhilarating. We travel on and soon we come upon a wedding. Every one in the village is in attendance. We are welcomed and I am touched by the kindness and hospitality of the people. The bride is wearing a large, grey fur coat. Music is playing. It is at once both oddly mournful and gay.

My traveling companion and I set off again. We walk along a very narrow and dangerous path, high above a deep ravine with a sheer drop off at the edge where we are walking. My companion slips and looks as if she is going to fall off the cliff but is rescued at the last moment by the innkeeper of the village near where the wedding has been taking place. He invites us to come to his inn because we are so cold. He is very hospitable and welcoming. I keep having to buy film for my camera because I am taking so many pictures, but I wonder why I am going through rolls so quickly. Then I notice that there are only 11 snapshots per roll; 11, a master number: balance, justice, harmony, the transformation of the physical into the Divine?

Once inside the inn, we decide to relax because it is warm and we feel safe. We actually decide to have a party and order the local liquor but the bartender brings us margaritas instead. They also provide us with some amazing bud. My traveling companion and I are at a table with two other men, one is a rector from my church and the other is a man who cannot stop complaining. He is quite annoying because the rest of us just want to have fun and relax after all our harrowing adventures. The man who is complaining gets a terrible bloody nose that simply will not stop. We get concerned about this because at these high altitudes such a bloody nose could be fatal. Then I can't remember if the rector from my church or another shaman-like figure reaches over and touches the man with the bleeding nose several times forcefully around the area of his third eye. The bleeding stops instantly, as does the man's complaining. I think it is all a special kind of Shangri-La: the beauty and magic of the Andes, to be treated with reverence and respect. As with everything.

October 14, 2005

Gracious Heavenly Whatever or Whoever You Are: You say to persevere but how do I discern the distinction between that and my own willful stubbornness?

You are learning to participate in a different order of reality, one that does not require so much efforting. Perseverance is different than efforting. Perseverance means action through time with the assurance that the outcome will be reached, but you do not know when that is. Efforting, on the other hand, implies a force of the will, a lack of trust. If you surrender anything, it must be the efforting. This is what you are in the process of learning. This is not as difficult as you in your temporal form believe.

Persevere with the knowledge that when right, things will open and move swiftly.

Your task is learning how to embrace your joyfulness, your capacity for play. It is essential that when you approach any work that you do so with eagerness, not dread. You are wise to not do anything as long as that negative feeling, however slight, arises. Wait until the eagerness is there. With the eagerness and excitement, you can persevere. Without it, you fall back into efforting.

What you need to understand is that the creative process is not about finishing a specific task. It is about learning to let go of efforting, while allowing the flowers of perseverance and trust to bloom. Remember the process and the product must stem from a state of congruence. And light! This is not so much a process of creating light, though there is an aspect of creating light in all that you do, but more importantly about dispelling the darkness. Playfulness is key.

You will know when you get there in a different way. You will sense it deeply within. This is a challenging transition for you but one that is required for further deepening. Remain mindful of these things and the little windows that open up within you. Let go of efforting, focus on playfulness, and trust this process through time.

November 3, 2005

I ditched yoga today to read and write. There is always a trade-off somewhere. I am actually getting to the point where yoga doesn't work for me the way it used to. My body is older and gets tired more easily and the problem with my left arm from the cancer surgery so long ago still bothers me. I also think that the body inherently wants, loves to move and yoga is simply too static at times for many of the body's needs. I had another golf lesson the other day, and my teacher says I could be quite good if I can get it through my head that it's not about hitting the ball – it's not about the bike, stupid – but about learning to move from my core and let the ball get in the way.

Middle age and golf: that says it all.

I am having to unlearn some bad habits, most of which have to do with thinking; it's not about thinking, actually, but focus, intuition, and applied intentionality, feeling one's way into things. This obviously has far-reaching implications and applications to other areas of life besides golf.

What else have I been up? Getting back into the rhythm of reading again: Kunkel's new novel *Indecision*, the *Magdalene Manuscript*, according to which Mary Magdalene and Jesus were tantric lovers feeding off one another's kundalini energy, Kahlil Gibran's *Jesus*, and Jung's *Answer to Job*. Also giving away books, donating money to various organizations, networking with others, socially and politically. Upcoming events: a Peace Alliance gathering next week about establishing a Department of Peace and a conference put on by Students and Educators Against the War. Thinking about writing, sort of; dealing with my father, a lot.

Monday was Halloween and two friends of mine and I met to do our quarterly ritual. For the past week or so, my mother has come to mind a lot, how I am missing her more as time goes on. I set up a ceremonial display over her ashes, cut out pictures of shoes, because Mom was an absolute shoe hound. Not only did she have dozens of pairs of shoes in her closet, some of which she had never worn, but because she also had an extensive antique miniature shoe collection of china, crystal, and cut glass. Mom was a true shoe diva.

As we three women were sharing, a small altar of candles and a carved flying goddess in front of us, I said, "You know, I've been thinking about my mom a lot lately and I know this sounds crazy but I'd like for her to join us." My friends were immediately supportive, so I went into my bedroom and brought out her ashes, complete with the cutout shoe decorations, and placed her in our women's circle. I think my mother felt so shut out most of her life, so disempowered by the events of her childhood and the time she was born into, that she never was able to work herself out of it; she was always so stuck in the mire of her past. It felt important to have her there with us, in spirit and ashes if not in body. Just my sense that she has been trying to get my attention, somehow.

Then the next night, the evening of All Saints' when I was cleaning up after dinner, all of a sudden out of the cupboard where I keep mugs and glasses, a coffee cup flopped out from the top shelf onto one of my grandmother's crystal wine goblets that was on the counter. Out of the corner of my eye, I caught a glimpse of the mug falling and tried to catch it but it hit the 100-year-old wine glass before I could stop it. Naturally, the goblet shattered into dozens of pieces, completely ruined. I had not put anything into the cupboard or knocked anything with my sometimes clumsy hands, nor had there been any earthquake tremors or sonic booms. It was as if the mug flipped out of its own accord.

For a brief second I was on the verge of tears, for I will not be able to replace my Nana's goblet. Why of all the objects on the counter did that particular one have to break? But just as the tears of frustration started, they also stopped, and I was at peace. It was as if Mom were acknowledging her presence and my trying to get through to her. Breaking her mother's wine glass was bound to get my attention. One thing I know at this point to be true: spirit never dies; it simply changes form. In light of this, there is no death, only the heartache and joy that go along with the surrendering of physical form and saying good-bye. I felt that Mom had communicated to me from the beyond. I am going to keep talking to her as much as I can. Maybe I'm finally ready to listen.

Also an incident with P. where he spoke to me in that punitive, angry, aggressive voice of his, in front of other people no less. I walked out. I was so grateful to have this little apartment to return to. I told P. the next day that I swallowed way too much of his verbal abusiveness while we were married that I shouldn't have, and that is my responsibility. But now that we are divorced I sure as hell don't have to, want to, need to, or will.

I am so grateful I can literally walk out on the explosions rather than retreat metaphorically the way I did for twenty plus years. It is this capacity for solidarity and firmness that I wish I had been a better role model for my daughters. But as the saying goes, better late than never. There is something, too, to be said about the female leading, inviting the male to greater consciousness. Now, more than ever, I think this is our job.

November 8, 2005

Yesterday I had a physical therapy treatment on my shoulder, and at one point during the procedure, it was as if the veils parted and I dropped into another window of reality. The experience last week feeling that my mother has been trying to get my attention, plus the feeling at night on several occasions of an entity sitting on the side of my bed and the sensation of this energy lifting as I started to regain consciousness; the ceremony on Halloween; the cup dropping off the shelf; lying there on the physical therapist's table, receiving the message that my mom really wants me to take care of my heart, both literally and figuratively. Take care of your heart! She never did and died of a massive heart attack, but also not knowing how to take care of her heart in so many other ways.

My sense that she was encouraging me to take care of mine in ways she never did or could or would or knew how to, and that she is okay now; that everything is all right with her, and that she is still looking over me, watching out for me, and how much she truly loves me. It is so sad that I never felt that love while she was alive. Of course, I know she loved me; I just didn't feel the love. What I experienced felt like so much negativity and criticism and invasion. Maybe I simply learned early on to block it all out, including the love, in order to protect myself. The physical therapist even said that my upper back is like one solid undifferentiated mass, a sort of early fixed cellular memory of holding myself upright and rigid; how my mom used to stick her thumb into the center of my spine with the admonition "Stand up straight, young lady!" Not to mention, the physical trauma experienced from all the surgery and radiation years ago.

Lying there on the table I kept sinking deeper and deeper into this mystery, feeling the thinness of the veils between the two worlds; the worlds of the living and the dead; feeling my mother's love for me and the sense that she is okay, that all is well where she is, wherever she is; realizing that only a single breath separates us all from these two worlds. Knowing, too, that my mother wants me to see a doctor about my heart and all the scarring from the radiation. It was by her insistence years ago that I went to see an internist for a physical examination that eventually led to the diagnosis of cancer, and it's all about finding things early.

That's Mom: taking care of me even from the grave.

November 23, 2005
Gracious Spirit:
I come before you today feeling as if I am falling back into old patterns. There is also the very real question

of needing more living space. Even though P. and I are still seeing one another, I'm not ready to move back. What to do?

Part of the reason you get pulled back into the world is that you have not had a certain inner strength or certainty of your value. While it is a gift to be able to give, it can be a subtle trap to undermine the importance of valuing yourself and your own time. Reflect on how you feel when alone vs. how you feel when you are in the company of others; you need to balance the inner and outer parts of you. Far too much is going out; have the courage to say "no." If you are to do anything right now, it is take care of yourself.

How do you take care of yourself? By being alone more, reading, and exercising; not being with others so much. When you are with others, you automatically revert to a giving mode because it is a habit and you usually have more to give others than they have to give you. This is part of your special gift but it also leaves you going unfed most of the time. You must feed yourself. Put yourself as the priority. Be of service to yourself. Treat yourself as preciously as you treat others. It is OK to let go of much that you have been involved with in order to concentrate on yourself. You have done enough for others to have learned the lesson of putting yourself forward and realizing that many times these activities are neither time nor cost effective in a number of ways.

As for the writing: Are you able to give yourself permission to focus solely on that? Become a virtual hermit if necessary? You have spent much of the last two years focusing on the past. Now is the time to focus exclusively on the words that are inside you waiting to come forth. Do not let your lack of success deter you from what is being called for. Continue to act as if it is already there; it will come to you when least expected. Say "yes" to yourself and

177

"no" to others. Your time is of utmost value. Set this firmly in your consciousness so you can position yourself purposefully in the New Year. You have shown your willingness to give and be present. Now you must show your willingness to be present and give to yourself.

December 3, 2005

If Mother Nature decides we humans are vermin or pests she has to get rid of, she will do precisely that. I am so tired of caring about others, the planet, causes, politics, whatever. I just want to perfect the art of having a good time and of being perfectly OK with that. At this point, my time is far too precious and for perhaps the first time in my life I feel absolutely no guilt whatsoever about giving it to me rather than to others, however noble and worthwhile the cause and those others might be. It is beyond time to shed the old patterns and baggage. No more axes to grind or issues to prove or causes to champion. I'm tired of reinventing the wheel.

I am tired of waiting to see when the books will sell or when I am going to get a lucky break or when Dad is going to die. The other night when I took him out on his 95th birthday he ordered a martini with vegetables (olives and onions), soup, fried frog legs, and a mountain of ice cream – and I do mean mountain; it must have been at least four scoops – then complained the next day that his stomach hurt and that the food in the restaurant, until then his favorite, was "no good." When Dad said he wanted to reach the milestone of 98 and then 100, I shuddered inwardly, please no!

Horrible daughter, angel daughter all rolled into one. The way I have been feeling lately is pretty darned grumpy and aggravated, and yet somehow these uncomfortable feelings are required: to remind me how human I am, that inner core of peacefulness deserting me. I am trying to remind myself of the truthfulness of the words: there is enough anguish, torment, worry, unhappiness and anxiety in the world; why not be happy on the spiritual path?

Why not indeed?

Laughing and smiling on the way: sounds like a good New Year's resolution to me. I am not sure what brought this to a head; the end of the year, moving into winter darkness, and the holidays. Looking back over the last few years, all the work and effort put forth with so few results: the addiction has to stop. I am no longer interested in doing anything that has to do publicity and the marketing mantra of visibility, visibility, visibility. I have a new mantra of my own: enough is enough is enough! It's time to pull the plug; the business isn't working. Yet like a gambler, the seduction of "just let me try one more thing, one more roll of the dice, one more marketing ploy."

I think at this point I will dedicate what time I have left to being a complete and total eccentric, and if God has something more in mind for me, He/She better make it pretty damned clear to this middle-aged with a bad left shoulder and arthritic hands space suit, otherwise I'm talking to my cats, reading books, puttering in my garden – if I have one – and the world can come to me.

And then, as if on cue, this dream:

I am trying on all sorts of dresses for a play. I am playing the part of Queen Cleopatra, and I need just the right outfit. But I cannot find anything that suits me or feels right. I try on long dresses, short dresses, fancy dresses, cocktail dresses, and still am unable to get the right one.

I see another actor who is also in the play, a girl-woman, developed physically but still somehow immature, wearing the dress I know is right for me and what I think the regal Queen Cleopatra would wear. It is elegant: a long beautiful multi-colored brocade skirt reaching to the floor with an emerald green velvet top and a jeweled cross in the middle. I tell the girl-woman: "You cannot have that dress. That dress is for a Queen!" But the girl-woman only snickers at me with a "too bad, it's mine, I found it first" look. I feel thwarted. I want to wear the clothes of a queen, to be a queen. But then I think: Isn't Cleopatra a queen no matter what she wears? To be regal is an internal event.

December 4, 2005
Dearest Guide:

I'm trying to understand P.'s declaring undying love for me and our love making Friday night, then within 24 hours he's hiding my things and pretending I have no presence in his life. What is he hiding? What am I hiding from?

Stillness. Your trajectories are moving in different ways, toward different things that each of you must accomplish in your own way. It is important to have no judgments here, and it is also necessary to address the confusion and mixed messages. P. is less concerned about the way he interacts with others; you hold to a higher standard in your engagement with people. This is how you are built, not he. While it is important to take note of these differences, it is equally important that you do not give the thought patterns of why this? why that? much energy. Humor and lightness are the best responses – and then do what you need to do to handle the situation rightfully for yourself.

You are learning more the call for stillness. You are sensing the need for this at a deeper level. Dealing with your father and his needs is more than enough for you right now. Continue to winnow and prune as much as you can from the outside world. This process may at times include P. Or not. You cannot and must not let his actions or non-actions deter you from your path. Getting yourself settled in another space will help ground you for when you are alone and no longer required to be a daughter. Your full womanhood awaits.

P., while so capable and proficient in worldly ways, is still very much struggling with his incarnation. He is learning through all these various interactions with others how to find himself. And this is how it must be for him. This requires the human in you to practice great non-attachment and trust that all will be well no matter what the specific outcome is for either of you. Keep focusing on what you need. Let P. do what he needs. Any dissembling or being less than forthright with you or others is for him to address, not you. Other than having to deal with the final stages of your father's life, you are entering your prime and your power.

In all things, be compassionate, first with yourself, then with others. You have spent the vast majority of your life dealing from the reverse mode. Your internal sense of self-worth and worthiness has grown strong enough to understand this is called for. It is imperative that you have regular time to set aside for scriptural reading and nurturing the stillness within. The past few weeks have provided you with ample opportunity to experience what happens when you do not do this. For it is out of this stillness that all, simply all arises. You must water the spiritual core. Your light is precious: do not neglect it, and do not squander it. Be mindful of P. and his actions but do not judge them. His journey is his journey; he is required to participate in what is required of him as you are required to engage in what is required of you. You are in the process of discovering your soul work – or of it finding and discovering you.

While much love is needed in the world, as you grow spiritually one of the hurdles you must cross is not wanting or needing to fix things; it is about the basic, fundamental acceptance of the goodness and providential nature of life.

Doing must be synonymous with love, otherwise the doing – in whatever form it manifests – often becomes about power and ego and control. This is not the way. Only love.

You are positioning yourself for the new order. Focus on this and be at peace. You say you have lost your peace, but this is not possible since your peace is always with you. The only way you can lose your peace is if you lose yourself. Being able to take a deep breath during turbulent times and say, 'Peace be with you' will help you through the challenges ahead. This is the original battery recharger, that one single phrase. Go about your business and do what you need to do to grow stillness, eliminate unnecessary interactions with others, and go underground as you call it. All is good.

February 6, 2006

I had to count on my fingers what day of the month this is.

I was going to make a list of things that have happened between my last entry and now but I can't remember much except the following:

My dad: It is mind-boggling how he keeps on keeping on. You come into the world needing to be burped and changed and held. You sleep, you eat, you poop. And that's exactly the way you go out. The symmetry is at once fitting, poetic, and exquisitely poignant. There is a rare beauty at work in so many things.

The children were home for the holidays and merriment and good cheer were generally experienced by all, young adults and middle-aged alike, with only the occasional hiccup that families reunited are wont to have.

I decided to move, but not back in with P. So I found a place in the mid-Wilshire district, close to the Miracle Mile and Hancock Park. Again, a certain poetic or existential irony is at work here: instead of getting out of LA, I am moving farther into its bowels.

Once all the boxes and furniture and lamps and desk and sofa and chairs and pictures and artwork were off-loaded from the moving van, I had to confront the stark reality of how much stuff I have accumulated thus far on my sojourn on this planet. I was – and am – appalled. It took me two weeks alone just to put away my books. I actually found it disturbing. I never have thought of myself as a particularly materialistic person but you have to confront at a certain, mid-point stage in life how much sticks to you as you go through. As relatives have died and left me things, the pile seems to bloom and grow without any specific intention on my own part to go out and buy things.

Sure, I'll take that old Victorian sofa from Aunt So and So. How kind of my antique collecting cousin to leave me x,y,z. Mom and Dad's insistence that I keep this or that for their grandchildren: dishes, silverware, pictures, you name it. All of a sudden, or so it feels because it is not so sudden at all, I am a ripe and moderately seasoned mid-lifer who has enough stuff to furnish a modest three bedroom 1920s Spanish style duplex. I even took ten boxes of books and fans and dolls and masks and knickknacks to the Salvation Army in the past week alone. I filled two large trash bins with papers and notes and magazines and catalogues and reference materials and graduate school notes and there is still more winnowing to be done. And my absolute horror when my next door neighbors, a young Korean couple, came to introduce themselves, only to congratulate me most sincerely on all my "stuff." To them, this was success. Inwardly, I cringed.

And so what did I do after the frenzy of unpacking and putting away and giving away and getting rid of so many things? I ordered another box of books (art). I had half a shelf of space left.

I have also decided there is not enough poetry in my life, so here goes for the New Year to get off to a good start. Two poems I came across that I like:

> If the angel/Deigns to come/It will be because/You have convinced/Her, not by tears/But by your humble/Resolve to be always/Beginning: to be a beginner. Rainer Marie Rilke

I may have quoted this in journals past but it certainly bears both repeating and rereading. Besides, I forget half of what I have written anyway. Better to be redundant than to leave out, say I. And another poem, this by Hafiz:

> Don't surrender your loneliness/So quickly./Let it cut more deep./Let it ferment and season you./As few human/Or even divine ingredients can./Something missing in my heart tonight/Has made my eyes so soft,/My voice, so tender./My need for God/Absolutely/Clear.

If there is not enough poetry in my life, there is absolutely way too much technology. I have noticed lately my intense, visceral reactions in public places where everyone – and I do mean everyone – is talking on his/her cell phone, LOUDLY, not making any attempt to be even remotely private or discrete. And all too frequently the one-sided conversation is about the most innocuous and inane things: "Like I'm so totally over it, you know, whatever..."

And if it's not cell phones, it's computers and/or palm pilots and/or everything at once. I feel as if I'm becoming a 21st century Luddite. However did we humans manage to exist for centuries, millennia even without all these technological accoutrements and encumbrances? I am coming to believe it is damaging, not only to our bodies, nervous systems, and psychological well-being but to our souls – this inability to be quiet, to get quiet. Someday, I swear to God, this whole high speed, cell phone, multi-texting, multi-tasking, Blackberry, Ipod, faxing, instant global everything is going to come crashing down, and I do mean crashing. We are not evolved enough as a species to handle it, and we are getting more shallow by the minute as each new communication device encourages superficiality and speed but no real depth. TV almost feels wholesome by way of comparison. At least people watched together, like sitting around the campfire absorbing the flickering flames. Now individuals just download whatever from wherever and watch by themselves.

Somewhere in my last entry I recollect the word "stillness" as being critical at this time, at least for me.

Stillness.

Interiority.

Quiet.

Patience.

Presence.

Waiting.

That's one of the many problems about celebrating the six week holiday rollercoaster between Thanksgiving and Christmas and then moving into January: there has not been a whole lot of time, still or otherwise, for any of the above. It takes such focused discipline to live at that level and depth of reality. And yet I feel that is part of what I am being asked to participate in.

My question: What now?

What kind of person do I want to become by the time I reach sixty, officially an elder of the tribe? What does the tribe need? What do I need to do to become an effective elder? Or perhaps more appropriately the question is, what does God need?

I scribbled some notes at church the other day: the whole question of where is the intersection of your deepest joy and what the world needs in order to heal. This speaks to the whole nature of calling: What is my calling? What I like to do – read, day-dream, think – is this what the world needs? The question is how our individual kingdoms, our individual lives fit into God's work, and how this leads each of us to living powerful, deep, and abundant lives.

So the question remains: What is my calling? Being a parent certainly has been a part of that, but the parenting I have known and participated in has shifted. Parenting is so very different once one's children become adults. My true calling: I thought writing was and maybe still is. But the feedback from the universe has been sparse on that front, for sure and true.

Being a therapist? Hardly. That stage is rapidly coming to a close. I have no desire to continue making that my life's trajectory, though I have learned much about myself and the human condition or comedy or tragedy in the process, especially being able to listen without judgment, at least most of the time.

I have been drawn more and more to different healing arts as my dissatisfaction with traditional therapy has grown. It does not feel right anymore. And I know my brushes with death have bred in me a sense of urgency and understanding about the finiteness of time that most people just don't have. The individual simply cannot be healed through the level of mind, ego, and talking experience. It takes too long. Very basic and necessary tools can be learned in traditional therapy that are useful, but that linear model simply is not enough anymore. We need to accelerate the speed at which healing occurs, and we can do this. I believe we have an incredible innate capacity to heal instantaneously; we just don't know how to access it. We are being trained, educated in the wrong things, in the wrong way. We need to be taught from the level of intention, intuition, and heart.

Again, the question: What is my calling?

My work on the Prayer Team? I certainly would not have picked that one, but it is the one area where the universe is providing some pretty clear and discernible positive feedback. And it isn't even about the people I pray for but more about my learning to accept the profound mystery and power of prayer. I have been a member of the Pastoral Care Team and Prayer Team at my church for several years now, and it is changing me. It has changed me. I am only just beginning to see and feel this truth.

Which makes me think of something I was mulling over on the way back from the airport yesterday: the exquisite fire of God's grace. Grace is not only a balm; it is a crucible of love's fire. It is up to me to let grace temper and tamp me into the place where my individual life becomes subsumed in God's. How do I allow this exquisite fire of grace to ignite and burn within me, to become purified by that?

With cell phones ringing and people yakking and scurrying around, getting and spending, myself most certainly included in that category: What does it mean, finally, to be human? To return to a place of what it means to consider being human and human identity as a sacred mystery and not as people who need to go out and show their patriotism by shopping. For connection and being human is not about what you do or buy; it is a profound awareness about how you live your life and engage with the world around you. And from that point of view, I suppose shopping can also be seen as holy. It depends. It's all a work in progress.

February 18, 2006

A rainy Saturday morning after record heat. I am beginning to feel half-way human again after a wicked attack of germs – in bed for the last two days straight, and that after three days of not feeling well. I am actually on a second round of antibiotics and still contending with a vicious cough. I haven't been this sick for years. Yet in spite of feeling as badly as I have, since Monday I have actually accomplished moving my piano into my new place, hanging more pictures and drapes, and driving out to Thousand Oaks to take my father to the doctor.

Yesterday I also took the time to reread all the messages and exchanges I have had with my Guide, and several things became evident to me:

I'm not "getting it" at the level I need to get it.

I still need to slow down.

I need to trust more, to trust absolutely.

I think too much and forget to listen.

My heart will always be more honest than my head.

I am on the path I need to be on, and I am loved every nanosecond along the way.

I am learning what I need to learn, although perhaps somewhat obdurately.

I need to have more fun.

I simply cannot lose when God/Spirit is in charge.

I have more courage than I give myself credit for.

It is all about LOVE! Love of self; love of other.

Hmmm...

Last Saturday I left my kitchen door open because of the heat, and as I turned around from the sink I spied a lizard – and I mean a very large lizard; at first glace I thought it was a small snake – scudding across the wood floor, the softest clicking noise of its tiny claws, unable to get any traction on the wood. After my initial EEEK!!! I gingerly escorted said lizard out the back door, shutting it tightly. No more reptile home invasions for me, despite the heat. I then went to look up lizard medicine, and lizard medicine is all about dreaming.

Dreaming.

Dreaming.

Dreaming.

What have I been dreaming?

What have I stopped dreaming about?

What do I need to start dreaming again?

Day-dreaming, nighttime dreaming, lucid dreaming, even nightmares. What dreams have I let slip? What dreams have I forgotten? From now on I want to grow old disgracefully and dream big, new dreams. That and learning how to sleep on sunlight. Lizard's message is this:

DREAM LARGE!

DREAM BIG!

JUST DREAM!

April 4, 2006

Sitting in bed looking out my bedroom window to a rainy Tuesday in the heart of Korea Town. In spite of the city sounds and noises, I can hear the rain splashing and spilling over the gutters onto the balcony and driveway. That vicious cold I had turned out to be walking pneumonia. I was much sicker than I realized. It has only been in the last couple of weeks that I finally have stopped coughing and hacking.

I feel as if some grand, mythic events are at play with this war, like a Greek tragedy, and must work themselves out in an irrevocable, inevitable, and inexorable way. The cost of pride and arrogance is high indeed. And America, or at least the part of America that is proud and arrogant and/or in denial, will be brought its knees, face down in the mud of our own misadventures. Humility, if ever learned, is hard learned indeed.

Right around the time I got sick, I went through a strange emotional phase, the whole idea of not trusting God enough and monkey mind taking over. Again. I remember it was after the bulk of the moving chaos had ended and most of my things, with a few exceptions, had found their way into their respective drawers, shelves, nooks and crannies, and rather than being elated about my new place I found myself curiously down and mildly depressed. A part of this I'm sure had to do with the fact that I was run down from the stress of the holidays, moving, and being sick. But not entirely.

So I went through the drill:

"OK, I have moved. Most of the arduous work is behind me. I have found the perfect place for me. When second son, W., graduates from college, he and his dog can land here. I couldn't have asked for more. And now I'm depressed – the exact opposite of how I "should" feel under normal circumstances. Why?"

And what did I come up with? What did I puzzle out? That I had somehow been "bad" or "naughty" for moving here rather than moving back in with P., that somehow I was "wrong;" that I hadn't done what I was "supposed" to do; that somehow my volition and choice didn't matter; that somehow I simply was not allowed to do what I wanted to do, regardless of how others reacted.

I was flabbergasted when I finally unearthed that layer. Not only that, but that I wouldn't even allow myself to be angry about the fact that my will was so beaten out of me as a child. I couldn't even allow myself permission to get pissed off about it. No, I had to squelch the anger and get depressed instead.

After I came to this revelation, I went through another drill, this time talking out loud to myself:

"Maurine, it really is OK for you to do what you want. It really is OK for you to have your own place even if you continue to see P. You don't have to live with him 24/7 if you don't want to right now even if the two of you are getting along better. You gave him a set of keys. He knows he's welcome anytime. It really is OK for you to choose what you want to do *just for you!* You don't have to feel invaded or manipulated or bad or naughty or disloyal or whatever for simply doing what it is you want and need to do. For you. It is OK. Really."

How repressed can a person be? Plenty. I learned to go so very far away as a child. I find myself actually practicing making choices and then watching my reactions: feelings of guilt, intimidation, anxiousness, that "you're-wasting-your-time" mantra which usually means I'm not doing what other people want me to do. It is a terrible but truthful thing to say but I need at this point in my life for Dad to go. I know Dad's leaving won't make all the old patterns miraculously disappear. But there is this urgent sense of needing to have the rubber band snap. It has been stretched way too far, too long. In his own way, Dad absolutely brutalized us, and Mother in turn manipulated my brother and me to make up for it, like a chain reaction of psychological trauma and abuse

Yet he is so old now, so frail, so genuinely out-of-it and in need of help. He forgets he said something, shared some story or fact right after he utters it – the other night he repeated the same statement twenty three times! I just nod and say, "Yes, Dad, we already talked about that," which doesn't help because he forgets what I say the minute I utter it, if he hears at all without my having to scream because he is almost completely deaf and refuses to wear a hearing aid.

Do I feel awful for writing this? No, it simply is the sad truth. On St. Patrick's Day, Dad had an eye doctor's appointment and as Murphy's Law would have it, it started to rain. No, not rain, pour. Instead of canceling the appointment – we were already on our way and Dad wanted to have his one good eye checked – on we went. As I was trying to get the wheelchair back into my car after his exam, it fell apart in my hands, bits and pieces of metal and wheels scattering onto the pavement in the rain. It gashed and bruised my leg as it collapsed and if it hadn't been for a young man with dyed green hair coming to my aid, I would have been in an even greater mess.

And when I finally got into the car, what did Dad say? Not "Are you okay?" or "Why are you rubbing your leg?" All he could talk about on the way home was isn't it great what the doctor said about his one good eye!

April 5, 2006

Hmm, the next day. What happened to interrupt me yesterday? Well, let's see. The electricity went out and I couldn't find the electrical panel to check the breakers. This required a phone call to my landlord, and awaiting his return call, to solve the problem. By the time that was dealt with I had to wrap a birthday present for a friend who was due for a very belated birthday lunch. That ate up both literally and figuratively two and a half hours before my friend left. Then I was off to the post office to mail another birthday present, then onto the market and drug store – all in the pouring rain. When I finally got back to my apartment, I could have chosen to write or play the piano but instead I spent the time I had before a dinner guest arrived organizing my taxes and shredding documents. My dinner guest stayed until 10:00pm, after which I cleaned up the kitchen, took a shower, and flopped into bed. I managed to read two pages of *Time* before I conked out.

And here I am: the next day; it sounds like Genesis. I finally unpacked the last two boxes of Mother's wedding china and lined the one remaining empty shelf in my closet with my journals. I had left them packed away in the garage but then thought: "Shame on you, Maurine! Be proud of your journals, be proud of all the work and time and words they represent. Quit hiding. Take them out of those boxes." So there are over nine linear feet of journals along my shelf. Every day, every time I go into the closet I see those journals, up close and personal. You might say I am in the process of unpacking the Maurine who was boxed up so long ago.

April 25, 2006

Easter has come and gone, along with a wonderful week in Paris with my youngest daughter who garnered numerous looks and two proposals of marriage. "Vous-etes la mama? Votre fille est tres belle." Merci and mercy; she is beautiful indeed.

Made two day trips, one to Chartres and another to Giverny, plus spending over six hours in the Musee D'Orsey alone – awesome, mind-boggling; even after six hours I still managed to miss the Gauguins – tromped up to the top of the Arc de Triomphe, huffing and puffing, lugging pounds of art books, an act of true motherly devotion. I did, however, draw the line about visiting the Louvre again – that Beast, the Leviathan of Art – and sent Mel. on her way while I strolled along the Quai St. Germain book stalls and bought some art books about Botero, on his birthday no less. When Mel. returned from the Mona Lisa and Venus de Milo she responded: "I understand why you didn't want to go. It's a monster!"

But I think the most memorable event was buying some food, cheese, a baguette, and bottle of wine and having lunch in a park near Notre Dame our last day there. Mel. and I spent nearly two hours talking about life and men and art and sex and dreams. She realizes as she gets older what a different kind of relationship she has with me than most of her friends have with their parents, especially her female friends with their mothers.

Was this conscious on my part?

Yes. Just wanting my children to be who and what they are meant to be, not what I think they should be or need them to be. The key words here are honesty and freedom.

We also talked about my mom and how very different it was for the two of us: Mom's rules and regulations and fears and control issues. Mel. made the sad yet poignant comment, "Just as Grandma was becoming a true resource for me, just when she was finally letting go of all her preconceived notions, she died."

Sad but true. We talked about death and the unexpected in life, how life can change in a matter of moments. Her confession about how unprepared she is at this point to deal with the death of either her father or me. I assured Mel. that neither P. nor I was planning on kicking the bucket just quite yet, but one never knows when or how that last breath will transpire. In the interim, the only appropriate response is one of gratitude and loving, compassionate stewardship of all the gifts life holds and brings. Such as April in Paris with one's radiant daughter when flowers and the earth are at their most fecund ebullience!

How lovely Paris! The City of Lights and café society. I sometimes wonder if, at any given moment, half the Parisian population works in the multitudinous cafes while the other half frequents them. One better understands French art and the seminal artists who created it after seeing all the cafes and cathedrals and flowers; how time and place and light so affect us all!

What a dichotomy: Europeans know how to live; Americans know how to work and get things done. How to combine the two? I have made a commitment to myself to live a more European life-style in LA, especially now that I am in a location where that is possible. I can walk to the county museum of art and stores and market. I even bought a little cart on wheels to use for grocery shopping. As much as it humanly possibly in La Cite du Automobile – and with gas prices now over $3.00 @ gallon – I am going to use my feet and SLOW DOWN! It truly is okay to enjoy life; indeed, that is one of the main reasons why we are here. Why or how is it I never learned that?

April 26, 2006
Gracious Spirit:
It has been a while since I have come before you. I thank you for the many blessings that are mine and mine to share. Every day I am more aware of these blessings and gifts. I feel it perhaps would be OK to let go of everything, especially writing, and yet I also know that if it is Your will for me to continue, I will.

If you do not enjoy the work you do, you are not fulfilling my will. This does not mean that the work may not be hard, even frustrating on the human plane. But you must feel a deeper alignment to the rightfulness of what you are doing and from this deep sense of rightfulness comes the joy. As you have gone deeper and grown, so too has your creative ability, what you have to bring to the task of writing. Do not let yourself be sidetracked by temporal issues; the creative process takes place outside time, though its manifestation comes through the time you put forth on a day-to-day basis.

What is it you want to accomplish? It is good that writing is no longer tied up with having to prove yourself; your willingness to let go of it even after all the time and mental energy is a good thing, a sign of your devotion and understanding that my plan and path truly are best. But consider also what this act of creation could mean. A gift that you, and only you, can bring into the world. You may even find yourself enjoying the process rather than approaching it with dread or anxiety or even more at this point a weariness that is understandable.

Pay attention to the difference between willfulness and willingness. In the past, so much of your energy has stemmed from willfulness, making it happen rather than from a point of willingness, of allowing it to present itself to you in a way where the efforting sloughs off, and you are present to the task in a different way. You become the vehicle but a different force is the driver. In a way, you don't have to be present at all; all you have to do is open up, the way an opera singer opens his or her vocal chords and lets the music pass through.

Let yourself reenter the world of creativity. Allow yourself to be surprised. Part of why this whole process has been difficult for you, so arduous for you – over and above the many people, places, and events you have had to deal with – is your false belief that you have to do this alone. You are not alone. You have joined with a source deeper and richer than you could ever have supplied from your human perspective only. Trust this source to guide you.

Every time you start to work, ask for help, ask for guidance, ask for clarity, ask for what is needed. It is appropriate to restructure time into each day for the work's unfolding. You realize that the time you have is the time you have; you and no other has this specific time allotment. Now it is time to say "yes" to this and still the voice of "I can't" or "This will never be right." It is imperative that you do not allow one iota of negativity into your energy field. When genuine fatigue and weariness set in to dull your capacity as a channel, stop, rest, refresh yourself, take care and tune your instrument for the next time you are called to play.

Be patient.

Be disciplined.
Be steady-minded.
Cull out all thoughts that are not conducive to fertilizing my garden within you.
Trust.

Right at the end of the above meditation, I heard something drop in the next room, my meditation den. I went in to discover three items on the floor that had fallen from the top bookshelf: *The Book of Runes, The Healing Runes,* and a pack of Tarot cards. Shades of the coffee cup popping out of the kitchen cabinet over a year ago!

Of the two Rune books, *The Healing Runes* felt like the right one to look at. I drew: Hope (past), Courage (present), and Forgiveness (future).

> Hope – the light that never fails, a feeling that urges you on...Hope is among the most abiding of God's gifts...Hope restores our optimism that tomorrow can mark a new beginning...With hope, we learn to keep on living our lives courageously and diligently...Hope is God's Love at work in our lives.

> Courage – Anyone who has been sorely tested knows well the courage it takes to heal...Are you being asked to make a leap of faith into an uncertain future?...If you react to the present situation with panic or denial, there is no place for Courage to take hold...think upon those who have faced great adversity with grace, and pray for their example to inspire you...the truest test of courage is to live.

Indeed. What's writing a book compared to being nailed to a cross or burned at the stake or gassed in an oven? And finally:

> Forgiveness – A life in transition draws upon forgiveness to make peace with the past...Who is it that calls out to you for forgiveness? [My mother? My father? P.?] To whom do you call out?

And, of course, that's exactly what comes next:

> Consider whether receiving this Rune...may be an invitation to extend Forgiveness to yourself...And if you have already begun, be gentle with yourself, it takes time to release the past.

Time to release the past indeed.

Which makes me think of something I read in *On Beauty* by Zadie Smith about time, the epigram at the book's beginning: "Time is how you spend your love." Or to put it another way, love is what you are meant to do with the time you have. Time. It is the only thing we humans can be said to own. None of us knows how much, none of us knows what our allotment amounts to – a few months, hours, days, years. But we all own some, not any of the stuff we spend a lifetime accumulating. That all gets given away, destroyed, lost, or left behind. Only time and how we spend it determines how much love we take with us in our hearts on the way out. Time is what we have and if we spend it wisely, we reap the coinage of love.

Time. Time. Time. This is what I am becoming more aware of now. Fingers beginning to bend; joints unable to flex as fluidly; eye glasses to read and see up close an absolute necessity; the veins on the back of my hands becoming more and more visible, like rivulets growing into a stream. I feel I am becoming less useful in the ways I have known and to which I have grown accustomed, more obsolete, and certainly more quirky and crotchety, wearing earplugs in airport lounges, wanting less, not more stuff, technological and otherwise. And it just is what it is. Time. Whether you are blessed with a lot or not much, it helps to mold both character and soul, especially if you can learn how to love non-possessively.

Another great line from Smith: "The greatest lie ever told about love [or the truth] is that it sets you free." No kidding on that one. Even God's love comes with a cross, individually inscribed and custom-made, should we choose to carry it.

May 4, 2006

Aldous Huxley once said: "Facts do not cease to exist because they are ignored," something many of us in America seem to forget, especially with regard to this war. Indeed, until each of us faces this truth, we will not experience the requisite humility, as the Twelve Steppers say, to make amends. And we all have a lot of amends to make. I certainly do, especially to myself. Talk about the New Jerusalem! The only message that feels of vital importance now, that needs to get through the thick skull of our collective and personal consciousness, is this:

- We humans are not objects; we need to learn how to treat one another as living, breathing entities who are different externally but internally the same.
- We do not own the earth. We have not been good stewards and we need to clean up our act. This has as much to do with how we approach the earth, what we hold inside our

hearts, as what we do externally to protect and husband it.

- We are failing our children. They and the planet and its resources have to be the No. 1 priority. Period.
- We are all going to die. If we truly meditated on this fact, I think we would be less inclined to hurt one another.

From this perspective, winning the war or the argument, however conflict manifests itself – person to person or nation to nation – becomes less important than celebrating the gift of life itself and trying to figure out cooperatively how to make this living experience, this human experiment a little less harsh and more loving for the largest number of people possible.

Perfect love casts out fear; once the fear is gone, true power enters. I hope we Americans can learn to not be afraid. I hope I can. Because we have the talent and resources to do a lot of good in the world if we would only commit to it; if we can let go of our fear, in whatever form it arrives. Our fear will not help fix or change anything, but our absence of fear can and will. And to learn how to not be afraid, we first need to face the truth of what and who we are. The truth may or may not set us free, but at least we would have a more accurate vision of the choice that lies before each and every one of us if we choose to make it.

May 16, 2006
In church on Sunday I prayed again for help around judgment, about not judging things and especially other people so much. I could probably apply some of that non-judgmentalism toward myself, too. But I asked for this particularly as I have been having what I call "old pattern reactions."

I am trying hard to understand the difference between judgment and discernment. Dealing with the responses of the mind, subduing – forget about taming – that weasely, slippery, cunning beast I am finding a difficult, if not arduous, task. Judgment, it feels, is so outer-directed; we judge others' actions, thoughts, behaviors. Whereas discernment is more about what actions, thoughts, and behaviors I need to engage in in order to live more rightfully, righteously, and joyfully on my own path.

All the judgments I have been having about my father and the past, then on Sunday, Mother's Day, he wanted to take me to the club for their special Mother's Day brunch. Some friends brought him and he was all decked out in suit and tie with white patent leather shoes, the works; the effort it took for him to walk to the table was visible. Then toward the end of the meal, Dad broke down, simply lost it, and started sobbing, not shedding a few sentimental tears, but sobbing, not only for Mom and her not being there, but knowing on an intuitive level that he was saying good-bye to his club, all that it has meant to him and represented in his life: the people, friends, and good times.

It was all I could do to get Dad out of the dining room and back to the car. He had to sit down on a chair to rest along the way. He collapsed in the car, still crying. I think he realizes he can't hold on much longer. And I looked at him and held him in all his tears and frailty and thought, "He really is a mensch. Still trying to step up to the plate to bat."

And all I've been doing is judging, judging, judging, all my thinly veiled irritation and impatience with his telephone calls and forgetfulness. I am so tired of judging! I am so tired of judging anything, anyone, everything, everywhere. What would this world look like and feel like if we didn't judge each other so much?

Last night I went to a Philosopher's Cafe meeting whose topic was about "the Other" and why we are so afraid of the other. We are afraid of the other because we judge the other as different, less than, not as good as we are, evil even. One of the speakers was a professor who presented a chronicle of how the Jews have been mistreated by "the Other" throughout history. And what he said was terrible and awful and sadly true. But to my mind, he completely missed the point, or the lesson, of the horrendous experience of that otherness; he, himself, was making everyone else into the other, Christians and Muslims especially.

Yes, we humans have done horrible things to one another throughout the course of history but it is not necessarily because we are Christian or Jewish or Arabic or Islamic or Chinese or purple with pink polka dots; it is because we are human and we frequently make very bad choices based upon pride, fear, ignorance, arrogance, laziness, egotism, and being mean-spirited. But it is we humans who have the opportunity to experience a change of heart, to make a different choice about how we respond.

Which brings me back to the issue of judgment: As long as we keep judging others as good/bad; you're in/you're out; I'm right/you're wrong that judging, dualistic energetic will continue to engender splits – psychological, emotional, political, and ecological – that will foster the sense of more and more otherness ad nauseam.

Fortunately, after the professor finished his litany of abuse, a wonderful Rabbi stood up and simply embraced the other professor's position; he didn't disagree or start arguing – which I, of course, would have been tempted to do – he simply said in all sincerity, "When I hear all these terrible things, I want to despair…"

Me, too.

This Rabbi went on to talk about the mediation work he does in Los Angeles, not the City of Angels so much as the dwelling place of mixed and varied tribes. He said it is not even about tolerance; he didn't like that word anymore. Rather, for him it was about attempting to understand the other and the concept of civility. Civility. Yes. Politeness, consideration, courtesy, patience. What the world needs is more civility and less judgment, and that goes especially for me.

June 10, 2006

My father called Wednesday and told me that he had diarrhea during the night without even knowing it. When I arrived later to see him, he was in such a deep sleep I could barely arouse him. I actually thought he might have slipped into a coma but he eventually came to. I believe he is practicing dying, going far, far away and then coming back. At this point, I think he is holding on out of sheer will. I do believe he wants very much to see all his grandchildren together again one more time, and this whole dying process no doubt is harder on me in certain ways than it is on him. Dad seems to be in a blessedly child-like state that protects him from any introspection or depression. He only says that he has been a "very lucky guy."

Lucky Bill.

I spent the afternoon helping him get a wheelchair, his admission that he needs one now, and his insistence that his insurance pay for it. There I was on the phone: first to one insurance company who informed me that they will only cover a wheelchair, and then with several restrictions at that, if Medicare refuses to do so in writing. Then on to Medicare and yes, they will cover the purchase of a chair but only after ten months of rental. Will he even be alive in ten months? The cost of renting a chair for that length of time is more than a brand new wheelchair would be in the first place. Just when old people need help the most, they get it the least.

There I was in Dad's little bed-sit with a phone in each hand trying to deal with the byzantine bureaucracy of the health care system – even when you have insurance – when Dad fouled himself, pooping everywhere while he was trying to identify himself to the insurance company because they wouldn't take my word for it. There stood my ancient father, naked from the waist down, clutching a clean diaper while the stench of poop filled the small room, confused and flustered but rattling off his name, address, and social security number as if he were still in the army.

Right, enough of that. After cleaning Dad up and calming him down, I took his credit card, lying through my teeth that the insurance company would reimburse him and that I'd handle all the necessary paperwork, and went out and bought him a brand, new wheelchair. When I brought it back to him, you would have thought my dad was five years old again, getting a new bike.

"Come on, Dad, I'll take you for a spin, so you can show off your wheels."

Down the hallway we went, with Dad gleefully announcing to everyone, "I just got this new wheelchair!"

He has already called me three times thanking me and how happy he is to have it. Imagine being happy about having a wheelchair! There is something to be said about the indomitable nature of the human spirit, that it can still respond with a "yes!" to life even in its twilight moments. I do pray that when the final moment presents itself that it will be peaceful for him and that he will just slip away to join Mom.

I have been brooding about time, chastising myself in the old way about "wasting my time," about putting things off – a.k.a. writing – until after the camping trip, until after this one last picture is hung on the wall, or rehung and readjusted several times. At some point there will be no more waiting, no more after, no more time left. The flow of moments simply runs out. And it is so difficult for me to have any sort of accurate, reasonable understanding about whether I am truly wasting my time and avoiding not finishing my novel for psychological reasons far too numerous and boring at this point to go into. Or, if I am actually being normal and it really is okay to spend an afternoon visiting friends or going to a movie, some of life's sweet pleasures.

It is a challenge for me to be loving and gentle. I simply never learned how and I'm having to teach myself to do this for me.

July 14, 2006
My "baby" girl turned 21 last Monday. She called, rather inebriated – or should I say quite merry? – from Rome in the wee hours of the morning. Italy had just won the World Cup in a shoot-out and the citizens of that city, as I am sure the populace throughout the country, were celebrating riotously. Mel. decided to go swimming in the Trevi Fountain to commemorate both birthday and football victory. Under normal circumstances, guards and police would not allow such wanton frivolity and disrespect, but Italy winning after two overtimes and a PK showdown encouraged the powers that be to turn a blind eye. What a way to start one's official adulthood!

More motherly duties involving both W.s, son and father. Son had knee surgery, and good ole Mom got the job of walking said son's beloved dog, a.k.a. the Best and Sweetest Boy Ever, around the neighborhood. Why is it we women always seem to have the job of cleaning up poop, in this case canine and decrepit parent? Is it our caring? Our seemingly biologically driven masochism, always putting others before ourselves? Or is it because we simply are the kinder of the species?

My father is beginning to talk about "I won't have many chances left" to do such and such and telling me what he wants in the way of a memorial service (play *Shenandoah*). After all these years a sweetness has arisen in him that is dear. It is as if the essence, the distillation of him has finally come forth and broken through the surface. It is noticeable, not only to me, but also to others. What I do not understand is why there was so much belligerence along the way. It is as if that old commanding, controlling self has sloughed off and this new – or old, in the sense that this sweet spirit is what my dad came in with in the first place – has resurrected itself just in time for the next stage of the journey.

Do we go out as we come in?

Do we come in as we go out?

It is all such an incredible mystery and witnessing it all the more mysterious still. This is something I was not able to do with my mother. She just left, and I do not know if it was a good leaving, a good death. Maybe in the sense that she was not in extended pain, and in certain ways that kind of sudden death, though immediately a shock, is ultimately I think easier on those left behind. But I was not able to experience my mother reaching the peace of acceptance that my father now has. Perhaps she never would have even if she had had a different leaving. She was really quite depressed toward the end, which is sad.

And my father constantly calling her The Prophet of Doom did not help. She questioned what her life had been for, a sense that she had not used it wisely or as well as she could have. The tragedy of my mother's life is she knew she hadn't used everything God had given her. Yet how I would have loved and treasured to see emerge at the very end the beloved little girl she was before her father died. Everything changed for her then.

I noticed something the other day that in certain ways felt quite subtle and yet in other ways, considering a near lifetime of free-floating anxiety and nervousness, that general sense of malaise and nebulous down mood, gone. I wasn't thinking about anything that had to do with the future or the past or writing or questioning why I wasn't writing or marketing books or anything. There was just – just! – this sense of profound internal stillness, as if I were finally learning how to be in the present and to be fully present to the present. The oddest thing about this realization was how below the radar it was; no fireworks, nothing dramatic, no luminous, numinous "ah–ha!" moment – just the sense that this feeling of profound difference was there.

What next? P. threw one of his anger fits the other night because W. and I arrived home from our camping trip early, thereby interrupting "his plans." His anger, fear, fatigue – I don't even care anymore what it is from – are pushing away those he loves the most. I left and went back to my place. When I finally crawled into bed, I luxuriated not only in the clean sheets and soft pillow cases but also the fact that it was my bed – no one else allowed unless I say so, unless I invite them in. My bed!

P. admitted to me he is still very confused about a number of things, and his relief that he is not tied to feeling responsible for being with me, someone with whom he so disagrees about the way life needs to be handled. And yet he says he adores me! Go figure. I told him that when all was said and done, we were not able to find enough love within ourselves to overcome this lack of acceptance of the other's world view. It all boils down to that.

So what's in this for me? What do I get out of this? A life-style? But that is only at the material level of existence.

I know if something were to happen to me, and I truly needed P.'s help, he would be there in a nanosecond, without hesitation. And he told me that watching me care for my father has brought him comfort that I could and would do the same for him. But what am I learning from our relationship? I know what I am teaching, or at least modeling, but what is he teaching and modeling for me? We make love every now and then – and great love-making it is, too – but then he goes off to do his thing and I do mine. Is this sophisticated or sick? Okay, maybe not sick but co-dependent and enabling?

I do know this: every step I have taken to honor my own path has been the right one.

July 17, 2006
Interruptions.
Interruptions.
Interruptions.
All the interruptions and stumbling blocks along the way. Originally in Hebrew that is what "sa-tan" (Satan) meant: an obstacle along one's path. Leave it to the early Church to make that stumbling block into something evil, rather than an expected part of life. And to make that stumbling block evil *and* female to boot.

Interruptions.
Obstacles.
Stumbling blocks.
They just are what they are, nothing more and nothing less. Sitting in my study feeling the heat of the day and the heat growing within, working on getting that writing backlog rekindled and burning. Went to yoga for the first time in weeks, and I could feel the heat, the fire in my belly and gut. Closing my eyes I could see the first and second chakra colors, red and burnt orange, standing for rootedness and creativity.

What are the stumbling blocks along my way?

Busyness. Once the practical aspects of life are attended to, what does busyness mean?

Not taking the time to get quiet, not making the time to be quiet. The importance of quiet to connect with the joy.

Why don't I take the time? Do I not think I deserve it? That somehow I'll get by without it? The whole idea of grabbing hold of my birthright to experience joy. This is what Spirit wants; this is what It plans for us.

Why can't I trust this more? What is it about not trusting? That I really, really, really do deserve to be joyful? That I am truly worthy of this and not being selfish for wanting it. How many times as a child and young person I must have heard that punitive, chastising voice! Or that by taking the time I am being selfish in the best way, a way that is honoring God. All the false idols we put in the way of joy, especially ourselves and our emotional woundedness. Why don't we feel we deserve the very, very best? Why don't I?

July 21, 2006

Just completed my sales tax forms for the past year. Book sales from July, 05 to June, 06 down almost a third from the year before. Between getting discouraged or simply moving forward, I guess there is not much of a choice. At least I sold something. It could have been zero. It all depends on which lens you look through.

Read an email from a friend on the principles of gratitude. To sum up:

- The universe is friendly and abundant; there is more than enough for everyone.
- Practice non-resistance. Whatever is, simply is; don't whine or argue about it. Good and bad are inherent in all things; it is up to us to

choose between the two. Better to choose the good, to choose life.

- Live with a state of mind that is grateful and joyous for what you have and who/what you are but also be enthusiastic about your ability to do better. Find the good in everything.
- Practice forgiveness; get rid of all resentments, complaints, envy, jealousies, victimhood, and covetousness. Acceptance must be 100%, especially of self. Acceptance = trust (refer back to the universe as abundant and friendly).
- Give as much as you can. Give of yourself and your possessions gratefully and continually. GIVE!

So I just got off the phone to see if I could donate more books to another organization.

A conversation the other night with P. at 3:30am in the morning. I heard him softly moaning, a few words of prayer "Oh, Lord!" escaping from his lips. I asked him what was the matter. This led to a two hour conversation about his concerns, fears, and needs about our relationship, whatever it is at this point. He wants us to be back together and is banking that the family foundation will be the glue that binds us. I felt for his yearning, his sense of feeling so unsettled, that time is slipping away. I feel the same way, too. What to do?

Be honest and truthful. That is a must, a given. I have spent far too much of my life trying at various times in a myriad of ways to talk myself out of that. I can no longer do this. I can no longer dishonor or neglect or rationalize away *my* experience. I know, at least from this particular vantage point and snapshot in time, that after going through the emotional rollercoaster of the past few years, my life is better now than when I was with P. 24/7. I don't have the care and concern and NOISE of overseeing a large house. I have more freedom. What would make me want to return? My love for P.? What about my love for me? I know what I offer P. spiritually and emotionally, but I keep having the feeling of waiting for him to catch up – no doubt a feeling he experiences reciprocally in other arenas about me too, especially financial ones.

What defines relationship at this point in life, after children are raised and financial pressures have eased? What inspires a relationship? What breathes life into it? Our love-making is as good as it has ever been, but all those other differences about how we choose to allocate our time and what we like to do as individuals still remain and are getting more pronounced as time moves forward. Children and family, while huge, simply are not enough.

The only thing I can do is be honest and forthright about what I am experiencing, as is true for him vis-à-vis me. I do not know what it is about having my own physical space that has made such a difference for me, has had such an impact on how I am and how I experience the world, but it has and I cannot pretend otherwise. I could live in this two household relationship for a while. I am at peace with it. But P. is not, and I must be sensitive to this fact. I do not want to lead him on, nor do I want to lie about the truth of my own experience and its significance. Could there be a third, middle way?

Then, of course, there is the old adage, never say never.

I never thought I would get divorced.

I never thought I would get divorced again.

I never thought I would move out.

I never thought I would stay moved out.

But there it is. Maybe I'll write a book entitled *How to be in Relationship With Someone Without Actually Living With Them*. It's a thought.

August 4, 2006
Gracious Heavenly Spirit:
I come before you with a sense that things are changing rapidly. In all ways I want to stay grounded in Your truth. What is the next lesson?

Death and rebirth: this is the pattern of all things. Every cycle and every season follow this command. Those who can witness this with acceptance align themselves to the greater purpose of things without the struggle that humans so frequently take upon themselves. You are at a great crossroad in your life. You have grown and changed on many levels; it is time to take these changes and what you have learned and share them. You are beginning to realize that the writing you have held to for so long as "the" way is only one of many. All is changing because you have had to surrender that narrower agenda in order to come more fully into your power.

Each season of life has its challenges and purposes. In your quiet way you can do more than you think without sacrificing the solitude that is so precious to you. Continue to open up to all that comes your way. It is not so much which path you take, but the way you walk on the path that is significant and determines the quality of your life. Keep constructing your internal mansion brick-by-brick. What will be challenging for you is to rest more and more in the space of compassion. It is compassion that communicates truly and effectively, not judgment, for it comes from a heart of love. Remember: all must be grounded in love.

Wherever you are, you make choices – small births and deaths in each moment, every day. Humanity's job, and yours being a part of it, is learning how to make choices and decisions that are aligned with the Above. The human in you sometimes wants no part of this, but the spirit in you is called to love. Give always, in any way you can. Generosity never seeks to get back, only to extend forward.

Do not worry about reciprocity. Trust in abundant Providence and be open to all the ways this comes back to you. This is not to say that taking care of yourself is to be neglected. A garden can only bear fruit if it is well cared for. You are realizing certain limitations of your physical vessel and these must be rightfully attended to without unduly dwelling upon them. Honor them so the well can be replenished.

In certain ways "dying" to the ideas you have held about yourself, particularly as a writer, will paradoxically allow "The Writer" within you to blossom and flower. Your journey is more all encompassing than you have allowed yourself to entertain. Concentrate on abundant life in whatever form it presents itself. The form is less important than the way you approach and embrace it. Your only responsibility is to light the way with loving-kindness and continue to fine tune how you walk on this earth. Be attentive to your contribution to the act of co-creation, but the rest is in my hands. You do not have to work as much as you think because you have a heavenly partner in all things. Life involves the constant changing of forms, but the one thing that does not change is the eternal truth, the eternal reality of spiritual being. Remember that always.

August 22, 2006

Today I woke up groggy, fixed some coffee, and decided to stay in bed reading. For some reason, I selected Volume V of Anais Nin's monumental diary. I haven't read anything of hers in years, but as always, her words resonated with me. I do so understand the depressive mood, the neurosis, the yearning; the compulsive need to talk with oneself, to unburden oneself of thoughts and language.

At one point Nin calls her diary the "only laboratory of truth" and of course I wonder immediately, is that true? There is so much that gets left out or forgotten, both consciously and unconsciously; things get changed and transposed; what is true one day can be the opposite of truth and downright false the next; a selection of words about a specific slice or perspective of reality that leaves out infinitely more than it takes in. What indeed is a "laboratory of truth?" The very act of diary keeping is a form of artifice. It is all through a glass darkly, all those qualities and behaviors that keep us, knowingly and unknowingly, from the truth about ourselves, the guides and mapmakers, the cartographers pointing our way toward, or away from, the truth of who and what we are. Perhaps a diary is not so much a laboratory of truth as it is one of personal courage to keep on poking and probing.

The other day I was invited to a barbeque hosted by my next door neighbor, a young writer/director, that was attended by a number of other young writers, agents, managers, all of whom are making it in Hollywood, along with some freelance writers and journalists who are also making a living by pushing a pen on paper, or at least by clicking their computer mice. And I felt *very* middle-aged, as if I had missed the boat, if I ever in fact had caught one, that sense of time and life passing by. I stayed a little over an hour and then left.

What is the right action now in my life? What is right action in my life now? What felt so right once – writing – in some ways no longer does. And the exquisite irony being I now have the time to pursue it; what I have lost, or misplaced, is the drive and discipline to do so – those lost nooks and crannies of passion closeted so long ago. But this sense of waiting for something to happen: I do not like it. Life continues to happen in spite of all the waiting. I don't know why I keep expecting some sort of sign or breakthrough. If Nin's diary teaches me anything it is about *not* being seen, *not* being heard, *not* being recognized. The hardest, most difficult truth of all, for me at least, is learning how to trust.

Trust.

Truth.

Two words so close and yet so far.

Trust the truth.

I can only trust my truth, and most of the time I go around clueless thinking I need to do this or that specific action rather than surrendering to the profound mystery around process. It means believing in the quality of effortlessness that arises from being grounded in abiding trust, the all-will-be-wellness of things. And today probably isn't the best day to explore this because of my wooly headedness and summer heat, both of which are giving me problems. Heat, along with pain, annihilates thought.

One line from Nin I loved and I ask the same question, too: "Whatever happened to joy in America?" Where is the joy? Forget about looking for it in America, or anywhere external for that matter. Where is the deep, abiding joy within? One quote I liked in particular:

> Life heals you if you allow it to flow, if
> you do not allow it to trap you. Freedom means
> that no one is able to destroy you, enslave you,
> paralyze you...How could I have felt so weak
> and passive at twenty and feel so strong now [at
> 69]?

I look forward to that feeling, too: liberation from within, even though I may still feel the blues. I remind myself that the blues themselves are a form of liberation.

August 27, 2006

W. and Mel. left early this morning to return to college, with huge sighs of relief all around. There is a time

215

when the kids must go and parents must let them go. I am so ready for them to not need me – at least as much – and for my father to not need me anymore. Tectonic plate shifts are required at this point. I am so ready.

At dinner the other night: my father's last big hurrah at his golf club with his grandchildren, but he barely ate. I sat next to him cutting his food and feeding him like a baby, all of six bites, before he asked to be taken home. The children were oblivious, though adept at pointing out my many faults and failings. How can such "perfect," know-it-all children come from such a flawed and fallible mother?

The evening was a disaster. What led up to it? A busy week, a busy day; still more phone calls to the police trying to sort out Dad's credit care theft which I discovered. Mel. packing to leave, W. packing to leave, dealing with his broken down car. (And tell me why you waited until the last minute before getting it fixed?) Not able to do much writing due to the fact that my right hand is in such pain, like an ice pick being jammed into the radial thumb joint; forget about taking Aleve and Napercin, they don't come close to helping. I can't even use my laptop anymore; instead I've had to jerry-rig an ergonomic one next to it, which of course required installing a sliding tray on my desk to hold it; treks to the Laundromat back and forth, my cell phone breaking down – the usual stuff – all those stumbling blocks along the way.

I was so angry and hurt at the children for not helping more with their grandfather; their "we're-going-to-do-what-we-want-when-we-want-so-don't-rush us" attitude – and wishing I had more of that *chutzpah* myself. I was ready to smack them all. And the irony is that of the four progeny, only the non-biological one who wasn't there gets it. When she asked me what happened and I told her that the others thought I was being belligerent, she shook her head. "You, belligerent?? That's a laugh."

Not belligerent, just tired.

Emotionally drained.

Frustrated and in pain.

Sad and anxious about Dad.

Subsequent conversations with the children made me realize that as smart and insightful as they are, they just don't get certain things. They can't. They are simply too young. So my advice to them all:

GO WITH FEAR AND TREMBLING TO SEEK YOUR OWN SALVATION!

You have my blessing. And don't send me any bills to pay for it or ask me for advances on your allowance or loans or can-I-just-borrow-this? You're so smart, college and soon-to-be college graduates, figure it out for yourselves!

I have decided to not get my cell phone repaired. Part of the agony in my right hand is due to dialing numbers with my thumb, but even more than that I am dropping out of the instantly available, cell phone culture. Everyone walking around, talking about their own little worlds, oblivious to others, creating noise pollution, encouraging even more bad behavior and non-existent manners.

I can already feel the addiction of reaching for the phone, especially while driving, leaching out of my system. Now if the pain in my hand and thumb would just go away, I'd be back to what? Back to something. Possibly even work? The dilemma of interacting with family and children for someone of a solitary, quiet bent. Why Nin never had children? And other reasons, too. The part of me that is so drawn to her world vs. the part of me that gets frustrated and annoyed. Thinking/feeling: you didn't have kids. Don't talk to me about art and artists and being a mistress; there are whole worlds you don't know about. And, of course, the same could be said in reverse about me, too.

When one does not have children, one remains to a certain degree, large or small, a child oneself, as Nin admitted. Not that all individuals who have children become mature but on the whole this is true; the experience of parenthood changes you. Those without off-spring can only see the world through the eyes of the child trying to break from or cling to the parental figures. But being both a child and a parent, an entirely different level of archetypal energy enters. You are transformed into a different being. It is not just about gaining deeper understanding of the same process about oneself and one's own dynamic. It is more about carrying multiple energetics and experiences of reality simultaneously. You simply cannot be as self-involved if you are going to parent half-way decently. And sadly, Anais did not have a balanced, healthy experience of her own mother and father in that regard. But then again, who does?

No, it is about sacrifice of oneself and one's own needs for another. Or, if not sacrifice, that sounds too much the martyr, it is about putting oneself on life's back-burner for twenty years or more. As a parent, you become in some ways the guardian of time, the protector of the future. It forces you to engage with reality differently, and that can be intense. As a parent, one cannot afford the luxury of neurosis, at least not for long; as an artist one can. Just try being neurotic and having kids; it's an E ticket ride to both heaven and hell. I personally do not believe I could appreciate my womanhood as well without having experienced pregnancy, childbirth, motherhood, and parenting; this experience – for better or for ill, for all the anger and all the love – connects me with other women and life in a way that Nin did not experience.

Nin talks about her refusal or lack of desire to become a parent because she could not bear to be condemned to the same experience as her mother with all the blocked anger and resentment, not to mention the sense of paternal abandonment she so struggled with. Who wouldn't at times be angry for having their life taken away? It's normal to feel that way. Even Jesus tried to get out of his sacrificial job.

Is it just sour grapes on my part due to envy about Nin's artistic life? Not really. Each of us is called on a journey of self-discovery, in one form or another, and perhaps even more than that, a journey toward self-mastery but most of us don't answer the phone. Answering the call doesn't necessarily make us any better or wiser or deeper, only different. Her myriad relationships with other artists and creative people? Yes, I would like more of that in my life.

In all fairness to Nin, she was pregnant once and had a miscarriage, so-called. She writes very movingly about this experience in her diary. But there is a big "but" about her "laboratory of truth." According to her biographer, Deirdre Bair, there were three possible fathers for Nin's child: Hugh Guiler, her then husband, Henry Miller, her then lover, or possibly even her own father.

After several ineffectual abortion attempts, Nin persuaded a doctor to abort the pregnancy at six months. For a brief while she considered having the child – a girl – and letting her mother raise her but decided against it. With her four lovers, including Otto Rank with whom she had sex as well, if you count oral sex as sex, around her in the hospital and with all her "eyelash stuff on," Nin delivered a stillborn daughter on September 22, 1934, whom she insisted upon seeing because she was "scientifically curious." When Henry Miller announced that one of his books was about to be published, Nin's response was,

"Here is a birth which is of greater interest to me." "For man, for love of man, for my life as a woman, I killed the child." The next day Nin drank champagne with her husband and fell asleep. But not before writing, "Glory, glory of deliverance. The sleep of deliverance."

Spoken like a true narcissist. As a woman I want to smack her; as a writer I think "good stuff;" as a moralist I am outraged; as a therapist and human being I feel great sadness, thinking how that little stillborn girl-child possibly could have brought Nin closer to man and humanity and art than any other activity or endeavor she might have engaged in.

But then I remind myself: some females simply are not maternal. No use trying.

August 29, 2006

Yesterday was another busy day. Got stuck in traffic for over two hours in the late afternoon after another 100 mile trek to see Dad. I started crying with frustration and fatigue. With no cell phone to keep me distracted, I analyzed the traffic patterns in silence.

The stench and smell of death when I was with Dad made me want to vomit; that at once sweet yet acid smell of decay, like gas given off by fermentation. How that smell was indelibly etched into me after all those days in the hospital battling cancer. After seeing Dad, I forced myself – and I do mean forced – to go walking for three miles out in Malibu, taking big gulps of fresh air, trying to clear my lungs.

While at lunch I looked across the table and thought, "He's simply not ready to go." In an I-don't-know-what sort of mood, I jotted down the following silliness:

We come in fresh and juicy;
We exit dry and pruny.
And in between,

We preen like queens,
Until Death, that Great Dean,
Snares our souls –
A Diosy!
A Dios: we go to God.
When we're ready.

Do we really have a choice in the matter, other than not engaging in completely self-destructive behaviors? Is the time of death encoded into our genes, programmed to check out on such and such a day at such and such time? I know we can will our own deaths, consciously or unconsciously. Cancer was my way of checking out, or my attempt to do so, when I sensed deep inside, but didn't know consciously, how unhappy I was in my own skin. At other times, though, death feels so random. Why this person and not that one? Why take a small child and leave my dad shrinking and shrinking?

I suppose like Frieda Kahlo, we can only say, "When I go, I hope it will be joyous and that I never come back."

****

The other day I was in Barnes and Noble to pick up a book and overheard a snatch of conversation between two men, something to the effect "even women in Nigeria are looking for a free ride." The two men, one white, one African-American, laughed loudly at this comment. I wanted to go over to both of them and rattle their cages. Let me tell you about free rides! Let's start with the first nine months when you're in a woman's belly, taking everything, literally everything that gives you life from her, totally rent-free, while she sacrifices her body that will never, ever be the same again after she goes through ten, fifteen, twenty or more hours of hard labor and excruciating pain to bring you into the world. Then after twenty-some odd years of cooking, cleaning, tending, mending, washing, mopping up food, slop, shit, vomit I personally walked away with less than a few percent of EVERYTHING, except my integrity and freedom. I kept 100% of those. I hope. Is that looking for a free ride?

Do you think the women in Africa who are stoned to death for having premarital sex are looking for a free ride?

Do you think all the young girls who are prevented from going to school to learn and who would gladly take care of themselves if they had a trade are looking for a free ride?

Do you think all the women who are not allowed to have dominion over their own bodies and reproduction are looking for a free ride?

Do you think all the women globally who still earn less, have less, and do more than men are looking for a free ride?

Do you think the female fetuses that are aborted and the young girls who are mutilated at puberty to prevent their experiencing their own eroticism are looking for a free ride?

And, oh, by the way while I'm thinking about it: Do you have a mother/wife/sister and/or girl friend who is at a job right now so you can sit here at Barnes and Noble on a work day having a little chat with a brother? Do you think they are looking for a free ride?

And another oh-by-the-way: I don't look out on the world today and see women as a majority in the corridors of power, at least not as these concepts are defined by men, and who is it that's doing most of the killing these days?

Don't get me started!

If I hadn't been in a hurry to get to a meeting, I might have joined these two men for a friendly chat. But things are going to change. The Goddess with all her intuition, power, and fierce love is returning. Soon. And she will expect anything *but* a free ride!

September 26, 2006

A woman after my own heart. Lysistrata lives on!

"We want [our boy friends] to know that violence is not sexy."

A quote reported in *Newsweek* by the girl friend of a gang member in Columbia, where wives and lovers are giving up sex in the "strike of crossed legs" until their men give up their guns. I only hope this woman and her female *companeros* don't get whacked for their display of feminine puissance.

Fall has arrived with the shifting of light and planets, including a lunar eclipse on the last day, the final degree of Virgo; it is a powerful time to recommit to personal transformation and affirm the healing of the world.

I am more than enough.

Right now.

Just as I am.

How we spend so much of our lives trying to be something or someone other than who we are, who we are meant to be. Why, for some of us at least, does it take so long to get to this point of self-acceptance?

Because it takes what it takes.

It is not about the darkness; it is all about doing what each of us can do, what each of us has been gifted to do to bring in more light. The darkness is only doing its job being dark. We need to concentrate on the light of love and compassion.

Some people stop having sex to accomplish this.

Some people give of their time and treasure.

Some people laugh.

It is all about generating more light.

October 2, 2006

Gracious Spirit:

P. is gone again with another female colleague. My reactions are mixed. A part of me is hurt; another part of me says, "Why not?" Where does the line of friendship cross over into inappropriate intimacy or my trust that he isn't sleeping with her? What am I to learn?

Rest in silence. Still your mind. Only then will the truth emerge for you. You must become very still. You must choose how you want your journey to unfold. There are certain areas where you lack clarity. When the clarity enters, it will become much easier for you to act. You still are trying to reach answers through your mind and your mind can only take you so far. The kind of clarity you require comes from a deeper place.

I know P. wants me to come back to live with him. This I cannot do now, and I'm not even sure why. Am I afraid of letting go? Are there sacrifices I must make that I am unaware of? Or afraid of? What is the spiritually correct path in this unconventional relationship?

It is all a process of choice. While there is a plan for you, you must still choose to embrace the plan. And what is that plan? To be loving. And what does that loving entail? Warm-heartedness: how you learn to live with warm-heartedness in all ways.

How do you treat yourself with warm-heartedness first of all? It is not a product of thought. Hence the need right now, for you especially, to seek the silence within your heart. When you enter the silence, you create the space for that still small voice to speak. Every day at this point in your journey you need to do this. It will help develop a calmness within you that will serve you well in the future. Sometimes answers to deep and disturbing life situations can only present themselves to you. If you submit yourself to this practice of silence and prayer, the answers you seek will unfold.

How do I learn which reactions to pay attention to and which to let go of? Those that are rightful and those that are emotional garbage from my past, old ghosts that simply must be put to rest?

Non-possessiveness, non-duality, non-attachment: this is the great paradox and challenge of being human. While it appears that you are separate from one another, you are not. How you treat yourself in this is how you ultimately treat others. Are your actions coming from judgment (right/wrong; good/bad; fair/not fair) or are they coming from warm-heartedness?

Warm-heartedness does not stem from a place of judgment, anger, self-righteousness, or hurt. So if you feel yourself in any of these emotional arenas you are not coming from a place of warm-heartedness. Warm-heartedness must be patient above all else. Patient and kind, reminding oneself constantly of non-duality. Coming from a place of warm-heartedness does not mean accepting whatever happens. Coming from a place of warm-heartedness means addressing what arises in a different way. You must remember all this is as much, if not more, about P. and what he is going through, than it is about you. You each have different lessons to learn.

What are my lessons now?

Non-reactivity. Discernment but not judgment. This deep discernment can only be cultivated in the discipline of silence. You must do more to facilitate this in your life. All the going and doing must stop. Silence first, then going. Listen carefully to what presents itself. Are they coming from the past, the "old" you? If so, pluck them out like weeds so new growth can emerge. Apply yourself deeply to this process. You need to be more consistent and disciplined without the punitive drillmaster of your past.

And remember to never forget the joy! Whatever outcome is to unfold for you, neither you nor P. is ready yet for what is to come. P. says he is waiting for you to decide, but in many ways he is waiting for himself to catch up, to come together internally. This internal integration you have by and large accomplished but you are catching up on the external plane. A reciprocal process is unfolding. Do the two paths merge ultimately or move farther and farther apart? In many ways, the choice is yours but you must feel deeply into that choice, not think about it. Only the heart and warm-heartedness can answer the questions you need.

Laughter, too, is the sustenance of warm-heartedness. Feed yourself and those around you with laughter. It is truly a blessing and a balm to heal many things. Be patient that all will ultimately be made right. There can be no other way, no other outcome on the Path of Love.

Love is not a thought.

Love is frequently a feeling.

But Love is always an action in action.

Be the loving vessel you can be, the loving vessel you are. Your primary task, your only "job" at this point is to meet me in the silence, listen, and learn. Do not be seduced by the appearances of external reality.

October 5, 2006

A dream about seeing my mother again and going to heaven:

I am in an old ramshackle house similar to the one I lived in in Agoura during the 1970s. It is out in the country and very run down. My dead mother comes to visit me. I am very excited to see her. She looks old and frail but I am so glad to see her. I hold her head in my lap and stroke her hair. I ask her what it is like to die. She answers, "Hostile. There are many evil spirits that try to hold on to you so you can't get to heaven." She tells me she finally did get to heaven and it is a nice place, a good place. She is happy, okay. I ask her if Nana [my grandmother] ever came to visit her after she died the way my mom has come to visit me. "Oh, yes," my mother replies. "Several times. We are all allowed to." I continue to stroke her hair and kiss her. "I am so happy to see you, Mom!"

There are a lot of comings and goings around the country cottage. During all this Mother is helping me. She is genuinely kind and doesn't criticize or find fault with me the way she used to. At last she says she has to go back to heaven. I will miss her. When will I see her again?

Then the dream shifts and I see Mother again and am happy. Then I realize I must be in heaven myself in order to be able to see her. I am not upset so much as surprised. I didn't think I would die so soon. I am still young, but it is okay. Mother leads me through all sorts of rooms and corridors. She tells me, "There are a lot of rooms in heaven." We keep moving. There are people milling around as if they are waiting for something, but there seems to be an absence of human emotions.

As we walk, the rooms keep getting prettier and nicer. The people start to look happier, more eager. Finally we reach our destination. We enter the room where God resides, the Inner Sanctum, and it is like a big party. We are the lucky ones who get to be with God. God looks about nine or ten feet tall; thin and wiry yet fit, with long grey/white hair and beard, magnificent and kingly without being overbearing. He is walking around, talking with the people in the room. Then He says He has to take care of something, that He will be gone for three or four days. He leaves and I look around still wondering how this all is happening but when I turn back God is there again. "I thought you were going to leave for a while." God chuckles and says, "I did. I'm already back." And I realize how different time must be in heaven. Eternity but in an hour kind of idea.

I am not unhappy about being dead and in heaven but I am rather surprised and miss my children terribly. P. is bereft mourning for me. This makes me sad. I want to comfort him, them. Then I realize that this will force P. to have a different relationship with the children; that if I am around he cannot or will not do this. But I still miss the children so much. Maybe I can visit?

I then ask God how I died.

"You drowned."

But I am a good swimmer. How can this be, I ask?

God answers, "The Apocalypse."

October 10, 2006

Just returned from a brief trip to Northern California to attend a cousin's wedding, plus a quick stopover in Santa Cruz to visit number two son. W. is living in a garage with his dog and has no source of heat but is at peace with his life. He said, "What else do I have, Mom, *except* my life?" He claims ownership of his life. At twenty-two he knows it is his to do with as he chooses. I am just now learning this at mid-life. I thought to myself, garage not withstanding, "You've done a good job. He feels he owns his own life and is at peace." What more is there, truly?

And how sweet the wedding! Held at the Old Schoolhouse Compound in Point Reyes Station, one of those tiny, quaint spots north of San Rafael. An intimate gathering of about seventy people, the ceremony held outside in the garden on a beautiful and sunny autumn day.

The audience members opened with an Indonesian monkey chant to warm things up, followed by a lovely ceremony and then reception under fairy lights with a full, full, full harvest moon, larger than most this year due to its location closer to the perigee. Fresh oysters and grilled salmon and lamb, a roast suckling pig the night before at the rehearsal dinner. Sleeping in my sleeping bag on the floor in between my cousin and his ex-wife, now separated twelve years but not legally divorced, while I am legally divorced for several years now but still sleeping with my "ex" while my younger cousin and her partner were in bed, sharing it as the mood struck with one, two, or all three of K's nieces and nephews – all while Pin Two, a miniature pincer and of course the ring bearer, looked on and barked at us all. Sometimes families can be a lot of fun.

Sometimes.

Driving down through the Central Valley yesterday on Interstate 5, listening to classical music on period instruments; harpsichords, recorders, opera, Haydn, Mozart, violin concertos, Bach piano concertos, Handel's Royal Fire and Water music, spiritual songs; six hours non-stop of music, music, music. No. Cal and So. Cal: not only two different geographical regions, but two different states and ways of life. And how sweet the air there compared to LA!

Had a conversation with FS about the ill-defined no man's land of my relationship. It is not about being in couples' therapy (been there, done that), but it is a spiritual issue; i. e. the deep conviction that love is a gift from God and how to acknowledge and honor that gift. We talked about what it means to participate in sacrifice, for that is what love can entail.

I hear the world "sacrifice" and I contract internally. I feel as if I have sacrificed so much already. What does it mean to be crucified for another? FS says we humans see crucifixion and sacrifice as suffering, bad, something we do not want to do, an activity we do not want to engage in. But he says God sees crucifixion as Love, the willingness to sacrifice for love. Am I capable of making this kind of commitment? Again? To what? I am enjoying for the first time in my life being self-centered and selfish – as much as I can still having four off-spring, a sometime partner, and an elderly parent to care for.

But then FS said something that left me absolutely rolling with laughter, tears streaming down my cheeks. In all seriousness he said, "Remember, marriage is only 'til death." In other words, don't worry; it's not for all eternity. The way he said it made me howl. Marriage is just until death; you can have a good time, a ball even for eternity. Now there's something to look forward to. Time passes through our awareness, not we through time. Death, eternity, the ever-lasting hereafter: what is it all anyway?

October 24, 2006

Had a wonderful experience with a client a week or so ago. While doing Reiki on this individual I held her head and said a prayer, asking God to hold her in His loving arms. This was done silently, of course.

Afterwards, this person shared that she had the sensation of her head being cradled throughout the entire session, which lasted about forty-five minutes, even though she knew I had moved my hands over other areas of her body. At this point, I shared with her what I had prayed. She started to weep, that feeling of being loved and held so foreign to her. So foreign to many of us, I am afraid.

It *is* miraculous but it is not a mystery.

How we who are built for Love can be so disconnected from our source! Myself most certainly included in that bunch for a long, long time. And how sad that by and large we do this to ourselves! Love never does. Ever. But broken relationships don't necessarily go away by themselves. Sometimes, frequently we have to work very hard at getting over our brokenness.

Sitting in church the other day listening to the sermon about what it means to live in community. My arrogance and the flipside of that my shyness and need to be quiet can make this relationship business a real challenge for me. What does it mean to be intimate with another? To be fully present? True presence is rare; we are all distracted by so many things: phones, noise, cars, sounds, lights, not to mention what goes on inside our own heads.

And permanence: how many of us experience that any more with all the moving around, traveling and changing jobs, professions, locations, and lifestyles? As Carol King wrote: "Don't people stay in one place anymore?" Not much. We are a transient lot, we Americans, and Angelinos even more so, quite literally.

Intimacy: face-to-face, soul bearing honesty, one heart to another.

Presence: the ability to listen and bear witness without necessarily having to put in our two or three cents' worth.

Permanence: continuity through time, if not location. One instance where the telephone actually helps.

This is how community is built, how we build community first within ourselves and then between one another.

Last Tuesday, after a particularly stressful day with Dad, I had to rush back into town from Thousand Oaks and then on to church to teach a class on Joy in Everyday Life – as I was cursing the traffic and wondering why in hell I committed to doing this. I left the 101 Freeway and drove over Kanan Dume Road out to the Point where the park reserve is, looking out over the sea and the necklace of the bay. It was late afternoon, around 5:00pm, with my having to be prepared to teach in Beverly Hills by 7:30pm that night.

But I just had to stop. I parked illegally at a bus stop and got out of my car. For all of five minutes, I stood there, arms out-stretched, palms open; praying for peace, praying to receive what it is I am meant to, praying to become the writer I am meant to be – or not – allowing the creativity in and in. Or out and out as the case may be. People passed me as I stood with arms open and mumbling prayers of peace, prayers of personal purposefulness, prayers for being open and for opening more. The biggest challenge, as always, to say "yes" and "no" when appropriate and to trust that this is absolutely the most critical and necessary action for both the planet and me right now.

Let your yes be a yes and your no be a no; all else comes to evil.

You must claim what you want in order to get it.

Ask in order to receive.

Keep knocking!

Then back into the car, driving south on PCH, reaching my place mid-Wilshire around 6:30pm, typing up some notes and running off material on my computer, then back into the car and off to church.

Again!

Please God. Please help get me through the next hour and a half, the next 90 minutes so I can come home and collapse. Please. Please. Please.

And yes, I made it through class. I made it through the night.

Then back on the road by 9:00am the next morning to go to the doctor for some blood tests and in two near car accidents by 10:00am, neither of which would have been my fault. Does that matter? You can feel the frenzy building. After witnessing two cars T-bone right in front of me, I gasped, "Oh, my God! Oh, my God!" The driver who had not caused the accident got out of his car and walked over to the one who had and started pitching an absolute tantrum about being late to the office. Not "Are you okay?" or "Boy, am I glad no one was hurt!" or "Thank God, that was a close call!" but an absolute hissy fit right smack dab in the middle of the intersection because his plans had been interrupted. Plans interrupted: just wait until you die!

Talk about the frenzy building; it is not dissipating, not getting any better, only worse.

Prayer.

Peace.

Frenzy.

Chaos.

How does it all fit together?

What is the personal velocity and vector of all this brokenness and heartache?

November 1, 2006

I am as tired now as I remember being as a young mother with babies and toddlers scampering around but I am some twenty plus years older and haven't the physical reserves and stamina of youth, none of those booster rockets to propel me forward. Now it is young adults running around graduating from college and building careers, plus dealing with a 96 year old baby in the form of my father.

Early last week he called in great distress. He had to see his doctor. Right away! So I hurriedly set up an emergency appointment, drove the fifty miles to pick him up, and took him to see Dr. D. And what does Dad do once I get him into the office? Why everything is fine, just fine. He doesn't even know why I wanted to bring him in for a check up. No problems with urination or bowels; no problems walking, though he did admit to being afraid of falling and therefore, prudently, stayed in his wheel chair.

"Don't want to break anything, you know."

And on it went.

As I witnessed this confabulation I motioned to the doctor with my finger and the two of us stepped out of the examining room while the assistant took Dad's blood pressure.

"Dr. D, let me tell you what's really been happening."

"So he's on good behavior here?"

"How much longer do you think this can go on?"

And what does the doctor tell me? For quite some time, perhaps years; that on a scale of elderly degeneration my father is mild to moderate only. I cannot fathom what severe must be. I almost grabbed Dr. D by his white coat to plead with him. "Tell me it's not true! Tell me I won't have to go through several more years of this!"

Dr. D's less than comforting comment:

"You'd be surprised how long some of them can last."

I was practically in tears, shell-shocked. And, of course, the wicked irony of it did not escape me. I always thought it would be my mother who lived to extreme old age, not my father. At least I could have carried on a conversation with Mom. It is almost as if the universe determined that I wouldn't be let off that easily; that I had been given the assignment that one parent would stay and stay and stay. I just got the sexes mixed up.

In that moment of standing in the doctor's office I had to confront 1) wanting – no, not wanting – but needing my father to die and expecting him to for some time and 2) there is a good possibility he could go on the way he is for quite a while.

I feel at this point I have been taking care of people, particularly old people, most of my life. I took care of my aging grandmother as a child and teenager because she lived with us half the time, along with my father's family, all those "command performances" as my mother called them. Since he was the youngest of eight, they were old, older, and oldest. And of course I took care of my parents psychologically from early on and for the last few years very hands on physically, emotionally, and God only knows how else.

At one point during my conversation with the doctor he said that Bill really isn't my "Dad" anymore; that a series of small strokes has affected him; that I need to approach him in a different way; that he still will respond to kindness and compassion. Well, who doesn't respond to kindness and compassion, young or old, senile or not?

I wanted to scream:

"But you don't get it. He's *exactly* the way I've always known him: expecting me to be there thinking about his needs." Obviously his body is deteriorating, but he's still pretty much the same, only the wants and patterns are more distilled. I cried on and off all the way home and had a shot of tequila AND a Xanax when I arrived. Time to regroup, needless to say.

So today I cancelled a morning meeting to stay in bed before facing another 100 mile round trip to see about Bill again. As trustee and executrix – forget about daughter – I have a fiduciary responsibility that must be fulfilled.

I need to stay in bed without moving.

I need a car vacation.

Already the phone has been ringing and I have been ignoring it. I actually went to a matinee yesterday to escape all the sound and noise when someone's phone went off not once but several times, and this person actually had a conversation during the movie! There just doesn't appear to be any escape anywhere, anymore. How to cultivate the internal quite, the peace and calm within all this chaos? And the holidays are rapidly approaching, that energy-suck time of the year that is at once both grueling and gay. What to do? I would take naps if I could but I've never managed the knack, except in a car, which of course presents obvious problems. I simply have to learn how to manage my life in a different way.

November 19, 2006

I tried going to church today but sat in my car at the stirring wheel incapable of moving. I looked down the street, saw cars and thought, "In the state I'm in, I'm not safe to be on the road." I went through my usual pep-talk. "But it will do you good. You know it always does." "But I think I might actually faint. I don't have the energy to say 'hello' to anybody."

This back and forth went on for a few minutes until I simply said no, got out of the car, shut the door, went back inside my house, took off my skirt, and lay down on the floor with my legs up the wall, a good yoga refresher pose. After a few minutes I drew a bath and lay down in the hot water. It was only 11:00am in the morning, but I felt so strange, as if I were going to throw up but not; faint but not. There was a quality of the surreal about it. I looked at my painted toenails and feet up against the bathtub tile and thought of Frieda Kahlo. If I had had my instamatic camera, I would have taken a picture of them and one of my pubic hair. I imagined the shower spigot vomiting.

After about half an hour of soaking, I got out of the tub and dried myself off and fixed some chicken noodle soup, always a comfort boon. I then read some scripture and started to feel better. Such a dissociative, out-of-body experience, thinking about the past and what it triggered.

How can a child be heard when he or she is not allowed to speak truthfully, when it is impossible in the family to do so? The capacity to ask for something, to make oneself understood is crucial to an individual's sense of being loved. Yet how many of us learn early on to censor ourselves, even without physical or sexual abuse, in order to protect others, especially our parents.

When we are born into a specific time and generation, we are "assigned" an unconscious emotional hole to fill from the previous generation. The lack in my family centered around mothering and parenting, and the expectation that the children (a.k.a. me, the daughter) would do the mothering that my parents never had. I had a "job" to do even before I was aware what that job was.

During the first years of life, as infants we unconsciously try to understand our mother's desires in order to make ourselves into a satisfying object. But the father or third party is supposed to intervene and say, "No, you cannot fill that lack." The father, in effect, says no to psychological incest. Or the mother must intervene, if the infant is trying to fulfill the father's needs. This allows us to enter reality in a healthy way by not having to fulfill the defeated longings of either parent. When we can't say "no" to this, our experience becomes traumatic. The neurotic child keeps trying to figure out how to fill the void – the way I've spent most of my life.

November 20, 2006
Gracious Heavenly Spirit:
Why have I needed to believe P. hasn't slept with others? Who or what have I been protecting with this lie? Reflecting on yesterday and my strange disoriented experience: how being the love object for my parents to fill their sense of loss when young, how much this has impacted me and my relationships with men.

My reaction to P. when I finally pinned him down, it was a relief. What I feared was somehow no longer a fear; the idea that I don't have to protect him and his needs anymore. What truth wishes to express itself?

You were so invaded as a child in your emotional and psychological boundaries and the sense that it was your job to protect others.

How has this played itself out in my relationships? It goes much deeper, something I have hidden from myself. Was my naiveté used to cover my fear that P. would leave me? And now that that fear has been removed, I can be free?

You have been trying to protect a full entering into your being but from a completely different level than the physical. The physical aspects of sexuality you have mastered but it is this deeper, erotic level that you have denied yourself because it would have meant betraying your parents and their need for you to be there for them. You were your parents primary love object and because you were their primary love object, it goes very deep and is hard to let go. Now the letting go can happen because you understand that there will be no punishment, no fear of withholding love.

Is this one of the reasons why I feel this immense need to create space around me, to have no one violate my space, my need to be alone – almost as if it were the last puzzle piece that I can be at peace now if I say "no;" P. will take care of himself; I don't have to fulfill his needs because I feel guilty or am expected to – that I can say "no" and do what is necessary for me?

Yes. It will take time for this to percolate deeply into your being but it is a large step toward the clarity you require and so desire. You know you are on the right path because you feel more peaceful; you are not upset. Upset indicates resistance to what is and you are embracing what is more and more with trust. This trust has been critical to learn because you did not learn it as a child. In many ways, your parents were most untrustworthy, hence your confusion when young. They were trustworthy in material ways but not emotionally trustworthy. In certain ways they "raped" you and you had to protect yourself from that; hence your comment that struck such a discordant chord. "P. would never do that to me, hurt me, violate me." – that is your parents' message to you about them! "Maurine would never leave us, hurt us, do anything to disturb us.

She is the good one, the caretaker, the girl." This role is now over. You have found your freedom.

Your sense that you have needed time away from P. since the divorce to create something healthier started something. Now you are stronger. Witness your reaction to P.'s revelation, something he has held as a threat over you in the past: I will sleep with other women if you don't do what I want, or I will love other women if you don't do what I want. Your relief about this knowledge is from letting go of the need you felt you had about taking care of him based upon what you learned from your parents. You must take care of you. Critical.

It is up to P. to learn how to take your "no" not as the abandonment he so fears but as a necessary part of the process of constructing healthy boundaries, something neither one of you learned while growing up. Your "no" will actually be a gift the way his being with others is a gift to you to release you from the burden of unquestioning fidelity so instilled in you by your parents to assuage their loss and fulfill their needs.

Afterwards, rereading what I wrote, I burst out sobbing. Does it all come down to that? Being relieved of something I have been carrying far, far too long. P.'s being with other women isn't something personal I have to fix or take care of. No longer personal. It's not just about me.

December 6, 2006

Sitting outside on my small back porch, 3:30pm in the afternoon, listening to the sounds of the city: traffic, building noises, hammers, and horns. Yesterday driving back from tending to Dad, I had a sensation of feeling so lost and the night before watching the sunset as it pulsed down below the horizon, a wave of such loneliness and sadness came over me – feelings I haven't experienced in a long time. It is as if I don't know what to make of things anymore; at this point I simply am incapable of making a decision about anything; that anything I would decide with my mind would somehow not be right. Just the sense of "What the hell am I doing here?!?" I still haven't found the right current, the one that is meant to carry me, the one I alone can navigate, and I am just floating, drifting aimlessly. I haven't felt this "off" in a long time.

FS advised me to check with my Guide, and no doubt he is right. Sometimes I wish I knew how to do life in a different way, but I don't. I only know how to do it the way I do it, flawed and lop-sided as it is. The process of discernment is so tricky at times. Humility always, trust in the Unknown, belief in Providence outside oneself – God, Spirit, whatever you want to call it – getting me to the place I *really* need to be.

I feel as if I am at the center of a great star, like the Etoile in Paris, and I could take any number of directions or paths. But the problem is at my stage in life, a misstep or misdirection going the wrong way is too costly. There simply is not the time for course correction the way there used to be. I feel like a pirate lost. If I haven't figured out my life's work by now, will I ever? I do not want to be on my deathbed still trying to figure things out. And knowing, too, that may be exactly what happens to me anyway.

What is missing within me that needs to come into being? I don't even know what to pray for anymore – selling books or a screenplay or getting an agent or more clients – all that just feels so beside the point, as if I am treating God like Santa Claus. "I've been such a good girl, so please send me…[fill in the blank]."

Rubbish. That simply will not do. Maybe I am destined or called to do nothing, and it is only my vanity that wishes otherwise. Perhaps C. S. Lewis is right: one cannot understand the ramifications of choice and time until one is beyond them both, which means dead. Well, we may not be able to understand, but we *are* called to be responsive and responsible to both choice and time while on this earthly plane.

Petition.

Petition.

Petition.

What am I to petition?

What do I need to petition for?

How much can one person petition? I feel I have petitioned so many times already, in so many ways. I do not doubt that there is an answer to the question of my life. My faith and trust have grown to the point where I not only believe but know that this is so, that this truth is reality. What I doubt is my being able to hear the what/how/when/where of being called. Things feel so different to me now, and yet I haven't the language to articulate the difference. It is almost as if I am getting dumb and dumber by the day. Maybe that is what I need.

In Your will is my peace.

But what is Your will? Unless I can figure that out, how can I truly be at peace? I have come so far in so many ways, and yet I still feel as if I have not deciphered this last riddle and that I need to decipher it to fully enter into my power. So close and still not there, like my meditation of long ago about my heart being cut with a knife. Personal velocity and vector somehow off. It is so hard, such a challenge for this mortal to live day-by-day with patience. I am not well built for it, nor well suited for it. I want some imaginary goal to be crossed, and yet I don't even know what that goal is. The feeling that so much is at stake now, so much on the line; bad choices waste precious time that cannot afford to be wasted, and knowing too, despite this human loneliness, not alone at all.

December 7, 2006

Gracious Spirit:

After all this work and the many words of comfort and encouragement You have given me, why do I keep slipping back? What now?

Still all doubt. To cultivate this deeper wisdom, you must actively seek it daily. This is where the human in you falls short. This is not a judgment about you, simply a statement of fact. In many ways you are just learning how to listen and this takes not only patience but practice over time. Patience and practice. You will find the patience grows as the practice does. A part of what is being called for, and we have talked about this before, stems from honoring yourself.

You have had so little training, so little experience knowing how to honor yourself. You never learned how to say, and more importantly to believe, that you counted, that you could be factored into the process. You learned long ago and very deeply that you stood outside of things. A most difficult task to engage in, especially without the aid of the inner well. Do you think Jesus did not feel alone on the cross? The transcendent call: to embrace the loneliness, even despair, while yet remaining in supplication with faith. You have tools now that you did not have before to navigate this earthly realm in a healthier manner. Use them.

There is something about being a creature, your creatureliness, your part in the play and dance of creation that you do not fully understand. This is part of the cross you have to bear. Your creatureliness is at times a challenge for you due to many reasons: the lack of training and guidance you experienced as a child, your sensitivity, your more ethereal bent. Ground yourself as much as possible in your creatureliness as well as your spiritual being. They are not as separate as you might imagine.

Be attentive to the boundaries of creatureliness and the boundaries of spirit. Old structures are in the process of breaking down; be gentle with yourself as these are among the deepest layers of your nature that need to be addressed. Be grateful that the truth about your life is finally emerging. Forgive your parents for so misusing you and be mindful that you do not misuse yourself out of unconsciousness or habit. You do not penalize or criticize a child as he/she stumbles to learn how to walk or master a new task. How can you know what you do not know? How can you be other than who you are? Never doubt that I will use all this for the good. There are rewards you do not know about, cannot know about from your creaturely perspective. But you can from your human perspective claim the abundance, the providence that is your birthright in spirit. Rest assured that what you truly need will be supplied in right timing. Remember it is my desire to help you in all ways and in all things that will bring you closer to me.

December 21, 2006

A friend from church passed away a few days ago and watching his death process was…what? Difficult? Curious? Different? Last rites administered amidst tears, hospice workers, and pain medication; how WM struggled so with his dying. It was anything but going gently into that good night. He called out "Help me!" on several occasions, arms raised in combat defense, jerking, to deflect whatever demons or apparitions or angels or delirium were filtering through his semi-consciousness – shades of what my mother told me about death being hostile.

The witnessing of death, how individual and idiosyncratic it is. One person drops dead; another dwindles, dwindles, dwindles into peaceful sleep that at some point turns into that Big Sleep; another fights and struggles; another gets whacked by a Keebler Cookie truck on the way to work or by a random drive-by bullet, never knowing, quite literally, what hit them. Why is it that personal death feels so much stronger and more compelling than all those other deaths from poverty, war, and disease?

I think what both saddens and bothers me about WM is that he originally was given a diagnosis of six months to live, and he outlived this diagnosis by five and a half years, as Raymond Carver would say, a gift of "pure gravy." And what did WM do with those five and a half years? Not much, holed up hibernating like a bear in his cave of an apartment, ranting against George Bush – an easy thing to do, I must admit – along with the horrible state of the world, ditto. So little, if any, joy.

Where was the joy?

And yet it is I who promised to witness his cremation, his fear of having his body mixed up with others or being burned with cats and dogs. Thinking to myself: "Dude, you'll be dead. It won't matter and you won't know anyway!" But saying out loud to him: "Well, if it will make you feel better, I'll watch." That pledge did bring WM some comfort.

I keep reflecting on something I heard the Dalai Lama say: about making good use of the one life you have. So I have booked a pilgrimage to the Holy Land, leaving the day after Easter, going with a small group from my church. It feels right for me to do this now. I have declined several invitations over the past few years to make the trip but now the timing feels right.

January 6, 2007

A quiet New Year. It is a relief, in a way, that the holidays are over. As the little fish, Dorie, says: "Just keep swimming!"

And so here I swim. It is curious, though, because I think less and less these days and in certain respects there is less and less to write about because of this. When younger, I thought so much about so many things, so much wonder and wondering about life. Now I am thinking less – I think – but hopefully observing more and being present with what I observe. It occurred to me the other day that I spend as much, if not more, time tending the sick and lonely, visiting hospitals and rehab centers, those homebound by illness, as I do writing or anything else.

And it just is what it is. At this juncture in life trying to learn how to be patient and loving is my work. Patient and loving. Curious how the former is both a noun and an adjective. There's some food for thought – if I were thinking more. Learning how to be patient with the patient. And aren't we all patients of one sort of another, all suffering from a terminal "illness" called life?

I look at my children: their youth, all the plans and ideas they have about their lives; what to do, where to go, whom to be with. And while they have so many more options than I did both because of their greater emotional and psychological well-being, the first and most important, and financial resources; again, important but not as much as the former, I am still glad to be where I am now, at this stage of life.

Youth goes by so very quickly and can corrupt you in a way like no other period in life can, always comparing things to when you were young. In reality that decade, give or take a few years on either side, is only one of several, or many, and is over very quickly. The false sense of freedom that youth gives you, that you can go and do whatever you want vs. the true experience of freedom that comes from within.

There is something to be said for youth – weren't the 70s GREAT! – but there is also something to be said for experience. In certain ways, youth can be highly overrated. I was far unhappier, at times quite miserable, while young. The tyranny of youth, or the idea of youth, that so many of us carry. But beauty turns inward and learns to express itself in other ways: what it means to have a beautiful soul and heart. It takes a long time – a lifetime? – to get the ego reined in and youth is all about ego. At this stage in the journey, something else is required.

I was talking with a friend the other day about love and not just the concept but the reality of love. It is a perfectly parsimonious and elegant system and only works if you are truly loving. When one is truly loving, everything, simply everything shifts. You can't be "sort of" or "kind of" loving; you must be truly and sincerely loving. To paraphrase Paul: it doesn't matter or count, or for that matter even work, unless you have love, true love in your heart. Love has no opposite. It just is.

We worry about teaching young people how to read and write, ways to get ahead in the world when so much more of our efforts should be about teaching them how to be loving with self, family, neighbor, community, and world. There is no force on earth more powerful than love. And it doesn't cost money to teach it; it does, however, require focus, patience, and time – commodities in sore lack these days with all the rushing about to get here, get there, win this, buy that, achieve something, and so on.

What most people do not understand is that time slows down when one is more loving, not linear time – yes, the clock keeps on ticking – but the *experience* of time. Love attenuates time, how we move about within it and apprehend it is different. Does that mean we will live longer if we are loving? Maybe, maybe not. But we will experience time in a different way. That is why love is the only operating system that is perfectly designed in every way, for both recipient and practitioner, for the fullest benefit of all. Love releases light and well-being to whoever comes into its energy field. Light is released when Energy is divided by matter. The most direct root for releasing one's light is for man/matter to be pierced by Love, to be drawn into Love. $E=mc^2$.

So, please let there be more light and more love. Everything, simply everything will flow, and does flow, from that. That's when the true chain reaction will begin. That is what resurrection is; i.e. the transformation of mind and matter, of mind within matter. That will be critical mass.

January 14, 2007

Something occurred at the beginning of the week that I do not understand and yet I do: how one small, seemingly inconsequential event can have such powerful ramifications.

P., D., and I met for dinner on Monday evening. We were going to eat and then go to a movie together. When P. arrived and I asked how his day had been, he said, "Terrible. There's a fire out on Malibu Rd." where his beach house is. He wasn't too concerned because the fire was over a mile away but thought he'd skip the movie and go check on the house.

"Will you spend the night out there?"

"No, I'll be back later."

The three of us had a nice dinner, then right at the end as D. and I were getting ready to leave, P. received a phone call. When he answered the phone he said, "I'm just finishing dinner with D." I looked at P., perturbed. Why not mention me? As I leaned over to give him a quick good-bye kiss, he turned away from me, his body language communicating "Don't bother me." It was a gesture of irritation and impatience, annoyance even. As we left, even D. commented on his father's reaction and not mentioning my presence. But we were in a hurry to catch the film, so we left.

When D. and I returned home at 9:30pm, P.'s car was not in the driveway. Both of us were concerned. If there hadn't been any problem with the house, he would have been home. So I called P. His cell phone clicked on and then off, indicating that he got my call but did not want to talk. Unbeknownst to P., however, the channel stayed open and I could hear that he was in a bar drinking with another woman and talking about going skiing. I kept saying hello, hello, giving P. a chance to respond but he either did not hear me or didn't know that he hadn't turned the phone off. I got very upset, wrote him a note explaining what I heard, and drove back to my place.

About forty-five minutes later, my phone started ringing and I knew it was P. I didn't want to talk with him. Another half hour went by when I heard knocking at my front door, and more phone calls, and more knocks. I finally went to the door and opened it. There stood P. saying, "I thought we were going to spend some time together tonight. D. said you were upset about my being with someone."

By this point it was after 11:30pm and I was tired. I didn't want to argue or get into a fight. I told P. it had really bothered me that he didn't acknowledge my presence at the dinner table, that I noticed how he pulled away from me as I tried to kiss him good-bye, that I tried calling him only to find him drinking in a bar with another woman, and if that was his idea of "spending time with me" I didn't know what to say. The next day I went back to P.'s and removed what few things I had left there and brought them to my place. I did not speak with him for the rest of the week.

****

P.'s response when we finally talked? That he had been out to Malibu to check on the house and had run into a friend at the Los Flores stoplight and they decided to go out for a drink at Duke's. Yeah. Right. More to the point: Why wouldn't or didn't he acknowledge to whomever was on the phone at dinner that he was with his ex-wife, friend, mother of his children, and supposedly love of his life? (Pick any of the above.)

So many things started to unravel. Not just all the time when P. is with others, in whatever capacity – business, pleasure, both – but the realization that somewhere, somehow, on some level I am what? So forgettable? Don't count? Will always be there? The one safe to come home to?

Thinking, too: P. rarely asks about my work and what I'm doing, what it was like to watch my friend die, my recent speakers training program. At least I try to interact with him and his world. I ask questions and have offered to participate more in his business activities if he would like. Really connecting to how patient I've been, such a good sport, laughing and joking about things that could really bother me if I let them.

I asked P. "What do you tell these other women about me?" His answer? That I am on all the documents, wills, etc. "That's the only thing they understand." What that communicates, however, is that his money is protected and they cannot get it. It says nothing about the emotional connection between the two of us. In the time of our being legally divorced I have always said to everyone – male or female, gay or straight – that P. and I are trying to extricate ourselves from the Gordian knot of our past. But I cannot pretend anymore that this pattern is okay, and it has as much to do with me as it does with P. My loyalty, my naïveté, my understanding nature: I am just fed up with the emotional dishonesty, especially my own, always rationalizing things away or trying to see things from P.'s point of view.

What about *my* point of view?

He can drive to Santa Barbara for New Year's with someone else, and when I've asked to come along, I'm told it's "business." He can fly to other cities for dinners and retreats but the traffic to my place is simply too bothersome to deal with, except on Saturday or Sunday when there is less. P. has yet to sleep through the night at my place, not wanting to disturb his exercise and tennis routine.

It is amazing how the universe works; it keeps sending you the messages you need until you get it. The same pattern in both my marriages: wonderful to come home to but not necessarily to have fun with? I am simply sick and tired of waiting for me to show up for me.

I keep reminding myself: "You are in your mid-fifties, Maurine. You really don't have to do anything you don't want to do." I'm not sure if it is sad or comforting that I have to remind myself of this. And after twenty-five years, I know P.'s process: as long as we're working on it, we're still in a relationship. But as a friend said yesterday, "If you stay with P., you'll be working on your relationship the rest of your lives."

What is the higher good here? That is the only real consideration, the only thing that matters or is of consequence. And this sort of consideration requires time and quiet. I continue to pray for P. and myself every day. I have felt good being alone, not anxious, this sweet pace of life that is mine.

When last we spoke, P. talked about a renewed and renovated partnership, not a relationship or marriage, but a true partnership. At this point in the journey, what would that look like? What are the qualities and requirements of a mature form of loving interaction? At what point can you stop talking about and working on "being in a relationship" and purely and simply *be* in one?

Maybe I am being naïve.

I probably am being stubborn.

I know I am tired.

January 23, 2007

Gracious Spirit:

I am now aware of two things:

1) how wonderful it is to not have to answer to anyone – except You, of course – and

2) already the pull from P. to work on our relationship; his concern that I am "erecting a wall between us."

What feels like a necessary boundary to me is a wall to him. I feel such a need for this time alone and yet I know, too, that I am called to walk a certain way because of my commitment to You. In church Sunday, the sermon was about mercy; the quality of mercy that requires taking time; that time and mercy go hand-in-hand, and this kind of union creates restoration. Help me understand.

Mercy is the heart's ability to see beyond the immediate here and now into a deeper reality, a reality that holds true through both distance and time. How can you be merciful toward yourself as well as toward P.? This is not as mutually exclusive as you might think. As long as you continue to reach deeply into your heart, you will discover that you cannot not be merciful because you will be taking the longer view, and the longer view stems from the compassion that arises from being non-judgmental.

This is difficult because the ego/mind is always trying to "figure things out," "to make things work" in a way that is pleasing to the ego. But what needs to unfold here is a deeper level. Be firm but loving in this process. This separation asks much of you as well: to believe in yourself,

251

you need to heal this part of you that was so invaded and/or silenced as a child. It makes exquisite sense that you would and do require silence and the ability to control your boundaries in order to be merciful with yourself and what was lost and buried so long ago. It is difficult for P. to understand the level of personal invasion you experienced, as it is equally challenging for you to understand the level of fear and abandonment he experienced while young.

That is one of the reasons why this separation is necessary for the healing of you both at a core level. It is healing for you in order to get a sense of and establish your true autonomy. And by true autonomy I do not mean only the ability to move around but to establish, or reestablish this core sense of individuality, which is your birthright. This was taken from you, you might say was beaten out of you, so long ago.

Remember that it is a universal field, a grand dance of reciprocity, a process of healing on all levels. It is not so much a question of what specific action you do or do not engage in. It is the quality of mercy that you bring to any given situation that counts. It is this deeper place, beyond ego and reactivity, that you are exploring. It is not so much a matter of doing this or that, of engaging in conversation or not but witnessing this deeper order. In all ways this movement needs to be honored but you do have personal choice about how you go about honoring it. You can trust your intuition and instincts more than you realize.

This process has a different dynamic, one of unfolding. Unfolding cannot come from the mind. It can only come from paying close attention to your feelings, reactions, and heart. All will be revealed at the appropriate time. Human time and divine time function differently. You are becoming more attuned to divine timing and this is good. Bless each moment of each day and learn to enjoy the unfolding. Your highest good is always as close as your own heart. Listen to it well. And remember that love enfolds you always.

January 31, 2007
Holy Spirit, Gracious Spirit:
Teach me more about the quality of mercy.

Mercy is of the heavens, an aspect of the Divine that if humans could implement to even a small degree would transform things to manifest the Kingdom of God in ways unimaginable from the present mired state of the vast majority of humanity. The key to mercy and being merciful is in the small moments, the small things and ways of being where the true power of mercy unfolds. In this sense, one who practices mercy holds great power.

Mercy requires time, even if just for a moment to be able to pause and ask oneself: How can I be merciful in this situation? True mercy is not a form of self-abnegation but of self-empowerment. It is the power that arises from the heart that desires to love and be of service. Mercy that comes from the heart and the call of God to incarnate His Kingdom is peace-giving and power-giving simultaneously. The call to be merciful is one of the most important calls in the Kingdom of God, yet one that can be easily confused with other actions. Doing good, while laudable and important, is not the same as being merciful. Good deeds can further the Kingdom but mercy is a quality of mind and more importantly a quality of heart that quite literally "grows" the Kingdom. "How can I do good today?" vs. "How can I be merciful today?" bring two different answers and courses of action. One can do good and still harbor an unmerciful heart. And God/Spirit always wants the heart to come from a place of deeper, or higher, disposition.

Mercy requires a radical restructuring of how one approaches each day. If you are called to be merciful in the

Kingdom of God, there must be a deliberate decision, a deliberate cutting away from what is old and less consciously chosen toward a way of interacting with reality that is focused and slower than the way most of humanity moves. This slowness is key. This is not to say that mercy cannot occur quickly within the moment but the unfolding of the power of mercy may require more time. Sometimes, even frequently one may never know the impact of an act of mercy yet the deliberate intention of being merciful, of being called to act with mercy requires a slower internal process. One can be merciful spontaneously but it also can be a studied art. There is no contradiction in this paradox.

Mercy is the platform beyond judgment. Mercy understands judgment and yet still chooses to move beyond judgment to a higher realm, a longer view. Love, too, can do this but mercy itself becomes a form of justice at work in the world. If one is treated with mercy; if one accepts the mercy freely given of a merciful God, then one cannot help but desire the call and furthering of justice. Mercy and justice, God's justice, not the justice of legal systems, go hand-in-hand.

Mercy entails knowing the truth of a situation on one level, usually set in a right/wrong; good/bad dynamic, yet still choosing to engage in a set of actions, words, and behaviors that transcend it and engage a different perspective. Mercy, while acknowledging duality, asks that the heart engage in non-dual reality. Self and other become one. This is true also of love but mercy requires that this manifestation of love then be set in motion by a series of acts. One cannot be merciful without setting love into action. Mercy then becomes the grand conduit of Love's action in the world. You don't just, or merely, love your neighbor, though this is good, right. You engage in merciful acts, both large and small, to demonstrate that love. Mercy is the mechanism of the Kingdom's unfolding, the practical conduit of Love in the world.

February 4, 2007

I just found out that I have to go under the knife again. This time for shoulder surgery, a result of complications related to the cancer surgery I had twenty years ago. The operation count at this point is nine.

Also renewed my business licenses, with both good and bad news: the good news is that I did not have to pay a fee this year; the bad news is because I earned so little money. Hardly any book sales for 2006. The city official who helped me chortled, "Are you joking?!" The good news is that I took it in stride. I realized that my tutelage is to remain positive and more importantly generous, so I've continued with my book giving spree.

But this has also been accompanied by paternal messages of doom and gloom that sank in so deeply. That constant, nagging voice of "What's the matter with me?" "What's wrong with me?" A neurotic can play that theme like jazz, riffing away, playing discordant sounds, the permutations and combinations as subtle and varied as the individual's cleverness and intelligence will allow. Rather than simply saying, "So what?" or accepting with laughter what goes on, or at the very least being able to tell yourself, "Oh, will you please shut up already!" The ability to accept with graciousness what comes in life is a much more useful gift in many ways than the ability to analyze and dissect, that kind of convoluted thought patterning in many ways simply reinforces our innate narcissism. Who hasn't been wounded? Just about everyone on the planet, in one way or another. It can be a long process getting over oneself.

I finally succumbed to peer pressure, a.k.a. my son W., and have reintroduced television into my world. Now it is back into the vortex of images and sound: channel surfing, news, shows, commercials, commercials, commercials. I still haven't figured out how to interface my cable server and my DVD player. The Geek Squad must be close at hand.

Is this a cause of comfort for those of us who are older and unabashedly non-geeky? I now have an IT guy to help me with my computer, a web marketing guy to help boost Internet sales and traffic to my sites – so far with scant results – AND an audio/visual guy to help with my TV, cable, DVD/VCR, CD/radio/tape player. Yikes! And soon there will be no generation on the planet that remembers what it was like before this technological tsunami hit.

Classes of the future:

Cell Phone Etiquette 101.

Advanced Solitude and Silence Behavior (limited to upper classmen only).

How to Use Play Station So Young People Learn Not To Blow Things Up.

How to Play Outdoors Without Taking Your Palm Pilot, iPod, Etc. with You (open to everybody).

A way of being in the world will be irrevocably lost unless we actively seek to preserve it, the way we preserve historical relics. We are biological creatures being forced into a non-biological world, a technological one that is calling the shots to a large degree about how we interact with reality and this process is FAST, FAST, FAST! The evolutionary rhythm of biology is much slower. Will we be forced out of expedience and/or survival to become less and less human – and how do we even define what that means? – OR will we of necessity have to become more and more human – again, define that – in order to carry on?

This is where the Grand Shift will occur. History and the future will look back upon this time as just that: the Grand Shift from the head ruling things – because, after all, technology comes from the head; it is a product of the mind, whether an atomic bomb to blow us all up or the cure for smallpox and cancer or AIDS – to the heart because the heart is what connects us all; it is the first thing to sound in the womb and the last thing to be silenced with death. How to train the heart so we can use the tools of technology to be of service to one another? Otherwise I think we really will blow ourselves up, whether through weapons or poverty or disease or hate. We will blow ourselves up unless each and every one of us, or at least enough of us, those goodness cells and "X" factor of will, participate in this shift where the mind/ego is put in its most useful place, not on the throne but close at hand. The heart has been exiled far too long and needs to reassume its rightful position as the true ruler of our lives.

March 11, 2007
Thoughts:
Shoulder surgery. Driving to the hospital in the early morning darkness, the rising nervousness just before going under. How many times have I experienced that unique sensation? Upon awakening, re-experiencing the particular and peculiar pain under my left arm, though to a much lesser degree of intensity, that I experienced with the original cancer surgery. Marveling at the body's cellular memory; how that pain-knowledge was still there, even as the physical fault created so long ago was being corrected; the immense knowingness and wisdom of the body existing outside time.

My absolute paralysis with writing. I had thought for Lent I would make writing my spiritual practice. So far, half way through the forty days, I have only looked at my novel manuscript twice – and that not even to reread it – but to look at others' comments and shred previous drafts. This book truly is my cross to bear. It feels like Jacob's wrestling the angel. I may need several reincarnations to get this particular writing mission accomplished.

More conversations with P. I have never seen another human being, except myself perhaps, so struggle with understanding and getting things right. How can I not admire the struggle itself, even though I experience some of the same "been there/done that" reactions? If I can silence the judge in me long enough, then I can find the patience to be more compassionate.

My father. I found a dead mouse in his room last week; had to buy more special medical equipment and supplies; had to replace his bed due to his ruining it with urine, despite rubber pads and diapers. I positively hate that my primary emotional responses around him are fatigue, impatience, frustration, and anger. It almost feels at this point like caring for an animal in a zoo, making sure the messes are cleaned up and the food is regular. The heartbreakingly sad reality is that most zookeepers probably feel greater affection for their charges. What has happened to me?

Had my half-birthday horoscope read and the overarching theme: Trust, trust, trust. Surrender, surrender, surrender. Trust, trust, trust some more. I guess that just about sums it all up: the Alpha and Omega of Everything.

Thinking the other day about something I heard about fasting, keeping the Sabbath, and tithing. If each of us on this planet were to engage in these three activities, in whatever capacity we are able, in whatever format our particular religious tradition encourages, how the world would be transformed. Giving more, consuming less, and keeping quiet, prayerful respect one day a week; if enough individuals were to do these three things, we would be living beyond war already.

A recent email that has helped me through some rough spots:

If you feel oppressed by someone or something, even by some aspect of your own personality that you can't seem to make 'obey' your conscious desires, go to that place. Feel that oppression. And tell yourself, that right there is a lie. Right there where you feel blocked and afraid and needing to do something, but just can't, can't start out...Tell yourself: I am free right here. Right here where I feel so unfree, I am free. Right where I feel frustrated and afraid and I don't know what to do: right there is growth.

March 20, 2007
Three weeks from today I will be in the Holy Land. I need this spiritual pilgrimage more than even I know. When P. offered to buy me a Trio to keep in touch, check my emails, and make and receive calls, I cringed. That is precisely what I do not want to be doing in Jerusalem. I asked P. to come with me but he declined.

I realized the other day that though I talk to God a lot, I do not pray enough, and I am understanding more the difference between these two ways of communicating. And while talking to God is fine, prayer is most important. Yesterday while taking a bath I prayed for the Holy Spirit to come to me.

Come!

This is such a profound mystery to me, and paradox, because while we are loved, we nevertheless are called to walk a certain way because of that love, reflective of the Creator's behavior toward us; to take up our cross and move on, with or without dust on our feet. How I long to balance the forces of darkness and light within me! Two steps forward, one step back. One step forward, two steps back. Endless it feels at times.

Met with a friend for another ritual, more an extended conversation than anything else. And as I considered what I want to unfold, what arena of action I want to concentrate my intention and attention on, it is that of the warrior within me, the warrior archetype in its finest sense; i.e. protector and defender, not as perpetrator of violence and destruction; rather the warrior as committed, strong boundary-keeper, an impregnable container, the holder of the peace and that which is good and worthy. Anything that tends to display or bolster the ego is a destroyer of spiritual integrity, and I feel I am being tamped on and tamped on and tamped on like a blacksmith tempering a steel blade until I get it. That is why the warrior energy feels so important to me now.

Clear intentions.

Firm boundaries.

Unwavering resolve.

Unconcerned about what others think.

Trusting my own integrity.

The Celtic triple goddess Brigit, standing for the light of truth, for what she believes is right, representing all aspects of womanhood: the young virgin, the nurturing mother, the wise crone who holds within the power of her blood, symbolic also of the beginning of Spring. So Bach and Brigit today! All those pagan Celtic and Germanic genes within me somehow firing in a different sort of Rites of Spring.

There is also the sense of the warrior following the command of his/her Lord. That's what I meant earlier about the ego being destructive to the spiritual journey. The warrior is only truly a warrior when personal ego is laid to rest. In a way, one can only be an instrument of truth, a true warrior in the absolute sense, when one comes from a place of profound humility and surrender. Being the recovering pagan and most perfectly imperfect human being that/who I am, this presents quite a challenge. I suppose the good news is that God already knows this about me and keeps tamping and hammering on the steel of my mind and heart anyway, preparing me for a different sort of battle, one which I am only now beginning to comprehend.

Sort of.

Everything else is details. It is, in many ways, a tribute to His/Her patient perseverance and my persistent willful stubbornness that She/He keeps right on tamping, no matter what. I guess I am getting enough metaphorical headaches to finally pay more earnest attention and take the spiritual remedy that has been so consistently offered and yet so consistently denied. Maybe denied is not the right word, rather misunderstood. The ego has a marvelous way of defending itself, but a different kind of warrior is called for now.

April 9, 2007

En route to Tel Aviv, Israel and then onto Jerusalem. It is hard to believe that I will be in that sacred city in less than twelve hours. How long a journey to get there in so many ways! Last night was restless and dream-filled. I even awakened myself with my own groans, afraid I would miss the flight. I am hoping and praying that these next two weeks will bring the clarity I yearn for.

En route, reading Paul Cousineau's *The Art of Pilgrimage*, a most excellent choice for the long plane ride. Some excerpts and quotes to focus me for what lies ahead:

Question: How far does forgiveness reach?

Answer: As far as your prayers allow.

Pilgrims are people in motion who seek completion, or at least a kind of clarity about something in their lives, Goethe's "holy longing" for a deeper quest. And more light. Mine is to hear the voice of commitment to words and language; a pilgrimage to recover that passion and longing within me.

Sculptor Henry Moore on the secret of life:

> The secret of life is to have a task, something you devote your entire life to, something you bring everything to, every minute of the day of your whole life. And the most important thing is – *it must be something you cannot possibly do.*

Hear that, Maurine: something you cannot possibly do! How I need to re-cultivate the art of listening because what goes on inwardly is worthy of my love. I need to value this more. Forget the world and its response. Listen to what you love, Maurine, and what is difficult for you. Dive deep!

An old Hasidic saying:

> Carefully observe the way your heart draws you and then choose that way with all your strength.

Learning once again – and again and again – how to break through the threshold of inertia and resistance. Time is dwindling and time is the enemy of power in *all* things. Mortal, mortal me. How to remove the guardians of habit and routine; those actions and rituals that keep me bound to the ordinary day-to-day of things?

As Cousineau writes, vacations are easy; pilgrimages are different because they invite darkness into our lives. He cautions to not be fooled or seduced by glamour and all that pushes toward that in the world. The word "glamour" is actually an old Scottish word for "spell." How to avoid the illusion? There is a spell of a different sort that needs to be cast now.

The ancient Sanskrit word for chess player is the same as that for pilgrim.

So I ask myself:

What is the next move?

And the move after that?

Embracing the concept of the labyrinth, its trial and ordeal.

My problem is I think I will get through the labyrinth and be done with it, once and for all.

Fallacious thinking.

Life is not linear.

It is cyclical.

Remember that always.

The labyrinth is an initiation to a different realm of consciousness. To get to the secret place that is "the real" within me. And learn to be grateful for the hardships along the way: this is the pilgrim's task.

From the Dalai Lama:

> If you utilize obstacles properly, then they strengthen your courage, and they also give you more intelligence, more wisdom. But if you use them in the wrong way, then you will feel discouraged, failure, depression.

This is not what most of us want to hear precisely because it is so true, an injunction against any and every form of self-pity and why me?

Why not me?

Why not you?

Why not any of us?

It's life.

Pilgrimage is a call to pay close attention to the sacred source of life, what gives life from within. It is about taking time, as Cousineau says, "seriously, elegantly." I like that thought: taking time elegantly, the elegance and eloquence of time.

April 11, 2007
My initial impressions of Jerusalem:
Besieged.
Beleaguered.
Occupied with guns.
Smaller, more compact geographically than I had expected.
Messy, garbage strewn everywhere.
Not particularly friendly.
Actually rather sad.

In my fantasies I had imagined Jerusalem to be a city of light beckoning from the hill, the mecca for so many people over so many centuries. I cannot say that it is a city of much light at all. There actually is a lot of darkness here. I understand why Jesus lamented "Jerusalem, Jerusalem, how I want to take you under my wings as a mother hen her chicks..."

(The next day)
6:00am in the morning as dawn begins with birds voicing their various songs. I've been awake for a while now – the expected result of going to sleep at 9:00pm. I just fixed myself a cup of instant coffee from the St. George College rec room, decaf no less. I must confess I'd give just about anything for a good fix of real caffeine! The local coffee is a dark, murky brew, thick and flavored with spice, cardamom I think, and not bad but nowhere to be found at this time of day by me.

Yesterday we visited a number of sites: the Wailing Wall, the Dome of the Rock and El Aska Mosque, St.

Anne's Church and the pools of Bethesda where Jesus healed, the Lithostratos where he was taunted and tortured by Roman soldiers, the Via Delorosa, and Ecce Homo convent where he received the cross and his crown of thorns. I think the quality that has impressed me the most since being here, over and above the amazing architectural and archaeological richness of this city, is not all the sites and monuments devoted to celebrating Jesus's divinity but how closely connected I feel to his humanity. Walking the streets where he walked; visiting the places where he taught and those where he was hurt. What quiet calmness and courage he must have possessed!

The Western Wall, too, was deeply moving as I prayed with my right hand touching its cool stones. How many prayers have risen to heaven from this spot? And also disturbing as armed guards paraded around the perimeter and excavation workers rattled and riveted around us. Then moving from all that chaos, women ululating, men praying, Bar Mitzvahs happening, jack hammers reverberating through security check points into the peacefulness of El Aska Mosque and the magnificent beauty of the Dome of the Rock.

It is hard to understand all the fighting and animosity over such small pieces of geography, and yet this is a city whose entire history has been one of constant conflict and fighting for territory, control, and ground. There is almost a quality of the absurd about it: "This street is ours, don't come near; that street is yours, stay away; this cemetery is for my people, bury your dead over there," and on and on. It is hard to not sympathize with the Palestinians when one sees how much the Jews have settled on and confiscated their lands, whatever the Bible says about it being "theirs."

What is theirs?

It is God's.

It is Everybody's and it is Nobody's.

One wonders if there ever will be a peaceful solution to this city and its many problems. It is as if blood, killing, and hatred have seeped into its very stones. Where can the healing come from if not from the hearts of the people themselves?

Today we are to visit Bethlehem and must take our passports with us in order to get in and out of the city. What madness is this? Or the twenty-seven foot concrete wall built around parts of Jerusalem to keep the "other" out. One would think the brutal lessons of the Holocaust and how not to treat the "other" would have rendered such separatist actions impossible, unthinkable but alas, no. In some twisted, perverted way it is as if the Jews are acting out on the Palestinians, to a far lesser degree of course, what was done to them in Europe by Hitler only decades ago. But the impulse behind these actions, i.e. revulsion over what is perceived as different, is the same.

For all its religious richness, Jerusalem is a sad, broken city – a testament to man's territoriality and need to be right rather than kind.

****

Finished reading a book entitled *The Pagan Christ* by Tom Harpur. I am not unaware of the irony of my reading this while on a pilgrimage in the Holy Land.

The author presents a compelling case for de-historizing Jesus and re-mythologizing the Christos archetype. Harper says early Christianity was never meant to be taken literally but was part of a long tradition of the ancient Mystery Schools and that Jesus was an updated version of this tradition. It was the Church Fathers of the 3rd and 4th centuries, wanting to consolidate their power and control over the illiterate masses, who destroyed much of the esoteric literature upon which the "new" religion of

Christianity was based, making it into a literal story rather than a symbolic one of spirit entering flesh and being renewed. Because it is all about awakening to the Christ spirit within, not about believing in a literal, historical God/man in the person of Jesus. An apt point:

> [It] is not that those ancient people told literal stories and we are now smart enough to take them symbolically but that they told them symbolically and we are now dumb enough to take them literally. (John Dominic Crossan, *Who is Jesus?*)

The central truth of human experience which Christianity alludes to, but which predates Christianity by thousands of years, is that we are embodied spirit, spirit housed within matter and destined for eternity through the love of God. Christianity, as opposed to what Harpur calls Christianism, is about recognizing the power of the Christ energy to quiet our instinctual natures. What he calls Christianism is taking literally (virgin birth, Jesus as the only Son of God, etc.) what was meant to be understood symbolically; i.e. the idea that physical birth must be followed by spiritual birth, the "birth from Above" that Jesus talked about. The early Church simply came along and destroyed Christianity's links to its Pagan roots in order to strengthen its power.

The whole point of early Christianity was to recognize the divine presence within and to recognize that divine presence in others. If you have this perception of reality, you cannot harm the "other" or allow the other to suffer injustice because you recognize there is a spark of divinity in that person, too. Christianity is not about being "rescued" by Jesus but about internal transformation. A good point along this line by Carl Jung:

If I accept the fact that a god is absolute and beyond all human experience, he leaves me cold. But if I know, on the other hand, that God is a mighty activity within my own soul, at once I must concern myself with him.

Indeed, a mighty activity within one's own soul. It is not about worshipping Jesus – even he said only God was good – but to *become* more like Jesus and if he is a god, and the only Son of God, how can this be accomplished? It is a contradiction in terms.

And as I sit here in this city where the three major monotheistic religions battle for the literal rightness of each of their causes and have been so battling for centuries, one understands completely why this inner transformation, this personal experience of the divine, as opposed to following religious dogma, is the only thing that will save us from ourselves and each other.

April 16, 2007

More sites visited:

The Garden of Gethsemane with its ancient olive trees, trunks thick and gnarled. Our guide informed us that the roots of these trees date back to the time of Jesus, over two thousands years old.

The Rock of Agony inside the Church at the Garden; a slab of stone surrounded by a cast-iron crown of thorns where Jesus prayed and wept for his cup to be taken from him.

The magnificent acoustics of the Church of St. Anne where the healing pools of Bethesda are located. Even our poor, off-key singing could not obliterate the beautiful sounds and over-tones. I could imagine with what splendor voices doing chants would fill that space. Music truly is of the Divine.

On our day trip to Bethlehem, we visited some small caves in the sloping hills surrounding the area, near the Church of the Nativity, catacomb-like hollows in the rocks where people lived and in which Jesus most likely was born. But there is a beautiful, mirrored star on the floor of a grotto in the Church of the Nativity to commemorate the star the shepherds allegedly followed. Hundreds of people were waiting in line to descend into the grotto, fall to their knees, and kiss that star.

Bethlehem itself is a walled city, a prison-like fortress cut off from the outside world. The people who live inside are required to have special passes to get in and out while we pilgrims from half-way around the world can come and go with relative ease. The irony that as one approaches, there is a sign about peace sponsored by the Israeli Ministry of Tourism painted in large, colorful letters on the outside of the wall.

And sadder still, on the inside, the graffiti: To Exist is to Resist. Protestations of Peace and Conflict, Conflict and Peace side by side; the insane contradiction as the guards man their guns and barbed wire is evident everywhere. The Palestinians of Bethlehem are for all intents and purposes under house arrest. There is sixty percent unemployment and poverty is rising. The streets have the feeling of a ghost town.

****

Other books brought along for this journey (particularly Goldsmith's *Practicing the Presence* and *The Infinite Way)* have stirred a lot inside me, especially the concept of duality and non-duality, the great theme of Genesis. While an objective reality, duality is also a choice we make about how we engage with reality. Because our first reality, our primary state of being is union when we

269

walked in harmony with God; so the grand choice before us all is between union and non-union.

Goldsmith says if we see God as the only Cause and Source, duality loses its power. It is all about being the conduit for things, not the recipient of things; to be a conduit of consciousness through which the Infinite Good flows to others. I know this is true; what I do not know, what I have not yet been able to achieve is making this reality stick for more than a nanosecond. As Goldsmith says in all seriousness: "You may say that [living in non-dual reality] is hard work, but it is much harder than you think."

No shit!

Like I said: a very fallen angel. I still look to the outside world for confirmation, feedback, and reward. We live in a culture that constantly and consistently focuses on what we do not have or what we need to get. Such longing, longing, longing always for something other. For the richest, most materially well off country in the world, one cannot underestimate the vast unhappiness of many Americans today.

All of this as a reminder that no good can come *to* me but good must flow *from* me. It is all about giving, never about receiving. My problem, of course, my nemesis is that I expect to receive something back. But that's not the way this principle works, and I will keep getting this lesson over and over again until I get it. *Until I get it!* Light only gives; it only expresses itself. From the point of humanhood and duality hard, hard, hard. From the point of union with Grace, the easiest thing in the world.

How do I train myself to withdraw the use of all force and opposition, physically and especially mentally, from the world? This is the only road to peace. As long as I am concerned with external forms and results, I will miss the mark (sin). Goldsmith believes the question of whether we are serving God or results must be addressed in order to deepen spiritually. Me: I still exist in the Land of Results, and one of the principle keys to spiritual development is to get rid of wanting results.

Wanting to get something.

Wanting to acquire something.

Wanting to achieve something.

Otherwise it is not about love but about trade and bartering. Goldsmith says true spiritual growth begins when you can train yourself to have no opinion whatsoever other than God Is. A major signpost in the spiritual journey is learning to transcend the desire to tell God anything or ask God for anything. I'm still working on that one.

Goldsmith emphasizes the necessity of relinquishing all censure, condemnation, and labeling of things as good or bad. The only thing you can know about God is that God Is. Period. Anything else is a thought or a concept about God and therefore limiting. There is no magic formula or prayer to achieve anything because all is already present in the spiritual realm. Nothing is being withheld from us; all that God is flows constantly to us. Anything else implies a lack of faith in the grace and abundance of God. Our supply or achievement is not dependent upon us and what we do but rather upon our connection to the divine vine. This is why we keep getting so screwed up because we pray for specific outcomes in the material world rather than focusing on our continuing connection to Spirit.

We cannot ask Spirit for material outcomes, only for spiritual ones. Render unto Caesar what is Caesar's (the material world) and unto God, God's (the spiritual).

The invisible vine, the Father, the Creative Principle, our Spiritual Mother, whatever label you want to give IT is continually supplying us with what we need for our unfolding. That is His/Her nature; He/She cannot do otherwise. So every time you return to the material stage of consciousness, you will be purged again and again.

And again.

And again.

Ah, me…

Abundant supply means giving, not getting – the exact opposite of what most of us think.

Getting = matter, flesh.

Giving = spirit.

It is not even rocket science; it is about training the mind how to think – or not to think as the case may be. You will demonstrate what you have in your consciousness; you will not demonstrate something separate from that. It is like learning how to connect with our own Spiritual Underground.

Keys to this journey:

Utter no need.

Do not tell God what to do.

Do not try to accomplish or acquire any outcome.

God is sufficient in all things.

The only real prayers are:

Thy Will Be Done.

I Rest in Thee.

Thank You.

April 19, 2007

Pilgerhaus, The Galilee.

6:30am in the morning as I sit by the Sea of Galilee and listen to the waves greet the shore. The birds welcome the day and one another with chants and song – if not a symphony, at least delightful chamber music. The beauty of this place and this area is compelling. I could learn to love Israel from this one spot alone.

It has been a busy few days: a trip to the ancient fortress of Masada where the last of the Jewish revolt was crushed by the Romans in 73CE. Yesterday we visited Caesarea Maritime with its ancient theater and Hippodrome, along with a smaller Crusader-built fort with protective moat. Even if one were to remove the spiritual and religious components from this country, the archaeological riches would keep any traveler enthralled.

Also a stop by the Dead Sea where some of the more adventurous in our group donned suits and walked in. Alas, I didn't bring one. The horrible sores I developed from a recent treatment to heal irradiated skin precluded my going in. Honestly, I look as if I have leprosy and have had to wear a scarf throughout the entire trip to keep people from staring and exclaiming in hardly masked revulsion, "Oh, my God! What is *that*?!"

But the moment so far that has been the most compelling for me, indeed surprised me, was what I felt at the Church of the Holy Sepulcher, the unexpected, spontaneous response that occurred there.

It is easy to fall into a skeptical, perhaps even cynical view about many of the things one sees around the "industry" of Jesus in the Holy Land; all the vendors hawking their wares from crosses and rosaries and icons to the cheesiest of cheesy Jesus junk. Then there is that segment of pilgrims who border on the superstitious; if I can just touch this, if I can only place my cross or icon or scarf where Jesus walked or preached or was buried I will somehow garner his mystical powers.

I was wandering around the crowds, watching and taking some pictures – yes, just like all the other idolaters – when several members of my group invited me to join them in a line to enter the place where Jesus was said to be resurrected. This particular area of the Holy Sepulcher is overseen by the Greek Orthodox Church as the church itself is divided up between various sects and denominations, even on the roof above the sanctuary where the Ethiopians pray. I joined my friends and waited, not thinking much about it; just another site on The Jesus Tour.

There are two chambers to this shrine: the outer chamber where the angel allegedly appeared to Mary Magdalene and the inner sanctum where the Resurrection occurred. As I entered the first space, I didn't feel much of anything. But as I entered the second, smaller chamber, the place where Jesus is said to have risen, I was absolutely overpowered by the sheer transcendent holiness of the place. The only possible response was dropping to my knees.

Holy. Holy. Holy.

The interior of that space was *so* holy. One could literally feel the sensation of being resurrected within oneself, of being drawn upward. It was visceral and real, simply staggering. That, along with the experience of utterly transcendent beauty. You could literally touch the beauty, or rather be touched by it. Beauty and light. I was on my knees before I knew what was happening. I looked above to the silver Greek Orthodox ornaments hanging overhead. You could feel the sensation of being pulled upward, upward, upward. It was absolutely stunning, even the more so because I had no expectations of anything happening. The exact opposite in fact. I was simply one of many people being shepherded into and out of the site. A priest manning the sanctuary made sure people entered and left promptly, like someone at a fair; you've had your two minutes idea, now time to get off the ride.

I came out of the space crying. I am still trying to figure out what happened because it is outside my ability to articulate in language. It was simply awesome and awe inspiring, beyond measure and time.

April 21, 2007

Back in Jerusalem after three days in the Galilee region. The call to Muslim prayers sounds from the nearby mosque. Such a sad, mournful cry it feels to me.

Yesterday I do believe was the finest day of our sojourn thus far. We started out in the morning at a leisurely pace and went to the Church of the Beatitudes, which is located not far from the place where we are staying. After wandering around the church itself, our group split off from the crowd and walked across the fields adjacent to the ridge overlooking the Sea of Galilee. This we did single file and in silence, taking in the beauty of nature, the early morning sunshine, its warmth, the sounds of birds and plants rustling in the soft breezes. After thirty minutes or so we stopped and read from the Sermon on the Mount. One can certainly understand why Jesus drew upon the lessons of nature the way he did, standing in a field surrounded by flowers and wheat. The view of the entire valley was panoramic, spectacular.

From there we went down to the Sea of Galilee for a boat ride. What would it have felt like to be a fisherman in Jesus' time? At one point the boat's captain turned off the motor and we drifted for several minutes on the lake, again in silence, feeling the gentle rocking of the boat and water softly lapping at its sides. I was asked to read from the Gospel of Matthew, chapter 14 ("Fear not! I am with you.") followed by a lunch of fried tilapia called by the locals "Peter's Fish." Of course.

Then we moved on to Capernaum where Jesus lived in a community of approximately 1000. We wandered around Capernaum for an hour or so and then visited the church where Jesus supposedly appointed Peter as the keeper of the Kingdom. This is the site where Jesus, after his resurrection, appeared on the beach before Peter and some of the disciples, cooked them breakfast, and admonished Peter to "feed my sheep." In earlier times, this church was called the Church of the Charcoal. There is something so endearing to me about that: Jesus throwing some fish on the "barby" for his friends.

Our final stop for the day was at the Church of the Miracle of the Multiplication of the Loaves and Fishes. How's that for a name! I have to admit, by this time I was churched out, so I wandered into the gift store where I discovered a marvelous book: 2000 years of history about pilgrimages to the Holy Land using "faux" newspaper headlines plus some exquisite art to chronicle the richness of the history here.

Angel Surprises Mary With Good News!

Jesus Arrested Without Bail!

Etc.

Honestly, it was the most wonderful juxtaposition of cheesy kitsch and beautiful art, so naturally I couldn't resist. John Lennon may have said, "It's all show biz," but I think it is just as likely to be, "Buy this, my friend, and you'll be happy."

My rector approached me and another member of our group to lead a communion service after our return. Because I have been so impressed by the wind through the various trees and palms around where we are staying, I knew exactly what Gospel verse I wanted to read: John chapter 3, Jesus's conversation with Nicodemus about being born from above by the winds of spirit. We held the service outside by the lake in a small clearing around 5:30pm in the afternoon.

As I read the verse, the breezes came up through the small area where the group of us stood as if on cue. And as the gentle breezes continued to move, we went into a silent mediation about what this trip has meant to each of us. The moment could not have been more magical: the breezes, the backdrop against the Galilean Sea, the sun lowering on the horizon, the sound of the water against the shore. It was evident as we shared the Eucharist that everyone had been profoundly moved.

This ceremony was followed by a round of drinks, much laughter and more laughter over dinner. I have been around more laughter on this trip and experienced more laughter over the past two weeks than I have in the previous year or so. There may be a balm in Gilead, but there is absolutely without any shadow of a doubt a healing balm in laughter. It has nourished my soul like an oasis in the desert.

Finally, to top the day off, as if it could have been any better, we met in the small chapel for Compline. One of the young women in our group graced us with her beautiful voice, singing several hymns a cappella. Afterwards we held hands in the candlelight. Such loving people, just feeling the simplicity and the sincerity of their love.

When I got back to my room I spontaneously burst into tears. I had been so touched by the day. Such a perfect day! Such a perfect, perfect day! A day couldn't possibly be any better than this day had been. I thought about the Native American saying, something to the effect, "This is a good day to die." It was a good Friday indeed.

God is.
God is.
God is.
God is.

Tomorrow we arise at 5:00am to walk the Stations of the Cross. And Monday is our last day before flying home.

April 22, 2007
Midnight, en route back to LA. Eleven and a half hours from Tel Aviv to Newark, a three hour stop-over, then another five and a half hours back to our final

destination. All in all, a marathon twenty-four hours in transit. Catching up with the last bits of our trip:

On Sunday we arose at 5:00am to walk the Stations of the Cross through the Old City of Jerusalem while the streets were deserted. It was wonderful having the walkways to ourselves and watch the day break. As we were passing the various stations and reading from a small booklet our guide had given us, it was positively uncanny how what each of us read fit the individual reading it to a "t."

One gentleman read about praying for those in prison and those accused unjustly of crime. His job? Chaplain at high security lockdown in the Twin Towers jail in LA.

Another woman read about mothers and to pray for those who have lost their children, either literally or metaphorically. She had a son who died of the same cancer I had when he was not even twenty-one, and she felt deep concern for her daughter and the challenges she now faces at mid-life.

As I was reading about how pilgrims frequently stop, kneel, and make the sign of the cross as they see people walking the stations, I swear to God the words were barely out of my mouth before a man fell to his knees right next to me, made the sign of the cross, and kissed the crucifix hanging around his neck. When I asked one of group members if he had seen the same thing, he nodded a vigorous "yes!" And I know the stranger hadn't heard me because I had been speaking very softly. It was much more than any serendipitous coincidence. Synchronicity doesn't even being to explain the perfect connection between words being spoken and the person speaking them. And we all had selected our individual parts and stations at random! No one had even seen the little pamphlet beforehand.

We ended our walk at the Church of the Holy Sepulcher. I had such a profound experience the first time I was there that a part of me was reluctant to go in again. What if I didn't feel the same transcendence and beauty? What if I was not moved the way I had been before? I hesitated about going back into the part of the sanctuary where the angel appeared before Mary (before me?) and into the inner chamber itself.

But I was spared the "what if?" That area of the Sepulcher was not yet open to the public when our walk ended. It was still too early in the day and the priests were moving around chairs and carpets and lighting candles "getting ready for business," so I was allowed to keep my previous experience intact. I smiled inwardly to myself, knowing that I had been willing to go into the chamber again and possibly have a most mundane reaction compared the first, or no reaction at all. But this I was spared.

After the above, our remaining time in Jerusalem was filled with cramming in as many activities as we could. I visited the Citadel of David where our guide talked non-stop for over an hour about the history of the land from the Canaanite Period to the present day, not once coming up for air. It was impressive. I walked along the ramparts surrounding the Old City while discussing current issues in religion and spirituality. I visited the Jewish Quarter again but unfortunately the Wailing Wall was off limits due to Holocaust Memorial Day and Israeli Independence Day. I had lunch at the King David Hotel, and on our way out of town as we headed toward Tel Aviv, we had the privilege of celebrating a private Eucharist at the 12th century Crusader Church in Abu Gosch. Our rector gave a beautiful homily about what it means to be a pilgrim, how we can bring a pilgrim mentality, even more a pilgrim spirituality, back with us to LA. He gave us each a personal blessing, laying his hands on our heads and anointing us with oil. I wish I could remember what he said to me, something about the Holy Spirit. It was as if I went into some sort of trance. I know it felt important and I know I was moved. This was followed by a beautiful Vesper service conducted in French song. I honestly do not know how we could have done one thing more in the time we had.

How can I be more attentive to this gift of spirit I have been blessed with? How to keep this pilgrim energy moving back in LA?

PART III
TO BE CONTINUED...
(Excerpts from Journals 100 – 106)

Without risk, faith if impossible. Soren Kierkegaard

April 27, 2007

I know my trip to Israel has affected me profoundly but I don't quite know how. It is as if my DNA has been altered; as if I am being reorganized from the inside out. A need for more prayer, certainly. A need for more regular prayer, certainly. I keep repeating the mantra "God is" over and over again. It is changing my perception and apperception of reality. Like *The Way of the Pilgrim* repeating the Jesus prayer, I do believe if I can continue to say "God is," I will get to the place internally I need to be.

I have been thinking more and more about Goldsmith's differentiation between the world of trade and the world of love. As he says: If you do anything that has a desire for any reward, recompense, or recognition, it is trade, not love; love has no desire for any return. It makes me realize how much I have been living in the world of trade rather than the world of love despite my sincere efforts.

Case in point: I was rummaging around my garage the other day, looking for I don't know what, when I discovered that some of the boxes of books I had stored in the back were water damaged and infested with termites. All that time, effort, money, organization, marketing, website agonies, typing, sitting, typing, editing – all that only to become food for termites. As I told FS, it is hard for me to believe that God really thinks that this is the best plan for my books. He nodded his head in agreement.

Prior to my trip, this would have rendered me mildly depressed. Not much, but enough to notice. I had a different response. I can still do something so they will not be termite fodder. I can give them away. I can let go of all that those boxes represent to me and simply be generous. I can surrender *my* plans, *my* ideas, *my* sense of right and wrong, *my* feelings, *my* pride – anything and everything that has to do with expectations of any kind – and let them go in order to allow life to unfold as it will. And to trust that it will unfold in a way that is better, indeed much better, than the one I could imagine or orchestrate on my own. I need to get out of the world of commerce and bartering and into the world of love.

Perhaps everything needs to be cleared out to make space for what is yet to come. I feel I am being trained to become a scribe to the voice within, that infinitesimal part of God that is uniquely me. It is hard to explain. The only thing that I do know is that I feel better, lighter, freer, more laughter in my life, not so sober and somber anymore, things feeling simpler, even though the external world appears as mindless, threatening, and chaotic as ever.

I am connecting to the Great Love within. It is all about radiating this Great Love, being a conduit for its Presence. We all have it; it's just that most of us either do not know it or do not believe in it or do not take the time to get better acquainted with it. Yet how different each of us and the world would be if we did!

So I am learning to be more generous.

I am learning to give away books without whining.

I am learning to silence that "yes, but…" voice.

I am learning to be more observant of the subtle ways in which Spirit moves.

I am learning to trust in a different way.

Previously, so much of the trusting I engaged in still rested on my own effort and efforting. The trust and trusting I now am learning are different. While they require attention and obedience, which I am both good at and not good at, they do not mandate so much efforting. Efforting is still a form of control; all efforting must stop! I think God is systematically stripping me of every last vestige of control around my work, perhaps even my life. The difference for me now is that I do not experience this stripping away as a failure or punishment. It has become a form of blessing; I think I'm finally getting it.

One never knows the outcome of anything; one can only engage in each act with love and perseverance, but perseverance without efforting. This surrendering of self to Spirit is quite something. Incipient joy in each moment begins to bloom.

Then last night, this dream:

I am in a house with some other people. It is nighttime and we are being attacked, threatened by two large snakes: one is a luminous, white cobra inside the house and the other is a gigantic python, more like a leviathan, dappled and colored, in the crawl space underneath. I, along with the others, but mostly me, work to defend the house. At one point, I am bitten by the white cobra; I watch its fangs go into my arm. After the cobra bites me, it dies. One of the people with me, a young woman, comes up to me and says, "You must be very mystical to not die from the cobra's bite."

I reply: "Let us put this house in order!"

****

Another check in with my Guide:

> ...but the Paraclete, the Holy Spirit, whom the Father will send in my name, will teach you everything and remind you of all I have said to you. (John 14:26)

Gracious Spirit:

It has been nearly four months since I came before you. Something happened to me in the Holy Land that I do not fully understand but a shift has occurred. What now?

Ground yourself completely in the day-to-day of things. Solitude and quiet are essential. Do not be deceived, in whatever manner, even for a so-called "good" cause, to relinquish these aspects of your life. The time you have allotted to you is sacred – indeed, all time is sacred – but you are ready now to go deeper. You must trust this going deeper. Embrace and love each moment. This is the true secret of life.

That is not to say that devotion and discipline are not required, but it is love that must guide you. It is the time, how do you say, to "get cracking." You honor yourself enough to feel gratitude, not guilt. You have by and large silenced the voice that unsettles you, that wonders "why this? Why that? What now?" Even why are the books being eaten by termites? You took something that would have upset you in the past and changed it into something positive. You became more generous. You expressed your faith in God. It is resurrection thinking. This is what you experienced in the Holy Land: resurrection thinking.

This is key to your progress. You already feel the shift and what you took away with you will continue to deepen. Humans can see only a small arc of the infinitely larger stream of consciousness. Honor your depth now in a way you have not before because you either felt unworthy or were not encouraged to do so. This sort of courage cannot come from the world. It can only come from within your own heart.

Your desire to find sanctuary away from the hubbub of the city is good. Placing yourself in the rhythms of nature will allow you to continue the process of deepening. Take all the tools you have learned up to this point and be selfish enough and courageous enough to use them. They are blessings for you to bestow upon you. Embrace them as fully as you can. Immerse yourself deeply into each day. This can be done with gentleness and humor, not efforting.

Remember to enjoy and have no thought to outcomes. You see that all manner of things will be well if you trust.

June 8, 2007
Gracious Spirit:
You spoke to me of solitude and how to guard this. I simply do not know how to be in the world and in relationships and yet protect the space and time necessary to do the work You tell me I need to do, indeed now am "ready" for, though today I feel anything but ready.

Distractions. Your mind is racing and you have difficulty focusing on what is necessary. There is a compulsion to do things, and yes there are actions that need to be taken, but the fountainhead from which these actions must arise is the well of silence within. The most critical components for you are silence and quiet. They are the only way for you to stay connected and you need to stay as connected to your source as possible. Stay connected to the quiet at the center of your being. This will feed you with the calmness you need to address the challenges in your life. It is the calmness stemming from silence that will be the true healing agent for you at this time.

You have faced much over the last few years. Are you not stronger precisely because of your efforts, sporadic as they sometimes are, to return to the place of silence and solitude within? It is the way to healing, healing of self and healing of others. Remember that as chaos unfolds around you, it nevertheless presents an opportunity for you to dip into the well. Trust the silence and solitude. That is not to say that you may not need to remove yourself time to time from others, even those you love and care for. Jesus did this, and it is well to emulate his actions. But Jesus walked among his brothers and sisters and still maintained a well-spring within of peacefulness, solitude, and calm. This was as much a part of his true teachings, his Mastery as the words he spoke. Pay attention.

All this is unfolding for a reason, part of a larger plan. You are being winnowed. And it remains your choice, as always, to pay attention or not. This alertness can only realize itself if you take the time to be silent and alone. This does not mean away somewhere physically, though this is not a bad thing and may yet present itself to you. It is much more about being able to go into your Father's house internally to be nourished and renewed. This can be achieved as easily and as simply as taking a few breaths and refocusing yourself on the source of all power.

June 9, 2007

And what happens the very next day? Playing with my oracle cards I drew Sige, the goddess of quiet time. I must confess I have never heard of her before. She is the Gnostic goddess considered to be the Great Silence or Void from which all creation sprang and the mother of Sophia (Wisdom). Sige counsels me to:

Quiet the mind.

Breathe.

Go into the space of silence within, that place of peace where the world cannot enter.

Spend time alone.

Do not attempt making decisions.

Action will be required soon enough but for now, be quiet and still and rest.

Always good advice, anytime, anywhere. Never avoid a good opportunity to shut up.

Shhh....

It has been a difficult week. My entire body hurts – my shoulder where the surgery was; my knee where surgery may be required. I have had a constant ringing (tinnitus) in my ears for the past three days which, while not painful, is driving me absolutely crazy.

Crazy!

Not to mention Dad threw a temper tantrum on Father's Day when I arrived ten minutes late with the family. The classical litany/barrage began:

"You're always late!"

"Can't you get anywhere on time!"

"Why didn't you take the freeway?"

"You know you should take the freeway!"

"Why don't you do what I tell you!"

And on it went. It was the quintessential story of my life, played out in horrible, graphic relief before P. and the children. I have never seen P. so angry with my dad in my life – ever! He usually defends Bill; it's *I* who have the problem. Finally, he saw what I have been trying to convey to him these many years about my childhood and upbringing. And I hurt all over and am no longer young with whistling and ringing in my ears.

I watch my daughter who is at the beginning of the curve leading to the height of her sense of self-empowerment. Traveling now in Buenos Aires on prize money she won for her senior thesis, she also just received news of being accepted for a Fulbright scholarship in Italy. Her unspoken words: I will *never* end up like you! I said the same thing myself when I was her age and look at me now.

Talk about the pull of inertia!

Talk about the forces of entropy!

Talk about needing Sige!

And yet I am told by others what a saint I am and how grace-filled I am and how the Holy Spirit speaks to me. But I sure as hell don't feel any of that today. Why am I almost congenitally unable to put myself first? Even more than that: to put the artistic life first? The artistic life is not about helping or being of service, though it might have that impact on others as a secondary or tertiary result. The artistic life is about BEING, about embracing one's life and being to the fullest; indeed, delighting in that joyously and whole-heartedly, or with suffering if need be. But it is first and foremost about being.

It is a kind of selfishness I do not have with any sustained consistency. And life is over before we can ask "what happened?" Can I possibly learn how to be of service to myself? Right now I just want to learn how to be quiet and take some tap dancing lessons.

Something I read recently from Judy Chicago:

> How many people in this world can stand up to the consistent rejection male culture subjects women to?...How many women are willing to face rejection and rejection and rejection and rejection and rejection and rejection and rejection and still insist on exposing their femaleness? (Female Rejection Drawing, 1974)

The key word here is rejection. If one operates from a sense of joy and groundedness, rejection is a moot point. I understand, of course, what Chicago is saying and as a woman I relate. On the superficial level all the rejection of work and effort, but on a much deeper level, at least for me, it is about participating in the rejection of my own femaleness; of not being valued and my own complicity in carrying on this pattern.

An equation for this riddle:

Individual context + compassion (especially for oneself) bring forth the power of artistry and miracles, which in turn leads us deeper into the mystery of life and self. It is this deeper mystery I wish to explore and give my heart to.

July 1, 2007

Went to see a lawyer the other day to talk with him about drawing up a living trust for my children and it brought up the issue of my parents' estate, all the monies they have given my brother over the years. Even if I count all the money Mom and Dad have gifted me AND all the money they have given their four grandchildren, it still doesn't come close to what my brother has received. The extent of the discrepancy at this point is over $100,000 and the lawyer said that unless my father stipulates his wishes in writing as a codicil to his will, I am basically shit out of luck. The lawyer said it has been his experience that once the parent dies, that's it. All bets are off. Get it in writing.

The lawyer said the only thing he could do at this point is talk to Dad in person to see if, in fact, his wishes are for me to receive an equal share and if Dad is mentally competent enough to know what the lawyer is talking about. And at this point, even I know this is a big "if." Plus the lawyer is going on vacation for two weeks and cannot see my father until after his return, and Dad could keel over any moment, this we all know.

All this has brought up so many feelings of anger and injustice and how we women just seem to get the shaft so much of the time. This situation with my family of origin has also rekindled many of the negative feelings I had with P. around the marriage contract and what I walked away with after twenty-one years of marriage, the disparity of it all in light of P.'s wealth, even though we had a "deal." And yes, I signed on to it, yet I have to confess that I have been surprised how raw a part of me still is over that – and only myself to blame.

And isn't it ironic that P. has been encouraging me to fight my brother on what I deserve and am owed from my parents' estate but he certainly did not want any lawyers involved in our divorce mediation. What is the difference, in principle at least? The difference is that when it is other people's money, not P.'s, I need to fight to "protect my rights and interests." But when it is P.'s money, well we had an agreement, didn't we, and an agreement is an agreement. Am I the only one to see the contradiction here? Okay to fight brother but not ex-husband?

So here is the current geography of the relationships with the men in my life:

A father who is hanging on with a tenacity that is formidable. Then there is P., trying so hard, loving me so much, and all I want is to be by myself, at least part of the time, and a brother who is far away. I look out at this personal geography and then I look at the geopolitical situation in the world and it is hard not to come to the conclusion that it is the men, by and large, who have really fucked things up. That is not to say that we women would do any better if we had the "power," which ultimately we do, it's just a different kind, but I would sure as hell like to see how things might be different if we ladies were more in charge. And the mythology, or propaganda, that we are the weaker sex?

I have come to a complete halt doing anything. There is something almost arrogant about trying to change or better the world, and arrogance and self-righteousness, whether from the right or the left, however well-intentioned, simply will not work, will not bring about the massive systemic changes that need to occur in order to shift the world to a new paradigm. Touching individual minds and hearts is important, worthy, laudable, yes. But the reality is that the vast majority of humanity hasn't a clue and couldn't care less, and that's just the way it is.

Period. The only way things will change for lasting impact is:

- Changing how we allocate our resources, especially money for weapons.
- Having the media transform the way they present the world.
- Taking better care of the world's children; they alone represent hope.
- If you are living in poverty, do the best that you can to stay alive.
- If you are not living in poverty, help those who are in whatever way you can.
- Learn how to listen more and talk less (myself included).
- When choosing between being right and being kind, choose kindness. Always.

That's it. That's my list of Things to Do to Help the Planet through the birth canal we presently are in. Simple and to-the-point. I don't know. I feel as if I have done a complete 180 on just about everything. Where is the line between trying to manipulate reality (control) and acting with quiet awareness (collaboration)? Manipulation is still manipulation, regardless what end of the spectrum you're coming from. And how do we avoid our own vanity in the process? How do I? How do we learn to act with humility rather than veiled or not-so-veiled self-aggrandizement?

Me, I'm still working on that one.

Rousing words indeed and variations on a theme of social consciousness that has guided me for decades. But I have come to understand that the only change I can make involves me; I cannot expect this of others because that denies the other his or her freedom of choice, even to be a jerk. I only need to embody the change I want to see in the world. If I can do this, I have accomplished my job, my task on this planet. Something that simple and yet that profound would change the world. What a concept tending to one's own garden!

July 8, 2007

I was thinking the other day about how unlucky I have been in my career, and I found myself immediately reacting: you ingrate! You bloody idiot! How dare you! How lucky can one person be!

If I had been born in 1940, I would be dead because at that time a diagnosis of Hodgkin's disease was a death warrant, incurable. Even being born in 1950, if the doctors had not discovered the tumor soon enough, I would be dead. If I didn't have health insurance, I would be dead. If I weren't married to P., who has the money to pay for these things, I would be dead. If I lived in any number of places in the world that don't have the doctors or medical facilities and technical sophistication to deal with my condition, I would be dead. If I hadn't awakened at 4:00am in the morning to the voice activated fire alarm in 1992, my entire family and I would be dead. If I hadn't been persistent over a period of months trying to find out what was going on with the sound inside my head, I could be dead or at least incapacitated.

How goddamn lucky can you get!?! You want to define "luck" as selling books? What are you thinking!?! Are you bleeding mad!?

Probably.

That, and an awareness of all the beauty around me, even in LA. The other afternoon I was sitting on my front porch, just feeling the gentle breezes and watching the clouds move overhead. I spent nearly a half-hour watching the play of it all as it passed before me eyes. It felt as if there might even be the possibility of a surprise summer storm. Just the feeling in the air, the special light and all the clouds on the march, a moment of such beauty, so freely given. Just there.

And here I am most of the time with my head up my ass wanting things *my* way. I do have a lot to learn. No, that's not it. I need to implement what I have learned with greater consistency. I need to put it more into practice and celebrate the good fortune I *do* have. Gratitude is something this human is not good at, and yet it is also an attitude that transforms our lives when we engage in it.

Like I said: How lucky can one single human being be?

July 16, 2007

Some thoughts that have been gnawing at me from a book I read recently about death (*Escape from Evil* by Ernest Becker), a topic we Americans, being death phobic, assiduously avoid, and how this relates to war.

Becker's primary thesis is that most, if not all, evil in the world stems from our trying to escape the "evil" of our own mortality. All other animals just go about their business of eating, pooping, copulating, and dying but in our desire to avoid the inevitability of death, we humans have wreaked havoc on the planet.

Primitive man did not need missile launchers; he had sacrificial mounds instead. Leave the sophisticated missile launchers to us moderns. And the accompanying irony, of course, that such efforts to avoid mass death – the idea that we're protecting ourselves with these weapons – actually end up creating the likelihood of more death occurring, all because of our desire to feel "safe."

Talk about the Fall! From being a "primitive" who engaged in a kind of mystical participation with nature to a consumer of TV, toothpaste, and soap. To go from being a sharer of goods within a group to being dependent on the redistribution of goods from outside. How do we get back a sense of authority within ourselves rather than trying to "prove" ourselves by projecting everything out onto the world, especially the fear of death? This is one of the core messages of Jesus' ministry: *take back your power.* Or to put it another way: if you're going to give your power away, give it to God and God alone. Ultimately who cares if I prove my point of view to you or you prove yours to me? We're both going to die anyway. That single bit of knowledge might allow us, if not to get over ourselves completely, at least to put things more in perspective and regain a sense of connectedness.

How very different primitive man's relationship was to the cosmos! We cannot begin to fathom it from our modern perspective. Primitive man observed a rhythm to things: day and night; sun and moon; seasons and cycles – there was no time being counted or ticking away on watches, calendars, clocks, or computers. But when the concept of time entered human consciousness, we changed. This speaks to the idea that once we become aware of time, we experience a sense of existential dread and guilt. And this makes us want to control and manipulate reality so that we can somehow fool ourselves into believing we won't die.

Becker believes most of the misery on our planet stems from our trying to avoid this fact. What is going on in the world today, particularly with the war in Iraq and terrorists and violence, is related I think to this process. Instead of isolated sacrifices on behalf of a fearful tribe, larger and larger numbers of people are being co-opted into what Becker calls the "dreadful ceremony" of war.

The logic, or illogic, goes something like this:

The more bodies that are piled up from the other side, the more money I have, the more I can beat or at least manipulate fate (death), the better able I will be to survive. Sacrificing others for an idea, or economic gain or war, all fuels the idea of providing the individual with a false sense of security that death won't really happen. No wonder that as a species we appear addicted to war: the paradox of trying to ward off our own death by heaping death upon others. War takes the fear of dying and places it on an enemy by making them into prey. We engage in the death of others so we can delude ourselves into believing that somehow, someway we can escape death ourselves.

Does it truly boil down to that? That all this evil and blood-letting are simply because we humans cannot tolerate the thought of our own blood and death and ultimate vulnerability as creatures? Maybe that is one of the reasons women as a whole are less violent than men. Every month we see our blood and yet we manage to live. I wonder if the young men and women who enlist in the armed forces "to protect God and country" understand that they may be sacrificed for something else?

August 1, 2007
Columbus Isle, San Salvador, The Bahamas.
Sitting on a balcony overlooking a pristine beach, listening to the breezes sound through the palm tree fronds. It is only 10:30am in the morning and already the air is so hot and humid it is difficult to breathe. I feel as if I am becoming a vampire only coming out when it is dark. Last night I had the beach to myself, swimming naked under a full moon, floating with the surf into and out from the shore. I could imagine our amphibian ancestors crawling out of the water. Skinny dipping with moonbeams dancing on a luscious, warm sea at night.

As impossible as it seems, this is the first time in twenty-five years that P. and I have been alone together for a week, except when we first met in London. Seven days with no kids, no relatives, no friends, no anybody. It is like the honeymoon we never had and it feels so sweet to melt into the soft laziness of having nothing to do except eat and sleep, make love and loaf around.

This morning I got up at 7:30am and was tempted to go back to bed at 9:00am. This points to a new goal of mine: learning how to take naps successfully. I have never in my life been able to nap guilt-free, and I have a lot of precious naptime to catch up on. My goal for the next year is to recognize what feels good and what doesn't without feeling I'm letting anybody down.

What feels good?

What feels better?

What feels best?

And to base the actions in my reality by simply – simply! – allowing myself to feel good.

For is that not what spirit wants: for us to feel good?

What a concept!

I do believe our Creator/Creatrix wants us to feel good and so many of us spend our entire lives getting in the way of feeling good. I wish I had figured this out earlier.

I told P. the other day that if he cannot or will not join me in this dance of feeling good, I am going to feel good anyway because more and more I believe it is an important part of our spiritual journey, our spiritual calling. While we humans do suffer, being on this plane of reality isn't about suffering.

Yet how many of us think that feeling badly is what we are meant to do? Well, feeling badly and suffering can provide the foundation for surrender and humility, both of which we need, though we may not want them. No doubt about that. But joy is of heaven.

August 22, 2007

At my place once again on Sycamore Avenue, retreating into the quiet. That odd sensation I had last night, dozing off in front of the TV, not the first time either that this has happened, but the recurrent feeling that someone is going to enter the room and demand something of me, want something from me, only to come out of my reverie long enough to remind myself, "You are alone, Maurine. You can relax. Nobody is going to ask you for anything right now. You can go back to sleep."

Spent Monday with Dad. Our conversation went something like this:

Bill: "I want you to transfer some money from my savings account into my checking."

Me: "I've already done that, Dad."

Bill: "And how are the boys? Making any money? Working hard?"

Me: "I hope so."

Bill: "Did I tell you I wanted you to get money from my savings?"

Me: "Yes, Dad. I've taken care of it. Don't worry."

Bill: "And the boys? How are they? Are they working hard?"

Me: "Yes, Dad."

Bill: "How many people are going to be at dinner Friday night?"

Me: "Thirteen, Dad."

I then go over all the people who are attending.

Bill: "Have you made reservations yet? I want you to make sure you do that."

Me: "Yes, Dad. I made them over a week ago."

Bill: "Now, so let me see. Are there going to be ten of us?"

Me: "No, Dad. Thirteen."

Bill: "Thirteen!?"

And then we go through the elaborate counting and naming ritual again, citing each person who will be joining us. We do this at least three times in the course of five minutes. And then it's back to:

Bill: "Did you transfer that money for me?"

Me: "Yes, Dad."

This conversation loop, with some minor variations, goes on for the entire three hours I am with my father. I help him find his misplaced urinal and make sure fresh batteries are in his transistor radio. I leave with a pair of his pants that need mending. As I walk out the door, there is one last question:

Bill: "How many people did you say are going to be at the dinner?"

It does absolutely no good to say, "Dad, we've already talked about that." I leave him weary beyond measure.

Yet a bright spot, an example of how God works in the world:

Went to see FS and mentioned a book drive I am involved with through Rotary International to help raise a million books for LA school children, ages 4 to 9.

Me: "If you have any books you might want to donate, that would be great."

FS, with a sly smile on his face: "You know, I just might be able to help. Follow me."

And out we went through the rectory courtyard with FS dangling some keys in his hand until we reached a door marked "Library," which he proceeded to unlock.

FS: "You can have all of these."

I went into shock. Shelves upon shelves of children's books, resource materials, and encyclopedias. Goosebumps came up on my arms. Talk about asking and ye shall receive! The words were hardly out of my mouth before the universe gave me an entire library to dispose of. Sometimes miracles happen that quickly. So as I give books away— several hundred since my return from the Holy Land – I am gifted back with an entire library that will go to helping kids. Now that's something.

The moral of the story?
It pays to be generous.
You do reap what you sow.

August 29, 2007
Gracious Spirit:
Despite all our efforts, something fundamental remains out-of-sync between P. and me. I know You intend only good and that there is nothing but love and generosity behind all Your actions. I do not want to dwell on anything other than Your will. How is this to be?

Calm. Quiet. Listen. Watch. Subdue the voice that wants to think, encourage the part of you that knows surrender is the only path, surrender to what spirit wills. You do not have to figure all things out; rather, you are required to remain present. When your mind manufactures pictures and scenarios of the future, you have the choice to pursue them or to let them go. There is nothing wrong with dreams and day-dreaming as long as you remain aware of where ultimate power resides.

Part of your concern stems from not wanting to hurt others, and all the effort you have put forth over the last few years to repair your relationship. But it is important for you to remember that only you can be honest with your own heart and it is that honesty you must cultivate. As long as the honesty is in place and you are not seeking a specific outcome, you can rest in the assurance that all will be well. What you need to pay attention to is the honesty. That is your personal responsibility. It is when you put others' feelings above the truth that your heart knows, the truth that you experience internally that you are led astray.

How do you experience this honesty? Feel it in your body, feel where tension increases or decreases. Remember how you felt better sharing with P. about not trying to protect him. You have done this so much of your life; now is the time to let go. You cannot, indeed must not worry about or anticipate others' reactions to what you say and therefore censor yourself unnecessarily. Your task is to focus on the honesty and what brings you increased peace or conversely increased discomfort.

Part of what you are still working through is the notion that some outcomes are "good" and some outcomes are "bad." You put these word labels on events and then try to conform your behavior to fit these concepts. And while it is true that discernment is called for and that personal responsibility is required, it is not so much as you might think from your human plane. There are forces at work outside human knowledge or manipulation, and that is why surrendering to and trusting these forces are critical. Your task is to be as honest as you can; it is time for this after a lifetime of deferring that internal honesty and sense of truth you have been blessed with. Focusing on the internal honesty is part of your spiritual path.

Part of being honest is being vulnerable to the fears and anxieties humans are vulnerable to but knowing that these frailties and vulnerabilities are not the ultimate Arbiter. Trust the Ultimate Arbiter. You are making progress, yet more is required. When you feel that moodiness start to descend, stop! Recalibrate yourself. The Lord of All Things, and not you, is Master. This is where surrender and trust must reside. Stay focused on the NOW right before you. And rejoice!

September 7, 2007
Frankfurt, Germany.

Sitting in the airport on a three-hour layover before my plane to Venice. Mel. is by my side. We are on her after college trip – three down, one to go! – two weeks of art and gallery hopping. That is what she wanted and that is what she planned. You might say I'm just along for the ride and to foot the bill. And it is with immense delight, great pleasure, and much gratitude that I do so. A mother and daughter adventure that will provide memories we both can hold in our hearts for years to come.

On the first leg of the journey, before meeting up with Mel., I read *Saints and Madmen* by Russell Shorto, and it speaks to the way I have been feeling lately: ecstasy and craziness and how close these two can be. The few moments I have experienced the Transcendent have fallen, if not between saint and madwoman, at least between grave illness and the humdrum, day-to-day of things, and both have been meaningful and profound. I suppose the moral of the story is that the Transcendent can break through at any time.

A quote from Nobel Peace Prize recipient and Belgian priest, George Henri Pire:

> What matters is not the difference between believers and unbelievers, but between those who care and do not care.

Caring and not caring. The glitch comes from how one defines that caring. Those who care profoundly for an idea, especially religious and political ones, can be willing to go to war and kill for that caring. Those who care from the heart are less likely to do so, in my opinion at least. Caring from the head vs. caring from the heart.

On the issue of pride vs. humility Shorto writes,

> This is where pride comes in. A lot of our problems come down to the fact that we're all such know-it-alls that we're closed to other people's views and styles.

It all boils down to creative listening, the ability to listen without feeling the need to stuff our ideas down

others' throats. When we can listen, it is infinitely harder to
hide our shared humanity. This type of creative listening
invites vulnerability, the absence or opposite of pride.

Along these lines, from a forty year old woman who
was repeatedly raped by her father and institutionalized
most of her life with MPD, multiple personality disorder
(a.k.a. dissociative identify disorder):

> I've learned that you don't need an
> abstract language to talk about spirituality. You
> don't even need to say 'God.' *You just
> recognize.* Recognize your children, give them
> your time, tell them they are real and valuable.
> I was made to feel invisible as a girl, and that
> was devastating. Recognize others. That's
> where spirituality is. (italics mine)

As you see others, you see God.
As I see others, I am seen by God.

The above points to the concept of witnessing, which
is fundamentally the language of the Psalms: Do you see
me, God? Am I seen by You? A part of me cringed when I
read "I was made to feel invisible as a girl." It felt as if I
wasn't even there a lot of the time, just gone.

I also like this from Martin Buber, how he takes the
valence off the words "good" and "evil":

> There is not, as we generally think in the
> soul of man, good and evil opposed: There is
> again in different matters a polarity, and the
> poles are not good and evil, but rather *yes* and
> *no*, rather acceptance and refusal.

Which one do you gravitate toward?
I like this thought, too: the Latin root for the word
illusion is *ludere,* which means to play. The illusionist

therefore is not one who tricks or deceives but one who plays. How we need to keep this playfulness, this "illusion" within ourselves! In this manner we protect ourselves from giving so much power to our illusions that they control us. Still working on this, no doubt.

September 20, 2007
Somewhere over the Atlantic Ocean.
Up this morning at 4:00am to catch a 6:20am flight from Marco Polo Airport to Frankfurt, Germany. After considerable ticket hassles in both Venice and Frankfurt where even I lost my patience, I finally managed to make my connecting flight. I am so weary I didn't even cry when I said good-bye to Mel., but now the tears come. I shall miss her terribly!

The past two weeks of traveling – what Mel. has dubbed our Art Pilgrimage – have been daunting for me physically. In the course of two weeks' time I have been on:

11 plan rides, including the next and last leg of my journey from Newark to LAX.

10 train rides, including the Football Express in Germany (rowdy!).

8 bus and tram rides.

7 taxi and car rides.

4 water taxi rides.

1 bicycle ride for an entire day.

And...

FEET, FEET, FEET: tens of thousands of steps looking at art, walking over Venetian bridges schlepping bags and luggage, in addition to loading and unloading said luggage at airports, train stations, buses, and hotels. Everything, and I do mean EVERYTHING, hurts.

Just call me Sherpa Mom or Mel.'s Mule.

This is the first "vacation" I've been on where I actually lost weight. I have to confess that while a part of me is looking forward to getting home – no more bags and luggage to haul around – another part of me dreads reentering that world. It has been so wonderful, such a precious gift being able to enjoy the female energy of my daughter. And mine, too. Awakening in the morning, looking at one another, and automatically starting to laugh. "I'm hungry." "Me, too." "Let's go to breakfast." "I was just thinking that!" Or watching how we selected the same pieces of art, how we were drawn to the same shapes, colors, and forms. And, of course, shopping.

What is it about women?? Men, by and large, feel so narrow to me, and yet they rule the world – for now – while women can go so deep and take in so much and yet are, by and large, in a subservient position throughout most of the globe – for now. Does it all finally boil down to:

Narrow (penis).

Deep (vagina).

?!

As much as I admire Freud for his insights, this is one arena where I think he got it completely wrong; it is not penis envy – spoken like a true Victorian male – but vagina envy. I cannot say that women are better than men because there is an equality consciousness that needs to grow on the planet now in order for us to survive. This is absolutely essential. And I do not want to patronize men anymore than I want to be patronized by them. It's just that...what? We need to raise women up more without men being threatened by that, the eternal fear of the maternal yaw, the devouring female. Raise them/us up!

And as I fly over the Atlantic, and then on to yet another plane to fly across the United States, I think of crossing over. All the crossing overs there are in life:

Physical

Emotional

Psychological

Spiritual

The most we can hope for while we are engaged in all these crossing overs is to be more playful, patient, and kind. If I can just cross over to that!

November 8, 2007

The dispersion of books, both mine and the library entrusted to me by FS, has taken on a life of its own. From FS's gift alone some fifty-five boxes of children's books have been packed for the Rotary International Book drive, another twenty-three have been given to a local high school for at-risk girls; and another three to a local boys and girls club. And I still have hundreds left! This is in the hands of a Force that is beyond me. My only requirement at this point is to show up. And trust.

What else have I been up to?

Trying to understand the he and she of things.

God may have built us as spiritual beings capable of choosing love, but as animals, as biological creatures we are built to insure our survival. For without this impulse to go forward, there is no life. But the problem is that after eons of our biological survival threat mechanism being built into our amygdale and limbic systems, the triggering of our psychological threat arousal is frequently experienced as the feeling of "I am going to die!" So we attack the "other," usually in the form of our partner, because that feeling of "I am going to die" is so deeply ingrained in us (see Becker).

Our brains were not built for love, at least not on the physical/biological level. Our brains were built for survival, to keep us alive. We fall in love because our brains are on drugs (a.k.a. hormones), and biology will have its way with us: birth, growth, decay, death. Being in relationships activates our warring brain systems, and we need to learn how to deactivate them, which takes presence and practice. And prescience and patience.

The moral of the story?

The part of the brain that keeps us alive is also the part that keeps us arguing, fighting, and defending against intimacy and vulnerability. While we may need the warrior archetype for self-preservation, the trouble comes when there is a misunderstanding of incoming arousal material. Not the War of the Roses but the War of the Battling Amygdales; the feeling that no one else is there for you, so you panic as our forebearers must have panicked on the savannah eons ago. All this takes place at lightning speed. So the animal in us responds one way while the spiritual being is called to respond in another.

Don't tell me God doesn't have a sense of humor or knows a good challenge when He/She sees one!

Animal = built for temporal survival.

Spirit = built for eternity and love.

How do we honor both?

All that by way of a very long-winded introductory statement about how I'm feeling these days; how I'm feeling is pretty damned old, or at least frightfully middle-aged. Earlier this week I thought: if I don't slow down, I'm going to collapse. I made myself not leave my apartment for an entire afternoon.

I also have been focusing on:

1) How I can be more in fellowship with myself. The fact that I haven't come up with any concrete ways of doing this is telling. (And writing doesn't count!)

2) How to create more art and artistry in my life, a sense of expansion and liberation, and not just writing or lamenting my failures and short-comings as a writer, which are legion (see previous entries).

I finally got into the back of my garage and sorted through more damaged cartons of books. I had to throw out thirty copies of the step-parenting book and salvaged a dozen more, using a toothbrush with a tiny amount of bleach to clean around the edges. That whole process took an entire morning. As I stood by the kitchen sink with toothbrush in hand I thought, "This is either EXTREMELY obsessive compulsive or an act of great devotion." I personally could not decide which. I'm leaving that up to God to correct the former, if true, and encourage the latter, if true.

It takes so long to "get" life and then it's over.

November 15, 2007

Finished two books by C.S. Lewis (*Virtue and Vice* and *Paved With Good Intentions*). Lewis reminds me of a crotchety old Oxford don who is ready to thwack you on the knuckles if you disagree with him theologically. Fortunately, or unfortunately, I juggle too many alternative perspectives.

Lewis appears to inhabit such a black and white, good and evil universe, and it is this very polarity that bothers me because it is the antithesis of the non-dual framework now called for. Lewis' position allows the individual to place evil external to him/herself. And while there are absolutely evil, bad things happening in the world, I believe the genesis for that evil resides within the human heart. Or at the very least in our laziness and the choices we make about how we engage with reality, what we covet and lust after. The devil doesn't pave the way to hell; we humans do with our fear, narcissism, envy, and greed.

Of the two books, I found the latter more compelling, and therein lies the rub. Why is "the bad" more compelling than "the good"? How do we go about developing the "coolness of mind" the Dalai Lama talks about, whereby we are not led around exclusively by our emotions and reactions to things? Because Lewis believes that as we become less dependent on our emotions, we become harder to tempt. True, but hard to achieve because our passions and imaginations are subject to so much change and flux.

The goal, for God at least, is to kill our animal self-love and replace it with a different kind of love: a love of charity and gratitude for *all* selves. God's whole purpose is to get our minds off the subject of our own value – or lack thereof – and put our attention on building God's Kingdom.

The primal questions Lewis says we must ask are:

Is it righteous?

Is it prudent?

Is it possible?

Of all the vices Lewis believes cowardice alone is purely painful. Hatred can have its pleasures. Courage, on the other hand, is one of the reasons God allows a dangerous world: so that moral issues come to a head and we must decide. Courage: the highest testing point of reality. How does goodness then within us ripen?

November 24, 2007
Another check in with my Guide:

> Never worry about anything; but tell God all your desires of every kind in prayer and petition shot through with gratitude. (Philippians 4:6)

Gracious Spirit:

I do not know why it is so difficult for me to pray. I know my time on earth is dwindling and there is the desire to use the time left in the most productive way. Or better said to allow my time to be used to Your best advantage and act. Speak to me.

Trust your journey. Relax and focus solely on the twenty-four hours you have been gifted with. This type of discipline is essential because it is only through the present moment that the Divine Will can break through and be made manifest. The Divine Will you seek is a flowering of spirit within; it is not a product of activity but the process itself. In this sense, it does not matter what you do – write, preach, teach, or jump – but how you go about doing what you do. You must remember that the eyes of the world ultimately are not the final arbiter of anything but the world itself, which will fall away.

There are many different journeys and many different pathways for all walks and endeavors of life. The only criterion you need to concern yourself with on your particular journey at this particular time is: Does this activity fill you with joy? Does it feel congruent with your being? If the answer is yes, continue. If the answer is no, stop. Only you can sense internally the truth of the answer, whether yes or no. Your Heavenly Father, above all, wants you to experience the joy of your desires; earthly rewards and recognition are not a part of His/Her concern.

That is why you must relax and feel your way into things. Is there a part of you that feels you still do not deserve? Is there a part of you that believes you cannot partake of this abundance or that your Heavenly Father truly wants this for you? You need to focus on the clarity of your self as an instrument. You must concern yourself only with the process of creativity and how you feel about it, not where it leads you or some arbitrary goal you want to achieve. The worldly part of you keeps stumbling on the obstacles of what the world puts before you as its demands. These are not your concern, but rather focusing on the internal, eternal rhythms as they move through you, what you call the Kingdom of God. You might be surprised what could happen, indeed must happen when you put these as your priority.

If you cannot or do not experience a quiet gratitude and joy, reassess. The experience of gratitude and joy is a signpost of right activity. Trust that the movement on the river of your life is guided by an Intelligence and Power and Love far grander than anything you can imagine. The only thing you need to ask yourself is whether you are experiencing joy. You may be surprised how concentrating on this will aid the manifestation of creativity in the world of form.

December 4, 2007

A lot of reflection and reassessment about being in the world, a large inventory taking place, both internal and external. Someone once asked me how much I was willing to sacrifice to be a writer. Well, by my reckoning, I have given some thirty years of my life and a fair amount of money. I have placed my time and treasure on the line for this word fetish business.

Sometimes I feel like Don Quixote chasing non-existent windmills or a salesman or gambler who's waiting for the "next big deal" or the win that will "set things right." When I added up all the money I have spent over the past three decades without breaking even, no business can survive with this as its plan. What is the critical line between perseverance and stupidity?

What is it that prevents me from stepping into my joy? I keep losing the larger picture, to my detriment and distress. Cicero was right: gratitude is the parent of all other virtues. And yet at the same time, the one that seems the easiest to forget.

I am becoming more and more aware of the finiteness of my life, my "leasehold of days" as Seamus Heaney puts it; far fewer left in my hourglass of time than those that have come before. The clock ticking on my father and P. and me and the children and the planet: how to make use of the remaining grains of sand? Certainly not by fussing and brooding about books rotting in my garage, or whatever else I stew about, but for the peace that passes all understanding. I remind myself of the principles of Reiki:

- Just for today, I will live with the attitude of gratitude. I will give thanks for my many blessings.
- Just for today, I will let go of anger.
- Just for today, I will let go of worry.
- Just for today, I will do my work honestly.
- Just for today, I will be kind to my neighbor and every living thing.
- Just for today.

Just!

December 11, 2007

The event:

At P.'s after dinner, around 9:30pm, a business colleague/friend of his dropped by to deliver some Christmas gifts, but did not leave, wanting to talk. She asked if the two of us could sit down. I kept thinking, "This is odd," and wondered why P. hadn't returned, taking much longer than the twenty minutes he said he'd be gone. When he finally did return and saw C. sitting on the sofa with me in my bathrobe ready for bed, he went stiff, his jaw clinching.

"I didn't know you were going to be here. I have work to do."

And with that, he turned abruptly and went into his study, closing the door. I walked into the kitchen to get some water and C. followed me. The conversation went something like this:

C: "So, it's okay with you that P. and I are dating?"

Me: "Dating?"

C: "Yes, we've been intimate for about a year now."

Me: "Oh, really? Do you know that he and I are still sleeping together?"

At this point my blood is boiling.

C.'s jaw dropped. "No!"

I was already on my way to P.'s study.

Me: "You've been sleeping with her?! For a year!?"

At which point I stormed upstairs to gather my things while P. was at the front door ordering C. out of the house.

P: "You have to leave. Get out. Just leave. You have to leave. Now!" He then lifted her up bodily and put her outside.

All the while C. was standing before P. in hurt, surprised tones:

C: "You lied to me. You lied to me. Why did you lie to me? You said you were just friends and that you had some financial responsibilities toward her. Why did you lie to me?"

At which point I butted in:

"It seems he's been lying to us both!"

I grabbed my purse and as I was walking through the front door I turned, furious:

Me: "I don't know who is the stupidest person here: You (pointing to C.), you (pointing to P.), or me (pointing to myself)."

I left with P. following me, ordering me to get back into the house, while C. followed him, trying to get him to talk with her. I refused to return and told P. to get the hell away from my car. In the meantime, C. stormed off, roaring down the street in her expensive Corvette. By the time I got back to my place, having to stop on the way for gas, P. was already parked in my driveway. I told him to go away. After I slammed the door, he finally left.

I had been praying for divine intervention regarding my relationship. Whoever thought it would be this? And P. and I were actually scheduled to meet with FS the very next morning to work on rebuilding our way together. Obviously, I bailed on that one. I didn't even want to try.

December 17, 2007

After numerous phone calls and a letter from P. placed upon my car window, we met at a park to talk. After an hour of dialogue, he left as if nothing had happened, as if everything was back to normal and business as usual. I was nonplussed.

One of the fundamental issues I see is that while P. and I love each other – there is no doubt about that – we are such different people, and I simply do not know anymore how to address that fact. There always seems to be something disagreeable between the two of us, somehow, someway, no matter how hard we try. And neither one of us, for whatever reason, appears capable of letting that go.

Last Sunday, only two days before C. walked in, P. took me to a jeweler, and I was flabbergasted when he intimated he wanted to get married again. I had absolutely no idea whatsoever that that was what he had in mind. While I had once hoped and planned that we would, I have to confess I don't feel that way now. What would getting remarried accomplish when we weren't able to get it right when we were married? He wanted to get divorced to fix things; now he wants to get remarried to fix things. How crazy is that?

I am still so upset about what happened Tuesday evening, and how blind I've been, trusting P. more than he is capable. And I wonder how it works for him that he could go to Mexico with C. and her two sons for three days after Thanksgiving while his own sons and I stayed home? Are they more fun, stimulating, relaxing, and/or enjoyable to be with than we are? And then after waiting three days for him to return and not wanting to wait any longer, I ended up being the one apologizing and sending flowers because it upset him that I didn't stay. It makes me sick to my stomach, like a total schmuck. He's gone three days with another woman and then is upset with me for not waiting for him? How sick is that!

While I believe P. may be sincere, he is not being honest. If he had been honest with C. or with me, Tuesday evening would never have happened. And now I feel I am in a no-win situation because it's not just about P. or C. anymore; it's about me and my sense of self-respect. C. clearly had no idea of the extent of P.'s and my continued relationship, nor I of his involvement with her. I simply cannot believe she would have said the things she did if the picture had been clear to her. She thought she had a chance, and I can't blame her for that. I hold P. accountable.

While I do believe in being in a relationship and the value of relationship, I don't have either the stamina or the energy to keep doing this toxic dance. I look out on my life, I feel its energy, and I like it. I've worked hard to feel this sweetness, and I don't want to let it go, and P. appears uninterested in sharing it with me. Or even asking about it. What is it about the men in my life? A part of me is so tired of the needs and neediness of men.

January 1, 2008

6:00pm in the evening. Dark outside. After removing all the Christmas and holiday decorations, I stood weeping uncontrollably at the kitchen sink, purging myself of all the pain. Sobbing, sobbing, sobbing. Cathartic. I must have cried half an hour. I feel like such an idiot! So dumb and stupid! Stupid, stupid, stupid!

Humbled, humbling.

Humbled and humiliated by all that has transpired.

My blindness and idiocy humble me, terribly.
What did I expect? That I could have it both ways?
Stupid, silly me!
Gracious Spirit:
The crossroads loom. I have never needed more support than I do now. Help me please!

Focus on your breath, your life-source. Breath and breathing, in and out. By focusing intently on your breath, it will ground you and slow you down over the weeks and months to come. Concentrate on your breath as your emotions and feelings work to overwhelm you; keep breathing in and out, in and out. There are no winners or losers here. Doing what is called for, however painful the process may be, does not alter right action. Right action is right action; nothing more and nothing less. If you remain focused on right action and use your breath as a grounding tool, you will move forward not with anxiety or dread but with purposefulness.

You see much more clearly now many of the patterns that you have been dancing to and struggling with in your relationship. Only you can make proper assessment of the steps toward healing. Do not judge yourself for the time it has taken, and the pain, for these deep structures to reach the surface of your consciousness. The divine intervention of which you speak triggered a new process of reflection and self-discovery. Embrace this. Once the revelation is presented, it is not possible to go back to the way things were. Or to put it another way: it is, of course, possible because in all things you have the power of choice, but by doing so you also know on some level that it would be a lie or dictated by laziness, habit, and/or fear, and this is unacceptable.

You already have been going through the mental process of stay or go, remain or remove, and you can feel internally the reactions that are elicited from each of these courses of action. You are realizing more each day how you have been bound up and how you have bound yourself up. Remember what your Heavenly Father wants for you: love and freedom. In many ways you have experienced these already; yet in some other profoundly deep ways you have not because you have held yourself back or deemed yourself unworthy. Pay careful attention to the level that is now erupting.

Ask yourself: "Should I follow Plan A?" (trying to repair things with P.) and see how your internal being reacts. Then ask yourself: "Should I go with Plan B?" (really separating from P. in a way that you have not done before). Merely living in separate domiciles does not mean that you have separated in other ways. That is why C.'s intervention was a gift, a gift for both of you. You are realizing in radically different ways the direction of the path you need to take. There is no couple at this point; only the external form of a couple, not the deep spiritual reality of joint sharing and communion and the true desire of sharing intimately with another human being. You understand more the external behaviors and attitudes you personally need to address. Do not let fear or habit or history interfere with this process.

It is good that you see this event as divine intervention. You are spiritual enough and more importantly desirous of following a spiritually guided path that in times of trial bordering on despair that honest spiritual yearning will sustain you. It is essential that you keep your mind in check as it experiences the reactions and emotions that you are experiencing. But for you especially it is vital to stand firm in the rhythms of your breath and being, your very life-force itself.

In so many ways, you have never learned how to breathe for yourself, and if you cannot do that, how can you expect mature, intimate exchange with another? It is the piece/peace that you have felt missing over and over again and a lesson of upmost importance. You have much greater clarity of what the stakes are; it is not just about your relationship with P. or anyone for that matter. It is about your relationship with yourself! If you were not such a seeker of right alignment with the God-force, this would not matter so much to you. But since you are such a seeker, you are required to engage in a level of reality that calls for focus, clarity, groundedness, and right action.

Have the courage to stay true to yourself. This, by far, is your most difficult challenge because you have had a lifetime of being otherwise, especially from your family of origin, but also because you are female in this earthly form. Concentrate on learning about your feminine energy. It has been used and abused many times and it is an essential demand now calling to be healed. Do not punish or chastise yourself for the things you have done wrong in your relationships in the past. Just say to yourself objectively, like a scientist investigating an experiment, "These are the behaviors I have engaged in that have not been helpful or have been counterproductive." Bless this information because it presents the road map to your healing.

Do not judge or anticipate any outcomes other than remaining lovingly expectant of the good that always comes to those who seek after spirit. Do not have any expectations of what that good will be or how it will look. Remember, you saw clearly C.'s behavior as a divine intervention, but it most certainly was not in the form that you could have anticipated, expected, or wanted. Yet a divine intervention it was. You are called to acknowledge the intervention, not orchestrate the outcomes. You must remain open to the form in which guidance is presented. Release all else and concentrate on the day before you, remembering your breath, your true life force and how it sustains you. Trust this process, however painful and confusing it might be, and know that you are loved.

****

Daughters of Jerusalem
Daughters of Jerusalem: weep for me.
I want to live without judgment;   ·
But it is the humility I lack.
Arrogance abounds with
Boundaries that have no end.
Supplicant that I wish to be,
The roots of this stubbornness run deep,
A fathomless distance and defense
Against that which my true heart desires.
Daughters of Jerusalem:
Weep for yourselves.
Keen and mourn for the inner light
That does not come,
But remains hidden in the dark recesses
Of this human heart.

March 8, 2008
An email from my youngest daughter. I honestly do not know how she can be so together at twenty-two while her mother seems so clueless and relationally challenged at mid-life!

"My only thought is that you must not consider Dad's comments, requests, pleas even until you have decided what you want for you, for your life, and your relationship with him. Look within before even considering looking out to second party entreaties. I know this is incredibly challenging, but put all of Dad aside and find yourself in the world. As Anne Morrow Lindbergh wrote, 'Woman must come of age by herself – she must find her true center alone.' Once you have located yourself at this stage of life, only then would I consider locating yourself in relationship to other people. You must give to yourself before continuing the cycle of giving to others."

I wonder at times what that true center will feel like, or if I will even recognize it when I get there. Maybe I just need to let EVERYTHING fall apart and see where the pieces land. When the great crises of life come, you don't have time to start working things out; what you have already become takes over. Who you are is how you react. Over time a small white lie becomes the character flaw of deceit, and you respond deceitfully because that is how you've grown accustomed to responding. Over time, refusing to look at things and taking the easy way out makes you a coward. The moral of the story is you'd better be damned sure you concentrate on living with integrity and authenticity of spirit.

Do you know what that feels like within you, Maurine? Authenticity of spirit?

And what about forgiveness? Boy, am I working on *that* one! Because forgiveness is about creating a new reality; it is not a one-time event but requires an openness to a continued relationship through time, and this requires courage and presence to relinquish the desire for revenge. Because revenge is always in some way premeditated, and it is the premeditation that must be released. I'm working on that, too.

Can I be forgiving and give up resentment and anger? Because if I cannot, in certain respects, I am not exercising my God-given creativity and power. And if I cannot relinquish these feelings immediately, I can at least choose to pray that we all come to fulfill our purpose in creation, which is never lying, cheating, or destroying.

So easy to say. So very, very hard to do.

Forgiving is one thing, but how do you forget?

March 17, 2008

War within me and war half way around the world. Unbelievably, the fifth anniversary of our invasion of Iraq. After five years, Nobel laureate Joseph Stiglitz estimates the war will cost $4 trillion. With interest on the debt, future borrowing for war expenses, and the cost of continued military presence in Iraq, plus health care benefits and counseling for veterans, the amount could go as high as $5 to $7 trillion.

Is going to war, at least this war, an exercise in freedom or futility? All those deaths and those wounded: what are they for? Greed? Hubris? Stupidity? Laziness? A fundamental out-of-jointness of our values? We simply are fighting the wrong war! Our soldiers are dying on the battlefield and by their own hands to get us what or where exactly? Oil? And the children are just dying, period. Where we put our time and treasure says a lot about us as a country and a species.

On Saturday, the Ides of March, Answer LA staged a protest against the war. The day was absolutely beautiful, billowing clouds moving at high speed, a windy, blustery Chicago-in-spring sort of day. I packed up my small carry-on suitcase with over ninety copies of *One Bomb Away*, made a sign that read "Free Books," put on my coat and hat, and headed down to the CNN building on Sunset Blvd. I am absolutely determined to not let these books rot in my garage! I didn't even bother to set up a table. I just planted myself on a street corner, opened up my suitcase, and started yelling against the wind and crowd and noise:

FREE BOOKS!!!
FREE BOOKS!!!
FREE BOOKS!!!

I swear they were snapped up in less than half an hour. Forget trying to sell them, just yell the magic word "free." I could have given away another suitcase full if I had had one. People were actually jostling and pushing one another to get copies. It felt so good to do that and also to see that the books were taken mostly by young people in their twenties. One girl actually left four crumpled one dollar bills as a donation; several others asked me to sign their copies. Ninety more book seeds: I wonder how many will sprout? But that is not my job; my job simply is to spread the seeds.

March 23, 2008
Easter Sunday – the first time in years that I attended Church, Easter Sunday and Christmas Eve being the two times I boycott services. But this year I decided to attend because I did not want to deny myself the joy of an Easter Resurrection. I need to feel the Resurrection!

Looking back over the year 2007, which I had hoped would be one of fruition, and to have it turn out so contrary – the exact opposite in fact – ending the year with the *coup de grace* of P.'s relationship with C. being revealed. Certainly not the year I anticipated. Thinking, too, about the 4000th American casualty of the war being recorded today, not to mention many multiples of that in the Iraqi population, on Easter Sunday, Resurrection Day. Will the mothers who lost sons and daughters in this conflict be able to do what Mary did? To experience the sacrifice of their children as an act of grace and joy?

I have been reading books to avoid thinking about P. and C. and just finished one by Eckhart Tolle (*A New Earth: Awakening to Your Life's Purpose*). I certainly need to learn this purpose now as my past life crumbles away. I do believe Tolle understands a profound truth about the nature of reality: while events do occur in the world of form, the world is not what ultimately defines existence. And the lesson that I came away with from the Holy Land: act as if you already are what you seek; abundance comes when one acts abundantly. This is God's operating principle: providential abundance and generosity. Always.

We work so hard to acquire things without understanding that our very efforting is what blocks the organic, natural flow of this deeper – or higher – reality. How I have had this lesson beaten into me! Not what can I get out of any given situation or person but what can I give, how can I be of service. I just wish I could manage this in my relationships.

Tolle writes about how much, and how easily, we confuse content with essence. Again, our pesky personalities keep us focused at the content level only. We must surrender what Tolle calls psychological time, past and future, in order to stay present in the moment; the paradox that while the present moment may be a discreet unit of time, from another vantage point that single moment contains all the time that ever was, is, or will be.

And I love this about joy, the state of joy we were created to live in and precisely what I have *not* been feeling lately:

> Unhappiness or negativity is a disease on our planet. What pollution is on the outer level is negativity on the inner. It is everywhere, not just in places where people don't have enough, but even more so where they have more than enough.

What I call the Idolatry of the Negative.

Eckhart talks about non-resistance, non-judgment, and non-attachment as a road map to freedom. Yogis have been talking about this for millennia; it is nothing new, and it is not even rocket science. For thousands upon thousands of years humans lived so much closer to this state; our psychic splits, while huge and seemingly growing at an alarming rate, are still relatively new in the grand scheme of time. We used to live in rhythm with nature and the cosmos before we started commandeering and commanding them to do our bidding. Tolle talks about what he calls object consciousness needing to be balanced with space consciousness; the resurrecting of space consciousness is the next stage of our evolution.

Tolle also talks about "awakened doing" – acceptance, enjoyment, and enthusiasm. We need to be vigilant that we are vibrating in one of these three states whenever we engage in any activity. For if we do not experience acceptance, enjoyment, and/or enthusiasm, we are most likely creating some form of suffering, however subtle, either for ourselves or others. It is all about giving, making things flow outward, not wanting things to come our way.

This is what Jesus meant when he said he was here to bring abundant life: the abundant life from within to manifest in the world of form. 'Tis a truth not universally acknowledged but universally true nevertheless. And eternal. Everything must change from within.

April 20, 2008

I was asked to speak briefly at a women's dinner about my experiences in the Holy Land. As I stood before a group of approximately seventy women, I realized it had been a year since I first stepped foot in Jerusalem, walking through the Old City at night.

I believe I have changed more in this past year than perhaps any other in my life. I told the women that for me the timing had been just right: finishing my third year as leader of the Prayer Team and the fact that D, the priest who oversaw my work, was in charge of the group; the fondness and respect I had for him made me want to join his gathering.

I said that my prayer, my hope as I traveled to this ancient city, the city that has been the focal point and destination for so many individuals through time, was to be open. And that I was hesitant to share some of the experiences I had for fear of building up any expectations as to what might happen should they, too, decide to make the journey. But I said that if they decided to go and if they prayed to remain open, I was sure God would provide each and everyone of them with what they needed for their heart and soul and spiritual journey. Of that I was and am sure. They would not be disappointed and perhaps even pleasantly – or wildly – surprised. One learns to listen in a different way. Visiting the Holy Land is the ultimate Magical Mystery Tour.

April 22, 2008
Participated in an Earth Day event giving away more books – approximately two hundred copies of *One Bomb Away* and one hundred of *Step-parenting Without Guilt* – plus over five hundred bumper stickers encouraging DO SOMETHING FOR A CHANGE! The kids in particular loved these, in addition to handouts from Beyond War and my own printed materials about Spiritual Activism and Reiki. I was glad to see how many individuals were interested in the latter especially.

I don't know how many hundreds of people I spoke with personally and all but one gentleman, not so gentle really, were quite lovely. The aforementioned man, a lawyer, thought we should nuke the Middle East – Iran, Iraq, and Syria in particular – in order to protect Israel. I did not argue with him. I just let him talk. He took a copy of *One Bomb Away* and informed me that he would probably disagree with everything I had to say. I told him that was fine. As this man was going on and on, a young woman stopped by my booth, listened to him for a few moments, and then said, "Do you know how hostile your energy is right now? You're really contaminating this entire space!"

Bless her heart!

The man didn't stop talking, of course, but the young woman spoke the truth while I remained calm. Funny or brilliant how the Universe works: energy, both positive and negative, radiates. I absorbed his negative energy in a non-confrontational way and she picked up on this and spoke out. The truth *will* out. I do believe more and more that love, not ego confrontation, will win both the argument and the day.

Which, for some reason, makes me think of something I read in Kurt Vonnegut's last book (*Armageddon in Retrospect*): a young gawky, inexperienced teenager who enlisted in World War II and then spent much of the rest of his life and professional career attempting to communicate the horror he experienced. Vonnegut writes,

> There can be no doubt that the Allies fought on the side of right and the Germans and Japanese on the side of wrong. World War II was fought for near-Holy motives...

A chillingly contemporary mind-set, that. Then dear KV redeems himself:

> But I stand convinced that the brand of justice in which we dealt, wholesale bombings of civilian populations, was blasphemous...

He continues:

> That the enemy did it first has nothing to do with the moral problem. What I saw of our

air war, as the European conflict neared an end, had the earmarks of being an irrational war for war's sake...But I felt as I feel now, that I would have given my life to save Dresden [or Tokyo or Hiroshima or Nagasaki] for the World's generations to come...

And then, bless his pacifist heart: *"That is how everyone should feel about every city on Earth."* (italics mine)

Which side do we want to be on? On the peace insurgency side or that of the terrorist, be that terrorist an individual who wants to nuke the Middle East or down the Twin Towers? Moving toward some form of moral, global integration or mutually assured destruction? The choice is ours and we had better get moving because we are running out of time. We simply cannot afford this addiction to fear and war and relentless competition and greed. Like any drug, if abused long enough, the drug will win in the end.

May 5, 2008
Blue Point Villas, Uluwatu, Bali.

Bali! I can't believe I'm in Bali, half-way around the world, the last of the four promised out-of-college trips. Staying near one of the holiest sites on this island, an 11th century cliff top Hindu temple dedicated to the spirits of the sea, where wave after wave after wave after wave cascade in rhythmic beauty toward the shore. How one feels the god and goddess energy here, the magnificent beauty of it all!

As I write by the pool, son W. is out surfing: my blue-eyed, golden haired Adonis. He does turn heads he is so physically beautiful and yet his true beauty radiates from within, a gentle peaceful spirit, connected to the rhythms of ocean and earth. He carried that special energy in with him from the day he was born. He has introduced me to the *argot* of those who worship the riding of waves and who organize their existence around the opportunity to do so. I made him write down some phrases so I could understand what he is talking about.

Macher (pronounced mocker) – surf that is really good.

Kook, barney, traney – someone who is not good at surfing but thinks he or she is.

Pig doggin' – grabbing the rail going backside vs. front side.

Tombstone – when a surfer goes down and is on the bottom and his board is sticking straight up out of the water, held by his leash.

Shifty – waves that break all over the place.

Rippin' – someone who is surfing very well; "killing it" also applies.

Snaking – going in front of another surfer who has the right of way, as in cutting someone off in traffic; also known as dropping in and not considered good etiquette.

Surf stoned – when a surfer is tired and delirious from surfing long and good and hard.

As in Bali! And what a ridiculous adventure it was to get here. After months of planning, W. and I actually missed our flight for reasons too utterly stupid to go into. Let's just say I misread the departure time on the tickets and leave it at that, not to mention the days leading up to our leaving: arranging for hospice care for my father, not that I suspect he will die while I am away, but at the request of the place where he is living. I actually believe having more company around will perk Bill up, more people to tell the same story about being a young boy in Tyrone, Oklahoma and how the winds would blow three days in one direction and then shift and blow three days in the other.

Aside from this, I had to get someone to walk and feed W.'s dog, take in the mail and water the plants, followed by a splendid frenzy of packing at the last moment when we realized we had missed our flight. W. and I were able to get on the next one out of LAX on Singapore Airlines – a kind attendant taking pity on this much distraught Mom – but which resulted in an eight hour layover in Singapore Airport before our connecting flight to Denpasar. I will never forget W.'s and my playing pool at 4:00am in the morning while he sipped beer and we chatted about politics with the bartender who was most gracious when I got on my soapbox rant about the war. He offered to make me a mean Singapore Sling, his specialty, but even I turned him down. 4:00am is just too early to drink, I don't care what time zone you're in!

We finally arrived at our hotel shortly after noon a day and a half after we left LA, not too much the worse for wear – and in truth only about twelve hours later than we would have been if we hadn't missed our flight – relieved, in one piece, with all our luggage in tow. Thus far, aside from W.'s surfing and tutelage in the language of his watery tribe, we have seen some traditional Balinese dancers in full costume regalia, visited the absolutely stunning Kintamani volcano in northern Bali and the magnificent rainforests we had to travel through to reach it, saw some of the traditional arts of batik cloth printing and intricate woodcarving in Ubud Village, with a brief stopover in Kuta, the Wikiki of Bali, to replace a broken board.

Aside from the physical beauty of this island, one cannot help noticing the unique spirituality of this place, a spirituality that is in many ways quite superstitious – gods for this, altars for that, and I do mean altars everywhere, from huge carved stone entities to small roadside make-shift baskets of flowers, incense, and propitiations to the local deities and spirits that be. Certainly not a place where free will and individual choice have much sway, a non-western calendar (8 months of 35 days each) with only four types of names for off-spring. If you have more than four children, you start repeating the names, and where men are still legally allowed to have more than one wife. Our guide said that in his village there was a man who had four wives and four separate households. In his Aussie accent: "Don't know how he manages it, mate. One's enough for me!"

And yet a people who feel very kind and gentle to me, greeting you always with hands in the prayer position of *namaste* – that is, when they're not riding their ubiquitous motor bikes or trying to sell you something. I actually saw a young couple the other day, the man driving with his wife/girlfriend behind him carrying a large cardboard box with a Motorola TV in it. However they manage it I do not know and if there is an accident amidst all the crazy driving and horn honking, it can't be due to ineptitude or carelessness but rather to some evil spirit at that spot, so up goes another altar to appease the malevolent powers.

All the stories and dances that abound here about the conflict between good and evil, between yin and yang. Even the gods and altars of the Balinese are covered with black and white checked gingham to represent these polarities and also to not offend the spirits by any nudity, though I think the Balinese are anything but prudish. One of the dances I saw the other day was as ribald and bawdy as any Shakespeare, complete with foot-long phalli being hacked off and images of anal sex.

May 7, 2008
A restless night, could not sleep. Still feeling out-of-whack and jet-lagged despite the slow pace here. I have written little about the unfolding of events with P. because I simply have not wanted to. I have been trying to reach a place of quiet within, to allow things to be presented to me

rather than trying to figure things out. I am so tired of trying to figure things out. A few things I have noticed:

After finding out about C., my inexplicable obsession over a period of several weeks with the film *Becoming Jane,* a fictional account of Jane Austen. I watched this movie several times while sick, violently ill at the beginning of the year, a result no doubt of all the emotional trauma and stress of the holidays. My inadvertent and repeated bursting into tears at the comment of one of Jane's suitors, "It seems you can neither marry with affection nor without it." Can't live with love and can't live without it: how that describes both my marriages with parsimonious exactitude! An overabundance of affection in one that ultimately killed that relationship and an under abundance of kindness and respect in the other that eventually contributed to its demise.

In this process of allowing insight to arise I also remembered a period of time when I was a little girl, somewhere between the ages of seven and eleven, when I suffered from insomnia and couldn't sleep. As with most children, I would go to my parents' room for comfort and a pattern arose where my father would come back to my room to sleep with me, but my mother never did. It was always Dad, and this went on for several years.

I wonder: Why did my mother never come to comfort me? Why was it always my father? Was it some relief for my mother to have him out of their bed and into mine? Could she just not be bothered with me? While I have no recollection of my father molesting me physically, it was inappropriate for this behavior to have continued so long. An important boundary was breached and in certain ways it has helped me understand P.'s infidelities in a different light, not to condone them but to better understand on some subtle energetic level perhaps a covert message from me communicating, "Leave me alone." This does feel right to me, though it in no way excuses P. from his lies and deception. But there is a sad poignancy in his longing to be with me that I could not fulfill because of these early childhood experiences of invasion.

I have grave respect for the power of the psyche to express itself and get its needs met in whatever way it can. The insight I had about the generational lack in my family; there is no hiding from or escaping these imprints of long go. There is only the choice and discipline of recognizing and releasing them through time. At this point I have no agenda that I can repair anything with P. Indeed, if I were to take bets, I'd say no, throwing in the towel. And then again, I cannot play God. I have absolutely no idea what the future will bring. All I know is that it is time for me to be alone, a certain type of aloneness I have avoided my entire life for one reason or another, but no longer to be avoided in any way.

Thinking, too, about my first husband, and my gratitude to him for the opportunity to experience that head-over-heels kind of love at least once in my life and for the opportunity of living in England and all that was learned from having a different perspective. And to thank P. for the opportunity of having children, a family, his absolute dedication and devotion to that cause even though we both suffered personally in other ways because of it. I would not trade my children for the world, not for anything. They are the truth about life and being here. P. and I just (just!) weren't able to transform ourselves to the next level as a couple. It was a knothole of soul we couldn't squeeze ourselves through.

An erotic dream last night, the first I have had in a long, long time. I could feel the lubricating moisture of desire between my legs. I have been praying that my dream life would return to me, praying to be sent the dream I now need to dream. I used to dream so much about so many things. Now only tiny wisps of nocturnal smoke arise, as if some inner fire has gone out. It saddens me that perhaps the time for that kind of dreaming is past. I don't know. Where is lizard energy now?

I think of all the young couples I have seen since being here who have gotten married – at least one a day and some days several – in the tiny limestone chapel overlooking the sea at our hotel. Indeed, marriage is a bumper-crop business here. All the young men and women, so full of hope and optimism, embarking upon a new life together, having thoughts and dreams and expectations, conscious or unconscious does not matter. Thinking: I was like that once too, young and eager and confident.

Now, at mid-life, I feel so different, not patronizing toward them, though some of the couples look as if they are play-acting at being adults. No, looking at them with a poignant wistfulness of all the work and joy and love and heartache and disappointment that are in store for them. They believe they are taking on life but they will learn, sooner or later, that life is taking them on. They believe now, being young, that they have so much choice and opportunity and puissance over the journey. And then you get to my station stop along the train tracks of time and you realize that your only true and lasting choice is the perspective from which you view the journey and pageantry of it all. That, and what your genes have bestowed upon you, over which you have absolutely no control, only luck, chance, and good fortune handed down through the DNA of time. And even that is changing now as scientists get their teeth more and more into the secrets of our biological heritage.

Yesterday I witnessed a magnificent sunset, perhaps one of the top five in my entire lifetime. Shafts of light, like star fingers, exploding from behind voluminous clouds as the sun peeked through and winked back and forth at intervals. I watched the entire process for over half an hour. And then as dusk set, taking note once again of the small fishing vessels that head out to sea to ply the waters for fish at night. By the time it was completely dark, there was a flotilla of small boats, lit up like a string of pearls on a necklace surrounding the bay. And then at dawn, as day breaks once again, they head back to their homes and families.

And on and on it goes.

Timeless.

Eternal.

Over and over again.

Wave after wave after wave.

May 11, 2008

W. left at the break of dawn to surf and I received a surprise phone call from P. to wish me a Happy Mother's Day, something I hadn't expected.

This process remains SOOOOOO hard, changing with each day. Peaceful and accepting one moment, wondering and agitated the next. There is a part of me that still loves P. and another part of me that feels I must be alone. Yet I appear incapable of shutting the door and saying I never want to be in an intimate relationship with him again.

It was so much easier with AD, walking away and getting on with my life. He and I were both so young and green in our own way. It is easier for me to forgive myself about that relationship precisely because we were so untutored.

With P. it is different. He has been apologizing, groveling almost, saying how sorry he is, how much he loves me, how much he knows he mistreated me. It breaks my heart seeing him this way. My head says, "Stay away!"

but my heart still cares so much. Yuck! My ambivalence is even pissing me off, and it's been going on for years.

Took a day trip to Nusa Lembougan – Bali the way it was twenty years ago. Turquoise green waters, sea weed gardens cultivated by the island's inhabitants, an underground cave carved out of stone over a period of fifteen years by a local holy man inspired by a passage from the *Mutabarata*, followed by ramshackle bamboo structures for business and homes next to elaborately carved temples. It appears that all aspects of Balinese life are permeated by this spiritual presence, the constant aroma of incense burning.

Our guide informed us that, among other Balinese Hindu traditions, individuals are selected for the priesthood by outsides forces. An individual does not necessarily "decide" to become a nun or priest but is chosen or appointed by a village elder or sage or mad person even. And woe betide the individual who does not go along with the plan! A story was related to me of one fellow who did not want to follow his selection and refused the call. He became ill and suffered until he changed his mind. Once he agreed to become a holy man, his illness and problems ceased.

Superstition?

Conscience?

Coincidence?

Social Pressure?

Black Magic?

For there are priests trained in Black Magic here, as well as White Magic, the forces of good and evil juxtaposed dramatically. I told our guide that I could understand the White Magic, wanting to help others heal, pray to be saved, uplifted or whatever but that I had a very hard time understanding the desire, and being trained how to do so, to wish ill upon another human being.

Why would anyone want to harm a fellow creature in that way, unless one was broken to begin with and wanted to spread the poison of his/her hatred onto the world under the guise of religious or political practices? The guide didn't have much to say about that except to comment on the feeling of reverence and mystery that he as a Westerner had experienced at some of the temple rituals he had witnessed with his wife who is Balinese and Hindu, rather than the Catholicism he was raised in.

I understand completely the awesome humbling and humbling awe we humans can experience, indeed need to, in front of the Divine, but to actually train in religious practices aimed to harm or destroy? Come to think of it, who am I kidding? We in the West just call it war; that's our "religion." We raise individuals with the injunction "Do not kill!" and then we turn around and give these same individuals the sanction to do so under specific circumstances, with the blessing of the state. I suppose this is our own peculiar form of Black Magic; we even call some maneuvers Black Ops.

****

Several days later.

Just finished Steinbeck's *East of Eden,* the last of five books I brought with me to read while away, and can only say it is a prayer, a symphony of a book; an act of obeisance to the time it takes to tell a story, to tell the truth about the human condition. Such a book is the absolute antithesis of the mini-morsel sound bites we swallow over and over again daily but that have no nourishment at all. So we eat more and more and do not understand why we feel less and less full and more and more hungry, dissatisfied for something, yet not knowing what that something is.

As I was reading, I thought of my father and the time he was born into, a world "touched with so much glory." Images of playing marbles and spinning tops, visiting neighbors down the road on horseback, large families and women working over iron wood-burning stoves; learning how to fish and catch game with a rifle or bow and arrow; how teachers were respected and revered at that time, the world before World War I. That is the birthplace, the place in time of the man who spawned me, and in some ways I do feel that world still circling and swirling in my veins.

Describing the shift in tone and feeling between the 19th and 20th century, "the great boundary that was called 1900" Steinbeck writes:

> Another hundred years were ground up and churned...For the world was changing, and sweetness was gone, and virtue too. Worry had crept on a corroding world, and what was lost – good manners, ease and beauty? Ladies were not ladies any more, and you couldn't trust a gentleman's word.

Or handshake. Now you have to have a battery of lawyers and reams of paper legalese before signing on the dotted line. How much more contentious and untrusting we have become!

> ...And even childhood was no good anymore – not the way it was. No worry then but how to find a good stone, not round exactly but flattened and water-shaped, to use in a sling pouch cut from a discarded shoe. Where did all the good stones go, and all simplicity?...Oh, strawberries don't taste as they used to and the thighs of women have lost their clutch!

The thighs of women have lost their clutch: I'd just about sell my soul to write a line as fine as that! Sweet strawberries and the clutching of an eager woman's thighs and the glory that can light up a man or a woman; that special kind of glory that brightens the entire world. Love, poetry, music, beauty, the heavens at night, dawn and sunset, the laughter of children, even loss and intense sorrow: all the myriad things and events that spark "the glory" within us; this is what makes us uniquely and truly human.

The best, the greatest and most lasting stories are about everyone of us; they are deeply personal and familiar, like the story of Cain and Abel. They are about love and rejection and hurt and guilt and expiation and propitiation and pain and longing and how they weave their way in and out and through this novel of fathers and children and friends and brothers and lovers, like a baroque bass note that resurfaces again and again. And the primal story of good and evil, well or ill that Steinbeck believes informs us all:

> I believe that there is one story in the world, and only one...Humans are caught – in their lives, in their thoughts, in their hungers and ambitions, in their avarice and cruelty, and in their kindness and generosity too – in a net of good and evil. I think this is the only story we have and that it occurs on all levels of feeling and intelligence. Virtue and vice were warp and woof of our first consciousness, and they will be the fabric of our last...A man, after he has brushed off the dust and chips of his life, will have left only the hard, clean questions: 'Was it good or was it evil? Have I done well – or ill?'

I think there may be yet another story, or at least a subtext to the one above: What about a life of plodding, quiet mediocrity that gets nowhere and does neither good nor evil? A life that is never so good as good can be and not as bad as evil can be? It is just not much of anything, one way or the other. I think that is the sad truth for most of us. But then again, better an unrecognized, piddling, plodding mediocrity than ball-faced evil, to be sure.

Then comes the master stitch of them all: *timshel*, Hebrew for "thou mayest." We may choose good; we may choose evil; we may choose a bland, safe middle road of neither but the point is we may choose. And the wise, wily, kind loving Chinese man, Lee, saying: "Can you think that whatever made us – would stop trying?" Yes, we are in a relationship with this Force whether we like it or not. We may choose to engage with this Force, for we have been blessed with the gift of *timshel*. And while we may let go of our Maker, our Maker never lets go of us. Of this I am sure even in our darkest moments of despair.

Tomorrow W. and I return to LA, and then it will be time for those Reentry Blues.

May 27, 2008

Gracious Spirit, Protector, Knower of what I need to know: Months have passed since we last communicated. It is not so much speaking, is it? Rather a kind of listening to something deeper. I feel as if I am at the last door to something, the last door before something deep within. What needs to open now?

Greetings sister daughter! You are loved. Calm, quiet. You still fill your days and at night your mind with far too much chatter and activity. Part of this is habitual keeping busy on your part; part of it is some fear of the last letting go. Letting go of what? What is your fear around this? You have all the tools you need. Why do you not use them in a different way? What is the garden you wish to cultivate? Do not be afraid. And fear is not the only component; indeed, it is a rather small one at this point in time. Rather, it is cultivating attentiveness to yourself in a more profound way.

We have talked before about slowing down, slowing down, slowing down. I know you believe you have slowed down and in some ways you have; in other ways, especially with your creative side, you have not. Now is the time to honor the cultivation of that part of you. You might surprise yourself. Or be surprised! The darkness that comes at times and begins to overtake you: you have the tools now to arrest it and keep it at bay.

You must be open to the mystery of unknowingness and surrender at the deepest of levels. You can gain a precious peacefulness from this process even though at times it may feel the exact opposite. Remember what new good can arise from painfulness and decay. Be as open as you can about the future. You know your heavenly Father/Mother has only good to bestow on all His/Her creatures. You are on the precipice of learning something old, something new in a different way.

Pay close attention to those around you who either rob you of your energy or add to it. This can be a blatant process or quite subtle. In whatever form it presents itself, guard your energy! Do not let your mind drift into the past or toward the future. The work you do may require reflection about these two aspects of time but do not let your heart get caught in either of those dimensions. Stay present.

Continue to bless yourself. You put yourself down for many things (how do you say? For being a chump? Naïve? Stupid?). You must stop this. You did what you did and all is forgiven. Now is the time to let go of all previous patterns, thoughts, habits, reactions; a new garden is growing. This mysterious creative Force is part of you; indeed, it is what you were created for. Allow it to come through you. Keep focusing on prayer and surrendering.

Greet yourself daily as I did. You do not honor yourself enough. This pattern must stop. It is no longer acceptable in any way. Know what you have, who you are. Own it! The more you do this, the more you will release your laughter and light. You exist for yourself; you exist for your Creator. You have existed enough for others. While you may not let the latter go entirely, you are at the door of existing for yourself and the pleasure of your Creator. This is good. It is better than you can imagine. Release all disturbance and fretting. You are carried now and always.

June 13, 2008

Reentry into LA was met with both relief and apprehension. Bali feels so far away now, the vibrational acceleration of EVERYTHING here in LA seeping into my bones again after the laid back pace of Uluwatu. All this stress is not good for the system. And yet glad to be home, too.

My father continues to dwindle. I can hardly be around him for more than an hour because there is nothing left of who he was, just a weak, frightened, confused man. It breaks my heart. The process of death can be very unpretty. And take longer than one can imagine.

P. and I have talked little since my return. I received this email from him shortly after I got back:

> I woke up with the realization this morning that you are the most kind, loving, and gentle human being I have ever met – a true Conduit of Spirit – and that I consider myself most blessed and grateful to have you as my partner on our journeys together, whether

together or individually. Thank you. Thank you
from the bottom of my heart.

How can he write to me like this and be sleeping with
another woman?

We have not been together for six months now. I am
very much taking to heart my need to honor myself. Never
before in my life have I been called upon to relax and trust
life's fundamental beneficence as now, not even when I had
cancer.

The only thing I have any control over whatsoever is
how I choose to engage with reality. And that engagement
can come from a place of trust, joy, enthusiasm, and
gratitude – which I sincerely want – OR it can come from a
place of anger, depression, and woundedness – which I
most certainly do not want. And that is not to say that I am
not feeling very vulnerable right now: I am. I am beginning
to truly miss having physical contact and touch with
another human being.

Then these two dreams:

One about losing all of my possessions. I come home
to find out that everything I have has either been sold in
some sort of garage sale or donated to the Goodwill. People
are moving around packing things up and carting items
away. A young man is in charge of all the activity. I go up
to him, distraught, yelling, "What's going on!?! What's all
this about!?" He dismisses me and continues orchestrating
the removal of boxes. I run around frantically trying to stop
him. Finally I come across a stack of boxes containing my
books. I am so relieved! At least my books have been
saved, at least my books are in tact, at least I still have my
books even though I have lost everything else.

Then a dream about a watch P. gave me. The watch
appears like the face of a Salvador Dali surrealistic watch,
melting. It has fallen apart in the dirt and I am frantically

trying to pick up the broken pieces to keep them from getting ruined. I want to put the pieces back together and fix the watch, but this can't be done.

How my books and the written word have sustained me through all kinds of chaos and change; how time and relationships are disintegrating now before my eyes; my habit of always trying to "fix things," to pick up the pieces and make peace instead of just letting go.

June 14, 2008

P. wants me back as he continues to sleep with C.

My father's march toward death continues. He positively looks like death; he just hasn't stopped breathing yet. The hospice workers have ordered oxygen for him. Some of them tell me it could be weeks; others say it could be months.

It has occurred to me that the three primary male relationships in my life – my father and two husbands – have been emotionally compromised, and what this says about me, being attracted to that kind of man. I am beginning to wonder what a reasonably healthy, emotionally mature relationship would feel like, would look like at this stage of my journey. Is that statement, in and of itself, an oxymoron: an emotionally mature male/female relationship?

A friend said he actually had great empathy for me and what I've been through. I looked heavenward when he said that. Thank God someone finally sees this and is supportive of me! I have been blaming myself for this whole situation when maybe it hasn't been all about me. And it just is what it is.

What is, is this:

I pulled a rune spread and Perth leapt into my fingers: the rune that symbolizes being beyond manipulative powers, standing at the heart of initiation: the spiritual warrior's quest. And did I not write about that months ago? About wanting the warrior's protective, positive energy. Perth is about reformulating the deepest level of being and can involve intense psychic death because the renewal of spirit is at stake.

No shit. Is there anything else to strip away at this point? I'm afraid to ask.

Then Sowelu: a time for regeneration down to one's cellular level; becoming conscious of one's true essence – something which perhaps only now I am connecting with. Again, the caution of Sowelu, which resonates with the advice of my Guide: guard your energy! Watch who adds to it; watch who detracts from it. Retreat from others cannot only be necessary at times but a sign of strength.

Oh, Lord!

Finally Algiz: protection. One of the truest and best ways of protecting oneself is learning how to surf the emotions, not collapse into them, as I have done over and over again during the last few months and years. Learning how to ride the grief and anger out, or whatever other emotion presents itself, is an important tool of the spiritual seeker.

Then wanting to know what animal wisdom I needed, I fanned out my medicine cards and out popped Otter. And, of course, that felt spot on, perfect. Otter standing for balanced female energy; the female elements of earth and water and playfulness are part of her message. Otter is the epitome of femininity: long, sleek, glistening, and graceful. At 5' 3" I'm not sure how "long" I am, but I'll take the other three.

Otter is always on the move and curious. She will not start a fight unless attacked first. That is *so* me; even when attacked I don't like to fight. We otter types assume that all other creatures are friendly until proven otherwise. Again, ditto. Balanced feminine energy is neither jealous nor catty.

Otter medicine understands that *all* accomplishments are worthwhile and benefit the tribe. And perhaps most importantly: otter people express joy. Envy and the fear of being replaced have no place in this creature's understanding of goodness. What a concept in a world that so frequently portrays women as catty and conniving, jealous and needy, or all of the above. How my world needs this balanced feminine energy now!

And finally a talk with FS, just in case the Runes and medicine cards weren't enough. He said the three things we absolutely need from God are protection, healing, and the "good news" of being called into relationship. How the three archangels Michael (protection), Rafael (healing), and Gabriel (annunciation) are what keep us in touch with our spiritual reality. Without this foundational grounding we humans have a tendency of falling into what FS calls the "ungifts" of the Spirit. Rather than love, joy, peace, patience, kindness, goodness, faithfulness, humility, and self-control, we descend into the Shakespearean elements of our being:

Unwisdom, i.e. choosing denial of what is

Folly.

Recklessness and its "I-don't-give-a-damn-about-anyone-else" mind set.

Wickedness, a premeditated maliciousness that has many social ramifications (as opposed to individual recklessness).

Ignorance.

And last but not least:

Insolence, the mirror opposite of humility.

Sadly how much more easily most of us respond to these "ungifts" than their positive counterparts. But in all things there will be a reckoning, of this I have no doubt. The laws of the universe may be fixed but our responses are not. Therein lies either our hope or our demise.

August 21, 2008

My father, William Howard Bollinger, died August 6, 2008 – only a few months shy of his 98th birthday. To my mind, he lived too long.

I was not with Dad when he died because I had gone camping with two women friends. He had held on for so long that being gone for three days didn't seem a problem. I understand from the hospice workers that he called out Mom's name and smiled when he passed. Did he see Mom on the other side beckoning him as he made the transition over? I like to think so. The hospice workers said that frequently right before death the person who is leaving will have dreams or conversations with loved ones who have already departed, extending a metaphorical helping hand to ease the soul from one realm of consciousness to another.

While I was in the mountains, a flood of tears emerged about so many things: the end of my relationship with P., the last child leaving home, my father on death's door – and how exquisitely true that feeling proved to be! Just so many tears flowing out of me while in the ageless beauty and serenity of nature, with dear friends supporting me, looking on.

It was fitting, in a way, that I was among the grand old sequoias when Dad died; he more than anyone else was responsible for introducing me to the joys of nature, camping and fishing in the High Sierras as a child; how to bait a hook, clean a fish, and build a camp fire. Those two weeks we went camping every summer as a family, plus the odd fishing trip here and there to Lake Crowley, are etched in my memory forever: some of the few truly happy times I remember as a child. I think Dad's spirit somehow was with me through all those tears, passing through me and letting go.

I actually got a call from P. the last morning my friends and I were in the mountains, informing me that Bill had taken a turn for the worse. When I asked whether I should return immediately, P. said no. He thought Bill had another 48 to 72 hours. When I returned home that evening after a five hour car trip, my son D. met me at my front door.

"Did you hear about Granddad?"

"Yes, your father called me this morning. I understand Bill's not doing at all well."

"No, he died this afternoon, just after lunch."

Me, shaking my head with tears. When the end of the last parent finally comes, even though you have been expecting it, wanting it, hoping for it even at such an advanced age, there is a click that occurs, the click of the closing of the door to a huge portion of your life and the click opening the door to the last chapter of your own, with the tacit understanding that you are the next one destined to walk off the cliff labeled "death."

The next week was a flurry of phone calls, appointments, and activity: arranging for Dad's cremation and memorial service; arranging for the big party he wanted at his beloved Riviera Country Club; disemboweling his room of the last remaining vestiges of his life. So many emotions came to the fore. For some reason, when I saw one of Dad's dress shirts, the white one he wore the most toward the end, I simply lost it. I cried and cried and cried, remembering that shirt and how frail Dad looked in it. Thinking about the last Father's Day we spent together with him wearing that shirt, sitting outside on the patio in the sunlight, having what would be his last glass of champagne. I developed a splitting headache and left with bags and boxes of items to either donate or give away.

Dad died on August 6th, the irony of that being the anniversary of the bombing of Hiroshima, Dad's involvement in World War II, the grand adventure of his life, my book about nuclear weapons and the fact that I had given a talk at a church commemorating this event just prior to my camping trip. By August 13th his tiny room, his last resting place, was vacated of all that was left of Bill. In the car on the way out to Castlehill on that last day to turn over his room key, I heard Pachabel's Canon in D and was reminded of the day P. and I married: that was the music they played as Dad walked me down the aisle. How quickly twenty-five plus years can flit by! And how much can go awry along the way.

Then the following dropped out of my purse, something from P. that I had carried with me for years, from the Sanskrit "Although I Conquer All the Earth":

"Although I conquer all the earth,
Yet for me there is only one city.
In that city there is for me only one house;
And in that house, one room only;
And in that room, a bed.
And one woman sleeps there,
The shining joy and jewel of all my kingdom."

No longer mine to either have or hold. He is with someone else now.

Talk about being washed clean!

On the last day I saw Dad before his death, I ran into P. at the retirement home. As we stood outside Dad's room, talking *sotto voce* in the hallway, I told him if he had only been honest with me about C. The honesty would have hurt so very much less than all the lies and lack of respect. After twenty-five years I deserved that much. When P. left I went inside to see my father, distressed and disoriented. I tried to feed him his favorite lunch but he kept shaking and saying, "Can't, can't," then spitting up his food. All he wanted to do was get back onto his sofa and lie down. His last words to me were, "Maurine, you've made my day!"

The weekend of the memorial service: Dad's eulogies, the elegant party afterwards at Riviera with his friends and family gathered round – he would have loved it all. At the service I was the last to speak. These are just a few of the words I shared: "Poets and philosophers for centuries have asked: What makes a good life? All I can say is: they should have talked to Bill." I went on to describe how Dad had the great and rare gift of being able to truly enjoy himself and his life without guilt. He loved his family; he loved his friends; he loved his golf and food and cocktails: *he loved his life!* What a rare and beautiful gift that was and is. I managed to hold it together long enough to get back to my seat. I don't remember much else.

Several hours later when the last hurrah of the after party was dwindling, P. saw me standing alone in the corner quietly listening to *Shenandoah,* which Dad wanted played at his wake. I had started to weep softly, finally letting some of the feelings out, and he came over to me and hugged me and said he loved me. How I appreciated him for that, even though there is no going back to the home of our relationship again. Still, death brings us together in the end and allows us the opportunity of joining at a different level, from a different space.

The following day after the service, going through all of Mom and Dad's papers and jewelry with my brother, some six exhausting hours of two lives now gone. Recycling all the flowers from the memorial service for daughter A.'s bridal shower the next day. In a span of forty-eight hours going from death's finality to the hopefulness of two young people sharing a new life together, even as the life of my last parent had come to its close.

August 28, 2008
Gracious Heavenly Spirit:

WHAT NOW???

My relationship over.

My father dead.

Is there anything left that hasn't been said or asked already?

You are realizing more with each passing day that there is less for you to "do" but more space and opportunity simply for you to "be," to honor your beinghood in a way you never have before. The only thing you need to know is the fecundity that arises out of this turning inward to the peace that truly passes all understanding. You are beginning to appreciate the power that resides there. For one who is truly peaceful is a blessing to all. It is the gift Spirit wants for all His/Her creatures; you are fortunate to realize this after a lifetime of lack. Or rather not lack per se but after a lifetime of concentrating on so many non-peace giving activities and thoughts. Now you are tapping into this deeper well. There is no agenda to this peacefulness. It just is.

It is also good that you have by and large relinquished any judgment around this. You are embracing beinghood in a way you never have before. You know this intuitively; you feel this at a deeper level despite the understandable sadness and grief due to the loss of the physical form of your father and your relationship with P. You rightly ascertain that all ultimately is for the best and that you are allowing yourself to be guided and grounded in this truth.

Out of this deep internal peacefulness true joy and liveliness, aliveness arise, genuine and pure, the ability to play and be playful. These are great gifts. You are becoming more aware that these are among your father's legacy to you: a joyful heart, an ability to enjoy, quite literally to bring joy into your life. This deeper joy comes from the beautiful and timeless childlike being who trusts in reality, who engages with reality in a spontaneous way. There is no agenda to this type of soul other than relishing what is right before them in the moment, the way little children interact with reality, until societal and other worldly forces teach them otherwise and dilute their primal joy.

This joy and peacefulness are not contradictory or paradoxical. Love, joy, peace: these are the fruit of the Spirit, the primary fruit. The peacefulness allows the joy to enter and the joy waters the internal peacefulness. There is a union and communion between these two parts of you that have been disconnected. Now is the time for them to walk hand-in-hand.

The fact that you are not fretting in spite of all the challenges you have faced is an indication that you are dropping deeper into this other mysterious reality. When you notice the sensation of deep internal peacefulness, express gratitude. When you laugh or relish as a child would an activity, even eating a sandwich, whatever it is that you are engaged in at the moment, express gratitude for the moment of recognition for the quiet, childlike joy.

Many people think of joy as something loud, ecstatic, the antithesis of quiet but this is not necessarily so. While there are times when joy is expressed with exuberance and sound, the deeper joy I am referring to stems from a quiet, centered calmness that is at one with what is. Indeed, the sound of laughter itself arises from this place within. This is the space where peace and joy intermingle and wed.

While it is understandable that you still need to take action in the world of form – buying groceries, doing dishes, whatever humans need to do to care for the body's needs – beyond that the only activity called for is to cultivate this garden of peace and the flowers of joy within. You have been through much, and the trials you have faced have not soured or tainted your spirit, nor your spirit's longing for these deeper regions. You have remained true to the trust and belief that ultimately goodness and abundance shall prevail.

Continue to focus on the peacefulness and the joy – the true handmaidens of a life being well-tended, well-lived. All else will fall into place in its appropriate time and way if you can but continue to honor and cultivate these gifts. You see more clearly how worry, anxiety, what if, feelings of unfairness, judgment – all those reactions that separate you from yourself and others, your joy and peace, their joy and peace – must be laid to rest. Allow the deep, quiet peacefulness to subdue all internal and external clamor. All else will respond because the energetics of this vibrational field will touch those around you. Be the water of peace and joy for yourself and you will be the water of peace and joy for others. Amen!

September 1, 2008

An early, timely birthday present from my youngest daughter: two pairs of very lacey and racy underwear. One was a conservative creamy white; the other a red – and I do mean fire engine red – thong. I tried them both on and they look much better than I expected. Maybe there is some sensuality and eroticism left in this old body after all! I had to laugh with the thong, though; in addition to showing off my lotus flower kundalini tattoo, it also highlighted the humungous flaming red spider bite the size of a quarter on my left butt cheek! If there is one thing for sure in this life, you've got to maintain a sense of humor.

Also this marvelous note from Mel., which was rather cryptic until I opened her package:

"With what is inside this box, you will be able to make a new statement, a declaration if you will. One more subdued than the other, but both proud nevertheless. I debated about colors and hope to have catered to your conservative side as well as the lioness in you. Perhaps the latter is less practical, but I thought I'd start you off strong (and it will look great with your tattoo!). You can always add to this, the first of what I hope will be a growing collection, with colors to match every mood! Happy birthday, my dearest Mother. May this be just the beginning!"

I am quite flattered that Mel. looks upon me as possessing a "lioness" within, and perhaps that is part of what all this death and rebirth, crucifixion and resurrection are about. Why it has taken me nearly three score years to get to this internal clarification point, I do not understand. I have allowed far too much bullying of myself because I did not grasp this fundamental truth of beinghood. And I have bullied myself far too much as well, that relentless taskmaster within. Talk about hard labor! And it is sweet too, that my daughter is so rooting for me, as if I am somehow vicariously carrying a special feminine chalice for her. Or passing on a very special and sacred baton.

Finished reading *The Art of Power* by Thich Nhat Hanh, and it speaks to a lot of what I am coming to. A story Hanh shared to show how we become slaves to our thoughts:

A father thinks his son has been killed by bandits while he was away. He comes home to find his house destroyed and the body of a dead child inside. The mourning father cremates the body, assuming it to be his son, and carries the ashes around with him in sorrow.

In truth, the boy had been kidnapped by the bandits, not killed. When the son finally escapes his captors, returns home, and asks to be let in, his father refuses. He has become so attached to the idea, the mental position that his son is dead that he tells the boy to go away and leave him alone. The boy finally leaves and the father loses his son forever.

Moral of the story: Be careful; be very, very careful what you think and how attached you are to what you think. Thai shares this:

> If at some point in your life you adopt an idea or perception as the absolute truth, you close the door of your mind. This is the end of seeking the truth. And not only do you no longer seek the truth, but even if the truth comes in person and knocks on your door, you refuse to open it.

The mind wanting to be right does violence to the truth, and the earth. Hanh continues,

> Ideas and perceptions should be abandoned all the time, to make room for better ideas and truer perceptions. This is why we must always ask ourselves, 'Am I sure?'

****

A sweet story, and true:

A few weeks ago I decided to put some of my step-parenting books out on the street next to the lot across from my house where people park their cars to attend a nearby church. I put out twenty copies on a folding chair with a sign: "Free Books for Parents and Stepparents." By the end of the day, eighteen of the twenty books had been taken, absorbed by the Universe.

So I decided to try the same thing the following Sunday. When I went outside in the early evening to collect the chair and whatever books were left, both the chair and books were gone. I thought, "Crap! The parking attendant must have thought they belonged to the church and put them away with the parking sign."

Two days passed, then as I was driving through my neighborhood what did I spy at the end of the block but my folding chair with the free books sign still attached to it, plus two books left. Since I had a squawking cat in the car with me – yes, I've inherited another grand pet, just as I got W. and his dog out the door, in comes a feline. I dropped the cat off at the vet, all of two minutes away, then circled back around the block to pick up the chair. By the time I got back to the corner, however, the chair was gone, but the two remaining books were on the ground, so I scooped them up. For two days the chair and books have been wandering around Sycamore Ave. and La Brea Blvd. Talk about the Miracle Mile!

Next time I'm writing: Free books (but please don't take the chair!).

September 14, 2008
Ah, me.

After the fun of my birthday and feeling good about the dispersal of more books; forty-five copies of *One Bomb Away* at a disarmament conference and thirty-six copies of the step-parenting book via the help of the aforementioned parking lot and chair, I slammed into a brick wall.

I was watching something on television and saw a commercial with a couple in bed, and it hit me hard that I don't have that special kind of intimacy in my life anymore; and it's not just about having sex or physical touch, though I certainly miss both, but rather the sober realization that I don't have a buddy anymore, a special friend to share my days and cuddle with, and a part of me so misses that.

I realize more and more the longer I am away from P. how much I allowed myself to be compromised in my relationship with him and how unhealthy this was, however well-meaning and well-intentioned on both our parts. And I also have come to the realization that you can love someone deeply at the soul level, but at the earthly, personality level you might not. Both realities are true, and both realities must be honored.

So since my birthday, more grief. I cried so much one day I almost made myself sick. I had to concentrate on not crying because my head and sinuses hurt so badly, not to mention going through a couple of boxes of Kleenex, and my nose was raw. Just letting go of it all: a complex relationship of twenty-five years, my father's death, dealing with his estate, W.'s moving out, A.'s wedding. There was a span of a few days where I could barely put one foot in front of the other. Okay, what do I do next? Mail this envelop. Okay, what do I do now? Maybe you should eat something. Okay, what now? There is stuff coming up from such deep places, a purging of everything, simply everything. And I must allow all this to happen.

I will be out driving the car and crying; walking down the street and silently weeping just to get it out, people noticing sometimes, others oblivious. JZ tells me it will "blow my socks off" when I finally meet the right person; that there will be a quality of effortlessness to it, of rightness and ease, whereas so much of my relationship with P. was the exact opposite of that; it felt like so much hard work most of the time. JZ says my being will be recognized and honored in a way that I have never experienced before because I now recognize and honor something about myself that I haven't recognized and honored before, especially my heart, and that the deep honesty of true relationship comes out of being truly recognized, truly seeing and being seen.

The energetics of this new vibration will spread and they cannot be lied to, the way P. lied to me and how I allowed myself to be lied to and how I lied to myself as well. This new relationship will honor the qualities and energies I possess, will celebrate them in fact, not try to change them as P. did almost from the very beginning of our marriage.

So now I am entering this period of being alone, really alone, not the play-acting at being alone I have been engaged in over the last few years. I don't know why it appears to be hitting me so much harder now. No doubt my father's death has something to do with it, has opened up new dynamics. A friend of mine recently said that if you can't be alone with yourself, then you must be with someone, anyone to fill the void. This need to not be alone can influence a person to be with others he or she doesn't necessarily love or even care for but who won't leave. Such a pattern comes from a sense of emptiness, fear, and separation from one's Source.

I am not afraid to be alone, though the other night I felt so lonely; it felt as if I were hanging on by my fingernails, just. And I know, too, there is nothing I can change about this process, nor would I want to change it if I could, even though I am tired of it. I simply must move through it. Prayer in this regard does help.

September 24, 2008

I am sitting in bed with a lousy, stinking end-of-summer, beginning-of-fall cold. And Buster, my newly acquired feline roommate, is on the bed trying to get my attention away from this writing business. In many ways, I do not feel as if I even keep a journal anymore. It has become such a slap-dash endeavor, scotch-taping snippets of this and that, here and there, chaotic and incoherent.

A lot like life.

I inherited Buster, Mel.'s cat, as she is off in Italy teaching. He and I are the same age, so I wonder what that says about the two of us? D. teases me about applying the term middle-aged to myself. "When are you going to get

over that, Mom? You're not middle-aged anymore, face it!"
All I can say is: just wait until you're looking at life from
my perspective. You'll refer to yourself as middle-aged,
too. Now Bill, at only a few months shy of 98 when he
died: that's what I call old.

At any rate, one adult child and pet gone, another pet
of another adult child in. Life is like that: one revolving
door after another and you never know who or what is
going to walk through or spin in. I must confess it has
helped very much having another living creature around to
touch and stroke and talk to. I am settling into the reality
that I am alone without a partner, lover, or shipmate. But
the truth I know and have known for quite a while, even
though it has taken me a long time to accept it, is that now
is the time in life to be alone. I need to be alone to become
what I am meant to be, to allow her to break through the
surface of life and flower.

How or when does a woman finally give herself
permission to be who she is rather than what others want
her to be? To paraphrase Adrienne Rich: to become once
again "the presiding genius of her own body"? Part of my
journey now is to learn how to incorporate the kind and
supportive words friends and others say about me. So hard
to let in at times. Did I ever receive a compliment as a
child? One that I could take in as my own? And no doubt
this was one of P.'s great frustrations with me: that I
couldn't do this.

Maybe it is all part of an inevitable, inexorable
process. And ultimately for the good of all. P. once said
that my naiveté is one of the things that attracted him to me
in the first place. And why? Because he said it made me no
"danger" to him. Danger: that's the way he parsed his
world. Well, watch out world, I intend to be as "dangerous"
as I can from now on!

Why did P. and I accept the lie? You cannot be in a healthy relationship with a lie. What to do? We're all struggling with the some kind of emotional and psychological challenge; financial woes, health issues, vocational questions, relationship problems. We are just humans being human.

I am accepting more that I can trust the process of life, that Love will see me through. I really don't have to do as much as I think. I am actually beginning to feel rather stupid – not in the sense of not knowing certain things but in not needing to know, but just let things be.

Learning how to be patient.

Learning how to be loving and accepting.

Learning how to let go into a soul free-fall, trusting that the ever-lasting arms of Love are there.

****

Days later.

Feeling better now, cold recovery helped along with a trip to a local spa, soaking in the hot mineral waters. I noticed while I was there how okay, even good I felt about my body. I have fought and battled with my body throughout so much of my life: weight issues, eating disorders, not to mention the very real and serious health problems I have had to confront; all the scars and marks my body has picked up along the way, including a self-inflicted tattoo.

But I found as I was walking around naked, climbing in and out of the water, sauna and steam rooms that I actually felt proud of my body, perhaps for the first time in my life. I wasn't at all embarrassed or compared my body negatively with those of the other women as they entered. To actually feel proud of my body: what a concept! And what a splendid way to start the honoring of my womanhood. This is something I did not fight for in either of my marriages.

And so, of course, what did I not get from those relationships? Appropriate honoring.

What did I receive instead? An insidious, corrosive lack of respect. I believe both AD and P. respected my capability to get things done and perform certain functions – indeed, they relied upon me for that – but on some fundamental level they did not respect me *as a woman!* Part of this is endemic to the system; women around the world are not respected on the same level, in the same way as men. And part of it was due to the fact that I didn't respect myself; I always thought I had to please the man. Even if I am never with another man again in an intimate relationship, I will learn how to respect myself. It is about emerging from what can only be called a sort of patriarchal gloom. It is as if a spell is being broken, and I am in the process of waking up.

Then this deeply disturbing dream:

I am with my mother and father and am a teenager about fifteen years old. I know the young girl in the dream is me but she does not look like me. She has dark hair rather than blond but I know she is me. She is my dark goddess.

I am subject to the most abject kinds of abuse by both my parents: physical, sexual, emotional, you name it. In order to deal with this I, the dark haired girl, start taking all kinds of drugs and drink. The drugs and alcohol mask the pain, and in the dream I appear happy, cheerful, bouncing and dancing around. This goes on for a while with my parents yelling at me and telling me what to do as they hurt and mistreat me. I remain high as a kite.

The scene shifts and I find myself buried alive under the linoleum floor in our kitchen. There is one tiny little hole for air but there is a white pill or tablet stuck in the hole. I try to get air through the tiny hole despite the obstruction but it is not enough. I end up dying beneath the kitchen floor, drowned in my own vomit. I awakened from this dream in the early hours of the morning with my heart pounding. Pounding!

Yes, how that young dark-haired passionate beauty died, went underground when I was that age, probably earlier. What died under the kitchen floor was the passionate, exuberant, lively, sexual, sensual, feisty me. How to resuscitate and resurrect *that* girl! How to get that youthful dark goddess back into my life! How to get the wildness that was buried so long ago to come out again! How do I conjure her back into the light of day from the darkness of her dungeon under the kitchen floor – the quintessential place of warmth and food and nurturance, of sustenance that I didn't get when I so needed it? How to nurture and sustain her now? How do I open up the air hole so she can breath again?

I need to rip up that goddamned linoleum floor. How a part of me was so suppressed in such an insidious way: the ultimate violence – who you are being buried alive until you cease to be alive, cease to be anything except a drugged-out automaton serving the needs of others.

Rip up that floor, Maurine, let your dark-haired beauty out!

October 5, 2008
A rollercoaster of ups and downs:
On Wall Street.
On Main Street.
For me personally up and down with another terrible cold for almost two weeks now. I hosted a book launching party for a friend, followed by an all day seminar on Law and Ethics, which is not the most interesting of topics at any time. This was followed by a wedding planning dinner

for my oldest daughter, the first gay wedding in the family, two Bridezillas on the loose. Then only a few days later, the 25th anniversary of the Spirituality Center where P. and I trained to become spiritual directors. He was there with C., and I could tell he was nervous, uncomfortable when he saw me. During one of the program breaks I went up to him to say hello (C. had disappeared). P. honestly did not know how to respond. I actually felt sorry for him, like a deer caught in headlights. I left the reception early, with "gladness and singleness of heart."

This was followed by another milestone: my 40th – gag! – high school reunion. I wore high heels, stockings, a tight black lace skirt, white blouse, and dressy black corselet. If I do say so myself I looked pretty damned good, even some six pounds lighter than when I was in high school, oh those most ancient of days! Out of the over one hundred people who attended from a class of 560, there were only a handful of individuals I remembered and/or recognized. The party was scheduled to go from 6pm to midnight – drinks, buffet supper, then dancing. I arrived at 7:00pm and left before 9:00. That's how much fun I had – NOT! Where did all those Pali High Republicans come from? Weren't we the infamous Class of '68 when everyone started smoking weed and taking to the streets in protest? Oh, what age can do.

Then a flurry of emotional turmoil and another rollercoaster ride:

P. and I had a huge fight on the phone that ended with my telling him to fuck off and slamming down the receiver. He basically accused me of sabotaging his relationship with our children. I told him his own behavior was doing that; he didn't need any help from me.

The night before the wedding P. threw a big party for all the visiting relatives and soon-to-be-married couple. He had C. there instead of me, telling the children I wasn't invited. This was one of the reasons for the phone fight. A part of me was so insulted, like a slap in the face; after twenty-five years of raising A. and contributing to her life (P. himself says I "saved" her from psychological death); twenty-five years of birthdays and holidays and sending presents to my east coast family, my nieces and their children, and P. had C. at this event. A part of me understands; they are a couple now. Still…You'd think twenty-five years would carry more weight, or at least more acknowledgement and respect. Even the visiting relatives were appalled; their exact word was "insulted" P. hadn't even told them C. was going to be there instead of me.

So that Saturday night, the night before A.'s wedding, I took myself out for dinner and a movie. I was okay. I had a good time being with me. The next day A. told me I was very much missed.

Reflecting on all the changes and emotional seismic shifts, I had another talk with JZ. The facts are these:

- Growing up in an intensely father-dominated environment, I learned to be subservient, taking care of others. This kind of environment brands you like an animal; it goes very deep, learning that love is conditional by making others happy. In that kind of environment, there is no alternative. "Do what I say or else!" How can that be called love?
- In my family I was not valued or respected, so I learned to not value or respect myself.
- Getting married and having children, the importance of children in my life and the sacrificial nature of parenting, putting my children first, allowed me to avoid looking at these deeper issues. I got my value from being a good parent.

- There was also the financial aspect. When I married P. I got used to living a comfortable life. When a woman is in a situation like that, her self-confidence can erode, i.e. the feeling that I was not good at being independent and taking care of myself. Plus there were four children to raise, and that was a strong binding force.
- Denial of the above allowed me to remain in the relationship – don't ask, don't tell – and this type of denial is endemic to our culture; the idea that if you don't feel secure, you keep quiet and don't rock the boat.

UNTIL...the Universe rubs your nose in it, i.e. how the divorce released me. But the legal divorce was nothing compared to this emotional one. Yes, awakening from that dream. Until a woman owns her own eroticism, not just her sex or sexuality but who she is, she is not fully empowered. She does not live the truth of the erotic in the world, the full embracing of life and self, and how knowledge of the erotic makes you know the truth. If a woman is empowered in her own heart, she is fearless! Fearless! The terror of speaking this truth can be great, but now is the time for truth.

I repeat: NOW IS THE TIME FOR TRUTH.

October 24, 2008

Visited some old friends after A.'s wedding and it was like watching a tableau of my ex-life, with a few variations. How much I do not, repeat do not want to get sucked back into that dynamic again. And yet knowing, too, how insidiously easy it could be as I learn to stand like a wobbly newborn colt on my own feminine authority, getting reacquainted with the "me" as she was when she first entered the world and before the prison locks clamped down: courageous, curious, and risk-taking.

I sometimes wonder if I am even fit to be in a relationship; there always seems to be that sparky friction at some point, somewhere. As you get older, you really do want things to calm down and get easier without all the hassles and jockeying for position or arguing and debating all the time. The longer I am away from P., the more I see how emotionally, psychologically, and intellectually undernourished I was in my relationship with him. P. was an outstanding provider at the material level, but there was such lack of emotional fulfillment underneath and me, being me, just always expected to *not* get what I needed, deferring time and again to him. Well, no more. I am going to get what I need, with or without a man. But I could sure use some good, sweet sex.

Apropos the above, I read a book by Don Miguel Ruiz called *The Mastery of Love*. How, indeed, do we master love? You'd think after two marriages I'd know. Ruiz's answer:

You love people the way they are or you don't.

You love yourself the way you are or you don't.

That's it: the secret to a fulfilling relationship.

I think about all the contracts and legal documents and iron gates literally closing others out and me in, all of P.'s objections to my friends and activities, the way I went about "doing" my life. His strained tolerance because he knew he should allow these things but you could tell he didn't like them. And I am guilty of the same dynamic in reverse: my trying to be "okay" with things he did when I wasn't. The trick in any relationship is learning how to be 100% responsible for your 50%. It's not about "getting the love you need," which is the focus of so much pop psychology today, but sharing the love you have inside.

Ruiz offers these tips:

- Don't believe any shaman or teacher or guru just because they are a shaman or teacher or guru. Believe what you want according to what makes sense *for you.*

- Don't believe all the lies you tell yourself, all the lies you were programmed to believe when you were "domesticated" as a child. Don't believe your own bullshit. (As George Carlin would say: "It's bullshit and it's bad for you!")
- Don't believe your internal Victim or Judge, the voice that tells you how stupid you are, or whatever else it tells you. Don't believe anyone else's either.
- Nothing but common sense will guide you to your own happiness.

That truly is Paradise. And freedom.

November 3, 2008

I was actually able to talk with P. the other day without getting defensive, crying, and/or going ballistic internally. I was even able to thank him for all that he has contributed to my life. Will miracles and wonders never cease? Ruiz is right: Once you find the love in your own heart, you don't need to look for it elsewhere because you already have what you need. What you can do at that point is to share what you have with others. Neediness, want, guilt, and judgment shift to the desire to share and spread the love.

Spread and share the love: that's all there is to do. That and accepting the way things are without fighting or resisting them. This acceptance doesn't mean you have to go along with another person's drama or trauma. The important thing is to not take the other person's "stuff" personally. Let them have the freedom to take care of their own bullshit and be idiots if they choose. I've got more than enough to handle taking care of my own insanity.

I heard the following a week ago that struck a chord: "You don't think yourself into a new way of living. You can only live your way into a new way of thinking." And I might add: you can only love your way into a new way of being. Once this deep, resonant love is ignited, it becomes a nuclear reactor of sorts, a log of love or a love log that just keeps going, perpetually burning and giving off light and heat.

And the contentment that comes with this is the absolute best gift of all! I am happy as a calm clam right now just being little ole me. Who would have thought! I actually am okay just as I am! What a radical notion! I am enjoying my solitude and having a love affair with myself. It doesn't bother me, at least not right now, that I am alone or that P. is with someone. But a "friend with benefits" as the kids call it sure would be nice. And even that isn't necessary right now, not a top burner priority.

I continue to give away books and the whole process has become a game. Where and how can I give away more books? And as I participate in this giving, I am presented with more and more opportunities to give at schools and churches and libraries and donation centers, to family members and friends. A while back I calculated that I needed to give away approximately thirty books @ week for a year – yikes, an entire year! – in order to liberate the boxes from my garage. At first this felt positively daunting to me. However could I possibly do it?

But as I align myself more with the flow and givingness of the universe – because that's what the universe does: it gives and gives and gives; it doesn't sell or barter in trade or expect a receipt for tax purposes; it just gives – have I been surprised! Last week alone I managed to spread almost one hundred book seeds around LA and my various travels. I carry several dozen copies in my car at all times and whenever an opportunity presents itself, out come more books. I have even left some on church doorsteps, like the little paperback orphans that they are, with a note saying, "Please put these to use or give them to those who can benefit from them or sell them at your book fair or bazaar."

And I feel so good afterwards. How such acts put a smile on my face, and better yet a smile in my heart. I never would have imagined that my *lack* of success in one arena could end up feeling so good in another. Whoever knew?

November 9, 2008
I made a list of the qualities I want in a partner and I realized as I wrote it that they are the qualities I must radiate from within myself. I must *be* the lover I want first before that lover will be presented to me. Indeed, I must be this lover for myself and with myself, otherwise what is the point of all the suffering and hurt and pain and hard come-by knowledge?

The Kind of Partner/Lover I Want/Need:
Funny! Someone with a good sense of humor, a wicked sense of humor even, but not mean-spirited or malicious, someone who will make me laugh. How I love laughter! It's the best of the best of the best: light radiating light.

Someone who is accomplished in his own right, whatever that endeavor might be.

Someone who has children (preferably grown), who understands being a parent.

Someone who is athletic and healthy, who likes to use his body.

Someone for whom his spiritual life is important, but not heavy. Light!

Someone who will accept and respect me for who I am and not try to change me, who will not *want* to change me.

Someone who is mellow and easy-going; someone who has a similar rhythm to mine, melodic.

Someone who enjoys books and music and plays and art and movies. (And golf.)

Someone who will be patient and tender.

Someone who has a similar sexual/sensual sensibility to mine.

Someone who has, by and large, done his internal emotional work.

Someone who has friends and for whom friends and the cultivation of friendship are important parts of life.

Someone who is my equal, my compatriot; someone who can challenge me to grow with love and humor, not anger and control.

Someone who likes to travel and travels well, not demanding or complaining about things all the time but grateful for what is right and beautiful.

Someone who is financially responsible.

Someone who is faithful and monogamous and who doesn't lie!

Someone who will pitch in with the mundane maid chores. I resign from being the maid, the chief cook and bottle washer.

And what will be the passion that the two of us share? What will be our life's work? Perhaps just loving being together!

November 16, 2008
I have been feeling a sense of moving forward until last Sunday while playing the piano, Mozart's Sonata in C Major. During the second movement I started crying for self-forgiveness; for all the times I have allowed myself to

be abused in so many ways, both blatant and subtle, by so many people. Crying for forgiveness for not taking better care of myself. It is so much easier, infinitely easier to forgive others. It is much harder to forgive the abuse I have allowed into my life. Crying at the piano: I'm so sorry! How or why the beauty of Mozart's music released this in me, I don't know. I had already been playing for a while when the crying started. How the feelings are just the feelings and the blues are just that: the Blues. And the blues of liberation perhaps the most painful of all.

Part of this weepiness is probably related to the upcoming holidays: the first time in twenty-seven years I will not be celebrating as part of a family, everyone going his/her separate way. It all came to a head when I talked to P. about getting some things of mine from his house. At first he was defensive but then relented. We arranged to meet on a Friday, and he looked so sad. A part of me felt terrible, almost as if I were kicking him while he was down. P. and his company have been slammed by all the financial upheaval that is occurring; credit lines frozen, deals gone sour. And yet on the other hand, they are my things: records going back to my college days, things left to me by my mom and dad and other relatives, even wedding gifts from my first marriage.

On the way back to my place I felt simply awful. I bawled like a baby most of the way home, so many feelings and emotions, sorrow mixed with concern. P. really did not look well, an air of defeat and resignation about him. I felt so sorry for him, damn my tender heart. I can't stay and yet I can't seem to let go, even after all this time. I felt so badly that I called him the next day and said that with a few exceptions I would leave the rest of my things, mostly artwork hanging on the walls, behind. It was just too depressing, like eviscerating a dead animal, no longer a home.

****

Another talk with my Guide.

What is it about me that elicits this "feeling sorry for the other"? How or why is it that I so lose myself? Where is the laughter I so long for?

Twenty-five years creates bonds through time that are real and need to be honored. Honored! You and P. went through a great deal together. There is no reason not to love this even though the two of you are no longer a couple. As time goes forward, this will be easier for both of you. You have such a tender heart it is hard for you to feel that your actions are causing pain in any way and that is also a part of the journey you have needed to embark upon – knowing that you must factor yourself into the equation as well.

Yours is a challenging journey because of this: because of the intrinsic gentleness of spirit that you brought with you into this realm and also because of how dishonored you were as a child and how you learned to so dishonor yourself. You must not allow the events that need to unfold to not take their course. You are on a journey of healing that must be followed to become whole within your own right. There is no genuine way of being with anyone unless you can stand apart first. This is paradoxically easier for you because of your quiet nature and need for solitude and more difficult for you because your tender heart loves to give and share with others. These two aspects of your nature need to come more into alignment before you can engage in a balanced union.

Your desire for more laughter in your life is critical and it is telling that you placed laughter at the top of your list of what to look for in a partner, even before not lying and telling the truth. Because one who has the capacity to laugh understands much about the balance of life, the balance of the darkness and the light. Your desire for more laughter is a call to your own healing. You need to honor your tears but as you do, know that joy needs to be a part of you as well, a part of any relationship you enter into because that is an indicator of greater balance and health.

As for the part that automatically feels more for the other than yourself: you must be very careful to cut away the part of that response that comes from the old wound vs. the spontaneous outpouring of loving feeling that is an intrinsic part of you. The former must be abandoned; the other is a treasure you must learn to guard and honor with all your heart. Because it is your heart, the very best of you.

Ask yourself, "Am I responding from the wounded part? Or "Am I responding from the part that is good and true?" There may even be times when the answer to these questions is a little of both, but in time and with attention you will learn greater discernment how to judge and calibrate the two. You must remember that in this process of change you are learning to honor yourself in a way you never could before, in a way you perhaps never even knew you needed before. Now is the time for the journey of inner honoring long overdue. Trust always in this meditation and prayer.

PART IV:
ON THE ROAD AGAIN
(Excerpts from Journals 107 to 112)

Women are the answer. They are.
If you'll only let them into the story.
Women. They are the answer.
Zadie Smith, *The Autograph Man*

December 2, 2008

Back from a trip to Northern California to visit family and friends that was bittersweet. No more gathering around the Thanksgiving table, everyone scattered now to the winds of time and change. I did see sons D. and W. in Santa Cruz. On Thanksgiving the three of us did a ceremony with Mom's and Dad's ashes out among the redwoods. W. took us to a beautiful cathedral-like setting among the trees, sunlight shafting through their branches. There was a small stream and I said a brief prayer as I dropped some of their remains into the water, Mom first since she died first, then Dad. I thanked them for the gift of life, the gift that allowed me to have the two young men who were by my side and the two young women who were not. I prayed for their peace and being together, wherever that might be.

Then the three of us went to the ocean and performed a similar ritual there, tossing a cup of each into the foam and waves. Mom always loved the Pacific Ocean; it brought great comfort to her, I know, on many occasions. Then I took off for San Francisco as the boys stayed behind in Santa Cruz and prepared their own Thanksgiving meal.

I drove north to Sausalito to spend the evening with some cousins, then the following day continued farther north to Sebastopol to see my dear friend, DC. I'm afraid I fell in love with another of her art pieces and negotiated a deal right then and there. From her place I drove to my surrogate mother in Lockeford, my mother's dear soul friend. On Sunday we performed another ceremony around a rosebush and some angels UP set out in Mom's and Dad's memory. The three of them truly were the best of friends.

Then back on the road south to encounter the journey from hell. It felt as if I had entered the Twilight Zone of Traveling; every route I attempted was somehow blocked off or congested or fog bound. It was positively surreal, starting on the Interstate 5 and hitting thick central valley fog, then going over to the 101 South – it was just as crowded – then back to the 5 again. After nearly four hours of being on the road I was literally right where I started. On several occasions I started pleading, "I just want to get home!" By the time I got back to LA at 10pm, there was Kleenex all over the car floor from my crying and having to blow my nose due to a cold. I slept until 9:30am the next day.

I was then met with the news from my cardiologist that the results from my stress test were inconclusive; there may be more problems. What did I say about there always being something? I have to undergo more tests to see what is wrong. I have been having funny feelings in my chest lately– fluttering and brief pains here and there. I have found myself rubbing my heart area, that old wound from years ago where the doctors excised the lymphoma. But then again, it has been a stressful, emotional year. Why wouldn't my heart hurt? You can have a pain in your heart from feeling too much, not only from disease.

I jokingly told a friend: "My epitaph will be: Here lies a woman who had more operations than anybody!" and in spite of that, in spite of all the heroic medical measures and interventions I'll still be dust and ashes, tossed hopefully into a beautiful mountain stream under redwoods or into the boundless sea. We are all dust and ashes in the end.

December 5, 2008
Gracious Spirit:
I am still struggling with feelings of hurt and betrayal. I find myself so angry at times. It is like having a chicken bone stuck in my throat that I can't get out and it's there every day bugging me and reminding me of all the what – I don't even know anymore – all the crap I put up with. It has

been a year now, and it feels as if this journey is getting harder. What am I not doing for myself that I need to do? How am I not cooperating with Your plan?

Do not judge that it has been "a long time" or "a year" or that you should be at a different place in your journey of healing. You are where you are and perhaps it has taken this time for you to truly tap into how much P.'s actions wounded you. Be open to the feelings; they are not "bad" even though you hate feeling them. They simply are what they are and feelings by their nature come and go.

Feel your feelings. Go deeply into them, befriend them, ask them what they are trying to communicate to you. They are not about being victimized or being the victim. You have every right to feel the way you feel. You were violated and lied to; and you accepted this on some level. Your awareness is growing, and you are tapping into this personal level of betrayal more.

You must believe in the light that comes after the darkness. Do not put a timetable on this or say to yourself "I should be over this by now and moving on." Healing has its own ways, its own demands. Your job right now is to allow this healing to move through you. If you are still hurt and angry after a year, so be it. Perhaps it has taken this long for you to be able to look at this deep heart wound.

You must not run from but embrace your tender-heartedness in all its anger and hurt and confusion and pain. Just embrace it. Let the tears flow as much as they need to. In time and with time you will not need them so much anymore. Now they are communicating to you to just be with yourself and the pain. Because underneath the anger is real, true pain.

Stay focused on your journey. Take care and guard your heart. It is talking to you almost daily now; you can feel its fluttering, like a butterfly trying to escape a cocoon, long overdue in certain respects, right on time in others.

Hold your thoughts in check but feel the feelings as much and whenever you need to. It is hard for you to admit how hurt you have been, and to a certain degree, still are. And though you may understand that your journey is no longer with P., that deep knowing allows the hurt to arise even more.

Allow all the residual hurt from the past to surface. You are learning that you deserve more, are worthy of more, and to stand up for that worthiness and the many qualities you have to offer and the knowledge that you have not defended your goodness enough, your goddess as you call her. Now is the time to honor the goddess within. Do not allow her to be neglected, disrespected, or dishonored again.

December 6, 2008

Saturday morning in bed. Still nursing a cold, though definitely better than the last couple of days. Buster just barfed all over my coverlet. Life is just plain messy at times.

A dream last night about P.:

We are together and I am having some feelings return for him. Could we possibly work things out? But I'm still not sure whether I can be sexual with him, make love with him again. We talk about sleeping together, just holding one another, skin to skin. He says he wants me.

At one point P. is holding me and talking so sweetly, intimately, and vulnerably to me. It feels very real, a new and different P. Then C. appears and P. shifts back to his old dominating, controlling persona, as if announcing an edict:

"I'll have either Woman #1 (me) or Woman #2 (C.)!" And then he walks off.

Moral of the dream: I guess it just takes a lot of time to get over some things.

I went to a special Advent carol service at my church, one of my favorite liturgical events of the year. I sat quietly and prayed for comfort. I was so glad I attended, such a sense of being grateful that I have this place of worship as a home, the sense of release: "Okay, this is it; this is me. It's Friday night and I'm lonely and I have a cold and something's not right with my heart and I'm feeling pretty damn punk right now and that's just the way it is and I'm in the thick of it. Lord, help me please just let it all go!"

Later that night when I crawled into bed after 11:00pm, as I lay in the darkness with Buster purring by my side, I had a calming sense wash over me that everything is going to be okay, that I'm going to be fine, that I will get through this and come out the other side. I am so grateful for my faithful heart! Thank you, God, for my faithful heart!

I have been thinking too about true love: how rarely, if ever, have I experienced this in my life. The only time I have really felt that kind of love was when I awakened from cancer surgery years ago and felt the absolute Presence of God, utterly compassionate and accepting and non-judgmental. True love is not about authority and obedience; it is about acceptance and feeling embraced. I do believe we females struggle with this more, with authority and self-empowerment, still treated as objects in so many ways around the world, and how we do this to ourselves as well. It feels as if there has always been some kind of subtle force at work to comply to the rules, needs, and standards of others. Rules cannot bring freedom; they only have the power to coerce and accuse. True love is about freedom.

December 22, 2008

I will not be sorry to see 2008 pass. It has been a darn-tooting, shit-hole of a year. I am still struggling to quiet my mind, to let go lovingly of P. and the past, all the hurt and misplaced effort and lost opportunities; to look forward rather than back; to stop bolstering my side of the argument, even if it takes place only inside my own head. I am having to learn how to trust and be open unlike anything I have ever known before. I so did not think or believe I would be where I am at this stage in my life: alone, single, family gone. I am sure there are many others just like me out there all over the planet. I know I am not alone, even though I am.

I just got back from a consultation with a financial adviser, and I am going to have to get a job to supplement my income. What's coming in is less than what is going out and 2009 will be, among other things, a year of belt-tightening for sure. As I was driving back from my meeting, I started in on "What to do now? Where to work? Teach? Substitute? What?" And then I said to myself, "You know, Maurine, you don't have to decide any of this right now. For today everything is just fine. The only thing you have to worry about right this moment is to get home in time to let the plumber in to fix the downstairs toilet. That's all you have to think about right now."

2009: a year of cleansing and purging of the old and embarking upon the new.

And what will be the adventure of my life now? Only God knows. I sure don't. All my efforts to "figure things out" or "do the right thing" haven't amounted to much, as in half a hill of beans.

I would like to live more musically as Van Gogh put it. And I would like to share this path with someone if that is meant to be. But for right now I simply want to get through today. It feels so much more real now, this being alone. Last December we still made the attempt to celebrate as a family under the same roof. This year not even the pretense of trying. After twenty-seven years of celebrating Christmas Eve, I now have been reassigned Christmas Day.

And so it goes.

I've come full circle: back to celebrating Christmas Day the way I did as a child.

And we'll all muddle through somehow, in whatever home for the holidays we find ourselves in. And hopefully we will be grateful for all the blessings we have, that I have especially: the good medical news I received a few days ago about my test results. The second set of tests revealed nothing emergent, at least for now. A couple of valves to be watched. And the pains I have been experiencing? The fluttering and skipped beats? Could they simply be the pain of a love dying? The pain of a tender heart letting go?

After trying to get me back on and off all year, P. sent me a Christmas card saying that he didn't understand the choices I have made but that I must believe my "long-term interests" will best be served by them. Because of this he felt any further approaches to dissuade me would be a "violation" of my wishes at this time.

He's finally letting go, too.

New Year's Eve, 2008

The last day of 2008: my *annus horribilus* to quote Queen Elizabeth, if there ever was one. As I said earlier: I will not be at all unhappy to see this year pass – to be buried in the vast, deep annals of time. Relentless time.

The holidays have been trying, the new Doerken order: Mom's house, Dad's house, and the family moving back and forth in between. W.'s 25th birthday was an absolute disaster because he didn't want C. at his party and P. refused to budge; if he's there, she's there. The end result: W. told both of us not to attend his quarter-century celebration. What life can be like when a family splinters apart and works to readjust to new dynamics and configurations. Not pretty.

I want, no I need mental release from all this. The near constant thought processing and chattering in my head about the past, what happened or didn't happen has become a form of torment. Torment! I can't even tell myself to shut up anymore, it has gotten so bad. I have been reduced to saying "Hush, Maurine, hush!" – like a parent trying to calm a distraught child and not having much luck at soothing the hurt. Hush, Maurine, hush. It's going to be okay. You are into the home stretch of the holidays. The first baby is always the hardest, the most painful to deliver. Next year won't be as bad. Hold your course!

How I do want this year to end, this horrible, horrible year! I want it to end with a prayer of peace in my heart. I long for peace within myself; that special internal calm that stills all chattering and doubt. I long for peace in this world: Arab and Jew; Christian and Muslim; Hindu and Sheik; men and women and parents and children: please, please, please let there be peace. Let peace be the tone that is struck at midnight tonight. Let the bombs stops flying, in whatever form they take: emotional bombs, literal bombs, bombs of hatred and mistrust, bombs of ignorance and fear. We must all participate in stopping the bombing.

I must stop the mental bombs that pummel my consciousness, that I pummel myself with, to allow the peace and quiet in that truly pass all understanding; that is my prayer for today, the last day of 2008, and my prayer for tomorrow, the first day of 2009 and the days that lie beyond that.

Let there be peace.

And let that peace begin with me.

January 9, 2009

First entry of the New Year. Just back from a brief visit to Seattle to see D.'s investiture, the priest I went with to the Holy Land, and visit with my dear friend, L., an experience that was at once nurturing and sad. On the plane ride I sat next to a couple who were holding hands and stroking each others' arms with affection. Looking at the hair on the man's arms – of all things – brought up such emotion I had to get up from my seat and go into the lavatory to cry. How I long for male contact and caressing and being with someone again! Then seeing both D. and his family and L. with hers underscored what I no longer have and no longer am part of. How the holidays especially have reinforced that truth as well.

And yet some sweet moments, too: seeing how happy D. is with his new church home; laughing and talking with L. on her birthday over lunch and wine; walking the streets of Seattle and it actually feeling like winter – what a concept after the monotonous sun and smog of LA. D. commented that he thought I would thrive in Seattle and a part of me thought, "Why not?" Throw caution to the wind and step outside the box and just do something, anything different. After all, there is an abundance of coffee shops and bookstores in Seattle, my kind of town.

Since my return I've had several fantasies of selling everything except my piano and books and heading north with my cat. But then reality sets in at all the effort that would entail and the question "Would I really want to live in a place where there might be a month of consecutive days of rain or dismal grey?" I remember how depressing the winters in England were. The metaphorical grass isn't always greener, even when it does rain a lot.

And yet walking the streets with the rain and mist caressing my face did feel good and the early evening darkness and the late morning light felt remarkably familiar to me. It is then that I realize I am absolutely incapable of making any sort of decision about anything at this point in time. I really need to be led by God to where I am supposed to be and trust absolutely that She/He will get me where I am needed.

January 26, 2009

Yesterday after church I drove out to Zuma Beach to perform a ritual of release. I felt the need to let go of the past symbolically and all that has come before. It was a stunning, glorious day: the sky a brilliant blue and clouds everywhere after a recent rain. The wind was fierce and chilly and the sea roiling with waves and white caps – the kind of day and natural beauty that take your breath away.

I was most grateful that I had my yoga blanket in the back of the car it was so cold. I wrapped it around me and started gathering small stones from a lagoon where pelicans and other birds were resting. I must have collected twenty to thirty stones, carrying them like a papoose in front of me. I walked along the shore for a while, relishing the wind and sun and magnificent beauty of the day, the gift nature is, thinking to myself, "I need to do this more, to come here and experience this power, even if it is a long way from where I live and gas is expensive. I need to do this for my soul!"

After walking for about twenty minutes with the wind whipping about me, hair flying, I stopped and looked up at the sun and sky and out at the sea, and said a prayer, talking out loud amidst the wind roaring and buffeting around me. I prayed to God, Lord of the Universe, Whatever Presence that creates all this wonder and beauty and complexity and variety, She/He who hears all prayers and to Whom all flesh returns in the end, to release me from the past. There were tears of such feeling and gratitude streaming down my face and drying almost instantly in the salty air. Thanking

God for everything, for listening, for being on the beach shouting out words of love into the wind, asking to be let go of all that has been holding me back, to let go, let go, let go. And then I started to heave stones, one by one, into the waves and surf and sea.

P., I release you.

All the pain from the past, I release you.

All the weight and rocks that have been holding me down, I release you.

All the stones I have been pummeling myself with, I release you.

Stone thoughts of inadequacy, timidity, fearfulness, I release you.

Mom and Dad, I release you.

Heaving stone after stone after stone into the sea through the howling wind with tears streaming down my cheeks, tears of joy and pain and sorrow and gratitude and not-knowing-what-comes-next. Throwing the stones as hard and as far as I possibly could, given the constraints of jacket, yoga blanket, and wind.

I release you!

I release you!

I release you!

After throwing the last stone, I stood frozen in place for quite a while. I simply could not move from the spot where I stood in the wet sand, my footprints like a bird's cuneiform scratching. I stood and watched and cried and prayed, "Thank you, thank you, thank you for this moment and the beauty of this day!" I stood still until the waves erased my footprints, releasing everything, simply everything into the sea.

After this I walked along the shore for a while, relishing the wind stinging my face and mussing my hair, strands dancing, wild and kinetic. I had long before removed my hat, no protection from that article of clothing in such a gale! I kept walking and breathing and crying, exhilarated beyond measure, thinking, "I'm so glad I did this! I'm so glad I took the time to do this!" Perfect. Absolutely perfect. I could not have hoped for, nor orchestrated, a more fitting ritual of release.

Watching the seagulls and pelicans and other birds floating on the wind, floating on currents of air, floating with wings outstretched but not moving, effortless and free. Yes, that is what it felt like to me: effortless and free. I finally walked back to my car, grateful to feel the warmth inside and brimming with...with what?

Energy.

Surprise.

Joy.

A sense of accomplishment, of rightfulness.

So glad I took the time to do this, to drive all the way out to Zuma Beach after church on a sunny but briskly cold Sunday to engage in this ritual of release.

Release!

※※※※

Days later and this dream:

I am in my childhood bedroom. I am in bed with my father. He's fully dressed and I'm naked but covered by my bed sheets. He is on top of the sheets, so he cannot see me nude.

I tell him what has happened between P. and me: the divorce, P.'s affairs, etc. Dad takes in the information but doesn't react much one way or the other; he's not upset, just very matter-of-fact, "I'm sorry to hear that." He then turns over to go to sleep, not particularly concerned about how important and momentous these events are in my life. I tell Dad to get out of bed and go back to Mom. He leaves.

I get out of bed and see some items of clothing in the dressing room area, a small hallway between my bedroom and the bathroom. The clothes are in baskets. I notice a white and blue striped shirt in particular. I wonder: Why that shirt? It reminds me of a sailor. Ahoy!

Some thoughts:

There is unconscious incest, yet I am firm in the dream: "Go back to Mom!" Dad is literally now back with Mom beyond the veil of death.

Being nude in the dream means being without a persona?

The sailor shirt represents a new journey?

I go to my father for some empathy and understanding about how I have been hurt, but I don't get any solace from him. He can't be bothered.

How my father was hooked into me energetically and this can be just as powerful as physical molestation, perhaps even more so because it is so unconscious, not acted out in reality. Is this representative of how I was abused by my father and men in general? And how my mother colluded in this process, how she taught me to be quiet and obey, to be the peacemaker and peacekeeper, and on some level imprisoned because of this.

I still must have some energy tied in with this pattern that must be released, but the sailor shirt also represents embarking on another journey. My life as a pirate? Because until this release is accomplished, my internal energy will continue to be off, with three possible outcomes:

A man who still is in the dominating energy field will attract me; or I will be attracted to him.

A man who is not dominated by that field will not find me attractive even if I am attracted to him.

I will be attracted to a younger man whom I can control and who wants a mother/son energetic.

None of these at this point is acceptable.

How this dream represents the combing out of the old incestuous dynamic from within my psyche. I need to appreciate that my psyche is still working on this and be brutally honest that this energy is present. I must acknowledge this in order to transmute it, like an alchemical process. I must be completely real and without judgment about where I am in order to emerge from bondage, both internal and external.

And what are the severance signs of this process?

I won't feel positive or negative toward P. All of that will feel part of another lifetime.

I won't apologize for myself or my past or where I'm at; there won't be any need for that.

I will remain more in the moment, not rehearsing or practicing what I'm going to say (not an easy task for this writer/judge).

There will be a spontaneous connection with men because there is a special magnetism when the archetypes are not dominating the psyche. I need to ask myself whether there is any archetypal "Velcro" left vis-à-vis men.

I will have a sense of well-being, of gratitude, of waking up with a feel-better feeling in the morning.

Also, I need to be on the look out for when I find myself getting caught in the old patterning, i.e. doing what the man wants and then ending up not knowing how I feel. I must pay careful attention to this.

Ah me, more work.

February 8, 2009

For some reason I felt compelled to draw a Sacred Geometry card. It never ceases to amaze me how accurate these divination tools can be, and I do not subscribe to the idea that it is our own projections only.

Out of 64 cards, I drew The Triangle or Trinity: the sacred three of so many religions: Beginning, Middle, End;

Father, Mother, Child; Father, Son, Spirit. How the cosmologies of so many cultures look upon existence as having three distinct levels: lower (tribe), middle (self, individual), upper (archetypal, symbolic, Higher Power, God); and how the synthesis of body, mind, and spirit is so important to our journey. And, of course, how appropriate this:

> Drawing this card denotes movement toward strength and completion. You are moving on a life path that puts you in touch with a synthesis of the elements of growth, joy, and freedom. Wherever you are on that path, take a moment to acknowledge the progress you are making, and renew your resolve to act in accordance with that which strengthens and assists you in enjoying and fulfilling you life's purpose.

For whatever it's worth, it felt good to hear something positive about what I have been through, even if it was from a random, or not so random, deck of cards.

Though I drew the Triangle upright, I also read the reversed meaning and nothing could have been more appropriate, considering what I have been through over the past year:

> This card reversed is also a triangle, but in this configuration it suggests that you may have become the third party to a situation where two was the appropriate number. Though it may represent a loss, the situation cannot stand for long, and you are advised to resolve it or leave as soon as possible for your own self-preservation.

My own self-preservation indeed.

February 9, 2009
Gracious Spirit:

It has been several months since we last spoke and a different energy is arising. You know I do not want to be alone, how I long for human touch, and yet there is also a part of me that feels I need to be alone now, am required to be alone for some purpose. I want to fulfill whatever this purpose is, but I also do not want to let wounds from my past inhibit the opening of my heart deeply and with love to another human being. Please guide me on what is being called for.

It is all about your being calm and resting in the calmness that is growing within you. You have become more proficient and willing to block negative thoughts, even the whisper of them. Consequently you have greater internal space for the seeds of calmness to grow. Do not fret in those moments that do come up about the direction of your life, alone or with someone. Know that when the timing is right all will be presented. You are still working at deeply embedding the lessons of the last year into your being, solidifying them as your foundational rock for the future. This is critical for you as you move forward.

It is also important for you to continue to release judgment. The hurt that you have experienced has a tendency to propel your mind into judgment or its lesser form, self-justification. It is important that you let go of judgment and the judging voice within you. This is a strong voice, a strong pull. You have by and large quelled the voice of worry and fear, but you need to pay greater attention to the voice of judgment as it arises. For judgment, wanting to be right or prove your case is yet another roadblock toward your freedom. Even if there is objective truth behind judgment, is still a way for the mind and ego to have their way, to be in charge, to feel satisfied or good.

It is important to separate judgment – wanting to prove a point and be right – from asking the appropriate questions "What do I need here?" "How do I feel?" This is an entirely different thought process, or better said questioning process, that is important for you to engage in. It is important for you because of your past and your lack of practice with, how do you say, checking in with yourself. This kind of judgment is very different than the lawyering voice that is so strong within you about trying to prove your case or bolster your side of the argument.

This is particularly true of your interactions with P. You still want to prove your point, to justify your hurt. And while it is true that you have experienced hurt and sorrow and pain, your job now is to learn how to place them in perspective, neither positive nor negative, but as something that happened and there are reasons events unfolded as they did and you participated in these events as well. These are the areas of judgment you need to let go of. This is very different from the honest grief you have experienced. Grief and the releasing of emotional pain are a necessary organic process. The judgment I am referring to comes from the mind, not the heart. Mercy comes from the heart. Can you find it within yourself to be merciful rather than judgmental? This requires attention and practice.

Part of your work now is being attuned to the judgments that arise about yourself and others. The rest truly is up to you. You have the freedom of choice. It is important as part of the checking in process to ask yourself how you feel. What are the messages you receive? Calmness? Anxiety? Eagerness? Confusion? This internal feedback will provide you with a roadmap how to move forward. This is such a new experience for you that you need practice to help cultivate making more connections with the feedback mechanisms that you have been blessed with but that you have learned over a lifetime to silence.

That is one of the reasons why being alone now, especially for you, is important. You have moved through much of the pain and hurt of the past year. Now as those feelings subside there is more space for you to listen. It is hard for you to accept doing something just because you want to or because it feels good. This is where your self-judgment comes in about wasting time or not being productive or whatever voice that infers you are doing it wrong or are not okay just as you are.

Be attentive to this self-critical voice; it can be very subtle and you have had years, a lifetime, perfecting it, allowing it such influence in your life. It truly is OK to enjoy yourself, whatever it is you choose to do. Life, all life is meant to be embraced with joy. Still the voice of judgment and be merciful and kind, especially with yourself. Judgment only narrows the expression of the full range of human life in all its nuanced complexity. Remember that love must be at the foundation of all things, not judgment. Learning how to navigate the differences between judgment and discernment is key.

Pay close attention to the feedback of your internal being.

Release judgment.
Learn to love your life just as it is.
In time and with time more will be presented.
Trust this all-abiding love.

February 23, 2009

I saw FS, the first time since Christmas, and came away as I usually do: feeling better but not really learning anything new; rather, having what I already know reinforced.

Slow down.

Stop thinking so much.

Trust the arms of Love.

He loves hearing from my Guide and agrees that it is not a disowned part of my psyche but rather the wisdom of my heart speaking. And indeed, it does feel exactly like that. It does not come from a place of unconsciousness or unresolved issues or lack of psychic integration; far from it. It feels like the best and truest part of me. After I left FS, I stopped by two churches and two schools, giving away another two dozen copies of my step-parenting book. When the last box is gone, I plan on throwing a BIG party!

One of the things FS and I talked about is love, the different kinds of love we humans experience, and I have come to realize that I have never been loved for myself, for just being me, not even by my own self. What would that kind of love feel like? And I'm not talking about the kind of false romantic notion that one will fall in love and that everything will be smooth and rosy and perfect. Quite the contrary, the exact opposite in fact. Rather, that one is loved in spite of or because of those very imperfections. What it feels like to be delighted in by another: I can honestly say I do not know.

What would it feel like to just be you in a relationship? And that's not to say you wouldn't piss your partner off or annoy the hell out of him or her at some point – that's a given, because we humans are an odd and cantankerous lot. But that you would still be loved and held with the deepest regard. I have never felt this except with God. Not from my parents or husbands; perhaps from my children but, in a way, they don't count; that is a different kind of bond than the one I'm talking about: a mature male/female relationship. I have not had one in my entire life.

I have been fighting another cold and feeling blue. And that's an interesting point: Do I feel blue or do I think myself into being blue, think myself into that down position? So I'm trying to keep busy. I've actually put out some feelers and resumes for part-time work. I need the income but even more importantly I need contact with community. Whenever I think about getting engaged in a serious, disciplined writing process again, I become paralyzed. All my obsessive/compulsive avoidance behaviors kick into high gear. Why all that effort if it is only to be given away? But the same is true of life, isn't it? All that effort – the love, the joy, the heartache, the strife, the confusion, the elation, the surprise, the serendipity – just to leave it all behind in the end. All the more reason to enjoy the ride along the way.

And yet these are serious times we live in. It is as if we are all being called to become more real, more honest with ourselves and one another, more true. We who are incarnated here now on the cusp of the Great Transition – from greed to generosity; from competition to collaboration; from pride and arrogance to humility; from plunder of our planet to thoughtful and loving stewardship – need truth talk. And what is that?

What does it mean to be emotionally and psychologically sober, let alone physically so? And I understand the allure of altered states of consciousness, no doubt about that. Some individuals are simply more inclined than others to push the outside of the envelope; this I know from experience. The problem is you may not know when you've gone too far until it is too late and you can't come back. This has applications to relationships as well. Time for truth.

Yesterday was the beginning of Lent. I forced myself to go to the evening service but am glad I did. The somber feeling of the sanctuary, the subdued lighting and flickering candlelight, the beauty of Palestrina and Tallis, no instruments, just the human voice, soaring.

What now, God?

There have been several moments in my life, a handful of occasions when that utterance, that prayer has gone forth to be answered with a speediness and swiftness that have been astonishing. But now, it feels on some level, that the answer to that prayer is WAIT! Be patient! Do you actually know anyone who *likes* being patient?

Milton's *Areopagitica*: "They also serve who only stand and wait."

Stand and wait.

No kidding.

I also heard someone say the other day that God answers our prayers in one of three ways:

Yes, which is what we all want to hear, all the time.

Yes, but not now.

No, because I have something better in mind for you.

We humans aren't too keen on answers #2 or #3, and yet if we are to be in a relationship of trust, #2 and #3 are the answers that call this forth more from within. I keep thinking about what my Guide counseled: to let go of all judgment; live with joy and remain calm; all will unfold at the appropriate time. Until then, be patient. Wait! It doesn't matter what for or for what; there is an important and necessary lesson to be accomplished in the interim.

March 4, 2009

My half-birthday. I am glad it is inclement outside; it fits my mood and I am grateful for the moisture, the fertile watering of self and soil and soul. And to celebrate: ten cases of books to be delivered to the Los Angeles Unified School District as a donation. I did actually sell one book last week, to pocket a whopping $2.50 after splitting the distribution fees with Baker and Taylor, and paying for the postage to mail the book. But at least all those books, six hundred of them, will be out of my garage and into someone's hands where they hopefully will be of some use. Only three cases left: imagine that! The mountain of books that was stacked in my garage two years ago now has been reduced to only a few remaining stones, easily manageable. What once looked like an impossible, Herculean task is almost accomplished. I honestly never thought I could do it and in moments of despondency I kept telling myself not bird by bird, to paraphrase Annie Lamott, but book by book. I am understanding more and more the meaning and demands of the word "perseverance."

I just got off the phone with P. It was a most heartfelt and honest communication about what happened with C. I also am learning more about the meaning of the word "reconciliation," both within oneself and with another. And it is not about our being together again, but about being able to address one another with openness, vulnerability, and respect. Too late for the repair of our relationship, bittersweet and poignant indeed, but a beginning at least.

Last Saturday I was in a place of such darkness and sad loneliness I went to see a movie at 10:30am in the morning just to get out of the house. Crying during the movie (*Slumdog Millionaire*), tearing up while walking home, struggling to stay emotionally sober but having a hard time. The mantra I had been repeating all day long and variations thereof:

"Lord help me!"

"Lord, let me trust You completely."

"Lord, please help me stay open!" and not become embittered or cynical, which would be so easy to do.

And then that night late in bed I felt something move within my heart, a sort of understanding beyond words, beyond mind – almost like a weird reverse sort of vampirism – an infusion going in rather than a sucking out. So difficult to articulate in words; rather than the blood being drawn out of me, something was being transfused into me. And, in truth, this transfusion process has probably been going on for a long time now, but it felt as if it finally reached the last drop or the last puff of air when you blow up a balloon. I understood without words and felt in a visceral way about allowing God to take over my life; what surrendering to God and the God-Force at the deepest level feels like; to be infused and transfused by Spirit. You are either all God's or you are not God's at all. A surrendering at the place where the first heartbeat began at inception, only this time a different kind of inception, like the last tiniest of tiny leaks in the dam of my heart being filled up.

So THIS is what it feels like when you truly become connected and grounded in spirit, to be bolted down to that foundational grid, and the sense that this feeling was the source of true authority from now on; everything else was or had become a dead-end; indeed this power is the only way out of the labyrinth of human folly and desire and attachment to any sort of outcome on this temporal, earthly plane.

Then again on Monday night when that chattering, judgmental, babbling, self-analyzing, self-justifying, nattering away about this and that energy-zapping voice started in again, I had the ability to silence it, to soothe it with this new energy, this new infusion, like my heart pumping, or being pumped, in a different way. This is what the spiritual journey is about over and over again; experiencing the darkness and complexity of being human but not surrendering to it; or surrendering to it in the moment because it is occurring but not being overwhelmed by it; somehow holding one's center in spite of all the buffeting of Hamlet's slings and arrows of outrageously unpredictable fortune which, by definition, is fickle anyway.

The sensation of really, really, really, finally, finally, finally handing over the reins of my life to Something

Other: no escape clauses, no exemptions or exceptions, no "only in the case of" caveats; no return in thirty days if not satisfied but an absolute ironclad non-negotiable, non-refundable guarantee where the ego becomes witness for Something Other rather than for itself, no by-passing things or side-stepping things, no weaseling around mentally but dropping into a level of trust that is without compromise.

I repeat: WITHOUT COMPROMISE!

How a calmness set in that was at once still and yet paradoxically filled with life, brimming – albeit quietly – with power, like becoming a zombie for Spirit. Choice and free will remain but do not need to be struggled with so; everything somehow becomes easier, lighter. The voice that counsels, "Stop the lawyering, Maurine. You can let go. Stop the rehashing, stop the whatever. You are not in charge; I AM!"

I AM THAT I AM IS IN CHARGE.

An okayness pervaded every cell of my being, like I felt in the hospital after awakening from cancer surgery so many years ago. Soul talk now, not mind talk. I understand what Paul means about being transformed by the renewal of your mind, what one might call the original cognitive-behavioral therapy. But this event was of a different order of reality, more a blossoming or flowering of the heart. "Did not our hearts burn within us…?"

And how utterly appropriate what I just read in my *Runner's Bible*:

> Blessed is the man [or woman] whose strength is in thee, in whose heart are the highways to Zion. Passing through the valley of weeping they make it a place of springs; yea, the early rain covers it with blessings. They go from strength to strength. (Psalm 84: 5-7)

In whose heart are the highways to Zion: that is what this infusion/transfusion felt like. My job now is to practice, like playing the scales on my piano so my fingers are more limber, living from this come from – not talking about it or writing about it or occasionally managing to do it – but to practice living by it bird by bird, day by day, moment by moment, book by book, event by event, challenge by challenge, person by person – this becomes the path of liberation, or rather a participation in a series of liberations, an ever-widening circle that embraces more and more life.

It also occurred to me the other night that the lover I need, the lover I have hoped for is precisely this Lover within my own heart. Once I get to know this Lover better, a lover in the world of form will present himself. The absolutely imperative issue for me is to embrace this internal Lover with all my heart and to trust this Lover completely. Completely.

****

I decided after doing the release ritual last January that I wanted to do an integration ritual to set the tone of my new path. I decided to dance and sing and play to the Four Directions with the ceremonial drum I made years ago, a tambourine, gourd rattle, and wooden recorder. I want to welcome with great joy the many parts of my being into wholeness, to honor all the gifts I have been blessed with, and put them before the altar of Spirit to be used as She/He sees fit.

On the way to the site in Santa Cruz where I scattered my parents' remains among the redwood trees, driving in the early morning through the forest on a windy road, an omen of sorts: a small deer ran in front of my car. I thought about deer medicine and what FS said about concentrating on my gentleness. Yes, deer medicine; it's all about gentleness, the power of gentleness to touch hearts. How I am being called to honor this gentleness within, the gentleness that heals all wounds, the gentleness that can love both the darkness and the light; learning to love myself and that centering place of stillness within.

When I reached the designated spot, I smudged with sage. I acknowledged the Four Directions and did a brief ceremony for each.

Starting with the North, I played my wooden recorder, praying to the male principle, to the mind and intellect, the wisdom of the patriarchs, the fallow season of winter, to the seeds dormant in the ground but about to open. I called upon these forces, the ancestors, all the energy of the North to help me with my healing.

Then on to the West, beating my ceremonial drum, calling upon the wisdom of the grandmothers, that deep, introspective feminine wisdom, the creative life-force, the wisdom of the body which cycles rhythmically, like the beating heart. I called upon the Western forces for that deep healing, of owning who and what I am.

Then I turned to the South with my turtle-shaped rattle, turtle representing our Mother Earth, the rattle representing a young child; turtle as the oldest medicine, the symbol of Gaia and its goddess energy, MY goddess energy, earth-sign that I am. South as symbolic of the wisdom of the child, of openness and wonder, the season of summertime and growth and play, of laughter and being carefree, the place of my own ancestors and lineage. Shaking that turtle rattle as if there were no tomorrow, shaking it in both hands, in rhythm and syncopation, Rattle, shake, rattle-rattle, shake, shake! Dancing and singing and hopping about.

I finally turned to the East, the last direction in my circle, and the one I wanted to end with, the sun still low in the morning sky. I chose my tambourine for this direction: jingle, jangle sounds plus beats, shaking and striking and jingle-jangling all at once. East: the voice of spring and rebirth, the season of new vision dawning, of empowerment, the planting of seeds for continued growth. I jumped and hopped and circled until I felt the energy subside; the entire ritual took slightly over a half hour, not that long, but it was enough.

Afterwards I burnt sage again to complete the cycle and played a little more on my recorder in honor of my parents. May they watch over me now in death in ways they were not able to do in life. Peace. May we all be at peace with one another.

March 27, 2009
Rome, Italy.
4:30pm in the afternoon. I write while Mel. rests. I can't believe I slept away my first day in the Eternal City but I was just too tired. After traveling all day and night, plus getting only a few hours of sleep the night before I left LA, restless and fretting that the alarm clock might not work or that I would be in too deep of a sleep to hear it, I was awake at 3:30am for a 9:00am flight. How good it felt to stretch out on Mel.'s bed! The next thing I knew it was 3:30pm in the afternoon. I am now vibrating after a cup of espresso and at the sheer joy of seeing my youngest daughter again after three months of not being able to hold her in my arms.

So much has transpired since my last entry. At long last, after two years, the mountain of books that was stored in my garage has been liberated into the world! I delivered the last three cases on Monday before I left to the downtown branch of the Los Angeles Public Library. Done. All gone. Mission Accomplished. This odyssey of dispersal has taught me the value of stick-to-it-tiveness, of

403

perseverance, of not allowing the voice of doubt or despair to infect or infest me. And at times it has been challenging not to succumb to it *but I did it!* I, or rather some force, has allowed me, encouraged me to keep on keeping on. Perseverance through time, and perhaps with a dash of stubbornness thrown into the mix: the "I-refuse-to-let-all-these-books-rot-in-my-garage" attitude and a commitment to the cause of giving away all that I have to give.

This accomplishment underscores a foundational truth that I am learning more about with each passing day: the *vision* that inspires each of us leads to God's *provision*. I am understanding at an exponential rate that God or the Source Force or whatever you want to label the Great Cosmic IT will provide the means to fulfill that vision, especially if it is in alignment with the principles of generosity and giving.

A case in point:

Two weeks ago I was sitting in church reading the news bulletin during the offering collection. My eyes happened upon a small blurb about the vestry deciding to sell a condominium that the church owned and would anyone be interested?

After the service I approached the head of the vestry and asked if the condo was still available. Yes, and they had just lowered the price to within my range. After I heard the asking price, I asked "How many square feet?" thinking that it would be the size of a postage stamp. But when I heard the answer I almost went into shock; it was actually bigger than the place I am now renting. Maybe I wouldn't have to sell my piano and/or dining room furniture after all.

Within a week the church had accepted my offer. I have never felt so carried by spirit in all my life, except when I had cancer. It felt effortless. As I sit here writing in Rome, half a world away, I am almost 50% through the escrow process and hence part of my fatigue: running around LA amassing the requisite papers for loan approval, arranging for inspections, reading reports, title documents, homeowners' association by-laws, CC&Rs. I already have a pile of papers that is at least three inches thick and I am not joking.

And here is an additional lovely wrinkle to the whole story: the condo is where D. and his family lived, the priest with whom I travelled to the Holy Land. It is absolutely brilliant how the universe works. My helping D. with search committee interviews on several occasions that ultimately provided him with his new parish home in Seattle opened up the space for me to find possibly the only place in LA in a half-way decent neighborhood that I could actually afford.

Then one day after taking the property plunge – the first time in my life I will own something on my own – the Voice That Worries started in: "What do you think you're doing? This will drain most of the assets left to you by your parents."

As the anxiety started to kick in I happened to look down at the pavement where I was walking and there before me was a dime. Message? Don't worry. All will be provided. The penny I found a few weeks ago at almost the exact same spot had multiplied ten fold. I have absolutely no doubt that when consciousness becomes aligned with the principle of trusting providence that everything, simply everything starts to unfold in a powerful way.

This unfolding might not be in the manner that we think or expect, but it will unfold. And more times than not, if we can learn to step out of the way and simply allow this unfolding to occur, we would be surprised how effortless – dare I say joyful? – life can be. There are angels at work, and they truly are on our side. There is a critical timing to all things. Too soon won't work because you're probably pushing and too late means your fear kept you hobbled from taking action or it wasn't meant to be anyway. But when you hit the "just right" current, it does carry you speedily toward resolution.

April 5, 2009

Palm Sunday. 4:30pm in the afternoon on a stopover in Philadelphia en route back to Los Angeles from Rome. My trip to see Mel. was at once wonderful and poignant; seeing her again made me realize how much I miss her. She is so beautiful and accomplished and capable and lovely. And how quickly a week goes by! I was only just settling in when I had to pack up and leave again. Rome, the Eternal City. I can see why Mel. loves living there. One week simply is not enough to get in sync with its rhythm. And how I love the sounding of the church bells! Whenever I am in Europe and hear the ringing of the bells I realize once again how much I miss that particular part of living abroad.

What struck me the most as I was wandering around is how much I miss sharing sights and smells and sounds with someone; watching couples walking and holding hands in the park, old and young, husband and wife teams traveling together, having an adventure together. I would like to experience a truly deep and reciprocal love with another human being in this life. I want to be able to open my heart again, to give and receive that special intimacy and laughter and vulnerability and buddyhood.

A true, true love. What would that look like? I have become at peace about being alone; indeed, I feel as if the answer to my prayers of last winter for a lover have been answered with "not yet," and I am okay with that. For now. I have come to the realization that I have given of myself too much, have sold myself short, both literally and metaphorically, in both my marriages, and will not, cannot make that mistake again. I have not honored myself enough, have not demanded enough for myself, and have put up with way too much I shouldn't have. If I am going to be in a relationship again, I want it to be one of valued equals, not one up/one down, or my being overly patient for the male to get it, or conversely for the male to take care of me in a way that is both infantilizing and patronizing. The goddess must lead the way. Now is the time for this deep internal strength to emerge into full flowering.

In both my marriages this may have been touched upon but was not the sustaining foundational core. We were either too young or busy or emotionally needy and off key. I would like to experience a sacred, whole and holy union with a man before I leave this earth. How I miss looking deeply into another's eyes! I pray to remain open, to not get bitter or shy or afraid to love again. In many ways, both subtle and blatant, I allowed myself to be taken for granted emotionally in both my marriages. I gave more emotionally than I received, and I finally grew weary of trying and probably waited too long to put my foot down.

I need to learn how to demand and receive more for myself. I need to learn how to fill my own space before I can know how to share it meaningfully and healthfully and honestly with another. I just wish my heart still did not hurt so, or my body ache for lack of holding and touch.

****

One day while wandering around Rome, I visited a small Tibetan Buddhist store. There was an incredible mask there, a turtle shell decorated with metal, symbolic of the world and our Earth. I fell in love with it, but alas, it was too expensive for my pocketbook. So instead, I selected a small goddess mask: a three-eyed red female deity. When I asked the shopkeeper to tell me about the goddess, he said she was the Vajrayogini: a powerful goddess in the Tibetan pantheon. When I had the chance, I googled her on the computer. This is what came up in a cursory review:

Vajrayogini literally means "the diamond female yogi." She is the highest Yidam, the supreme deity of the Tantric gods and parallels the Western concept of a guardian angel in that she inspires, guides, and protects. Vajrayogini transforms everyday experiences into a spiritual path and is considered a female Buddha. She is visualized as a translucent deep red form, a young female with the third eye of wisdom on her forehead. Apparently no male Buddha approaches her in metaphysical or practical importance.

Every aspect of Vajrayogini is designed to convey some sort of spiritual meaning. Her red-colored body represents the blazing of her inner fire. Her face symbolizes that all phenomena are subsumed in emptiness. Her arms represent her realization of the truth, and her three eyes symbolize her ability to see everything in the past, present, and future. In Vajrayogini's right hand is a curved knife to show her power to cut through delusions and obstacles, and in her left a skull cup filled with blood, symbolizing her experience of the light of bliss, cutting reality with her "cleaver of wisdom" and consuming it in "the cup of inseparable bliss and void."

As the Divine Feminine, she has no shame or fear; she is feisty and beyond limitations, qualities I could certainly use right now. She also is able to control both her anger and her lust. She is the fully enlightened female; the wild, fiery aspect of Buddha along with experiential, existential wisdom. She is the one "Who is the Essence of all Buddhas."

I realized I need Vajrayogini medicine far more than I need turtle. I need to blaze with her wisdom and fire.

April 13, 2009

The day after Easter. From Good Friday to Easter Sunday a remarkable seventy-two hours. On Friday it was dark and brooding, clouds in the sky suggesting rain. At church the service was somber and quietly reflective "Were you there when they nailed him to the cross? How I tremble, tremble, tremble…" And, of course, right in the middle of this poignant hymn, a cell phone went off – LOUDLY. I actually felt sorry for the person to whom it belonged. How mortified and embarrassed he/she must have been! One more reason why I dislike cell phones. Then Easter Sunday morning was glorious and bright; you could literally feel the earth bursting forth with the energy of spring and new growth.

From last Monday to this one also a transformation of sorts. After being up nearly 24 hours traveling back from Rome, I awakened to the news that my pre-approved loan had not been accepted after all because of the financial chaos going on, and my broker's shock that this had happened.

Him: "I just can't believe it. In any other market, your loan would have been a slam dunk, approved in ten minutes. You have money in the bank and an 815 credit rating!"

Me: "Well, this isn't any other market now, is it? These are crazy financial times and your shock does me absolutely no good. You really dropped the ball on this one."

With which he agreed and which did me absolutely no good. I was furious: once again listening to someone else's authority rather than my own. So I called P. to see if he could help at the 11th hour to pull a loan rabbit out of the bank hat, and I so did not want to make that call. For the next three days I scurried around resubmitting all the documents and information I had gathered previously for the broker recommended by P., frantically working to get everything done for the second escrow to close, and not sleeping at all well due to stress and jet lag.

By Wednesday morning I was a mess. I woke up at 5:30am, couldn't go back to sleep, had a client scheduled at 9:00am, so why bother trying? I fixed some coffee, ate some oatmeal, and went to work on my computer – did I mention also having to pull together the final tax returns on my father's estate because his accountant had "forgotten" something? By 8:30am I was puking into the toilet from sheer exhaustion and nerves. I managed to stop heaving only minutes before my client arrived.

On Thursday I spent three hours walking around my neighborhood doing errands and later attended the Maundy Thursday foot washing service and The Watch. I think of all the services in the Christian year, Maundy Thursday moves me the most. Thinking about that last meal, what would my own last meal look and feel like? Would I be able to lay down my life for my friends and those I love? Then spending that lonely and agonizing night praying in the Garden of Gethsemane: how alone a single human being can be and what I imagine the abject terror of the animal part of us knowing he or she faces imminent death. Such visceral fear that blood mixed with sweat quite literally appears on the forehead of the condemned man, condemned but no crime committed, except the willingness to die for love.

Something also happened between P. and me that provided yet another piece of the psychological puzzle I've been trying to figure out since we parted. He called saying he wanted to talk about one of the children and asked if he could come over, and I said yes. But I realized shortly after he arrived that talking about the children was not the real reason he wanted to see me. What he did want to talk about was the condo and his reactions to something I said.

Before I left for Europe to visit Mel. and before I even approached P. about finding another broker, I showed him the apartment. I can't remember if I offered to show it to him or whether he asked to see it. It doesn't matter. While he was looking at the new space, he made the comment, "I know you'll make this into a place of beauty." I turned to him and said, somewhat humorously, half-jokingly, "Thanks to Bill's help" meaning the money I am using to buy the condo is money I received from my parents' estate.

But what P. really wanted to tell me was this:

How hurt he was by my comment. He realized I had not said it to hurt him, that there was nothing malicious intended by it but he was hurt nevertheless, not only by what I said, but by what I did not say about him. He went on to tell me that if I get the condo, every time I walk through the door, it will be because of what he has done, what he has contributed to make my lifestyle happen.

So many complex and contradictory reactions went through me at that moment – and how P. struggled visibly to articulate what he did: anger and hurt and very much wanting to convey his feelings honestly, choking back tears. My first thought reaction was: "Oh, my God! What have I done wrong? How bad of me! I'm so sorry for making you hurt! How thoughtless and awful and terrible of me!" I literally had to arrest the impulse to rush over to P., take his hand in mine, kiss it, and beg his forgiveness on bended knee, just the way a loyal subject might ask for clemency from the king. Fortunately another voice inside me said, "Don't you dare move! Just listen to him and what he is saying. You haven't done anything wrong."

So I stayed put and listened. Finally I said: "I can see how you might feel that way and I am sorry if you were upset. I am most truly grateful for the help you and your colleague have provided getting me this loan. I really do appreciate it."

Then P. went on to imply that the reason I could live the way I am living is because of him; that if it weren't for the money I got from him in our divorce I would not be able to do anything, that all this was made possible by him. When would I recognize what he had done, what he had provided? He said with great effort that he wasn't going to require that I sign any promissory note regarding the real estate deal, though I offered to do so. After all, isn't that how business has always been conducted in our relationship? By signing pieces of paper?

I didn't say much else. I just let P. talk. When he left I thanked him for his honesty.

And then I started to get mad and called him. "You know, I really do appreciate your help with the loan. I really do. There is no doubt that the deal would have fallen through without your help. So I really want you to hear that. But the money I am using to purchase this condo is from my Dad and Mom, it has nothing to do with you. But that's beside the point. When does the money I have – from whatever the source, our divorce or my parents – become MY money? When is it no longer anyone else's but mine?"

So rather than feeling even somewhat obligated to help his ex-partner of twenty-five years and mother of his four children get a loan for a two bedroom condo, maybe just maybe to make up in part for the inequity of the divorce settlement itself and the fact that the last year we were together he lied to me about being with another woman, it ended up being about P. and all he had done and how hurt he was that I didn't see this.

After I hung up the phone, I started in on my lawyering voice – "How dare he!" – then a trap door of grace opened and I fell through it. I realized in rapid succession how painfully difficult it must be for P. to be in the world, to be that much in need of recognition, to be that fragile and sensitive to an off-hand remark about my dad.

And then I had the following insight:

P. was reacting exactly the way my mother always did; no matter what the situation, whatever the event, whatever the circumstance, positive or negative, it had to be about her; it could never be about anyone else. And when I reached this moment of realization my heart cracked open for both P. and my mother, how lonely and isolated and alone each of them must have felt in his and her own way most of their lives.

My mother lost her father at the age of two and a half; she lost her mother emotionally at the same time. P. lost his father at the same age to cancer, and although his father did not die physically, he died to P. in every other way and he lost his mother emotionally because she became the caretaker/nurse of a physically and psychically broken man.

I realized I was not as deeply wounded as either P. or my mother. My wounds stem from invasion, like trying to swat gnats away from constantly buzzing around my head. Or trying to brush red ants off my skin so they would not bite with their constant, stinging criticism.

But at least someone was there!

And having someone or something there provided a sense of safety. At least someone was there; however they botched the job, at least they were there. P. and my mother did not have that experience, and the huge existential loneliness they must have felt and carried with them throughout their lives, I felt compassion for them, a deep compassion and sorrow that stems from understanding something in a different way. I realized after my anger subsided how deeply sorry I was for P. and my mom and the immense isolation of their journeys.

So in church on Good Friday I said a prayer of thanksgiving. I can't even say it was from a place of forgiveness; it felt more like a profound acceptance and an epiphany of "I get it." I got P. and my mom in a way that goes beyond anger and hurt, beyond the lawyering and judging voices inside me, to a place of deep healing acceptance. Every one of us really is doing the best he or she can with the tools and experiences at our disposal. As long as you still get angry and defensive, you remain stuck. True freedom is about uncoupling the internal chains.

Then this deeply disturbing dream about P. and my mother:

In the dream it feels as if they are lovers, though my mother appears much older than P. They are kicking me out of the house. The feeling in the dream is ugly, ugly, ugly, and ominously dark. They are yelling at me and harassing me, calling me all sorts of names. I'm worthless, no good, bad. They want me out. Get out! Out of their sight! They throw things at me. When I try to take my things, they fight me for them. "That's not yours! You can't have that!" One of the things we struggle over is a hat rack that I am finally able to wrestle from them. I argue with them and try to defend myself against the injustice of their actions, but it doesn't do any good. I finally leave with the hat rack (an indication of saving my head and sanity?).

Grisly! Somehow in my psyche P. and my mother have been having an affair, and this infidelity finally throws me out. How utterly creepy is that! The collusion between P. and my mother, the incestuous relationship between their two wounds binding together to fight me. And yet too how being kicked out in the dream, however much it hurts or is unfair, ultimately represents my freedom.

Ugh! An ugly, ghastly dream, one of the most unnerving I have ever had. The feeling tone in the dream was terrible, simply terrible. It makes the one where I was buried alive under the kitchen floor tame by comparison. I haven't been battling my Dad in P., the way P. has always thought and complained about, but the much deeper mother wound, how hurt they both were at such a young age; how P. and my mother shared *that* dynamic, and perhaps that is the reason they never got along. The dominating male framework was an easy cover-up for this more insidious level of psychic invasion.

April 19, 2009

Journal 109: added together, numerically $1 + 0 + 9 = 10$, $1 + 0 = 1$: representative of new beginnings. Also in the sign of Aries: the first in the wheel of the zodiac, new growth, strength, energy, courage, activity, and fire. And it does feel like that in many ways: the literal heat outside; the bright sunshine and spring light and extended evenings; feeling within me an ongoing process of change. Today may actually be the day that I sign the loan documents on the condo that I have been working to bring to resolution since March.

New beginnings indeed.

In addition to the above, over the past few weeks and months, I have become increasingly interested in the Tarot. On the way back from Rome, I read a book by Paul Case that was recommended by a yoga teacher and was impressed, if not somewhat overwhelmed, by the many levels of interpretation and meaning that can be revealed, the subtleties and nuanced information contained within the images and arcana. A rich field indeed, the Tarot's complex interweaving of astrology, the Kabbalah, the art of numerology and other principles of mathematics and geometry, not to mention ways of decoding our psycho-spiritual journey. The master key to Hebrew wisdom is literally "The Name" translated as "Lord" but really the Hebrew verb "to be." IHVH: "That which was, That which is, That which shall be." That, not He, no gender assigned. God is the ONE REALITY.

- That Something which has always existed behind all forms.
- That Something which exists behind all present forms.
- That Something which will be the foundation for all future forms throughout time.
- IHVH.

I want to learn more about this system of thought.

May 5, 2009

Finally closed on the condo. On Earth Day no less. I now am a property owner. My very own little space of earth, at least for a while. Can we ever really own anything? But mine for now nevertheless. What is it the Bible says? How happy to have a small plot of land and a few olive trees? Well, at least I have a balcony with a view of some palms. This means more to me than all the mansions in the world.

Have had numerous sub-contractors over to provide estimates for demolition, painting, plumbing, flooring, tiling, and electrical work, plus putting the utilities in my name, donating the old appliances to a women's half-way house, etc. But it doesn't feel as if I have accomplished much at all. Though the above list sounds impressive, no work has actually started, and the money clock is ticking.

In addition, only five days after close of escrow I found out that the income stream which I have been relying on to finance the mortgage, property taxes, and HOA may be drying up. It's almost as if the universe is testing me with this new change in fiscal events: "Can you really, really, really trust that all will be provided as necessary when the time comes?" I'm trying not to panic but at this age taking on a thirty year mortgage, I hadn't factored into the equation that this might entail going back to work full-time. It is taking a lot more grit than I previously imagined.

One bright spot:

The first evening after escrow closed, I met with some women friends for a picnic at my new place, and while eating we drew some medicine cards. I picked eagle and it was perfect, just what I have been feeling, symbolizing connection with the Divine:

> Eagle is a reminder to take heart and gather courage because the universe is providing me with the opportunity to soar and broaden my sense of self beyond the visible horizon. This may involve a spiritual test; it does require attacking fear in whatever form it takes and trusting that the wings of soul will be supported by spirit. Eagle's message is to conquer fear and jump into the adventure of co-creating with the Divine.

I repeat: co-creating with the Divine.

May 30, 2009

Since my last entry, my life has changed irrevocably. On May 13th – unlucky number! – I found out that most of my life's savings were lost, evaporated overnight by an illegal Ponzi scheme. The money I had been investing and counting to live on is entirely gone. This represented two-thirds of the money I received from my divorce. The life I have known and the life I have been planning have been ripped out from underneath me. Not just marriage and relationship, but everything, simply everything. It feels surreal even as I write these words. I cannot believe how prophetic my eagle medicine about spiritual testing would be!

Some Frantic Transmissions to and from friends:
On Friday, May 15, 2009 8:00am Maurine wrote JZ:

417

"I am writing this to let you know that I, along with a thousand other individuals, have been victims of a Ponzi scheme, and I have lost two-thirds of all my assets. Everything started to unravel right after we last spoke. I closed on the condo and a week later the shit hit the fan. I have witnessed most of what I was counting on to finance my future disappear overnight. I don't know at this point what else could possibly happen to me, and I'm afraid to ask. I'm letting you know about this so you'll know why I haven't called. Trying to figure out what went wrong in my relationship pales in comparison to this. Please keep me in your prayers."

On Friday, May 15, 2009 at 12:02pm JZ wrote:

"Oh, Maurine! What a horrible turn of events. Of course, I will hold you in my prayers. Is there any chance of recovery of at least some of the funds? I hope we have a chance to talk soon."

On Friday, May 15, 2009 at 4:35pm Maurine wrote JZ:

"It does not look good. It is truly a very, very difficult time. I'm trying to hold on. I will let you know what transpires as more information becomes available."

On Friday, May 15, 2009 at 5:41pm JZ wrote:

"Thanks for the quick response. This is one of those life-changing 'shadow intrusions from the Universe.' As you deal with the mess and have time to reflect, understanding can arise that affords you a context for healing. May it be so."

On Saturday, May 16, 2009 at 7:55am Maurine wrote JZ:

"I did a dialogue with my Guide that I will forward to you when I have the chance. Right now dealing with the physical and emotional stress of all this is paramount for me. I've got to keep some semblance of calm in order to move forward. I've let go of the general contractor and designer I hired to help with the condo rehab. At this point I will be doing the absolute minimum in order to move in. Crazy, crazy times. I would like to talk with you at some point; I simply do not know when I'll be able to schedule something. Hopefully after a week or two I'll have a better feel for things."

On Saturday, May 16, 2009 at 12:22pm JZ wrote:

"Yes, calm, and also looking for what this all means, which I expect is what your Guide explored with you. I have been attuning to you and see that something is stirring, something important. That does not take away from the critical nature of the situation but ride the wave of crises into new territory. More later, when the time is right."

****

Lord:

Help me to understand what I am to do now? Overnight I have lost over 60% of my life savings. I thank God – You! – that I have been spared the rest. At least something remains. For this I am profoundly grateful. But what now?

Sometimes no action can be taken other than prostrating oneself before forces and events that are out of your control and to be completely in the moment of your devastation. There is no action, no doing in moments such as these, only profound unmitigated surrender.

There is a part of me that does feel anchored in all this, that ultimately I will be okay. And I know I am not alone in what happened. To have most of one's life savings vanish instantaneously: this has happened and is happening to so many people right now. But at this stage in life with less left ahead than behind, what am I to learn?

Creativity: the infinitely resourceful and mysterious well of creativity. In the world of form events can appear catastrophic and indeed they are on that level of the material world. But if you remember to align yourself with the superior power of the creativity of the Universe, of the Divine Principle, Divine Mind, the Logos and Light – whatever name you want to attach to this Ultimate Power and Mystery – this is what you must continue to focus on.

You and so many others like you are being called to a level of creativity and surrender that the planet has never seen before, never witnessed before. It is impossible for you to fathom how this darkness will be transmuted into light but transmuted it will be. The out-workings of the Divine Infinite Mind always – I repeat always – move toward realignment with the God Force and healing. While tremendously bad events occur in the physical world – either through human miscreation, mismanagement, greed, passivity, inattention, or whatever word you wish to affix to the outward event – everything, simply everything arising now and occurring on the planet is an invitation to reconnect with this principle of beneficent creativity, calling this creativity forth from each and everyone who is bearing witness on the earth today.

Allow the devastation, the tears to flow and work themselves through your physical being but sense too the burgeoning strength. That is the creative life force coming to the fore; it can never be stopped. You humans can block it for any number of reasons and in any number of ways but the creative life force will always send forth new shoots after the devastation of fire, flood, famine, economic chaos, or whatever disaster that is presented. This is the pattern and lesson of the universe and of God for those who can allow the co-creating, co-facilitating life force to come through and be honored, however difficult or menacing or unexpected the change agent might be.

You must remember especially now that this Divine Creativity and Love are always at work, no matter what occurs in the world of matter. You are seeing, more with this core strength you have within, that this has been and is the best investment you have ever made. This investment can never be taken away or stolen or lost or misused once it is in place. You feel this truth at the core of your being that is unshakable despite or in spite of the understandable grief and confusion you feel as a human right now.

What you have reached within you can never be lost; you can return again and again to this well. Even a few months ago you would not have weathered this financial catastrophe as you are now; you have also touched into this deeper place through the hurt and wounds experienced from human love, or perhaps better said, from human misunderstanding in love. You have moved through these many obstacles in your journey; this too demonstrates the principle of creativity and the ongoing out-working of divinity through creation and created things.

Things will be presented to you that you do not know. Your ability to stay present to this unfolding rather than trying to force or manipulate it but to listen and watch with different eyes and hear with different ears – all these actions are critical now and you are doing this whether it feels you are or not; you have aligned yourself with this path. Try not to judge yourself in any way; this will not serve the creative self that yearns to express through you, that wishes to create new sprouts of growth through the rubble that is your financial world at the present time.

You are being called to live more simply. You are being called to live more creatively. You, like so many others, are being called to let go of a lot of things: material things, ideas about what should be, attachment to things and thought processes; there are so many ways in which this new creativity, this new earth will present itself and unfold. Remember this is a time of great creativity, especially for you and especially at this time in your life. Do not allow external appearances to inhibit the bringing forth of this creativity. You are being called. Allow this unstoppable, creative life-giving love to help you through these treacherous times. You have no idea what is in store. Keep calming yourself and reminding yourself of the absolute, unending, unwavering truth of this ongoing Divine Creative Love.

****

More Frantic Transmissions:
On Saturday, May 16, 2009 at 1:47pm Maurine wrote JZ:

"Over the last few years I have given away nearly 20% of all that has come to me in an effort to be an open channel. I do not look upon myself as a greedy person, but I can see now where perhaps a certain complacency had set in on my part – the idea that something would continue that I had grown to rely on and depend on in a certain way. Obviously, that is not to say the perpetrator of this crime is not to be held accountable for his actions. I never had any malicious intent, but the expectation that I had somehow dodged the economic tsunami that has affected so many others and that things would perk along the same for me – I can see now how that complacency and that expectation had to be shattered. The thing I am struggling with the most now is knowing that a young man I told about this investment scheme has lost his children's college fund. I feel simply terrible about that, worse in a way than what happened to me. I don't have a spouse or children to care for. I may have a condo I can't afford and may go into foreclosure – I hope not but at this point who knows? But to have a family whom I care for so affected just kills me.

That's what I've been losing sleep over and what keeps tearing me apart. My children have been amazing, simply amazing, calling me every day, several times a day. I feel so much love around me. I will get through this."

On Saturday, May 16, 2009 at 2:56pm JZ wrote:

"Ho! You are dealing with this in a creative and powerful way. I hear you about the complacency. Your heart is so open, to tears and to helping others. I'm so glad that the family has rallied around you. That is a blessing."

On Sunday, May 17, 2009 at 10:37am Maurine wrote JZ:

"I think part of all this for me is to finally let the love of others in, to really let others love and care for me after spending a lifetime of caring and giving to others. I can see how I really need to learn this lesson at this stage in my life. Thank you for your encouragement and kind words. I am doing as well as can be expected, even though I still feel as if I've been hit by a truck – wobbly but at least conscious and not on life support."

On Saturday, May 17, 2009 at 9:50am Mel. wrote:

"I was thinking of you the entire day and found these two quotations that brought you to mind, from Ruiz's *The Four Agreements*:

> Whatever life takes away from you, let it go. Whenever you surrender and let go of the past, you allow yourself to be fully alive in the moment. Letting go of the past means you can enjoy the dream that is happening right now.

> The angel of death takes the past away in order to make it possible for life to continue.

"Perhaps the money was the past and all this has happened to really slap you into letting go. Perhaps this has unlatched one more choking chain. I love you!"

And not just the children, the chicks now uplifting their mother hen, but other family members and friends have been wonderful. I received a gift massage from one; a Starbucks coffee card from another; my brother even offered me his most valuable family heirloom to sell to keep me going. I have received dozens of supportive and consoling calls. When an event of such devastating proportions is experienced, it does make you realize that the only thing of value that cannot be lost or stolen or taken away is the love you have in your heart for others and the love others have in their hearts for you. That's it. And yet the mortgage payments remain and the bills continue to come due. That's another truth about reality as well.

A few days later I received a card from Mel. by artist Cildo Meireles entitled *Zero Dollar*: on the front and back Uncle Sam and Fort Knox replace George Washington and the White House.

I wrote back:

"I got your card and the irony. What am I not doing because of the financial cushion I lost? A very good question. The only thing is that I am fifty-eight years old and you're only twenty-three. I have a very different perspective toward time than you do, my darling. At this stage in life we look for a little comfort and cushion. That now has been taken away and I feel I have been thrust back to my twenties, having to start from scratch all over again. Time makes such a difference, Mel. What can I say?"

In the intervening days since the world I knew collapsed, I have been on a rollercoaster of emotion. The only thing that has even marginally soothed me has been painting a carved wooden elephant on my back porch. Looking at the colors and watching my hand hold the brush somehow allow me to go brain-dead, and how I need that right now. Simply everything has been turned upside down. Talk about disorientation! Running around buying tile and bathroom fixtures and carpet and paint for a place I may have to sell before I even have a chance to live in feels futile. No, I will move in but I may have to sell the condo shortly thereafter and go back to being a renter; the American dream of owning my own home gone and not even a home but a two bedroom condo at that.

****

Dear Lord, Gracious Spirit, Still Small Voice Within:

The loss of my nest egg for old age and retirement has left me reeling. This is one of the heaviest blows I have ever sustained – it feels almost mortal in its severity. Just when I was getting my head above water again, finding a place to live that I could actually afford, looking forward to restarting my life, this happens. It has taken all the joy out of my move; it's hard not to look upon the condo as a burden now because I can't afford it. I am trying so hard to hold on, but I honestly do not know how much more I can take. I cannot see how Your hand is working in this. How is the loss of all this money somehow for my good? I am trying not to panic, but the gravity of what has happened is really setting in.

Comfort! You have received a difficult task, there is no doubt about that but it will serve you well to not focus on the difficult part but on how to comfort yourself in the days ahead. This self-comforting and self-soothing are the first part and for now the most important part of whatever plan you unfold. Remember what I said about creativity; there are many avenues through which this creativity can and will arise. It is not all up to you to untangle the knot that is your current state of financial affairs. Forces are at

425

work to rectify this shift in energy. You must not allow your mind to wander and run away with thoughts of what now? What next? What am I going to do?

Remember about listening and being present in a different way. Keep focusing on the Above. Remember that by yourself you can do nothing. The human you can act, of course, but the human you will be greatly aided if you remain calm and listen. I understand that this is a difficult challenge; all the more reason to center over and over again, as many times a day as necessary, to realign the human you with the divine aid that is available. For now your largest task is to keep recentering. Do not think about the future; do not allow yourself to wonder or question what will happen next. Ground yourself moment by moment in the comfort that is here for you, the Great Comforter at all times and in all things.

You are called to trust now in a way you have never trusted before. There are universal forces at work, so remember to realign yourself with these forces and that aid will be provided. This is why thinking too much about your current situation will not serve you as well as remaining open, watchful, returning to the Source for comfort, that calming balm – this more than any other action you might take is the important action now. You are called, especially now during this state of emergency, to slow down, self-care, self-soothe, focus solely on what can rightfully and reasonably be expected to be accomplished in a single day with gratitude

Remember that doors will open at the right time, in appropriate ways. You believe that it is you who must be responsible for all the doors opening; this is not so. You need to watch and be alert as doors are opened. If you are lost in thought or anxiety, it is easy to miss opportunities that are presented. It may feel counterintuitive but doing as little as possible could serve you more than you think. You must balance the pull toward action with quiet receptivity and gentle care of self.

You do not need to figure everything out all at once; indeed, this is impossible. You simply cannot right now, so do not waste time trying. Your ability to bring joy into your life during these challenging times is an important key for setting the tone of what is to come. Even being able to look upon the work at your new home with joy, rather than it being the burden you described, will facilitate the flow of energy both within and without. Your mental/emotional attitude needs the utmost attention. God's mercy is there. Keep calling out for it and drawing upon it. It is not God's intention that you suffer, even though you have been suffering. Keep believing in the good despite all external signs to the contrary. Do not judge by the eyes of the world but by the eyes of the heart and believe in the good, your good. It shall arise.

Thinking, too, that my "still small voice," my Guide has been telling me pretty much a variation on the same theme of comfort and trust for years now. How much trust can a single human being muster? As my Great Uncle Lawrence used to say: "There is a limit to human endurance," and I am at the breaking point.

Among other things in all this chaos, I called the people who helped liquidate Mom and Dad's estate when they moved. I went through all my belongings and stacked the dining room table with crystal, china, linens, jewelry, and artwork in the hope that I could sell them and make some money to pay my bills. Sadly, they were not interested in 80% of what I had, referring to the items as "high end garage sale" stuff.

Stuff!

Among the few items they were interested in were some family portraits, that Southern tradition of capturing the "landed gentry" in oil on canvas and mostly interested in the elaborate frames, not the paintings themselves. As the estate agents walked out the door with Mom, Aunt 'Rine, and Cousin Guyton, I thought: "So it's come to this: selling the family portraits and entering what Southerners call, with both disdain and commiseration, a state of 'gentile poverty'." As I closed the door I felt like Scarlet O'Hara "I'll think about that tomorrow" and wondered if I'd have to make a dress out of my old draperies. It actually brought a sardonic smile to my face. If Mom and Aunt 'Rine only knew, they'd be turning over in their graves! But you do what you have to do to survive. What is the intersection, the interstice between ethics and manners and morality and survival? A question each of us must answer in his or her own way. I'll think about that tomorrow.

June 3, 2009

A death has occurred, not only the divorce but everything, the death of my previous life and its personal velocity, the Maurine I was only three weeks ago gone. In bed the other night simply aching for someone to put his arms around me. Forget about the sex, just someone to hold on to at night and to be held by during this radical time of change. I am in the midst of a complete nervous breakdown and I know it. The only good that has come out of this catastrophe, this financial rape is I'm not thinking as much about P. and C. Forget their fucking relationship! I've just lost over a half million dollars in cash. With no way to recover it, no way to sit on stocks or real estate investments until the economy improves. The money is simply gone, vanished. Poof! I might as well have burnt it.

To say that this blow has been devastating is the Mother of All Understatements. It has been the *coup de grace*. And it is not only I who am suffering. I got to thinking about all the charities and causes I can no longer support. All the people and organizations I believe in will also be impacted, even if only to a small degree, because I can no longer give of my time and money to support their causes. The ripple effect is astonishing.

I can't say that I am struggling with my faith – why me? – a useless question at this point, or ever really. There is no answer to why. Actually there is: I got swindled and lied to by a group of greedy sociopaths; the crook at the head of the Ponzi scheme blew his brains out with a shot gun in a parking lot right before the shit hit the fan. That's the answer to "why?" I have been the victim, along with many others, of a criminal financial fraud.

But I am struggling terribly with: What does Spirit want of me? That, and my sense of fatigue and weariness at the thought to having to go back to work full-time just as I approach the age when the joys and pleasures of retirement are supposed to be opening up. And there is nothing I can do about it. Nothing. I simply have no choice in the matter.

Message to Maurine: Join the Global Financial Disaster Shakedown Cruise.

Yesterday I got on the phone to six private schools and the Beverly Hills School District where I worked umpteen zillion lifetimes ago to see about starting the job application process. Not much encouragement and, of course, it's the beginning of summer vacation, but looking to get a jump-start on the fall. I am trying not to feel sorry for myself; feeling sorry for one's self never helps, it actually makes things worse. The life that I knew and was anticipating, and to a certain degree counting on, is over. Again like Scarlet O'Hara: Gone With the Wind.

And I know, too, that a part of me has died, and I don't know what to expect. The last time I felt this sort of death I got cancer. I can only hope and pray that the hard psychological and emotional and spiritual work I have done in the intervening years will help me meet this incredible, extraordinary challenge in my life rather than checking out through disease. What I don't have as much of now are time and the physical stamina to help me through these demanding times.

My Guide keeps telling me to hold on and trust, but I don't think even Job had to suffer and wait this long. If this is supposed to be a relationship with the Divine, that implies some sort of reciprocity, doesn't it? When does something start to come back? I simply do not know how to surrender anymore, what more do I have to give?

Relationship gone.

Money gone.

No job.

Time left dwindling at an alarming rate.

Alone.

It may be true that I am a spiritual being on a human journey, but I am also a human being who is making/taking this spiritual journey, and right now this human being is hurting badly. Bloody badly and bloody hard!

June 5, 2009

I am still reeling from the shock of what has happened, the vector of my life redirected fiercely. Sometimes when I am in the car driving I forget where I am going and end up somewhere I hadn't planned. For the past four or five days I have been crying on and off uncontrollably; so many lies and so much betrayal over the past months and years. Hard, bitter pills to swallow. And there is absolutely nothing I can do to change what has happened except move forward.

And tomorrow is the commemoration of D-Day and the landing on Omaha Beach. I feel as if I am experiencing my own sort of D-Day (a.k.a. Operation Overlord) as in "Lord, be in operation over me!" There are no bullets flying, but I do feel as if I am fighting for my life, and I do not know how the battle will come out. Right now I'm just in the thick of it.

I finally pulled the plug on AWOL Ink Productions. After seven years of trying to run my own publishing company, I have officially gone out of business, returning my resale license to the State Board of Equalization. Zero money earned for the last fiscal year. All that time and effort and work only to arrive back to Zero Dollar, Mel.'s card more prophetic and fitting than one could imagine.

Zero dollar.

Zero sum game.

I feel as if God is doing a huge CONTROL/ALT/DELETE on my life.

CONTROL

ALT

DELETE

CONTROL

ALT

DELETE

Reboot. Reboot. A massive rebooting process overtaking me, all systems collapsing right before my eyes. I have no idea what the new system's hard drive is going to look like or how it is going to work. I'll either crash to smithereens on the rocks or somehow be brought safely to shore. Talk about riding the wave of tempestuous seas! Talk about being hacked into – financially, emotionally, psychologically, physically – the whole magilla, the entire nine yards and then some. I am completely at God's mercy. Completely.

July 12, 2009

My first entry in my new home.

As always, moving is taxing and tiring beyond measure on top of all the other obstacles and hurdles I have been facing. When the movers arrived at 7:45am on June

26, along with the rest of the household plates, dishes, pottery, art work, and stuff, stuff, stuff, I had already made a dozen trips moving smaller items, had all the new appliances installed, bought three news rugs, and then an overall cleaning in preparation for the final move, plus making more phone calls than I can remember dealing with this and that, the job and task of living.

Moving, simply put, is an absolutely horrendous expense of time, energy, and money. And once the movers were gone, all the unpacking and resettling and reorganizing still remained. Now where did I put my toothbrush? Underwear? Coffee filters? I have been here over two weeks and still have brown wrapping paper on my bedroom sliding glass doors because I haven't had a moment or the energy to think about curtains. That's on next week's "to do" list. But then again with this middle-aged body, why should I even care? Look away, all you Peeping Toms. Come and get it!

I started a new journal right before the chaos of change descended and of all the things that shifted location, it is the only thing I lost. I searched everywhere for it but finally gave up. It simply disappeared into some sort of moving limbo. Why that one thing, I wonder? Fortunately, I had made only one entry, something to the effect how losing over half a million dollars had not focused my mind as one would think such a catastrophe would. Not exactly a psychogenic fugue state but scary nevertheless. In one of my more darkly humorous moods, I had this brief email exchange with a friend who had been thinking about me and all that I've been through and wondered how I was doing. This was my sardonic reply:

"Up and down. One day okay, a total basket case the next. I've officially diagnosed myself with PTSD from the end of the my relationship with P., ongoing and intrusive thoughts of C., plus Acute Stress Disorder from the loss of over a half million smack-a-roos. This Acute Distress Disorder will officially end tomorrow because the diagnosis is technically applicable for four weeks only, at which point I will have dysthymia – ongoing depression, moderate – and Adjustment Disorder Mixed, which is probably self-explanatory. How's that for psychobabble? Except in my case, it's true. I had a meeting with a couple of therapist friends the other day and told them I was worried about myself because all I want to do at the end of the day is have a couple of glasses of wine and zone out in front of the TV, testing my rapidly deteriorating mental capacities on *Jeopardy*. This may or may not also be accompanied by imbibing some bud, depending upon how low I feel. But then again, the movers stole most of my medicinal stash so I don't have any left.

"They both said, 'Are you kidding?? Drink and smoke away after all you've been through. If you're still doing this a year from now, we'll send you to AA. But until then, RELAX!'" Oh, to get by with a little help from one's friends! Because it has been rough of late and I'm feeling so alone, even though I know I have a lot of people who love and care for me. But it's different. This is the longest I have been without a partner since my early twenties, and that's a LONG time."

I'm glad I can make other people laugh; I wish I could do that for myself. I actually have been doing a lot of crying lately. The direction I was headed in has careened against a brick wall of emotional and financial meltdown and I have absolutely no idea where I am headed, only that minute by minute I have less time to live. I think about Mel.'s question, "What space will this loss open to create something that you might not otherwise have attempted?" What space indeed.

Some of the things I wrote in that abundance book I kept last fall for forty days about trust, relaxing, letting go, what true prosperity means: how all those words and ideas and thoughts are now most decidedly being put to the test, where the rubber, or the dollar, hits the road. I have withdrawn from my church pilgrimage this October. I have eliminated as many extras as I can. The only luxury I have allowed myself to keep is my gym membership at $35 @ month to alleviate the stress I am experiencing. But I have been so busy over the past few weeks that I haven't been able to make it in to lift weights. And, of course, the irony of that too: the one thing I *do* allow myself to keep I haven't taken advantage of.

In the middle of all this turmoil and change I have sent out over a half dozen resumes for teaching positions and have had one interview to be a substitute, which is a start certainly, but I need full-time work. And even with a full-time job I will barely be able to make ends meet on a teacher's salary. Not at all what I imagined or envisioned for my life as I round the corner on sixty.

And so it goes and goes and goes. A part of me still gets upset that P. is with someone and I haven't even had a cup of coffee or a ten-minute conversation with another man in over a year and a half. I had no exit strategy, no back-up plan or partner waiting in the wings. My life has deteriorated to banging nails into the wall to hang things and then after I have done that obsessing about whether they are off by a quarter of an inch. Ah, the challenge of being both an obsessive/compulsive neurotic AND a Virgo!

All this change and loss and upheaval finally got to me a few days ago when I experienced the most terrible disequilibrium, a sickening dizziness, true vertigo when you feel the world whirling even when you are lying flat on the ground; that nauseous feeling of spinning, spinning, spinning. I actually thought I might have to go to the hospital I felt that bad from sheer physical, psychological, and emotional exhaustion.

Where is the good in all this, I keep asking myself?

Where is the good in losing all that money?

Where is the good in having to go back to work full-time at this stage in life when most people my age are looking toward retirement?

Where is the good in being so alone and lonely when we humans are built to be in intimate relationship?

Where is the good? Where is *my* good? In Romans 8:28 I am told that "God works with those who love him, those who have been called in accordance with his purpose, *and turns everything to their good.*" Boy, if this is what God calls "good," I'd sure hate to see what He/She classifies as "bad!" The last seven years of my life – with the exception of some wonderful trips with my children – have been dauntingly relentless with challenges and heartache and confusion and change.

I honestly do not know how much more I can take. I keep wondering: Where, God, is the good you have in store for me, that you have planned and promised and ordained for me? What am I missing? What am I not seeing? What is it about me energetically that prevents this good from entering into my being or prevents me from seeing the good that is there? I feel as if my back is as far against the wall as it can be or as close to the cliff's edge as possible without falling off.

Maybe that's it. Maybe I just need to fall, or jump, off. The only thing that is keeping me here at this point is my children, even more than my love for them, their love for me. That's it. If something were to happen to me, I know they would be broken-hearted. And while they will have to face saying good-bye to me at some point, as we all must do on this human journey, I know it cannot be now. I must dig deep, deep, deep from that well of strength and sustenance I know is there somewhere. I simply have lost or misplaced my divining rod. It must be here somewhere; I just don't see it or feel its presence now.

July 13, 2009
Lord:
You know how I awaken in the middle of the night restless. It is so difficult for me to find the place of gratitude and thankfulness in my heart, not to mention still having to confront looking for a job and all the financial pressures that have overtaken me. I don't know how to move forward, how to be filled with confidence and joy that all is moving as it should. I do not want to play the roll of victim, but I don't know how to reach the final comfort and liberation. Why can't I move on?

What is it about moving on, as you call it, that bothers you so? You make the assumption that moving on means losing something – and perhaps that is true on one level – but it also holds the possibility of gaining something as well, something that in time may prove to be more precious and more valuable than what is being left behind. You have been blessed with a tender heart and it is so difficult for you to protect your heart and defend it. You need to learn how to harden your heart in a way that allows you greater mastery, greater flexibility with life. I know that may sound contradictory: how to harden your heart when the vast majority of humanity needs to learn how to open and soften theirs but for you individually this may be a necessary task.

Perhaps the word "harden" has the wrong connotation. Perhaps the words "fortify and strengthen," as a bulwark of appropriate defense, are more appropriate. Even Jesus talked about how to care for oneself amidst the crowds. This is where you have a tendency to lose yourself in your own humanity rather than learning how to distance yourself from it while at the same time embracing it. This is a difficult challenge for the spiritual sojourner: how to be fully in the world but not of it, not subsumed or consumed by it.

Focus on bringing peace more into the moments of your days. You do this at times when you are truly hurting and feeling alone but the true spiritual practice is to walk in peace, walk in love. What happens is that you forget to implement the behavior in your day-to-day, moment-to-moment life. What you forget is to bring more of this spiritual realm into the physical arena to aid you with the challenges and demands of the physical domain.

There are no winners and losers here. You have a tendency to look upon yourself as losing something and while something is transforming into a different level, that transformation does not necessarily imply loss but rather a more neutral change. It is the human in you that looks upon this as a loss and therefore "bad" or "wrong" or "unfortunate," whatever word of judgment you affix to this current state of affairs.

This is only personal judgment on your part from the particular place and vantage point from which your mind views things. The mind is obsessed with codifying and classifying life experiences into categories of good and bad, better or worse, this and that. As you work to harden/protect your heart, also work on the practice of quieting your mind from focusing on what is gone, what is lost, and what is no more. Look to what is immediately before you in the moment and find the peace and beauty that are inherently there if you will but open your eyes, quiet your mind, and stay present with what is.

You make the erroneous assumption, often very subtle, that what is to come will be less than what has come before, and yet this has not been the pattern of your life. The true pattern has been just the reverse; each successive unfolding of the flower of your life has brought more to you, not less; more abundance, more care, more joy, more love. I know your life feels the exact opposite of this right now as you face being physically alone and confront financial and monetary realities. Focus on the unfolding of abundance because this has been the pattern in your life thus far, has it not? When the human emotions overwhelm you, remind yourself of this reality.

Allow yourself to be the beautiful, joyous child that at the core of your being you truly are. Allow this childlike joy to arise. Nurture it, care for it, cultivate it, embrace it. There are more resources within the child than you imagine and there is a reason in the grand scheme of things that all creatures are children (little) first because that childlike quality teaches an important lesson about how to walk through the days of physical and spiritual life: playfully, joyfully, spontaneously. Do not allow human despair to overtake you even though as a human you have been feeling despair. It is ultimately only a feeling, not the final truth.

July 20, 2009

And, of course, the lost journal finally surfaced. A comparison of the other entry, dated Wednesday, June 17, 2009:

"Early in the morning. I have been awake on and off since 4:00am. Finally got up at 6:30am and made coffee. Another restless night, another day…of what?

"I am not in very good shape. I am seriously depressed on top of still weaning myself away from P. I wish I could say that the loss of over half a million dollars has focused my mind, but nothing could be farther from the truth. I am distracted and frazzled and in a state of shock. A friend of mine told me the other day that I will never get over this event; that I have been financially raped and will never recover from this loss. He is right. I have been raped, and I won't see that much money in cash ever again.

"I am working to get the condo fixed. I have been packing boxes upon boxes and getting estimates for moving, in addition to sending out resumes for work. Some days I awaken in tears and continue to cry intermittently throughout the day. Other days I manage to make it through without too much weeping. The only thing at present that I have to look forward to are a couple of glasses of wine at night and seeing how many questions I can answer on *Jeopardy*. Not many. I usually end up falling asleep on the sofa not only from physical fatigue but from a soul weariness that has overtaken me.

"What the hell happened to my life?? I have been trying to wrap my mind around how this catastrophic loss could be working for my good, but I have to confess I am having a very hard time parsing this out. To say that God works in mysterious ways is the understatement of eternity. How much does it take to be humbled? How much winnowing of self and ego is required? At night when I am tossing and turning and hot and sweaty in bed and cannot sleep, I keep saying to myself: "Comfort! Comfort! God's peace be with you. Trust!" Occasionally this helps a moment or two before my mind goes haywire again, back to its default button of disturbing, unsettling chatter.

"It is hard at this point, almost impossible, for me to be excited about my future, the rest of my life: moving, having to go back to work, being alone; certainly not what I had in mind only a few short months ago, let alone the past few years. Everything, simply every single thing is being swept away and in the process of transformation. The feeling I had about a tsunami coming; how prophetic that proved to be! But there is a limit to human endurance even if you do have a willing spirit and heart. Even Jesus died on the cross. I simply do not know how much more I can take."

July 27, 2009

I thought I'd spend some much needed restorative down-time by the sea, the mysterious magnificent rhythmically pounding and sounding sea. All the pressure of the water against the shore, wave after wave: it made me think about the sermon last week in church about the spiritual power of pressure, a pressure that helps keep us focused, ever-moving toward the heart of God.

- How the wind and waves pressured the fishing boats on the Sea of Galilee to move in the water and how this, though scary at times, was actually a good thing. "Fear not! I am with you!"
- How the pressure of the crowds around Jesus produced miracles of healing and profound teachings that still hold true; the woman touching Jesus's cloak and feeling his power course through her.
- How pressure in the earth over time molds carbon into diamonds and the irritation of sand in oysters creates pearls.
- How we all at some point must leave the shore of comfort and familiarity in order to experience the pressure of spirit and how God uses this pressure to move us, thrust us, catapult us forward, whether we like it or not, understand it or not.
- How Jesus represents the great counterbalance to all these various pressures that storm around us, literal ones on the sea, but also figurative ones within the sea of hurting, broken humanity.

Boy, oh boy is that me!

How I have thought about this pressure of late:

The pressure of C.'s presence in the children's and my life; the pressure of the loss of all that money; the pressure of being alone; how all these pressures are propelling me toward a radically new way of living and being.

It's all about the pressure of God and spirit working in my life to form pearls and diamonds out of financial destruction and personal loss. I honestly do not know how people make it through the vagaries and challenges and unrelenting pressures of life without God. Suicide or profound catatonic withdrawal or schizophrenia or addiction appear the only other options. I just don't understand how else people get by.

August 8, 2009

I went to pick up Mel. from her dad's and saw a picture of C. and P. together, all dressed up at some party looking happy, and a primal rage surged through my gut. It took all I could muster to keep from breaking down and allowing it to spoil my day.

I keep hearing from others to forget about him, that I've got so much to offer. But if I am so great and wonderful and beautiful and strong, why am I alone? And yes, I have family and friends and people who love me but this is different. Twenty-five years with P. have left a mark on me. I wonder at times if I will be able to trust enough again to allow someone else in. It's about wanting to share my soul at the deepest level. P. and I, each in our own way, were so hurt, so damaged while young.

Crying in the wee hours of the night, with the cat as my only companion – shades and whispers of memories from England with my first husband so long ago. Praying to God for mercy, please help ease this animal-like pain.

Thinking: "Fuck Erkhart Tolle! It just bloody hurts!" At one point Buster actually reached out his paw and laid it on my arm. How our pets know so instinctively what we need!

I keep telling myself I need to concentrate on gratitude and beauty, gratitude and beauty; shift thoughts from the past, the hurt, the anger, the loss. Focus on gratitude and beauty, moment-by-moment-by-moment-by-moment. I wish I could do an exorcism or lobotomy on that part of my brain that carries all these memories and thoughts, some sort of electric shock treatment that would fry those particular neurons from my cranium and allow me to move on.

And then what happens? I get a phone call from P.

October 15, 2009

In the Laundromat the other day, reading while waiting for my clothes to dry. From *An Imaginary Life* by David Malouf:

> We barely recognize the annunciation when it comes declaring: 'Here is the life you have tried to throw away. Here is your second chance. Here is the destiny you have tried to shake off by inventing a hundred false roles, a hundred false identities for yourself. It will look at first like a disaster, but is really good fortune in disguise, since fate too knows how to follow your evasions through a hundred forms of its own. *Now you will become at last the one you intended to be.* (italics mine)

To become at last the one I was intended to be. Remember who you intended to be. Remember who you are. At this point in my life the only thing I care about achieving or doing or accomplishing is to be able to love one single human being well; to love honestly, sincerely, deeply, humorously; to love one other human being; to receive and accept love back: that's it. That's all I want to do; that would be the crowning achievement of a successful life, a life well lived. All the other things I have striven for do not matter. I just want to get love right once. Full stop. I hope and pray the universe will allow me one last chance to get it right before I leave this plane of reality. To make just one someone happy!

November 8, 2009
Gracious Spirit:
Help me be at peace. So much going on, too much to understand.
You have done more than you think and traveled farther than you know on the road of healing. And everything, everything on the planet today and in your life in particular, is about healing, healing from a place deep within. Once this internal place is settled, you will experience an energy and vibrancy that will bring in the new phase. Continue to have faith. Faith is more important for you than any hopes or fears you may have about the future. Your prayer for trust and surrender is rightful. Continue in this vein.

The fact that you have been growing in a sense of peace and acceptance is important. It is your new foundation. You need this in your life in order to be able to build a healthy future, for yourself or with another. Trust your instincts. Your heart will know what to do and how to respond when the time comes. How can you expect to be in a relationship with another without this loving acceptance of your own being first? You are moving farther away from the old structures. There remain a few more tasks, some minor attention to the last residual remnants of the past that are coming to conclusion. Nothing in this process, or the process of life itself, can be pushed or forced.

You are flowing on a grand river. While you do need to keep your head above water, and by that I mean monitoring your thoughts, however they may pull you down, the current of life will carry you. You are cared for more than you know. You forget this. You must not. Every moment of every day must be grounded in spirit.

Your job now is about love, spreading love, being loving. This energy will direct you to the next phase. Physical intimacy will flow naturally once this heart space is activated. You are closer than you realize to heart activation. You are learning to think with your heart. It is the heart, not the head, that must lead. You are learning how to listen to your heart and allow it to guide you.

November 20, 2009

I found a job! Or rather, it found me. After not having much success with employment as either a teacher or a substitute, a friend of mine passed on some information about a job opportunity working part-time for a foundation that does bereavement counseling for children. The husband and wife who founded the enterprise lost their only son a few years ago in a freak home accident, and they wanted to turn their grief into something positive by helping others. I realized in the instant I heard their story that there are far worse calls than ones telling you you've lost all your money. If money is all you ever lose, consider yourself lucky.

I interviewed for the job and was hired at $22.50 @ hour. From globe trotting and charity dinners and not having to work full-time to $22.50 @ hour. And proud of it! My job is to go into various schools in the Los Angeles Unified School District and provide grief support for elementary school children who have lost a loved one, and sadly many of the children in my groups are there because of gang violence. So now I work in East LA in a predominantly Latino and Korean community. It is almost as if I have been propelled back to my twenties going from classroom to classroom, school to school carrying all my materials with me, only this time in a suitcase on wheels rather than a black attaché briefcase. Amazing.

The place where I have my office is in a day-care health facility for mentally compromised adults, surrounded by a barbed wire fence and iron gates. To keep the crazies in or lock the crazies out, I'm not sure. One patient has decided to call me Donny and Marie; another, a friendly mute, shakes my hand whenever he sees me; another asks me if I'm Connie Stevens. Not infrequently when I'm in my office I hear loud voices and verbal scuffles and calls for 911 when patients have an episode or bad day. But mostly they just wander around, smoking cigarettes, clutching some precious object, or nodding off after taking their meds, with sounds of snoring reverberating down the halls.

The people who run the center are mostly Russian and I can't understand a word they say; it's almost like being incarcerated myself behind a locked door in a windowless space. Then when the patients leave, the "keepers" themselves sometimes go crazy: shrieking with laughter or hurling incomprehensible invectives at one another or dancing around singing folk songs to the tune of an accordion. Life has some interesting twists and turns, no doubt. And yet I am so grateful for that paycheck every two weeks, without or without the warbling Russians.

November 29, 2009

Is hope a lesson in endurance? Like the lyrics in the folk song: "How long and how much must we endure?" Is there no real creativity without this waiting? A sort of pregnant hope to carry on the torch of life and love and art? Perhaps this enduring creative spark within IS a redemptive moment, *my* redemptive moment. Such active waiting! Waiting for the divine inspiration, the divine in-breathing to occur. To breathe life into Life itself. In time there will only be the fullness of this Creative Love. How can it be otherwise? As Dante writes, it is the love that moves the stars. Chardin, too, understood this about the cosmos: Love births us into being, like a gigantic volcanic eruption.

A curious and interesting tidbit I came across while reading: how the Divine Self extended the feminine aspect of Being into consciousness and that the word "rib," from which Eve is supposed to have been formed, can be traced to the root of the word for crown. So in this sense, consciousness is crowned or fulfilled with the investment of feeling into our human nature; in other words, this feminine principle is the "crown" of creation and the jewel of our humanity.

How I like that! The idea that we women and what we bring to the table of life are primary, essential gifts to creation, not second class citizens who brought western civilization to its knees through our rampant, unrestrained sexual impulses. For without the feminine feeling nature, we all suffer the loss of something precious; it is this feeling nature that separates us from collapsing again and again, which we all do anyway, into animal instinct.

To let ourselves back into the story of our lives and remove the mask of personal consciousness: how I feel so mired at times at this level of personality and ego! And I know, too, from all the reading I have done about spirituality that this loss – or better said, this letting go of ego consciousness – is a vital stage in the spiritual journey, in the evolution and development of spiritual chops as it were.

I'm so not there yet.

Two steps forward.
One step back.
One step forward.
Two steps back.
That's just the way it is.
And apropos the above, rereading some of my Siddha Yoga Correspondence Course:

> There is really nothing we can do to prevent our eventual spiritual evolution. It is our destiny to merge back into that Light from which we originally emanated. (Vol. 2, Lesson 11, pg. 6)

Let go and let God as the saying goes. My problem is I keep wanting to grab it back. Letting go is a process without destination. Except perhaps death, and I'm not sure about that either.

New Year's Eve, 2009
All hell broke loose last week when P. announced his engagement to C. In two years time, going from "This woman means absolutely nothing to me!" to "We're engaged to be married."

Lordy, lordy! What next? A friend sent me something about this New Year being a Blue Moon Lunar Eclipse, supposedly one of the most powerful New Year's Eves we have had in a long time, a powerful time to release the past and call in new energies.

So in the spirit of renewal I went out onto my balcony and prayed to the Blue Moon, this special moon. I prayed for continued release. I prayed to be able to trust and open my heart. I prayed for someone to love. I told God I don't know how much longer I can go on alone. I prayed for

Him/Her to hear my prayer. And then I bowed my head in surrender to the Divine Will. Is there any other way?

Unbeknownst to me, my son D. was inside watching me. Three of the four "kids" asked if they could spend New Year's Eve with me: how's that for a compliment from your adult children? The fact that I provided sushi and champagne may have had something to do with this. D. told me later he had been watching me pray and how hard all this C. business has been on me. Yes, it has been hard.

January 8, 2010
Dear Heavenly Spirit and Gracious Guide:
The news of P.'s engagement has hit hard, these oh-so-human emotions still there. What do I need to learn at this stage in my life that I have not yet learned, somehow, someway?

Living and active within: I am living and active within, every moment of every day. The need for kindness in your life, treating yourself with a type of kindness that has not been demonstrated to you, your need for kindness is large and because you are alone it is you who must supply the kindness you need.

Most humans expect this kindness to come from other people and while this type of kindness is vital to move the world forward, more importantly for you is how to generate this kindness from within. Now is the time for you to demonstrate all forms of kindness to your self.

How do you go about this?

By being more patient. By not having so many things you think you need to do. Witness and embrace the twenty-four hours that are unfolding before you RIGHT NOW! You have a tendency to lose this daily focus by thinking "I am alone, I will be alone, I don't want to be alone," thereby in some manner reinforcing the aloneness itself. You need to continue to train your mind to stay grounded in the moment, and the eternal reality that you are not alone. I am living and present within.

This is a part of being kind to yourself. Think of the courage you have demonstrated in the face of P.'s unconsciousness, in the face of financial loss, in the face of uncertainty. While you may not feel very hopeful right now, there remains a part of you that does hope and this part carries the kernel of new growth.

Water that kernel.

Be kind to that hope seed.

Be as patient and kind with yourself as you can and honor every day all the things you have managed to accomplish. There are times truly when it appears the most dark before new light and life stream in. You need to spend more time in prayer, as many times a day as necessary to quell the waves of loneliness and uncertainty that occur on your human plane. What part of you is still judging another part that you somehow are doing it wrong or that things should be other than they are or that on some level you expect things to be different rather than accepting what is? You must learn to reach through the tears to the joy and gladness that are on the other side of life's dark challenges.

Hold fast to the last remnants of the life raft that has been carrying you and allow it to drift you into the new, or rather, next shore. Bow before God's time and economy rather than your own. God's good for you will always be better, more good than anything you can orchestrate on your own. Bring this truth once again to the forefront of your consciousness.

Do not judge by human time.

Trust only in God's time.

Allow God's timing to flow through you.

Husband it wisely.

Steward it with care.

For you especially there is no other way on this spiritual path.
All shall be well.

February 6, 2010
Alone on a Saturday morning, a dreary day outside. It has been raining for the past twenty-four hours. Yesterday I basically played hooky: spent the morning reading (a new novel called *The Unnamned*) and went to the movies in the afternoon. Then last night went to a supper club in Hollywood to see SZ, a tap dancing, singing, standup Jewish comedian. An entire day devoted to doing nothing much, with the exception of washing the dishes, emptying the trash and recycling, and changing the sheets on my bed. Like I said: doing nothing much. It has been a long time since I've spent a day like that, an experiment in being kind and gentle with myself.

I got the last remaining possessions from P.'s house – Mom's silver tea set and sterling flatware, Nana's de Havilland wedding china, an antique clock from my cousin G., plus some of his water color artwork. It took me most of the day to accomplish this task, loading and unloading the car, carrying everything three floors up on the elevator and then unpacking everything and putting it away. By 5:00pm in the afternoon I had had it. This process of disengagement, of disentanglement has been long and arduous indeed.

I try not to dwell on being alone. Some days I'm better at it than others; some days I barely get through. I honestly cannot fathom spending the rest of my life by myself. And yet I am alone and this may be it. The odds and statistics are not in my favor at this age and stage of the game. I was thinking the other night while fixing dinner that judgment is a luxury of youth, and I am most decidedly no longer young. Judgment must go, especially self-judgment. Coming closer and closer to facing one's own mortality really does humble you.

HUMBLE.

YOU.

I have been three months already at my new job and am so grateful to have work to go to, for the paycheck certainly, but also for the structure of having to show up and be present. Otherwise too much downtime becomes burdensome, oppressive even. And I know this job is temporary at best, a fuel stop on a highway I am traveling to somewhere, I just don't know where. Hopefully it will include some great sex and wonderful lovemaking and laughter. I feel at times as if my body has gone dormant. Sleeping Beauty but without a Prince. Or a penis.

Some loose papers I found in my closet when putting things away. I don't even remember writing this, something about truth unfolding within each individual consciousness. The truth as it unfolds within me...Am I open to this particular and peculiar and uniquely idiosyncratic "me" truth? The truth that is contained in the fluttering movements of my heart? The heart: fourth chakra, half way up the scale, the midpoint, the balance point, the fulcrum, the doorway and portal between heaven and earth.

Ask.

Seek.

Knock.

Ferreting out crossed wires and repairing damaged ones to reinstate the flow, the electricity of Spirit, to remove the blocked energy of unconditional love, all the blocked energy caused by misunderstanding, self-pity, judgment – I'm the queen of that – grief and resentment in personal relationships – the princess of that – all those blockages around the heart.

This heart!

How to let the love in?

By dismantling all denial systems, all the lies I
believed and the self-deception that allowed me to believe
the lies, especially my own. I try not to look back at that, so
clear in hindsight now. Then the thought: How am I lying
to myself now? Does the lie never end? Or does it just keep
transforming through time because we cannot tolerate the
pain of truth? Parsing the broken heart of humankind, at
least this broken heart. On this journey called life I am
discovering that the heart can be broken a lot.

I have been doing a lot more praying lately, actually
taking time on my days off to walk to church and kneel
before the altar in the small chapel to pray. Pray with
thankfulness. Pray for guidance. Pray for peace. Supreme
Being, Primal Energy, Universal Love: You know what I
need. I am here before You on my knees. Please bring me
what I need. And what You need for me.

I think about these blues of absolution, the slow blues
of liberation. How do I transmute the loneliness and
aloneness into my teachers? How to be liberated from
within while the blues float around? Freedom does come
with a price, and it can be bloody.

February 12, 2010
Gracious Spirit:
It feels as if I'm withering away, like a plant that is
not getting enough water. How can heavenly love replace
the physical one?

*Concentrate on being gentle. You cannot be with
another until you learn how to love and care for yourself.
In this way you learn the gift rather than the neediness of
love. Most people end up in relationships because of the
neediness rather than the gift. You are working at building
the gift that can be shared openly and freely rather than
from the point of lack, the idea that something external will*

complete you. You must complete yourself first before you can genuinely and truly and deeply share with another.

You must be vigilant to let no down feelings or thoughts take hold of you. That is not to say that you deny the reality of what you are experiencing on the physical plane but to remind yourself that the physical plane is only one part of a far greater and more mysterious whole. You need to discipline yourself to bring the sweetness in more, to focus on and savor the sweet moments that do present themselves and to express gratitude for the sweetness, gentleness, and kindness in whatever way they manifest. Once you strike this tonal vibration, you will find that its frequency will send out waves that communicate to the energy field you wish to attract.

You must ask, "Am I manufacturing anxiety, any form of darkness whatsoever, thoughts that decelerate, that bring me down or am I generating the energy field of kindness, gentleness and sweetness?" This must become fully grounded within your being. The love is indeed there. You just have a tendency to believe that the love won't be complete until you share it with another. And in many ways, this thought process is true; that is, wanting to share the love. But you can only share the love you already have. You cannot get love from another; that kind of getting can be nothing more than a mask or camouflage for neediness and that kind of neediness, stemming from a sense of lack, must be abandoned altogether at this point. The love you so want to experience, the love that you so long for you already have within.

Now is the time to find the shelter of that love. It is on this foundation that any external form of relationship will be built. Self-love, not needy or narcissistic, but genuine self-love is the only key. Concentrate on paying more attention to this internal love, this interior Lover. All will follow from that. Build the love fire within and its radiance cannot help but be attractive in the world of form.

February 27, 2010

Coming out from the other end of the wormhole, it feels like to me. I have been praying for God, the Universe to bring me to the next relationship in my life. But something has shifted and I realize I still was voicing what I longed for from a place of lack, that something was missing. And while this may be so in one sense, it is not the come from I need to express; i.e. the idea that loneliness and being alone are somehow "bad" or "not right;" or that things will be "better" when I am with someone when it's all about learning to be at peace with what is.

Last Sunday the sermon felt as if it were tailor-made for me. And the irony, too, that I almost didn't make it to the service, having lost track of time working on a manuscript. At the beginning of Lent: the forty days of wandering in the desert, whatever that desert is in our lives. And it hit me: the point of the desert is to FACE IT!! Not to run from it or flee from it but to embrace it fully and completely. I realized that until I accept right where I am – alone – just as I am – alone – my life still will be off, somehow amiss. The desert is all about being who you are, where you are, and at peace with whatever is, in my case aloneness, but not necessarily loneliness. Aloneness is a physical fact but loneliness is a psychological/emotional choice. While I am indeed alone in the desert, I do not need to be lonely as I am wandering. The point is to move from choosing loneliness to gratefully accepting the gift and beauty of my solitude.

I repeat: the gift and beauty of my solitude.

This shift has created a sense of spaciousness within me. God/Spirit does show up in the desert of our lives to lead us out of loneliness and into this sweet solitude.

Indeed, loneliness can only be conquered by those who can experience and embrace solitude. I may be alone but I also am positively and absolutely not alone. I, and I alone – no pun intended – can embrace this paradox lovingly and tenderly. Wandering in the desert does eventually lead to the feast. I must trust that God hears me even if I do not hear myself. It is all about making peace about being in the desert, making peace about being in this desert alone, but not lonely.

What I have noticed, and this happened almost immediately once I got this concept, is how much more aware I am of the immense beauty surrounding me, both large and small: the movement of the wind through the trees; how raindrops sparkle against the backdrop of street lights; the way sunlight shifts and moves through the day; the multitudinous shapes and forms of people and their faces, my profound gratitude for my home, having such a wonderful space to be in; the beauty of my tiny terrace and balcony garden. Just so many, many things. There is immense beauty in the desert, whatever that desert is for each of us, if we face it and allow it in.

My prayers have shifted, too. Now it is all about being open and receptive. Maybe I am better off alone? How do I know what is in store for me? How can I pray for what I think is better/best in my life when there is a far kinder and stronger and more intelligent Force guiding me that positively *knows* what is best and has been telling me this for years? It is not about getting through the desert; it is about wandering around with open, grateful eyes.

The other night over dinner with a friend, she said the main message she got from her family was "What will the neighbors think!" and how this fear of judgment by others had colored so much of her life. I got to thinking about the predominant messages from my family while growing up and I came up with:

No one listens.

No one cares.

You are an object that gets ordered around.

I realized afterwards that the second statement was not true. My parents did love me very much in their own way. It may not have been healthy; it may have stemmed from great neediness on their part, but they did love me. The other two messages, however, held true.

How do I learn to listen to myself in the desert of my own life? How do I learn to not treat myself as an object? Or to think/believe that God treats me like an object as opposed to a most beloved part of His/Her creation? In many ways, I feel as if I am only just beginning to understand what love is, what love means and how it works.

The internal peace that arises from this "desert" experience is at once grand and spacious and brimming with quiet life. Surrender, like wandering in the desert, is a process. Prayer aimed at outcomes – other than wanting to follow Spirit – can very easily drift back into ego manipulation, and this can be *so* subtle! Yes, ask for what you want but never forget the foundation of and for that asking: Thy Will Be Done.

So face the desert, Maurine. Allow God to show up and be present in Her/His own way. And enjoy the beauty as you wander. This, and only this, truly is The Way.

April 28, 2010

Gracious Spirit:

I realized the other day that all this human stuff is not going to go away. Rather, it is up to me to look at all the same old stuff differently. The meltdowns still occur, and here I have this amazing resource – You! – that I don't use either wisely or well. I come so often crying, whining, scared, in pain and I am grateful that I can do this, but it feels like time to mature more in this process. I need to approach Spirit differently – not just or solely for comfort but for tutelage and instruction about deeper things. The word that has been in my head is humility. I need to learn more about humility and how to walk humbly on this earth.

Humility is a way of learning how to walk with Grace, the knowledge and awareness of Grace before you at every moment. Feel how the internal energies shift even as you write that; you can feel the movement away from self-focus to that which is around. And that which is around at all times is God's grace. When you turn your attention to that reality, you cannot help but walk with greater humility on this earth.

And what is God's Grace? God's Grace is carrying with you at every moment a profound understanding of the beneficent loving transcendent Reality, that every moment of every day, that every molecule and every atom that comprise external reality are made from the grace of God's love. There is nothing separate or apart from this grace and this love. It is truly within which you live and move and have your being. There is no separation! When you learn to fully implant this awareness in your consciousness, you will walk with greater humility because you realize the unearned gift of this grace. It is all gift, nothing earned in the sense of self-striving. Appropriate pride is one thing and there are times when it enters in a rightful way. But the focus on gift begs that you acknowledge a different source of being than most of the self-willed energy that moves so much of the planet in the world of form.

Notice how the internal thinking process shifts when you contemplate the words "gift" and "grace" leading to thankfulness and gratitude and ultimately to humility because they acknowledge a Transcendent Power at work in all things, in all ways. This acknowledgement allows the individual to switch vibrational frequencies almost

457

instantaneously; a shift that paradoxically allows more power to enter the small self which then becomes transmuted into the power of the larger Self within. Humility is the ongoing process of this transmutation of power. One must trust absolutely in order to make this shift. One who cannot trust in all ways will never walk humbly. Trust becomes a cornerstone in this process, trust in the gift of Love and the ability to relinquish control. The tendency to drift back into inordinate self-focus and survival mode is crafty and fierce. That is why humility is always a process, never a goal. Indeed, one can never reach humility; one can only walk humbly, day by day, trusting in Love, the foundational vibration of all matter, every single thing. It is tapping more into this Love – and trusting it – that will allow you to move through your days with humility.

Humility: the letting go of the ego-driven self, the emptying of self so that something greater and more powerful can enter. You have seen for yourself that the thoughts and judgments you make move you either closer to or farther from humility. Judgment especially hinders humility's path because judgment artificially splits reality into disparate components when reality is a seamless whole. Self-judgment must stop if humility is to grow. This is very different from the process of discernment. Humility and self-judgment are antithetical. Humility implies an acceptance of reality as it is. Judgment implies wanting something to happen a certain way.

That is why practicing kindness and gentleness with yourself is the first step for you on the path of humility because it means accepting – and loving – yourself just as you are, just the way your Creator/Creatrix does. Experiencing this type of loving acceptance allows you to move forward with more humility because there is no judgment behind this love and this gift. And if this is your *foundational core – which it is – how can you not at some point learn to embrace it? Indeed, without embracing this truth, you remain stuck.*

You have relinquished more of the controls than you think, but it is important to fine-tune this process. Do you not think your Creator knows how to manage His/Her creation? Answering "yes" to this question frees you up. It allows you to grow more organically, which in turn fills creation's role for you to be continually creative.

One who walks with humility is in right relationship with Creation and Creator: not separate or smug but conjoined, commingled, not in charge but invited to participate in the Dance. Focus on acceptance and the fundamental okayness of things, even though things paradoxically may not feel okay at all; remember that everything ultimately is just that: okay. Accept this truth. Remind yourself of all the many gifts bestowed upon you, internally, externally, materially, spiritually. Relinquish the reins of self into the hands of the Master Chariot Driver.

May 7, 2010

Early afternoon at Temescal Canyon Beach. I told myself I was going to go to the beach today no matter what. No more TV or mindless channel surfing.

At work my boss quit unexpectedly, leaving me to take up the slack by overseeing her bereavement groups in addition to mine. This means more money in the short term, which is good, but does nothing for my long-term employment prospects since I do not want to be director of the foundation.

I also found out that two of the full-time jobs I applied for are no longer available, and I wasn't even considered or asked for an interview. Didn't even get to first base. People take one look at my resume and say, "You'd cost us too much." I am not unaware of the exquisite irony involved here. We tell kids their future depends upon getting a good education, that it's the single most important thing they can have or do. Then you get to my stage of life with a world of experience and an impressive list of credentials and suddenly you're "too expensive." What was all the effort for?

On top of all this, if looks as if my daughter A.'s marriage is on the rocks after less than two years, and she is in crisis meltdown. My other daughter is looking for work and struggling too, both daughters upended by life for different reasons, in different ways. A nine hundred point drop in the stock market yesterday, the largest single day decline ever. Everything, simply everything, is breaking down before our eyes. Earthquakes, explosions, volcanic ash spewing, an oil leak wreaking havoc in the Gulf with no end in sight. I honestly do not know what's what anymore, how much of the chaos is in me and how much is in the world around me or both. I am so weary, and it's not even really or only about being alone anymore. I don't know if you can actually die of loneliness but I wouldn't be surprised. I believe some people probably can and do. But I know you can die from lack of love and loving. I don't know if God's love is enough anymore. And I know I would be positively suicidal without it.

So I brought myself to the beach today, another desert of sorts to wander in, a much healthier choice than CSI in the afternoon. I brought this journal to write in, a novel to read, and some writing to proofread but I may do nothing for the next few hours except listen to the waves and smell the sea breezes coming in off the shore.

****

I saw FS yesterday, and he asked me whether I had talked with my Guide recently. I said no, that It/He/She/They probably would just tell me the same thing again. FS said, "Don't assume you know what your Guide is going to say." And he is right, of course – my tendency to think I "know it all." So I ask: What is the next best step in the design of my becoming, in Your design for my becoming?

Becoming, becoming, becoming: it is an ongoing process of the unfolding beauty of creation and the power of that unfolding beauty in the world, from the smallest of things to the expanse of entire galaxies and the cosmos. You need to train yourself to be more attentive to beauty. This trains the heart to be a powerful force for love in the world.

When you are able to concentrate on the beauty around you, you will experience an expansion. This may sound contradictory when one is aware of all the strife and miscreation taking place within the world, but the essence of that creation started from a point of beauty and profound love. It is this exquisite beauty and love that are the driving forces behind matter, not the misuse or abuse of matter which is so prevalent today and which seems to be the focus of most manners of communication – this dwelling on what is NOT beautiful and true.

Discipline yourself to focus on beauty. You are becoming more aware of this but every day you must look for beauty, recognize beauty, give thanks for beauty, be astounded by beauty. This practice also develops a more humble approach to life because you realize you had nothing to do with the creation of this beauty; it is all gift! Reverence for the beauty around you is a powerful practice. It will aid you greatly in what you so desire: a partner with whom you can share your path, because by focusing on beauty, your energy field is outwardly, not inwardly directed. It creates a more attractive energy because it is in alignment with the principles of creation: outward, giving, abundant, expanding, purposeful.

It is important for you to add this practice of attention to beauty. Start by focusing on the beauty within yourself. Stop immediately any form of self-judgment or criticism. This must be eradicated completely at this point in your journey because it is a sly but corrosive form of energy-sucking pride. Once you have become more grounded in acknowledging your own beauty, turn to everything else that presents itself to you and ask:

How is this object/person/event beautiful?

What is the beauty being presented to me now?

Concentrate on the beauty, along with grace. Silence all criticism. Express gratitude and acknowledge beauty at all times, in all ways.

May 31, 2010

Yesterday I was standing in my living room looking out the sliding glass doors opening onto the balcony. The jacaranda tree across the street was in bloom, purple lavender in color, surrounded by the blood-red of some near-by bougainvillea. And it occurred to me: I have actually survived the last year! Twelve months ago I lost the vast majority of my life savings; I had just closed escrow on the first piece of property I have ever owned not knowing what would happen, if I would even be able to move in. I didn't have a job and had been without a partner for the longest period in my life.

Twelve months later, I have actually managed to pay the mortgage and the homeowners association dues and all the property taxes, not to mention other living expenses. An entire year! In the last couple of weeks I received some unexpected money, some of it from a tax refund, some from one of the few investments I had left with P., another for being a first time home buyer – more than enough for me to live on until the fall. I thought to myself: "See how the Universe is supporting you! You are better off now than a year ago in spite of losing all that money. You are paying your bills, you've got a job, you are surviving! Imagine where you may be a year from now." Still sailing! And ship indeed it feels like at times, or high in a crow's nest look out when the wind blows fiercely across my balcony bow.

I realized that if I don't start living from my heart at this point in time, I've only got myself to hold accountable or to blame. Right now I'm just working on my heart and head singing a more harmonious duet. I never thought I would be where I am at this point in my life, but I am where I am and with luck and a little more pluck on my part, who knows what other adventures are in store? I thought about the new tattoo I had emblazoned on the tip of my kundalini serpent: the Wheel of Fortune from the Tarot with the Sanskrit symbol for Wisdom at its center. And I reflected once again on my potential talents as a pirate. No, not a pirate exactly, more like a spiritual expeditionary or pilgrim adventurer. In many ways, I feel as if I have only begun to scratch the surface of this journey.

As utterly painful as the last few years have been, I actually am grateful for what has transpired in this middle passage of life, how the Universe has forced me into a completely different understanding of reality; that somehow what happened had to happen in order to liberate all the energies around and within me. Because that's how the universe works: it moves toward greater and greater liberation.

And love.

www.ingramcontent.com/pod-product-compliance
Lightning Source LLC
Chambersburg PA
CBHW071401090426
42737CB00011B/1308